Postmodern Winemaking

The publisher gratefully acknowledges the generous support of the General Endowment Fund of the University of California Press Foundation.

Postmodern Winemaking

Rethinking the Modern Science of an
Ancient Craft

Clark Smith

UNIVERSITY OF CALIFORNIA PRESS

University of California Press, one of the most
distinguished university presses in the United States,
enriches lives around the world by advancing
scholarship in the humanities, social sciences, and
natural sciences. Its activities are supported by the UC
Press Foundation and by philanthropic contributions
from individuals and institutions. For more information,
visit www.ucpress.edu.

University of California Press
Oakland, California

ISBN 978-0-520-28259-9 (cloth : alk. paper)
ISBN 978-0-520-95854-8 (e)

The Library of Congress has cataloged an earlier edition
of this book as follows:

Library of Congress Cataloging-in-Publication Data

Smith, Clark, 1951–.
    Postmodern winemaking : rethinking the modern
science of an ancient craft / Clark Smith.
      pages cm.
    Includes bibliographical references and index.
    ISBN 978-0-520-27519-5 (cloth : alk. paper) — ISBN
978-0-520-95526-4 (e)
      1. Wine and wine making.   I. Title.
    TP548.S6874   2013
    663'.2—dc23

                                    2012045797

Manufactured in the United States of America

23   22   21
10   9   8   7   6

In keeping with a commitment to support environmentally responsible and sustainable printing practices, UC
Press has printed this book on Natures Natural, a fiber
that contains 30% post-consumer waste and meets the
minimum requirements of ANSI/NISO Z39.48–1992
(R 1997) (Permanence of Paper).

À Susie

Contents

PART TWO. PRACTICES

PART THREE. TECHNOLOGY

PART FOUR. PHILOSOPHY

Preface

The heresy of one age becomes the orthodoxy of the next.
—Helen Keller, "Optimism" (1903)

I have been making and selling California wine since 1972. When first I drove into the Napa Valley, I encountered a billboard that quoted Robert Louis Stevenson: " . . . and the wine is bottled poetry." For me, that was a little over the top. I thought, "Sure, I like wine, but 'bottled poetry'? Give me a break."

I have since come to believe that this statement sprang from more than the flowery prose customary in his era; that the wines of Stevenson's time were actually altogether different from ours. The modernization of wine-making in its every aspect has left us with clean, solid wines of greater consistency than ever. But they are missing something.

I hope not to bore you, my reader, while I briefly recount the professional journey that led me to this conclusion.

In 1971, I dropped out of MIT and came to California. After six years selling wines at a well-stocked East Bay retailer, I spent the next thirteen making wine in the modern way. I started off dragging hoses for three years at Veedercrest Vineyards, and in 1980 enrolled at the University of California, Davis, where I learned the principles of modern scientific enology. In 1983 I began applying those principles at the R. H. Phillips Vineyard, where the Giguiere family and I took the fledgling winery from 3,000 to about 250,000 cases in seven years.

At Phillips, I set up an extensive small-lot vinification and sensory lab and, with a series of hardworking UC Davis interns, began delving into quality enhancement in the nascent Dunnigan Hills region, presenting at the American Society for Enology and Viticulture a series of seven papers on vineyard variables affecting wine quality, based on the reductionist methodology I had learned at Davis.

A simple example. We were making White Zinfandel that had more of a canned tomato soup aroma than the fresh strawberry notes I was seeking. Accordingly, I conducted a series of small-lot duplicate trials to test a variety of vineyard variables and winemaking procedures, presenting the resulting samples to a trained panel in a double-blind setting, asking the panel to rate the samples for the aromas they found as defined by the two standards I supplied: fresh strawberries and Campbell's tomato soup. Compiling the scores and running ANOVA (analysis of variance) statistical analysis, we determined significant differences due to both greater grape maturity and four hours of skin contact, which led to substantial improvement in the following years.

But toward the end my stint at Phillips, I began to hit a wall. I considered that I had learned how to make very good white wines, but my reds were, well, pathetic. Even when I sourced excellent syrah fruit from Estrella River and old-vine mourvèdre from Oakley, the wines had no sex appeal. A trip to South Australia only disheartened me further. I admired the plush, deep, finely knit structure and provocative, soulful qualities of their Cabs and Shirazes—and realized I had absolutely no idea how it was done.

So I did what any journeyman winemaker would do who wants to perfect his craft: I opened up a consulting firm. I had the incredible good fortune to be taken on by the Benziger Family and their winemaker (and spiritual guide), Bruce Rector, as my primary client. Like Phillips, the Benzigers' Glen Ellen line was growing very rapidly, and Bruce needed to outsource several R&D projects.

These projects were to become the foundation for everything I've done since. The first was an elaborate feasibility study on what was to become the Glen Ellen Learning Center, for me a crash course in teaching, learning, collaborating, and innovating. Second was the making of an International Claret, a global project in which I worked with the Australian Richard Smart, the Chilean Alejandro Hernández, and Pascal Ribéreau-Gayon, our project chief and director of the enology faculty at the University of Bordeaux. This project opened up for me a whole new understanding of tannins, high-pH winemaking, and red wine site selection and viticulture, besides polishing up my high school French.

The third project was the pursuit of a decent nonalcoholic wine, a dream conceived by Bruno Benziger shortly before his death, for which he had purchased a reverse osmosis (RO) filter. In nonalcoholic wine, we could work outside the federal restrictions for standard wine that forbid flavor additives, and thus I was permitted for the first time in my winemaking career to fool around with flavors.

We would choose a bland base wine and use the RO to remove all its alcohol. If it was a Chardonnay, we might then add essences like apple, pear, pineapple, and butter; if a Merlot, we might add cassis, orange peel, and vanilla.

But it didn't work. The flavors didn't blend. We ended up with what tasted like a bland base with a bunch of flavor notes sticking out as bizarrely as spiked hair. This was my first hint of the true nature of wine that this book discusses. I would spend a decade scratching my head before I understood the problem.

I now know that what was missing was the aromatic integration that good wine structure supplies. There was nothing wrong with the technology; rather, because the base wines weren't made artfully, they could never accept the flavors and meld them together into a soulful singularity.

My work with RO was to earn me several patents and formed the basis of Vinovation, a wine technology company I established with Rick Jones in 1992 and operated until 2008, by which time we had over a thousand clients and had expanded our research to a wide variety of membrane technologies (see chapter 18). More interestingly, we attracted the attention of Patrick Ducournau, founder of the French innovator Oenodev, who assigned his right-hand man, the remarkable Thierry Lemaire, to train us in their system of structural *élevage,* which includes micro-oxygenation, lees work, and a sophisticated understanding of oak. These fundamentals are the basis of postmodern winemaking (PMW) and are summarized in chapters 1 through 6.

In 1993, I got interested in applying what I had begun to learn to the making of California wines according to European principles. Simply put, this involved less emphasis on impactful aromatics and more on texture and balance. Launching the tiny brand WineSmith, I focused on Cabernet Franc, the most challenging of the Bordeaux varietals, which Pascal once confided was better suited to California than Bordeaux ("In Bordeaux," he told me, "it's so refined, it forgets to exist"). In 1999, I expanded into Pauillac-style Cabernet Sauvignon, and in 2001 I began with Stephen Krebs at Napa Valley College to make minerally Chardonnay that I called Faux Chablis and a sulfite-free Roman Syrah from Renaissance Vineyard in North Yuba County, exchanging grapes for consulting with Gideon Beinstock (see chapter 13).

These wines showed me that Stevenson's description of wine as bottled poetry was not a flowery fantasy but plain reportage.

Post–World War II winemaking has seen more changes in production practices than the previous eight millennia combined. We are led to believe that on the whole, this is surely a good thing. But to call it progress requires that what was gained outweighs what was lost.

This calculation is not straightforward because gains tend to upstage losses. While the benefits of innovations are easy to see, what we have forgotten is, well, forgotten. Out of sight, out of mind.

However sweeping their impact, adaptations to fleeting changes in conditions don't constitute durable value. Cassette tapes and Super-8 video were a big deal in the '80s, but they held no lasting lessons. We have begun to see that the whiz-bang innovations of the twentieth century centered largely on exploiting suddenly abundant resources such as oil, stainless steel, aluminum, copper, and so on—all temporary circumstances. History will judge if we spent these resources wisely by whether we created lasting value or merely squandered them on short-term prosperity.

Contemporary Americans lead lives of unparalleled leisure and convenience. But have we built to last? The miracle of modern antibiotics may well be a fleeting bubble, outstripped by the superbugs these drugs encourage. A discovery like Gore-Tex or the silicon chip is worth a hundred Hoover Dams that may lie crumbled and useless a century hence.

Modern innovations in electricity, microbiology, and chemical engineering have facilitated powerful and profitable changes in winemaking, but as the demands of sustainability loom large, we may regret our failure to preserve old knowledge. When the oil dries up, we may soon wish we remembered more about horses. Chapter 17's hilarious account of tail-chasing in wine press design reveals much about the modern developmental process, which often seems unencumbered by the thought process.

Modern science is slow to correct its own follies. Scientists have banished Pluto on the grounds that it deviates from current theories of planetary formation. In so doing, they have misappropriated the word *planet,* twisting it from its original sense of "celestial wanderer." That is to say, planets deviated from the then-prevailing cosmology. Ironically, scientists now seek to banish the ninth planet from this company on the basis that it deviates from current theories of planetary formation. Equally comic is the misapplication of dilute aqueous theory to the making of fine wine, which has misinformed our inquiry into quality for the past half century.

Postmodern winemaking calls apparent progress in modern enology continually into question, and in so doing resurrects some key notions that have gotten lost in the shuffle:

- Wines depend upon good structure for their soulfulness. The *deviation* from our cherished solution-based chemistry model is a pretty good working definition of quality.

- As in all other foods, a complex natural ecology provides distinctive and soulful character to our wines that we could never hope to manufacture. Distinctive flavors of place require a living soil nurtured through a cautious approach to herbicides and pesticides.

Unlike the naive and poorly informed Natural Wine movement, postmodern winemaking is not "hands off." To put natural flavors first requires diligent application of intelligent observation and informed action. Winemakers must work very hard to become invisible.

ORGANIZATION

The book consists of twenty-five chapters, two appendixes, and a glossary. It is largely based, with publishers' permissions, on material compiled from my monthly columns in *Wines and Vines* magazine and articles published by AppellationAmerica.com and *Practical Vineyard and Winery* magazine, reworked to include a lay audience.

In this volume, my task is to articulate to my fellow winemakers the guiding principles of a new view of our work. But the language is plain English, because it is essential to make this discussion accessible to a broader readership. Tragically, today's consumer environment has become hostile to an honest discussion of production winemaking. Winemakers lie low while the Luddite paparazzi fire live ammo over their heads. Honesty is nowhere to be found, and platitudes like "We do the minimum" are standard fare.

Winemakers are earnest, hardworking men and women who are never in it for the money. They deserve respect for walking the hard walk from critics who merely talk the easy talk. But to survive in today's competitive environment, most choose to do one thing and say another: to work like dogs and give nature the credit. By allowing wine lovers to eavesdrop on our conversation, I hope that together we can coax these heroes to begin speaking proudly and openly of their real work. I want to thank lay readers for your curiosity and courage in picking up this volume, and to encourage you to hang with me when the discussion occasionally flies over your head.

This book is organized in four parts: Principles, Practice, Technology, and Philosophy.

The initial chapters explore the principles of postmodern winemaking, beginning with the surprisingly limited degree to which wine's aesthetic properties derive from its composition. As with architecture, the properties that please us are less a function of the number of bricks than the manner in which they are arranged. I next address soulfulness and longevity, knitting together the secret life of wine colloids by touching on critical factors in each stage of winegrowing, with analogies from the kitchen. In the subsequent chapters, I examine the decisions the winemaker must make concerning fruit maturity, the conduct of fermentation, the oxygen regimen, oak influences, and bottling choices. These remarks culminate in their application to microbial management and a practical discussion of minerality, followed by an opening into the realm of the human psyche that every winemaker must address, however mysterious its portents.

The four chapters on practice are devoted to the work of some extraordinary practitioners. Every postmodern winemaker proceeds in a different way. It would be fair to call PMW an aesthetic without a manual. No particular set of instructions or ethical stands is recommended, save that winemakers ought to make consistent products and tell the truth. In many cases, winemakers experiment with such techniques as micro-oxygenation and ultrafiltration as a means to comprehend and verify for themselves *what wine really is* rather than to use them in commercial practice.

The four chapters on technology elucidate winemaking innovations of the past two decades, their value to winemakers, and their impact on the marketplace. Many of these are membrane applications for the introduction of which I am justly notorious. But while these tools are used by large corporate wineries to make clean, standardized wines, they are also employed by many thousands of small artisans (WineSmith included) to produce sound, well-made wines with distinctive character of place. Lest I be thought disingenuous for bemoaning the narrowing of style that my own innovations have helped to create, I must argue that these technologies are not responsible for the sameness at Safeway, any more than a hammer is an architect.

Distinctive wines of place still need to be sound and balanced. As Jamie Goode and Sam Harrop say in *Authentic Wine*, "Vigilance [is necessary] to prevent wine faults that obscure sense of place" (3). I have contributed to making cleaner wines by developing tools to remove excessive alcohol, volatile acidity, dry tannins, *Brettanomyces* character, and vegetal aromas. In many California wines, true ripeness is accompanied by excessive brix, leading to high alcohols that obscure sense of place. Alan Goldfarb remarked that my 12.9% "Faux Chablis" exhibited more *terroir* character but was less authentic than its hot, bitter original 14.8% version. I think that this is insightful but that Jamie and Sam's advice is closer to the mark. If I had picked at 21° brix, I would never have gotten the lemon-oil aromas I was seeking, any more than the French should hang their grapes until they raisin in order to avoid chaptalization. Nor should they tear out their splendid vineyards and plant elsewhere. Instead they should get the grapes ripe and then take steps to balance them in a way that showcases the flavors of place.

There is nothing postmodern about the technologies I present here, and this book is not a justification for them. They can be misused. But open discussion of them is very postmodern, and is, I believe, the key to getting wine lovers the same degree of comfort with them that they have with stainless steel, electric lights, and the countless familiar manipulations such as picking, crushing, and pressing.

For such a discussion to occur, my single voice will not suffice. What is needed is an open forum in which winemakers from the largest to the tiniest tell their own stories concerning these tools. I have provided such a forum at PostmodernWinemaking.com.

Winemakers are both blessed and cursed by the limelight we enjoy. If we live in glass houses, at least we are not ignored. It seems too much to ask that critics stick to the work for which they are qualified—to report and judge what they find in the glass. Like football fans, critics are unrestrained in their opinions and advice, often with little reference to the realities that professionals face every day. If a vineyard does not yield perfect alcohol balance, it should be torn out, a celebrated Natural Wine advocate recently proclaimed, thereby condemning in a few keystrokes all the vineyards of France.

Much of the conversation about innovation in winemaking centers not on whether the new tools work but on whether we will go to hell if we use them. While I too distrust anything with a power cord, I find much of this diatribe rather insubstantial—seeking to persuade through emotional appeal rather than reasoned argument. Many of the players in these discussions are more interested in selling books or padding their page-view revenues than in a serious and balanced exchange of ideas. My purpose in the final section on philosophy is to provide distinctions and perspectives that can inform more profitable deliberations about real issues.

In chapter 22, I challenge the studied reluctance of Natural Wine advocates to place on themselves any tangible definition, seeking through vagueness to hold together a constituency with widely disparate objectives. Certifications such as organic, biodynamic, and kosher, for all their faults, are at least precise, and provide winemakers something specific to shoot for beyond mouthing platitudes.

While scientific enology has virtually eliminated spoilage, it has failed to inform the making of interesting wine. Having dispensed with its easy problems, winemaking has become a theater in which we can stretch our philosophical muscles and learn to grapple with mystery. Many of our best minds have turned their attention to an investigation of biodynamic winemaking, despite its shaky foundations. The delicious controversy surrounding its advent illustrates the inefficacy of reductionist science to organize inquiry into holistic realms, the subject of chapter 21. Perhaps the most valuable outcome in this area will be to refine science's enthusiastic skepticism toward the appreciation of complex systems as they exist rather than the manner by which they came about.

Postmodern winemaking is science in service to art. The aim is human pleasure, soul to soul. Organized knowledge is not our goal, and formulated wines inevitably fall short. The same subtleties that inform both the performance and the appreciation of a musical piece are present in the process in which winemakers are privileged to partake—that of bringing a vineyard's expression to the glass.

While Nature herself is the author of every wine, it is the winemaker's job to present the timbres of terroir in a fashion that resonates in the taster's breast, guided in doing so by our mutual humanity. Nothing is more exquisite than to be deeply known by another through an offering, be it a Syrah or a symphony, that touches us beyond mere words.

I conclude in the last chapter with a defense of my own working hypothesis: that wine is, for all intents, usefully regarded as liquid music. Its capacity to embody the spectrum of emotional modalities, to exhibit harmony or dissonance that we collectively apprehend, and its power to transport us from care and circumstance are the properties that wine and music share. Attention to nuance guides the best work of the gifted winemaker no less than the virtuoso musician.

Each chapter concludes with take-home messages—points drawn from the discussion that I believe are of particular importance.

The thoughtful reader will not find himself constantly nodding his head in these pages. I am often told, "I like your writing, but I don't agree with everything you say." I should hope not. If you are constantly in accord with my assertions, I have wasted my time. Just as in every line of musical melody, resolutions in postmodern thinking are always the child of the tension of discord.

A few notes about usage. Varietal wines are capitalized throughout; varietal grapes are not. Foreign words are italicized the first time they are used. I have taken the liberty to capitalize such semiformal movements as Biodynamics and Natural Wine. Reflecting the strong role of professional women in my industry, the gender pronoun is alternated.

Acknowledgments

I have done very little original creative work. If I have a talent, it is for creatively considering the inventions of others and devising applications of worth. This is distinguished from simple stealing of ideas only by way of acknowledgment.

I omit many persons to whom I am extremely grateful, and to them I will deliver thanks personally. I seek here to serve the reader by mentioning the names and works of my intellectual benefactors who contributed in important ways to the observations this book contains. Of the hundred people acknowledged throughout its pages who contributed to my understanding of wine, I have chosen my greatest teachers for elaboration here.

No greater professional good fortune could have befallen me than the tutelage of Patrick Ducournau of Oenodev/Vivelys, who (I dare anyone to contest) is the twentieth century's most important enological innovator. His view of *élevage* would never have dented my consciousness, however, were it not for his lieutenant, Thierry Lemaire, the most remarkable postmodern winemaking ambassador to the English-speaking world that can be imagined, and his equally brilliant colleague, Jimmy Betheau.

Years before Oenodev, I benefited beyond measure from the wisdom and faith of Bruce Rector and Pascal Ribereau-Gayon, the insights of the late Don Blackburn, and the patronage of Joe Benziger, my last and best boss. At Benziger, I was introduced simultaneously to reverse osmosis, wine structure, and the international enological community—the hand of destiny obvious only in retrospect.

Since my entry into the postmodern winemaking world, my perspective has been enriched by research collaborations and generous sharing from enologists throughout the world far too numerous to list. Principal among them were the members of the OIV Groupe d'Experts sur la Technologie du Vin, in particular, Art Caputi, Jay Behmke, Michel Moutounet, Véronique Cheynier, Alain Bertrand, Terry Lee, Mario Bertuccioli, Monika Christmann, and Santiago Minguez. I have also been schooled extensively through my relationship with the Australian Wine Research Institute by Peter Godden, Paul Henschke, Richard Gawel, and Leigh Francis, among many others. Among the current faculty at UC Davis doing considerable postmodern groundbreaking are Linda Bisson, David Mills, Andy Waterhouse, Mark Matthews, David Block, Anita Oberholster, and Hildegard Heymann.

Of my colleagues at Vinovation and its licensees, I would have been fortunate indeed to have worked with only a single one of these splendid partners: Rick Jones, Kay Bogart, Domingo Rodriguez, David Wollan, Gary Baldwin, Michael Paetzold, and Gianni Trioli, all of whom advanced my understanding of wine technology immensely. From among the thousands of winemakers who have had faith in us, highly useful insights were returned by David Noyes, Richard Carey, Bo Barrett, Randall Grahm, Michael Havens, Jon Emmerich, Barry Gnekow, Bob Broman, Peter Mathis, Peter Allan, Doug Nalle, Glenn Andrade, Paul Dolan, Paul Frey, Gideon Beinstock, Randy Dunn, and John Williams. The wine industry owes a great debt to the inspired compliance innovations of BATF's enology star, Richard Gahagen.

Otherwise unmentioned in the text are many others who deserve my appreciation for their contributions to my understanding of wine's nature and its interaction with human perception.

For my grounding in the many aspects of modern winemaking, I am ever beholden to my professors at UC Davis: Ann Noble, Michael Mahoney, and Rosemary Pangborn (sensory sciences); Dinsmoor Webb, Cornelius Ough, and Michael Lewis (fermentation science); Martin Miller and Herman Pfaff (yeast); and Mark Kliewer and James Cook (viticulture). I was especially privileged to learn from phenolics guru Vernon Singleton and the brilliant and passionate wine production engineer Roger Boulton. I am most of all grateful to my microbiology major professor Ralph Kunkee and distillation ace Lynn Williams, who gave the department a richly human face.

A decade earlier, I was lucky to receive undergraduate instruction at MIT from giants: Noam Chomsky (linguistics), D. S. Kemp (chemistry), Jerome Letvin (biophilosophy), and Hans-Lukas Teuber (psychology). Before them, I learned writing from R. J. Stegner and chemistry basics from E. Leland Watkins of Indian Springs School, where any parent ought to send their children.

We learn best by teaching, and wine historian Jim Lapsley, who vastly expanded my awareness of pre–World War II enology, also contributed to my winemaking fluency by sponsoring my idea for a condensed class on wine chemistry fundamentals at the UC Davis Extension, where I taught from 1984 to 2008. Ken Fugelsang, Jim Kennedy, Barry Gump, and Susan Rodriguez played key roles both in creating my adjunct teaching position at CSU Fresno and in contributing to collaborative research; and at Florida International University, Mike Hampton, Simone Champagnie, and Chip Cassidy continue to sustain my efforts at screwball postmodern research.

In preparing this text for publication, I must first acknowledge Jim Gordon of Wines and Vines for supporting many of the initial articles as a monthly column in *Wines and Vines* magazine and Roger Dial, who published most of the rest on AppellationAmerica.com, where Dick Peterson has generously contributed endless hours to the Best-of-Appellation panel. UC Press sponsoring editor Blake Edgar has been an encouraging and instructive ally throughout the book's rendering, supported by talented production editor Rose Vekony. The illustrations were mostly rendered by Jennifer Shontz, except the multipanel cartoons (figures 1 and 9), which were done by Brenda Cornett. Anne Canright and Sheila Berg supplied over a thousand editorial suggestions, deftly balancing my tone between the scholarly and the insouciant, continually impressing me with their compositional acumen and tolerance of, shall we say, my artistic temperament. Marilyn Flaig's skillful index can be read alternatively to the table of contents as a guide to the issues I address.

Thanks for their insightful reviews of the text to Jamie Goode, Bruce Zoecklein, Lisa Granik, and, above all, Joel Peterson, who was kind enough to really whack me on the shaky parts.

While any writer benefits from a supportive family, few are as fortunate to receive technical insights in their chosen field as I have been from my now-deceased clinical psychologist wife, Susie Meyer-Smith, and from my talented systems engineer brother and partner, Brian Smith.

Introduction

I perceive today an ever-widening gap between winemakers and consumers. As in any marriage of long standing, we sometimes go for long periods without talking as much as we should, especially when changes are occurring that we can scarcely articulate. The fine folks who pay good money for wine are disconnected from wine production people, so distanced are wineries from their customers. Even at the winery, as winemaking matures as a business, visitors to the homes of the familiar brands are far more likely to encounter marketing and salespeople than actual winemakers.

The intimate relationship that is part of the promise and the appeal of an essentially artisanal industry also suffers from a growing distrust of winemakers, fostered by a mounting awareness of unexplained and suspicious-sounding winemaking technologies. What's with all this manipulation? In our increasingly competitive world, winemakers, when heard from at all, tend to deliver soft soap that pegs our malarkey meter, and even in one-on-one conversation the boutique winemaker will often be less than frank about treatments the wine has undergone.

All too often, a technological path chosen for making the best wine is not divulged publicly. It is no simple thing today for winemakers to tell the truth. Under pressure from their marketing departments to produce that special something while appearing to do nothing, winemakers commonly chicken out, claiming to "do the minimum," unaware that this apparent duplicity casts an odor of suspicion on our profession.

With a dizzying availability of wines of every stripe, it's little wonder the buying public has turned to supposedly unbiased third parties to make their choices for them. Critics have assumed a powerful policing role despite, with rare exceptions, an absence of any serious winemaking training.

In the midst of this chaos, a revolution is taking place within the winemaking community. Precepts of the modern winemaking system we were all taught in school simply don't support the making of the great wines the market demands, and as a result, some of our most successful winemakers have strayed quite far from conventional dogma.

My intention in this volume is to articulate concisely and systematically the new paradigm of winemaking that dominates the forefront of research and practice. Although this is an insider's view of today's wine industry and I speak to my fellow winemakers in our common language, I have chosen a style that is also digestible for the engaged lay reader driven by curiosity, supplying enough chemistry and microbiology background to clarify the conversation as generally as possible. In elucidating our new way of looking at wine, I hope to enable winemakers to articulate more powerfully the methods and tools they choose, and to elicit some sympathy on the part of the consumer for the devil of technology properly employed.

In each chapter, I focus on a specific arena of our work, teasing out the complexities and philosophical dramas that an experienced winemaker confronts. These different threads are all part of one cloth. The Postmodern Winemaking movement seeks to reconnect with winemaking's ancient aesthetic, much of which was inadvertently left behind in the technology revolution following World War II. I hope that what emerges is a new vision of the winemaker's task and a clearer understanding of what wine really is.

Since the text is addressed to the practicing winemaker, the eavesdropping lay reader will encounter enological terminology that may be unfamiliar. Whenever possible, I have expanded my explanations to make technical winemaking concepts available to a broader audience without derailing the discussion's logical flow. The reader who feels left behind despite these efforts is directed to the appendixes, which include a brief summary of winemaking basics and a glossary short enough that it can be read from beginning to end in one sitting (I recommend the online version). Your best move, when these fail, is to seek out a real production winemaker and quiz her over a glass of her best.

Because even for professionals the principles presented here compose an unfamiliar picture, I have found it useful to repeat certain notions in the text to facilitate a global view. I hope I have struck a tolerable balance between excessive redundancy and leaving too few breadcrumbs.

WHAT IS POSTMODERN WINEMAKING?

How can he remember well his ignorance, which his growth requires,
who has so often to use his knowledge?
—Henry David Thoreau (1817–1862)

In the past few years I have been employing the term *postmodern* to refer to the paradigm shift in winemaking that I have observed and in some ways instigated. In my experience, postmodernism is not well understood in its general sense; instead, it gains meaning mostly through its diverse manifestations. Consequently, colleagues often wonder what connection could possibly exist between this new winemaking school of thought and other expressions with which they are familiar such as postmodern painting, architecture, theater, film, music, and philosophy.

Since postmodernism is by its very nature polymorphous, such confusion is to be expected. For readers wishing to gain a working understanding of the movement as a whole, I recommend *A Primer on Postmodernism* by Stanley J. Grenz, a concise map of postmodernism's origins, principles, mind-set, and diverse embodiments.

All winemaking is a fundamentally postmodern sort of endeavor, touching inevitably on many key postmodern notions: the manifestation of Nature both in wine's production and its appreciation, a broad diversity of localized style goals, the primary importance of collaborative groups, and the relativity of truth. Fine wine is a theater in which deconstruction occurs naturally and modern scientific practices are inadequate to guide extraordinary work. One cannot avoid becoming immersed in environmental concerns in the growing of wine grapes. A winery is a team, and an appellation is a tribe. Truth worth knowing is largely local rather than universal, for wines vary widely from place to place in the characteristics that are expected and extolled—a great sherry is a terrible Riesling.

Wine is formless, assuming the shape of its container, but it interacts with its containers, both the barrel and the glass, in complex ways. Its message is pure experience conveyed without language. Just as any theatrical performance is unique and ephemeral, the qualities of any particular wine are neither universal in appeal nor fixed in time. Defining and quantifying wine quality has proven extraordinarily elusive, and its complex chemistry has yet to be thoroughly characterized and rationalized.

But I am getting ahead of myself. Here I will provide a basic grounding in postmodern thinking and then spotlight, one by one, a variety of postmodern principles that have guided my wine production consulting work and compelled in this book its ever-shifting focus on assorted topics.

ORIGINS AND PRINCIPLES

From its roots in the experimental music, theater, painting, and architecture of the late 1960s counterculture, postmodernism has come to pervade all walks of life and fields of endeavor. Its sundry and sometimes contradictory manifestations derive in part from its origins as a rejection of modernism, which caused it to range out from that central dogma in various directions.

At its core, postmodernism questions the modernist optimism that fueled the Enlightenment, when Francis Bacon declared that knowledge is power and Descartes proposed his idealized vision of the rational skeptic, essentially today's trained scientist. Armed with generalized laws such as Newton's mechanics, this dispassionate and unbiased hero is charged with shaping an ever better world by uncovering Nature's secrets and exercising dominion over her. Four hundred years later, we are beginning to sense that this plan is not working out so well for us.

In our lifetimes, a cavalcade of technological missteps—nuclear proliferation; destruction of the ozone layer; the meltdowns at Three Mile Island, Chernobyl, and Fukushima; failures of the works of the U.S. Army Corps of Engineers; wholesale global species extinctions; and the continuing erosion of the right to privacy all come to mind—have led emerging generations to lose faith in the infallibility of science to competently coordinate technological central planning. Postmoderns seek instead to move beyond rationalism as the sole determiner of what is true, beautiful, sustainable, and good. More room is allowed for intuitive leaps, the wisdom of myth, and the workings of natural forces that we neither control nor fully grasp. If the inner city is the symbol of modern power over nature, the virgin forest symbolizes postmodern cooperation with Nature, including respect for her power to manifest complex, balanced ecologies that are robust, sustainable, and aesthetically appealing with scant help from humankind.

One problem with Descartes's vision of the ideal rationalist is that pitfalls inevitably await any human ego steeped in decades of training and study. *I worked so hard; surely I must know something!* In principle, we should be able to count on Descartes's ideal skeptic to be as skeptically rigorous inwardly as outwardly. He must also be unswayed in his evaluations by considerations of endowment funding, tenure, or personal exigency and immune to loyalties and enmities.

He must, in short, know himself. But this is seldom the case. Such training happens over in the humanities, way across campus.

Modern confidence in rationality is vulnerable to an additional pitfall. In the sciences, it's a thin line between the rationalistic axiom that all understanding is, in principle, accessible to the human mind and the conclusion that what is inaccessible is unreal or even fraudulent. Otherwise rational and dispassionate winemaker colleagues have devoted endless hours to websites such as biodynamicsisahoax.com—a phenomenon explored in chapter 21, "Science and Biodynamics." My argument in that chapter is that no outside observer is in a position to take a solid stance on biodynamic winegrowing, either pro or con, and I make no such attempt myself. I have much bigger fish to fry.

Postmoderns question that human ingenuity can, or even ought to, be dominant in guiding our lives and works down a path of inevitable progress. In contrast to a faith in the boundless resilience of our home planet, which led moderns to hang portraits of belching smokestacks in their corporate boardrooms, postmoderns see the Earth as fragile and vulnerable, with the extinction of the human species very much in play. The postmodern vineyardist, more specifically, is a steward of Nature rather than her master, seeking to foster a balanced ecology of unfathomable complexity rather than a simple monoculture that may be easy to manage but is vulnerable to opportunistic pathology and disappointing in terroir expression.

What's done is done. Postmodern winemakers are generally not Luddites seeking to turn back the clock. Winemaking typically takes place in very tough circumstances, and we prefer to keep our technical options open. By and large, we seek to work within the conditions of modernity, incorporating what is useful while moving beyond the hubris of the modern mind-set. To paraphrase 1 Corinthians, postmodernism believes all things and hopes all things. Few winemakers want to give up electric lights, pH meters, stainless steel, or Google, but we do increasingly reexamine the hidden impact of these conveniences. (See chapter 16, "Pressing Matters," for a humorous postmodern fable along these lines.)

Modern scientists view themselves as having shed allegiance to myth and superstition and believe that they have been trained to see the world rationally, as it "actually" is. After decades of dedicated study, they feel qualified to answer press inquiries, testify in legal actions, and serve on government task forces as reliable, dispassionate experts in their fields.

Postmoderns, in contrast, assert that science draws its legitimacy from myths of its own: the capacity of the rational mind to comprehend the natural world, the inevitability of progress, the universality of Nature's laws, and the power and freedom inevitably gained by knowledge of them. In addition, every expert is seen as having an ax to grind, often tied to grant money, corporate patronage, or legal retainer. Knowledge is not seen as always good. Many would gladly return to a time before we obtained knowledge of the atom's secrets or biology's terrorist potential.

In their skepticism of modern science, postmoderns aspire to break down the wall between the professional and the amateur. In this book, I strive to address both groups by using language that is as simple as possible, but no simpler, respecting both the lay reader's intelligence and the need for clarity, even seduction in my prose. I have often found that it is much easier for laypersons to relate to such postmodern winemaking concepts as structure, mineral energy, and soulfulness than it is for many professionals. Wine lovers are in fact often astounded to learn that these holistic terms are in professional disrepute, while concrete sensory component descriptors (e.g., berry, citrus, tar) are considered more relevant in academic circles.

APPLICATIONS TO WINEMAKING

In the eleven chapters of Part I, I articulate my own picture of postmodern winemaking, largely in technical language, though I've done my best to make my thinking accessible to a broad lay audience. For readers who have not made wine before, I recommend beginning by reading Appendix 1, "Winemaking Basics." All readers should keep in mind the "Glossary of Postmodern Terminology" as well, particularly the interactive online version, for insight into technical expressions. There is merit in reading the online glossary from beginning to end, A to Z, taking advantage of the links.

In the following discussion I will elucidate the winemaking applications of postmodern techniques, including construction, deconstruction, and juxtaposition. In addition, I will explore the application to winemaking of such postmodern themes as environmentalism, collaboration, localized and transient truths, subjectivity, holism, transparency, authentic scientific inquiry, and courageous uncertainty.

Many postmodern art forms juxtapose disparate worldviews, often interweaving elements of high technology with classical aesthetics. Scandalously, my own work is characterized by a willingness to apply winemaking's new power tools, some of which I invented, to the making of classic European styles, for which I am affectionately known in Natural Wine circles as Doctor Evil.

In my WineSmith Roman Syrah project, which Jamie Goode referred to in his insightful blog, wineanorak.com, as "the surprising juxtaposition of wine technology and natural wines,"[1] I utilize high-tech tools as needed in order to make sulfite-free reds of wonderful aromatic expression and remarkable longevity. These tools include reverse osmosis (see chapter 18), which facilitates balanced wines of perfect ripeness and maximum antioxidative power and is useful to trim occasional volatile acidity. In creating a refined structure that can integrate microbial aromatics and stabilize tannins, I then routinely employ micro-oxygenation (MOx) (see chapter 3) in reds just after fermentation in order to exploit the very phenolic reactive power true ripeness imparts.

Any winemaker will tell you that serious discussions about wine begin and end in the vineyard. That is where the magic happens. It is the winemaker's job, through skilled artisanal effort, to become invisible, the better to clear the way for the influences of provenance that are the sources of regional character: climate, soil, altitude, latitude, cultivar, vineyard practices and local social traditions.

I think winemakers get a bad rap. Yes, it's our job to appear invisible, to stay out of the way of natural expression, but that involves a very intensive sort of doing nothing. The artisan, though ignorantly despised for his stealthy conjurings, remains the secret agent without whom all is lost, for it is through the skillful winemaker that apparently naked flavors of place become manifest in the glass with the same apparent ease and weightlessness that years of effort lend to the graceful, seemingly effortless fluidity of the prima ballerina. Naturalness in wine is an illusion borne of much study and struggle, and winemakers ought to be proud of what they do instead of pretending to do nothing.

We have come a long way from the ridicule and marginalization that initially greeted Rachel Carson's *Silent Spring* in 1962. Millennials entering our industry today insist that environmentally friendly practices such as Integrated Pest Management can and must be the rule. While I am disappointed by many details of organic certification for U.S. wines, as I discuss in chapters 5, "Vineyard Enology," and 8, "Speculations on Minerality," I support the notion of living soil and believe that such vineyards not only support environmental concerns but also make better wine. I go on to propose the adoption of a similar philosophy in the cellar in chapter 10, "Integrated *Brettanomyces* Management."

While I find that these "better wines" have more palate energy and dimensionality, are more resistant to oxidation, and hold up longer in the cellar, they also have their own special problems, which I discuss in chapter 7, "Redox Redux." They are better in a technical sense, in the way that an athlete has a better body. But wines resulting from organic practices are not to everyone's taste, and thus are in no universal sense ideal.

IDEAL WINES

Postmoderns question the utility and virtue of generalized universal truth discovered through rational inquiry and manifest in formulas, equations, and laws. Modern enology has been organized into a set of fundamental best practices that enable wines in commerce to be more dependable than ever before in history. Large corporate wineries with the marketing muscle to enter the three-tier distribution system (producer to distributor to retailer to consumer) are now able to put on retail shelves tremendous volumes of Merlots, Chardonnays, and Pinots that feature precise and consistent flavor profiles.

The triumph of modern standardization is that Annette Alvarez-Peters, chief wine buyer for Costco and one of the six most influential people in the wine world according to *Decanter* magazine,[2] was able in 2012 to opine, quite correctly, that wine in Costco is a commodity no different from toilet paper. "In the end, it's just a beverage. Either you like it or you don't."[3]

Costco restricts its offerings to 300 brands, less than a tenth of a percent of the wines on offer nationwide, with $1 billion in sales annually. Another force in U.S. wine sales is the mega-distributor Southern Wines and Spirits, which dominates U.S. distribution with fewer than 10,000 labels, a mere 5% of the total selection approved for sale by the U.S. Alcohol and Tobacco Tax and Trade Bureau (TTB). These wines succeed in the three-tier system largely to the extent that they precisely fit the standardized model for flavor and packaging associated with their standard wine type. If they are "interesting," they fail. Enologix, a highly paid Sonoma-based wine database enterprise, thrives through advising wineries how to scientifically reverse-engineer *Wine Spectator* scores, instructing winemakers how to make standardized wines that will garner top reviews.

If you're looking for diversity, you will have to get in your Prius and seek it out. Despite rumors of its impending demise, there is another, separate wine industry with perhaps one hundred times the labels and one-hundredth the sales volume. But you have to go there.

Postmoderns focus on truths that are local, particular, and transient, and on honoring diversity and pluralism. What industry could more vividly embody these notions than the multiplicity of individual vineyards throughout the world? *In vino veritas.* Each terroir has its own truth, its own story to express in its own way. My work with AppellationAmerica.com's Best-of-Appellation evaluations program seeks to compile a Blue Book that articulates the regional characteristics of all 312 appellations in North America so that we can move beyond varietal labeling to a consciousness of the vast variety of available choices. Our goal is to foster a growing comfort level with such delights as Sandusky Gewurztraminer and Iowa Frontenac Port.

The last thing that a postmodern wine should do is conform to expectations. Nowhere is the specific more vital than in the making of wines of distinctive terroir expression. That is the antithesis of the modern corporate winemaker's job description, but for the 99% (okay, maybe it's only 98%), the small and struggling wineries on the D list that have no chance at national distribution, it represents the only hope for salvation.

The division between modern corporate commodity winemaking and boutique postmodern distinctive terroir expression is not doomed to persist. Retail channels will adjust once consumers begin to demand the same access to the diversity of New World styles as they do for European wines, where flavors of place hold sway. No one would liken a St. Emilion to a Chinon simply because they are both Cabernet Francs. In the same way, Long Island Merlots may earn a separate shelf space alongside those of California, and the Chardonnays of Napa, the Santa Cruz Mountains, and Lake Erie may come to be independently displayed and understood.

RELATIVITY AND QUANTUM EFFECTS

Postmoderns reject the notion of the objective observer. Particle physics, with its uncertainty principle, contingent realities, superstring theory, multiverse, and quantum leaps, was the first of the modern sciences to cross over into postmodernism, abandoning half a century ago any notion of mechanistic objective observation. The Enlightenment viewpoint just doesn't carry any water in this discipline. The existence of universal truth and objective reality are not prerequisites for functionality, and you've got to admit that physics seems to have muddled along pretty well without them.

Rejecting both the existence and the value of objectivity allows us to shed the pejorative connotations of subjective experience. Strictly speaking, for an experience to be subjective means merely that it is perceived by humans. But this pure sense has been perverted in modern parlance, and when we say, "That's just subjective," we mean to imply a finding that is random, unknowable, and unverifiable. Yet when *all* experience is understood to be subjective, we are compelled to look for patterns and areas of agreement—which music and chaos theory's fractal images alike illustrate to be quite striking and beautiful.

The postmodern view is that the experience of a wine is not actually in the bottle; rather, wine resonates in tandem with its consumer according to the environment of consumption. This interaction possesses features of resonance, harmony, and dissonance that are strongly shared and for which predictive strategies can be employed. This is the art of serving wine.

One of the greatest intellectual challenges of postmodern philosophy is to reconcile, on the one hand, the notion that everything is connected to everything else, with the equally firm principle, on the other, that every experience is unique. This is accomplished by abandoning the reductionist false friend that moderns so often employ: division of experience into manageable little pieces that can be studied, then reassembled in a sort of plug-and-play philosophy. Insistence on working only with whole experiences frees the investigator to explore patterns within complex systems, often with unexpected results such as the well-substantiated existence of harmonious "sweet spots" obtained by altering alcohol content as little as one-tenth of one percent, a topic introduced in chapter 11, "Harmony and Astringency," and developed in chapters 18, "The New Filtrations," and 25, "Liquid Music."

Attention to holistic systems guides the viticultural modeling of Bob Wample and David Gates (see chapter 15). A willingness to work outside the rationality box has supplied many of our field's key discoveries, which I explore in chapter 12, "Winemaking's Lunatic Heroes." In chapter 21, "Science and Biodynamics," I discuss in particular an eccentric path inexplicably chosen by many souls admired for their shrewdness and perspicacity. I confess that I have a chip on my shoulder here concerning the oft-asserted modern claim that homeopathy has no scientific basis, the refutation of which ties together Biodynamics, micro-oxygenation, and Singleton's vicinal diphenol cascade in a delightful postmodern thematic juxtaposition, a sort of running joke throughout the book. My goal in all this is not to defend Biodynamics or homeopathy per se but to open the minds of scientists.

The legitimacy of homeopathy (that is to say, a challenge to a system by a small amount of a harmful substance, which the system learns to resist) is a pet peeve among modern scientists, held in about the same regard as astrology. Yet we have plenty of examples where a homeo-pathic approach is demonstrably valid, vaccination representing a prime example. The wholesale adaptation of this principle to every natural system, as the Biodynamics evangelist Nicolas Joly extols in his lectures, does indeed seem both simplistic and risky. But this is wine—essentially playful, seldom a matter of emergency. Before we declare scientific mar-tial law banning new ideas, we had better have a clear and present danger. In my judgment, no imminent threat exists except to contempo-rary science as Mr. Know-It-All, in which case I fear that, until they come to get me, I must declare for the other side. I defend the concept of homeopathy not so much because I entirely accept it, but more because its mere mention makes modern scientific blood boil.

The experience fine wine affords, for which we shell out the big bucks, does not arise through scientifically delimited natural processes controlled by technical best practices; rather, it is a dance between spe-cific, unknowable ecological particulars (climate, soil, microbiology) and the peculiarities of human perception that are brought to bear when the cork is drawn, all orchestrated through the invisible guiding hand of the winemaker. This is the postmodern view.

Postmodern winemaking seeks to deconstruct the embedded myths that shape modern winemaking but fail to serve winemakers well. These pedagogies include the application of the solution model, the direct link between chemical and microbial composition on the one hand and fla-vor on the other, and the use of component aromatics as preference drivers for quality.

In his penetrating review of the manuscript of this book, Ravenswood founder Joel Peterson asked an excellent question: "Do we really have to give up the Enlightenment to move ahead?" My answer is yes, I'm afraid we do. By this I do not mean abandoning the tools of skeptical inquiry, experimentation, and hypothesis verification; we do, however, need to foster an awareness of the limitations of these techniques. We must question the whole notion of objective universal truths, and even cast a skeptical eye on their value. We have every reason to be suspicious of the capacity of the human mind to comprehend and conquer nature. What evidence do we really have that knowledge expands and progress is certain? The Enlightenment anticipated a gain in clarity as we approach universal truths. Postmoderns instead see growing paradox as we knit together a picture of how things are, as in the case of the wave/particle duality in atomic physics.

The UC Davis–spawned Aroma Wheel™ is a familiar example of modern enology's reductionist attempts to manage sensory impact by dissecting aromas into their constituent pieces. There is no evidence that varietal characters or any other constituent aromas are compelling drivers for lovers of structured reds. For Riesling and Muscat, surely the flowery linalool and geraniol terpenes drive sales—the more, the better. One can point to vanillin (an oak extractive) as a hook for novice red wine fans. But these are regarded as cheap tricks in the big leagues, where an inarticulable profundity in great reds is what has connoisseurs reaching for their wallets, just as with the great unpasteurized cheeses of France and Italy.

Flavors of terroir receive much ink in reviews, evoking the intense joy that comes from being shown deep places in one's own soul. Embodying a unique communion of taster and place, such flavors—whether of a fine red wine, an earthy Guatemalan coffee, or a perfectly spiced Thai soup—evoke profound connection, of being thoroughly known by someone far away. But these aromas are by nature unique, never to appear on a standard wheel.

The appreciation and evaluation of wine, the subject of chapter 24, presents intricate intellectual challenges that baffle novices and can perplex the most experienced professional. We cannot judge a wine unless we know the tradition in which it was made, yet to maintain objectivity, judges taste double-blind and are not told if a particular Chardonnay, for example, is from a nationally distributed brand of half a million cases or a tiny lot sold only out of a tasting room in an obscure location.

Postmodern philosophy offers useful tools for peering into the wine tasting process, concerning itself very much with perception, art, and language. Novice wine drinkers have a very different, one might say, a purer, sensory experience of what is in the glass than trained professionals do. As they try more wines, they naturally accumulate a growing vocabulary to parse their experience as they connect, through their own invention and through instruction, colors and flavors with sources such as varietal characteristics, oak, microbial activity, and aging. When tied to a wine genre, usually sprung from a European antecedent, this language may allow agreement with other tasters and a capacity to rate quality in the context of accepted style rules.

But these are human cultural constructs that quickly come to dominate perception itself. In appellations with well-established style traditions, wines are experienced through the lens of local custom. As with English speakers in rural Scotland, New Jersey, or the Deep South who do not perceive themselves as speaking with accents, the locally familiar becomes invisible.

It is only when compared to other regions that the local becomes colorful or eccentric. Just as television-speak occurring as a global unaccented standard renders local dialects peculiar, quaint, or even unintelligible, so today have globally distributed "expected" styles of Merlot, Chardonnay, and Riesling restricted the commerciality of small local producers in climatically unique areas. Global styles are not the pinnacle of quality; they provide consistency at the risk of a boring uniformity that has led to a recent appetite for diversity. Sorting among these wines with no fixed standards to guide us is a considerable challenge from which established reviewers such as the *Wine Advocate* and the *Wine Spectator* have, for the most part, shrunk from leadership. The coming-of-age of a surprising panoply of well-made wines from regions throughout the New World calls for a shift to a postmodern mind-set that respects and celebrates diversity. The theme of the birthing pains of New World identity is explored more fully in chapter 24.

Hans-Georg Gadamer's hermeneutics concerns itself with the way language arises as individuals experience art in a social context and maps the interplay of experience, thought, and language, threading a path that accepts both the objective reality of Enlightenment thinking and each individual's unique creative interaction with that reality. The wine exists, but each person's experience of it is unique, subject to personal interpretation, the opinions of peers, and the context, sometimes sterile, often romantic, in which it is served. Without question, the surest way to appreciate a wine is to share a glass with the winemaker at its place of origin.

LEVELS OF UNKNOWING

Jean-François Lyotard proclaimed in his seminal work, *The Postmodern Condition: A Report on Knowledge,* that "postmodernity is not a new age, but the rewriting of some of the features claimed by modernity, and first of all modernity's claim to ground its legitimacy on the project of liberating humanity as a whole through science and technology."[4] I have drawn much from my scientific training at MIT and Davis and receive regular thanks from winemakers for having applied it to the general benefit of our industry. I want to state definitively that I am entirely in favor of the courageous, skeptical inquiry that science represents. I am not anti-science, any more than I am anti-Christmas, but I am saddened by the commerciality and autocracy that today characterize both. I love enology and would like to see its practitioners clean up their game. I am anti-hubris and anti-arrogance but pro-humility and pro-inquiry.

The proper place for science in postmodern winemaking is in service to the winemaker's true purpose: to bottle something that when opened months or decades later satisfies human appreciation. It is clear that science has made tremendous advances, but still it must be admitted that our glass of knowledge is far from half full. Our ignorance can be parsed into three categories.

1. *Uncollected information:* that which we know we don't know but have yet to discern, investigate, or verify.

2. *Invisible ignorance:* that which we have not the language even to ask questions about, let alone delve for answers to, restricted as we are by our fixed way of thinking. Richard Feynman said that to see the limitations of current science we need look no further than the mysteries of fluid flow in a pipe.[5] Physicists will tell you that their work is so bizarre that the mind really cannot grasp it; instead we retreat into mathematics and machine calculations for our predictions. If we build machines that grind out accurate predictions, can we then claim these as prizes of science, when in truth they are not really within our grasp?

3. *The experiential imponderable:* that which is either fundamentally mysterious or otherwise unknowable. Scientific understanding works from underlying generalities, so it is not experiential in nature. It can state how to construct a major chord but cannot explain why it is cheerful while a minor chord is melancholy. It can explain why the rain precipitates but cannot capture the apprehension of autumn's first rainfall under an ancient elm with a special someone.

These lyrical, disorderly, unscientific phrasings point to a different kind of truth, a human truth, the apprehension of which is critical to the human condition and not at all the business of science. The actual experience of drinking wine falls into this category and cannot be published, posted, or televised.

The postmodern respect for diversity is also a characteristic of our craft. Each winery is its own separate world, which is what makes them so much fun to visit one by one on a day's outing.

I offer no formulations for making wine, nor do I advocate any particular tools. Although I describe the use of oxygen (chapter 3), barrels and oak alternatives (chapter 4), alcohol adjustment (chapter 17), many uses of membranes (chapter 18), flash détente (chapter 19), and yeast inoculation (chapter 23), I present these for winemakers to consider in their own unique situations, as items in their tool kits, and for lay readers better to understand what they are and why we might use them.

If critics are no longer trusted as arbiters of right action, postmodern practitioners need to explain their reasoning in making their winemaking choices. I recommend that you never use a tool that you are unwilling to disclose. This is really what is meant by manipulation. If you know a wine will improve by lowering its alcohol content with reverse osmosis, be a *mensch* (you too, ladies) and own up to it, explain yourself—and make the better wine. Until we stop sweeping our best work under the rug, we will forever be under the lash of poorly informed, ill-intentioned paparazzi.

My own bent is neoclassical. I make very Pauillac-like Cabernet Sauvignon; Cabernet Franc in a style somewhere between Graves and St. Emilion; a minerally Chardonnay that I call Faux Chablis; and a sulfite-free Roman Syrah. I pick my grapes ripe but not overripe and will, if needed, lower alcohol content, usually below 14%, with reverse osmosis. I generally like to structure my reds with Phase 1 micro-oxygenation. My goals are to show that California grapes are very well suited to European styles and that they are capable of great longevity if properly balanced.

Not all postmodern thought seeks to recapture the wisdom of the ancients, but in wine there is every reason to attempt to do so. Winemaking is far, far older than our knowledge of chemistry and microbiology, and no inquiring mind can remain incurious about what our antecedents knew that we have lost.

Indeed, the most radical and exciting activity in winemaking today is the rediscovery in post-Soviet Georgia—where the technique originated—and other hot spots as widespread as Friuli and Brooklyn, of the ancient method of burying, for many months or even as long as a decade, sealed clay *qvevri* (giant earthenware vessels) filled with white grapes, skins, seeds, and stems.

The premodern classic eras in which European appellations established their characteristics are creative bedfellows with postmodernism's challenges to contemporary convention. Like grandparents and grandchildren, they are united against a common enemy.

You have already seen my definition of postmodern winemaking: "the practical art of connecting the human soul to the soul of a place by rendering its grapes into liquid music." I know this sounds limp-wristed at first glance. My goal in this book is to persuade the reader to embrace this definition as a down-to-earth working mandate that directs our daily endeavors.

A final key element of postmodern thought is a willingness *not* to know. It would be a sad waste of time for me to attempt to replace the fallacies of my modern forerunners with pontifications of my own. I am quite sure that this book contains nothing that is "true" in the modern sense. As the postmodern pragmatist Richard Rorty famously observed, "Truth is simply a compliment paid to sentences seen to be paying their way."[6] This does not mean that the postmodern practitioner holds all points of view to be equally valid. One goes with what works. Truth is looked for in local functionality rather than in some universal objective reality.

The winemaker's goals are not perfectly aligned with academic realities such as grants, tenure, and peer credibility. Chapter 12 acknowledges the debt owed by rationalists to the crackpot visionaries who have done the exploratory heavy lifting that has always preceded organized research.

Far from discarding the scientific tradition that has brought us so much knowledge and power, I seek to incorporate its most useful findings and approaches, the ones that prove coherent with our human goals. This book is not intended as a declaration of war on modern enology, or a wine technologist's apologist diatribe against those earnest voices speaking out for Natural Wine, but rather as a love letter to all those who toil in and around winemaking, and an invitation to every person who has read this far to jump into the deep end. My hope is to convey a perspective that illuminates for each reader a path to your own truth and, more important, a useful model for making sense of the messages that wines themselves may transmit in connecting winemakers and wine lovers.

PART ONE

Principles

1

The Solution Problem

Progress has never been a bargain. You have to pay for it.
Sometimes I think there's a man who sits behind a counter
and says, "Madam, you can have a telephone, but you'll lose
privacy, and the charm of distance. Mister, you may conquer
the air; but the birds will lose their wonder, and the clouds
will smell of gasoline."
—Jerome Lawrence and Robert Edwin Lee, *Inherit the Wind*

Louis Pasteur's 1857 discovery of yeast as the mechanism of fermentation ushered in a century of discovery in the new science of enology, replacing the trial-and-error approach of traditional winemaking. In 1880, research stations in Bordeaux and Davis, California, were established to apply the fruits of scientific advancement to modern winemaking.

The advent of electricity altered traditional winemaking forever. So welcome were the advantages in lighting, labor savings, and refrigeration that one would be hard pressed today to name a winery without electricity anywhere in the world. As time-honored methods and equipment were rapidly discarded, a holistic system painstakingly developed over millennia was abandoned in the wink of an eye.

As easy as it is to praise the advantages of these sweeping changes, there was a downside.

Replacing empirical systems with theoretical methods devalues hundreds of years of specific knowledge and practice, tending to bring a squeaky-clean sameness to all wine. Before electricity, much greater care and attention was devoted to every step of the winemaking process.

When twentieth-century tools such as stainless steel, inert gas, refrigeration, and sterile filtration became widely available for the first time just after World War II, a modern winemaking revolution exploded out of Germany. A completely new way of making Riesling—fresh, sterile-filtered, completely without oxidative characters—rapidly became the standard for white wine making throughout the world.

It is hard today to appreciate the impact of this new type of wine. Sterile filtration came about as a product of nuclear energy, for the first integrity-testable filters were etched in atomic piles. The idea of a light, sweet, fresh, fruity wine like Blue Nun was as world-changing as color television.

Not to be outdone, Bordeaux installed its own stainless steel, refrigeration, inert gas, and sterile filtration, creating new possibilities for fresh white wines and as many problems for reds when oxygen was declared its bogeyman. In *The Taste of Wine*,[1] University of Bordeaux Oenology Faculty Director Emile Peynaud wrote in 1955 that "oxygen is the enemy of wine," a "blunt definition" unfortunately often quoted out of context. Technical progress banished the old guard from the caves, replaced by followers of Peynaud's solution chemistry–based scientific enology.

The modern approach spread from Germany first to Bordeaux and then across the ocean in the late 1950s. It sounded like a good idea at the time. In retrospect, it has become clear that using Riesling techniques on Cabernet led us away from red wine's soulful, integrative properties. The 1961 Bordeaux vintage is still tough drinking even today. Who knew?

It was to take half a century before people once again recognized oxygen's power to elaborate and refine structure. Without this knowledge, wines of normal maturity exhibited excessive reduction, malformed tannins, poor aromatic integration of vegetal, oak, and microbial notes, and unfortunate aging behavior. By the 1970s, the châteaux were coping by pressing fermentations early and stripping tannins with aggressive egg white fining, which resulted in drinkable styles that lacked depth. In the 1980s, Australia's flying winemakers introduced extended hang time techniques to the South of France; this overcame reduction problems through field oxidation, leading to fruit-forward quaffs that enjoyed a fad in the United Kingdom and the United States.

The poor longevity of ultra-ripe experiments in the 1990s at prestigious properties in Bordeaux and Barolo, coupled with a sea change in enology from solution-model thinking to an appreciation of tannin structure through research undertaken at Montpellier, Bordeaux, and AWRI (Australian Wine Research Institute), led producers to consider a return to prewar practices.

In the late 1980s, the idea that good tannin structure was capable of integrating aromas began to be explored two hours south of Bordeaux in the tiny hamlet of Madiran, where modern vinification techniques had wrought disaster. If the postmodern movement has a father, it is a peasant *vigneron* named Patrick Ducournau, who toiled to discover what had gone so terribly wrong with the region's traditional tannat variety. These huge, tannic wines had become incredibly dry, harsh, and prone to overt expression of microbial defects. His neighbors were busily tearing their tannat vines out and globalizing to merlot.

It was Ducournau's genius to recognize the real problem: without the use of controlled oxidative polymerization, the art of building structure had been lost. Protecting tannat from oxygen was killing the wines. His development of micro-oxygenation was the first step toward reviving a methodology of *élevage,* a suite of practices devoted to the "raising up" of refined structure capable of supporting integration and soulfulness. The complete package eventually included an advanced understanding of the use of lees and a complete rethinking of the role of barrels.

THAT'S NO SOLUTION

Scientific enology starts with the idea that wine is a chemical solution. This simple, seemingly obvious statement guides all phases of modern winemaking. It also happens to be false.

Solution-based thinking has shaped our view of wine and how we work with it by bringing to bear the powerful tools of analytical chemistry, chemical engineering, and sensory science. If wine is a solution, its sensory properties derive from the concentrations of substances dissolved in solution. The greater its concentration in the liquid, the more intense that substance's odor and taste. If this relationship is exactly linear, the solution is said to behave "ideally."

If wine is a solution, the goal of grape growing must be to maximize good flavors and minimize bad ones. We have only to identify the substances involved and determine which are positive drivers and which are negative. More fruity, less veggie, and so forth.

If red color is dissolved in solution, the way to extract more of it from the skins is to work the cap in a gentle way, which maximizes color but prevents excessive harsh tannin extraction. High alcohol is viewed as increasing the solubility of red pigment.

Tannin is viewed as the price we have to pay for flavor, so we press as gently as possible (or just use free run) to minimize harshness and allow the palate access to fruity flavors. Everything in winemaking becomes about selective extraction.

If excessive harsh tannin is dissolved in wine, the way to decrease its sensory effect is to remove it through selective fining, taking care to minimize concomitant decreases in color and flavor.

If wine is a solution, it can be sterile filtered without changing its sensory properties, removing particulates without affecting the solution.

In general, solution theory leads to an analytical (sometimes called "reductionist") view that wine flavor is the sum of its pieces. Off-aromas are connected directly to root causes: horsey aromas require more microbial control; excessive woody notes lead us to use older barrels or shorter durations; veggie aromas mean pulling more leaves to minimize shade. To manage the whole, you manage the pieces. You break wine into its sensory constituents (using the Aroma Wheel™, for example) and figure out ways to amp up the good stuff and dial down the bad stuff. That's quality improvement.

In the postmodern view, every one of these beliefs is injurious to wine quality.

There have long been hints that the solution model doesn't work. Early anomalies included the sparing solubility of anthocyanins, wine's red color compounds, reported by Pascal Ribéreau-Gayon in 1974.[2] Beyond a light rosé color, it seems, red wine is theoretically impossible. My ultrafiltration work begun in the early 1990s showed that anthocyanins, which have molecular weights of around 300, will not pass through a filter with a porosity of 100,000.

"Ideal" solution behavior predicts that the concentration of a compound in solution corresponds to its aromatic intensity. But when we micro-oxygenate Merlot, its bell pepper aroma decreases without any change in its pyrazine content. Why do pyrazines, Brett characteristics, and oak components, even in very high concentrations, sometimes marry benignly in the aroma, yet in other wines stick out as annoying defects?

The solution model was a powerful starting point, one that led California winemakers out of a wilderness of largely defective wines in the '60s to our present world of nearly defect-free wines. But aesthetically, we have hit the wall.

I may be going out on a speculative limb here, but I am convinced that wine used to be a lot more exciting. I believe that postwar modernization has cost us fifty years of clean and comparatively soulless wines. I believe that what we are drinking today is not the compelling beverage the Romans used to stabilize their empire. Those were free-range wines. Today, we hover over our wines like helicopter parents, shielding them from the essential experiences that develop depth, character, and strength.

Neither boomers nor millennials have experienced wine as Stevenson's "bottled poetry" or Ben Franklin's "proof that God loves us and desires us to be happy." When I first encountered these quotations in the '70s, I thought they were a bit over-the-top. There was no way to know for sure if wines had something more special in Stevenson's and Franklin's day, or if the rhetoric was simply of a different age. We are as ignorant of such wines today as the East Bloc, with no one old enough to remember prewar capitalism, was of free enterprise.

But today, if you look hard enough, there are many examples of postmodern wines that convincingly bear out these extravagant phrases. We will meet in future chapters a host of postmodern winemakers, and when we do, I urge you to seek out and try their wines as you read their views.

From two decades of postmodern retrospection, an aesthetic construct has emerged that not only holds the solution model to be false, but considers the extent to which a wine deviates from "ideal" behavior to be a pretty useful working definition of quality. Solution model behavior is not just incorrect; it is undesirable.

In the movie *Annie Hall,* Woody Allen's character tells an old joke: "A guy walks into a psychiatrist's office and says, 'Doc, my brother thinks he's a chicken.' 'Well, bring him in and we'll put him on the couch and cure him,' says the shrink. 'I'd like to, Doc, but I need the eggs.'" This is the position of the winemaker with modern training who might consider letting go of the solution model. If manipulating concentrations isn't effective, what will be the new way of working? The answer starts with a new language that interconnects the concepts of a structural model of wine and addresses the very human goals at the core of winemaking. In the rest of this chapter, I present the language distinctions that embody this alternative perspective.

To begin with, it takes some getting used to the idea that it's okay that we don't actually know what we're doing.

FUNDAMENTAL MYSTERY

The new view begins by accepting that enology has fundamental limitations. As useful as modern winemaking has proven in eliminating gross defects, it has done little to promote excellence. Its central tenet is that a clean wine will show varietal character. This is fine for Muscato, but when it comes to great reds—pardon me while I yawn.

Winemaking is really just a branch of cuisine—the ultimate slow food. Our job is not to explain but to delight. If music is any indication, the ways of the human psyche are often unpredictable and quite nonlinear (see chapters 11 and 25 for more on these ideas). In chapter 21, I'll explore the hilarious clash of Biodynamics and science to illustrate this theme more thoroughly.

AROMATIC INTEGRATION, REFINED STRUCTURE

A 2005 review by Roy et al. in *Materials Research Innovations* hammers home the point that the properties of systems depend less on their composition than on their structure.[3] In Japanese samurai swords, hard and soft steel are folded like puff pastry until there are millions of layers in the blade, resulting in steel that is flexible yet holds an edge. A lump of coal, a graphite tennis racket, and a diamond are all 100% carbon, but their sensory properties are entirely different because of how the atoms are structurally arranged. Consider the house you live in. The agreeability of your home's architecture depends less on how many bricks it contains than on the way they are put together.

Structured foods like bisques, reduction sauces, and emulsions are at the core of great cuisine. Aromatic integration is how sauces work, and why the *saucier* is the most important chef in a French kitchen. A great béarnaise doesn't smell of tarragon, mint, fresh onion, and vinegar; it just smells like béarnaise. The finer the emulsion, the more surface area between the fatty beads of butter and the aqueous phase that surrounds them, so in a great sauce there can be square miles of interactive surface in a tablespoon. The result is aromatic integration, because the intimate contact of fatty and aqueous regions provides close contact for the diverse flavor components.

I like to think of wine structure as similar to that of a samurai sword. Swords need two conflicting properties: the ability to hold an edge (conferred by the hardness of high-carbon steel) and the flexibility not to chip and break (conferred by soft, low-carbon steel). Around seven centuries ago, Japanese swordsmiths hit on the idea to weld together both kinds of steel, which resulted in a bar that could be sharpened on one side and had a flexible back. Then they found that a better blade, one that had both properties, could be made if they flattened and folded the blade several times. A blade with four folds, for example, would have sixteen (2^4) layers. The finest blades had as many as four million layers, held an edge forever without sharpening, and were also unbreakable.

In structured wines, similarly, tannins, anthocyanins, and other aromatic ring compounds, which are almost insoluble in solution, aggregate into colloids—tiny beads of various sizes and compositions. It is this fine colloidal structure that allows interaction between the aqueous and phenolic regions in a wine, blending the aromatic properties as if the wine were home to all things.

Winegrowing choices at every stage have profound consequences for the textural and integrative properties of these colloids, as well as their stability. The way the wine feels on the palate, the soulfulness of the aroma, and its longevity in the cellar are all determined by the wine's colloidal structure. (The brilliant work of Patrick Ducournau and his colleagues at Oenodev in developing tools and methodologies to enhance structure is described in chapters 3 and 4.)

The fineness of a great sauce is the source of our word *finesse*. Wines with finesse *feel* good. Their unified flavors are able to touch us deeply by soothing the thalamus in the midbrain, creating a sense of harmony, peace, viscerality, and profundity. (The phenomenon of harmony and its strongly shared nature is explored more fully in chapter 11.)

Figure 1 depicts in cartoon form the notion of aromatic integration. The first panel shows how a modern white wine works. Winemaking techniques that minimize tannin content result in an alcoholic solution containing apolar terpenes and esters that are hydrophobic. The polarity of the water drives these compounds into the aroma. The lower the alcohol, the greater the aromatic expression. By contrast, red wines contain a confusing excess of aromas: varietal fruit and vegetal elements, nuts and phenolic aromas resembling herbs, tea and cocoa, oak constituents, and microbial by-products (such as the horse sweat aroma of *Brettanomyces*) depicted in panels 2–4. These are largely composed of benzene ring and other double-bonded ring structures that are driven into the aroma by water, resulting in a cacophony of conflicting scents.

A properly formed tannin colloidal structure is capable of providing a home within the wine for these aromatic compounds. The shorter the tannin chains, the finer the colloids and the greater the interactive surface area for intercollating these compounds due to their affinity for ring-stacking among the tannins, as shown in panel 5. The result is an

FIGURE 1. Aroma projection in whites compared to aromatic integration in structured reds.

aroma that is primarily varietal fruit, with oak, vegetal, and microbial notes in a supporting role as muted, integrated elements (panel 6).

HOLISTIC APPROACH

In the postmodern view, better wine doesn't result from adjusting intensities. We do not seek to pump up the positive Aroma Wheel™ attributes and suppress the negatives. Instead, we try to merge all the wine's flavors into a coherent whole, like a well-conducted orchestra producing a unified, soulful voice.

It is a useful technique in modern science to pull a phenomenon apart into its constituent pieces, a technique called "reductionism" (not to be confused with "reduction," which is the converse of oxidation and is often employed to refer to sulfides and "closed" characteristics in wine aroma). Reductionism has come to dominate modern enology at many levels, from monoculture in the vineyard to draconian microbial eradication in the cellar. Simpler systems are easier to grasp and manage, but they do not necessarily yield preferable results.

Wine sensory scientists have attempted to define wine quality through reductionism, often mapping specific aromatic "drivers" of competing products and matching consumer preference groups within quadrants (www.tragon.com/news/articles.php). But wine's virtues are greater than the sum of its parts. The notion of high performance is best investigated by *driving* your Porsche, not by examining its disassembled parts laid out on your driveway. The interaction of all elements results in a whole whose functions cannot be predicted except as a single integrated phenomenon. Holistic examination is highly challenging, but it is not categorically unscientific. The lively "deliciousness" debate in 1995 makes for entertaining reading on this issue (see http://winecrimes.com/UC_deliciousness.pdf).

Modern sensory science insists on concrete terms such as those in the Aroma Wheel™, often evoking the old adage that you can't manage what you can't measure. But poetic terms like *harmony, austerity, generosity,* and *balance* are all essential to wine experience and cannot simply be shown the door by deterministic reductionism. I have witnessed many enology students held up to ridicule by their sensory professors when attempting to employ these terms. Better to consider the sign in Einstein's office that read, "Not everything that counts can be counted, and not everything that can be counted counts." In the postmodern view, we should learn how to work artistically with, and even to apply science to, holistic properties instead of pretending they do not exist.

MICROBIAL EQUILIBRIUM

Similar to the now well established vineyard practices cumulatively termed Integrated Pest Management (IPM), a balanced ecology can also be pursued in the cellar. Once the importance of structure is recognized, one is much more reluctant to sterile-bottle red wines. This means that the microbial dramas of the wine must be played out in the cellar prior to bottling. Thankfully, structure is useful in integrating the resulting complexities. The principles of Integrated *Brettanomyces* (or "Brett") Management are the subject of chapter 10.

LIVING SOIL

Wine quality was eroded in the modern era also by the replacement of organic principles of viticulture with the facile but destructive farming solutions of petrochemical agriculture: herbicides, pesticides, and convenient but unsustainable mechanical methods of soil manipulation. These have robbed contemporary wines of flavor interest as well as longevity.

The promotion of soil health and the encouragement of a complex soil ecology have a wide range of benefits. Living soils buffer seasonal variations in water and temperature, prevent erosion, and minimize mineral depletion. Vines in symbiosis with mycorrhizal fungi receive more complex nutrition and are more easily brought into vegetative balance. Wines from these soils exhibit enhanced flavor interest, palate liveliness, and antioxidative potential.

The hands-on, boots-on-the-ground approach to achieving vineyard health, vine balance, and proper maturity is called "Vineyard Enology" and is the subject of chapter 5.

LIFE ENERGY

An aspect of wine inexplicably left out of modern winemaking training is the central problem of reductive strength. Randall Grahm of Bonny Doon Vineyard (profiled in chapter 14) taught me that wine has *qi* (pronounced "chee"), Chinese for life energy. When it is young, it is best served to exchange qi with the world around it. When it is old, it must then guard its qi. Life energy diminishes during aging, so starting out with an excess of qi is a good thing. I used to consider sulfides a defect. Now I worry about young reds that don't have them.

Postmodern practice eliminates many problems that conventional winemakers obsess about, such as excessive tannins, bitterness, vegetal aromas, and microbial spoilage, all of which are much more easily handled using postmodern techniques. In place of these difficulties, new challenges emerge.

Several emerging practices direct our attention to wine's reductive vigor. Picking ripe but not overripe (and the resulting phenolic reactivity), enhancing structural finesse through the practice of lees incorporation, and the use of organic principles with their resulting minerality all combine to produce wines with substantial life energy. On the positive side, these practices result in wines of structural integrity, liveliness on the palate, and graceful longevity. The downside, however, is substantial antioxidative vigor, which tends to impart youthful austerity and even reductive aromas, thus delaying release dates and cash flow. Youthful mean-spiritedness can be overcome by careful balancing of the wine's energy.

HARMONY AND DISSONANCE

Much discussion in modern sensory science revolves around how subjects differ in salivary rates, taste bud densities, aroma and bitterness thresholds, and specific anosmias (aroma deafness). Postmodernism sees this work as important but asks for a balancing voice that recognizes shared experience. Subjects who differ in hearing acuities can still appreciate music together, and differences in visual acuities do not preclude appreciation of paintings and movies. The commonalities that individuals perceive, though more difficult to characterize, are essential to the artistic process.

Everyone perceives that a major chord is cheerful and a minor chord is melancholy, whereas played together, they constitute noise. As we shall see in chapter 11, there is strong evidence that the qualities of harmony and dissonance are as mutually perceived in wine as they are in music.

BEYOND THE LOW-HANGING FRUIT

In the chapters that follow, I explore each of these realms in more depth. Like any dogma, modern winemaking has solved the easy problems but left behind the more challenging ones. The postmodern notion is to return to a quest for technique based on human values rather than scientific principles, guided less by theory than by keen observation of what actually works. It is trial and error but assisted by modern tools. Eye on the prize: the elusive soulfulness, profundity, and harmony that consumers go crazy for and critics demand. To get there, it is time for less theory and more technique, care, and attention.

In retrospect, it's clear that modern progress has taken us down some blind alleys, while some of wine's obvious and important behaviors have been completely overlooked. Don't you think somebody should have told me in college that a cabernet, on the day it completes fermentation, can consume fifty times the oxygen a barrel can give it, yet three months later only a twelfth as much? The fact that wines in general vary a thousandfold in their individual oxygen uptake capacity is pretty big news. The observation that ambience, particularly background music, completely alters wine balance has vast implications for wine appreciation and for the work of sommeliers.

The regimented thinking of modern enology has much to answer for. Yet we would be foolish to abandon the innovations and insights of the past century. Instead, we need simply to place recent gains of knowledge in their proper humble context. Technology has given us power tools, and now, like any craftsman, we want to understand how and when to use them, and what their dangers are. As a first step, we must become intimately familiar with the surprising attributes of our base material, the subject of the coming chapters.

TAKE-HOME MESSAGES

- Louis Pasteur's 1857 discovery of yeast as the mechanism of fermentation ushered in a century of scientific discovery for winemakers.

- Neither boomers nor millennials have experienced wine as Stevenson's "bottled poetry" or Ben Franklin's "proof that God loves us and desires us to be happy."

- Wine has qi, life energy. When it is young, it is best served so as to exchange qi with the world around it. When it is old, it must guard its qi.

2

Creating the Conditions for Graceful Aging

Every wine has one of three purposes: to delight, to impress, or to intrigue. Generous, pleasant wines make us smile (the "yummy" style). Big, impactful wines with aggressive tannins and high alcohol are designed to blow us away (the "wow!" style). These styles have grown in popularity in recent years, paralleling the trend in cinema, with comedy and action/adventure films now surpassing dramas in popularity.

Box office receipts have waned for the third style: wines that make us think. Distinctive wines-of-place that call on us to ponder new experiences are not the rage. Yet these wines represent the core aesthetic that makes wine special. Distinctive wines of place carry the torch (we might call these the "hmmmm . . . " style or perhaps the "Aha!" style) for the entire wine industry, and without them, we might just as well drink vodka. They don't run with the traffic, and that is their appeal. When you serve them, expect way more head scratching than giggling.

While Internet chatter about the importance of this type of wine far exceeds the public's interest as expressed in dollars spent, it's the genre most winemakers get in the game to make, and also their path to being taken seriously by sommeliers and critics. And although these are not the grocery store commodity wines that move all those boxes, distinctive wines-of-place produced in tiny quantities in every corner of North America today make up the overwhelming majority of wine labels.

I like the term *wines of discovery* for these wines, whose purpose is not to shoot your basket but rather to make you dribble down to their end of the court. Here you are in the age of convenience, encountering wines that need age. Balls. Now you have to go out and rent cellar space.

The test of time is an important dimension of these wines of discovery. The pursuit of enhanced maturity allows us to choose between making *vins de garde,* which achieve greatness after extensive aging but are troublesome in the cellar, and *vins d'impact,* well-behaved young musts that require little attention and are easily bottled in youth but lack longevity and distinctiveness.

Every wine has a trajectory in time. If wine were baseball, a fruit-forward vin d'impact would be a pop fly, compared to a line drive reserve-style vin de garde. Generally, the better a wine tastes in youth, the shorter its life expectancy. Every winemaker would love to produce wines that drink well both in youth and with age, and widening the arc of a wine's trajectory is certainly the winemaker's Holy Grail. It is also an attempt to defy gravity.

The wise winemaker chooses the wine's purpose early on. Choices favoring one or another style begin in the vineyard years before harvest, starting with its location and varietal selection and culminating in harvest maturity decisions. In recent years, many techniques have been developed in both the vineyard and the cellar that can push wines into early affability or instead increase longevity and profundity. With skill, and to a limited extent, it is possible to do both.

The aim of postmodern winemaking is to capture what Nature has put in a vineyard's grapes and present it with grace and balance. As a branch of cuisine, winemaking, the ultimate slow food, has much in common with the making of sauces, because the soulfulness of flavor integration is a result of refining its structure. Granted, wine is not an emulsion like mayonnaise: the particles that make up the structure of a wine are not tiny beads of oil but instead are made up of phenolic chains that aggregate into tiny globs called colloids. But in both cases, the particles' shape and size affects their power to integrate flavors. For this reason, wine's texture is strongly related to its aroma.

Control of tannin polymerization is a central postmodern skill. Small, stable colloids not only impart finesse and soulfulness in youth, but they also prolong wine's longevity. Poorly formed tannins precipitate readily over time. When this happens, just as in the curdling of a sauce, aromatic integration is lost. Elements previously married become individually apparent, resulting in wine that seems over-oaked, vegetal, or Bretty. Wines with well-formed structure can carry much higher concentrations of these aromatic elements without offending the nose.

The willful formation of structural integrity by the winemaker is termed by the French *élevage,* and successful wines are said to have *race,* or good breeding. Like all good cooking, élevage methods require training and attention to detail. Good structure begins in the vineyard with vine balance.

Winemakers will always say they do the minimum. Try that on your three-year-old. Still, a good winemaker, like a good parent, strives to become invisible. The final product must sing its song of place, and the skill of the winemaker, like that of a good piano tuner, should go unnoticed.

CONNECTING THE DOTS

Over the past two decades, a picture of the nature of wine structure has slowly emerged that we will explore throughout this book. While much of this mental construct lacks direct confirmation, the same could be said for many embodiments of modern science such as the Periodic Table of Elements, which lacked direct evidence in its first hundred years. It has been my privilege since 1997 to work closely with Patrick Ducournau's OenoDev group, based in Madiran (Hautes-Pyrénées), who painstakingly knit together a working hypothesis that guides postmodern practice by combining empirical observations of many thousands of wines with recent advances in phenolic chemistry, largely centered at Montpellier under Michel Moutounet and Véronique Cheynier but also involving the Australian Wine Research Institute's Tannin Project and work at UC Davis by Roger Boulton on copigmentation and polymerization studies by his colleague Doug Adams, all founded on Vernon Singleton's life's work on phenolic oxidation, the focus of chapter 6.

I was able to contribute to this brain trust Vinovation's trials with ultrafiltration, through which we obtained direct evidence of noncovalent bonding that empowered investigations of colloidal behavior in red wine. Through my consulting work, I have also had the opportunity to road test the emerging theory by working with hundreds of winemakers and thousands of wines over the past decade and a half.

I am the first to concede that this view of wine structure is little more than a useful working construct, but I have found in it substantial utility for guiding winemaking decisions. Scientific verification is not the engine of progress in winemaking today; it is the caboose. As in any cooking technique, empirical successes initially drive theory. What follows, therefore, is probably not true in all its elements. But there is no doubt of its usefulness as a guiding schema.

BUILDING BETTER WINE

Tannins already exist in the ripe berry skins and seeds as polymers. Much attention has been focused on the ingenious and laborious work done at Montpellier on the degree of polymerization (DP) that exists in grape skins and seeds. But these polymers are unlike those we are trying to build in finished wine. As soon as they hit the highly acidic grape juice, they break down into monomers, which collect into colloids, later reassembling into wine polymers through a variety of pathways. Anything we might learn about grape tannin polymerization is lost in the chaos of fermentation. Over months and years, these monomers reassemble like Lego blocks, forming two kinds of permanent chains (nonoxidative and oxidative) with very different sensory properties.

Nonoxidative polymers have a soft, nonintrusive mouthfeel in young wine but tend to continue growing until they become harsh and eventually insoluble, falling out of the wine. We don't like these polymers.

Fine colloidal structure depends on the promotion of early polymerization while at the same time preventing it from getting out of hand. It turns out that the key to good structure is a good concentration of red anthocyanin pigment. Color caps off tannins, leading to wines with more finesse. In effect, the more color that is present, the shorter the resulting polymers and the finer the colloids (figs. 2 and 3). Driven together by the polarity of water, these chains aggregate into colloids whose size is related to the chain length of its constituents.

If oxygen is delivered to a young red wine, a different kind of polymer results that is more expanded. In much the same way a wire whisk creates meringue from egg whites, skillful introduction of oxygen to young red wine creates a mouth-filling, light structure that is stable and can form a foundation for soulfulness and graceful longevity. That's why the Aztecs taught the the Spanish explorer Cortés the use of oxygen ("conching") to convert cocoa powder into chocolate, still a standard practice in the finest Belgian shops (yes, that chocolate waterfall in Willy Wonka's Chocolate Factory really exists!).

In red wines, prompt action is critical, because color molecules (anthocyanins) are easily lost to precipitation, yeast adsorption, and enzymatic attack. Successful oxidative structuring is best begun within days of the completion of alcoholic fermentation, sometimes even under the cap.

Poor anthocyanins lead to long, dry polymers

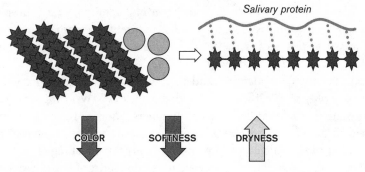

FIGURE 2. Polymerization with poor color.

High anthocyanins lead to short, fine polymers

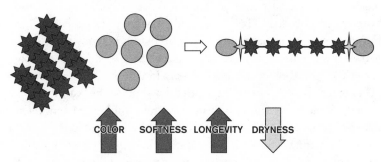

FIGURE 3. Polymerization with good color. High anthocyanin ratios result in short, soft, stable oligomers.

The mechanism of oxidative polymerization was elucidated in 1987 by Vern Singleton, who found that certain phenols found in grape skins could take up an O_2 molecule and become highly reactive, linking up to other phenols.[1] Singleton discovered, bizarrely, that the starting structure gets re-created at the end of the reaction in an increasingly reactive form, available to react over and over, resulting in a cascading polymerization effect. The reaction is homeopathic: early introduction of oxygen actually increases the wine's antioxidative power.

Understanding the ins and outs of the vicinal diphenol cascade is essential to a grasp of red wine's fundamental chemistry, and I have dedicated chapter 6 to exploring its mechanism and implications. Here I'll just touch on the high points.

The Golden Ratio

It has been empirically determined that a molar ratio of 4:1 total phenols to anthocyanins is ideal for good structure. Since anthocyanins are
phenols too, this means the ideal polymer has about six units, with
anthocyanins on each end, with a total molecular weight (MW) around
2,000. Yet these covalently bonded polymers aggregate into colloids
that pass only with difficulty through a 100,000 MW ultrafilter, demonstrating that several dozen such oligomers (short polymers) are contained in a single colloid and hinting at the destructive potential for
sterile filtration, which typically operates near this size range.[2]

Intentional encouragement of oxidative polymerization in nascent red
wine is referred to as Phase 1 micro-oxygenation, which requires high-
performance diffusion equipment that produces extremely small bubbles
of pure oxygen that readily dissolve before reaching the wine's surface.
Splashing will not suffice. Since tannin polymerization is energetically
favored over oxidative ring cleavage, it is critical to introduce oxygen at
a rate slow enough to be entirely taken up by this reaction, thus preventing oxidation. Patrick Ducournau was the first to develop an oxygen
diffuser that could regulate the extremely low flow rates necessary.

Oxygenation at this early stage does not shorten the wine's life; paradoxically, it increases antioxidative power by stimulating latent phenolic
reactivity. In fact, stopping abruptly will stimulate reductive behavior,
causing the wine to close up aromatically and produce stinky sulfides.
This is not a bad thing but rather a sign of longevity potential. Oxygen
treatment may be extended to balance reductive strength as desired,
depending on the intended aging trajectory. Tannins move from green to
hard, lose their graininess, and gain volume in the mouth due to an
expanded structure, eventually softening into a plush, stable mouthfeel.

While color is critical to creating refined texture, the winemaker
should not be fooled by highly colored musts that have experienced
field oxidation due to extensive hang time. These do not form stable
structures. Only monomeric (unpolymerized) color is useful in refining
structure.

When conducted prior to the addition of sulfur dioxide (SO_2), Singleton's cascade includes a second reaction, one that also stabilizes color.
Hydrogen peroxide is a side product of the reaction, which, in the
absence of sulfites, will oxidize a molecule of ethanol to acetaldehyde.
This compound, responsible for the stale apple aroma in fino sherries, is
problematic in mature wines but a godsend in young red wine. It bridges

pigments to tannins, doubling the rate at which oxygen stabilizes color. Once incorporated into polymers, the anthocyanins become protected, also shedding their susceptibility to sulfite bleaching.

Even if oxygen is not employed, color will still improve structural finesse. Despite its high tannin levels, Syrah texture is dependably soft, while Pinot Noir, though much lighter, is notoriously susceptible to the coarse, dry mouthfeel associated with overpolymerized tannins.

Pinot is a tough town. Anthocyanins contain a glucose molecule that stabilizes their structure, and in most grape cultivars this is protected by an attached two-carbon acyl group that blocks attack by most glucose-loving enzymes. But Pinot Noir pigments lack acylation. Moreover, the grape's weak tannins are insufficient to promote good yeast settling. Yeast and suspended grape solids not only adsorb pigment but also have a voracious appetite for oxygen, much greater than diphenols, thus thwarting polymerization and color stability.

A Season in Heaven or Hell

Although each vineyard has its own charms and virtues, it is a universal concern that red wines with low color/tannin ratios form coarse, grainy structures that lack integrative properties and shelf life. The path to sound, integrative structure and graceful longevity involves

1. balancing the vine;
2. picking at the proper moment;
3. facilitating effective coextraction; and
4. stabilizing structure.

Any misstep in this chain of events means that little can be done to enhance structure without remedial interventions in the winery such as component blending, lees incorporation, or even sugar addition.

Vineyard Enology

Within a growing season, efforts are generally focused on vine balance, a topic of great complexity that merits its own discussion (see chapter 5). For now, let's focus on optimizing the development of flavor, tannin, and color.

Pigment and flavor elements are formed in grapes beginning at *véraison* (the onset of coloration) in order to attract birds to ingest mature seeds. This shift in the vine's attention from green growth to reproduction is known as Cycle Two. The vineyard enologist strives to encourage a marked shift into Cycle Two by balancing crop load, judicious nutrient availability, and moderate water stress, thereby promoting light exposure, air movement, and moderate temperature in the fruit zone. If Cycle Two does not proceed enthusiastically, it is well to have highly colored components available for blending. If all goes well with Cycle Two, then choosing an optimum moment for picking is the next critical step.

Ripeness, Style, Nature, and History

There is no single definition for the right degree of ripeness. Ripeness per se does not exist outside of the winemaker's intentions about food functionality, fruit-forwardness, flavor density, structural integrity, and longevity.

The Loire appellations have become known for chenin blanc picked in three styles (remember, my convention is to capitalize the names of varietal wines and lowercase the names of grapes). The crisp, fresh, floral wines of Vouvray are gathered in early maturity before the mown hay/ summer meadow notes of Savennières develop. Coteaux du Layon requires extensive hang time and botrytis to produce its honeyed *vins liquoreux*. Heat summation and season length to some extent dictate what can be done, but doubtless Vouvray-style wines could also be made in warmer upstream areas. In California, where no regional *régisseur* is looking over one's shoulder and there is no fear of rain, we can do as we choose, targeting an off-dry, stainless steel–fermented quaffable wine for mass appeal or a complex *sur lie,* barrel-fermented, age-worthy Chenin Blanc aimed at the connoisseur.

In reds, control of tannin polymerization is a core postmodern skill. In determining ripeness, attention is centered on creating a good concentration of unpolymerized anthocyanins in the finished wine that will restrict tannin polymerization, leading to wines with finesse.

Optimum ripeness is a complex determination. Underripe grapes may not contain the optimum concentration of anthocyanins, may be difficult to extract, and also may lack desired fruit flavor density. Cellular breakdown in the skin, which releases pectinases that greatly aid extraction by reducing pulpiness and releasing pigment, may not have occurred. Malic acid reduction occurs throughout ripening and is advantageous to mouthfeel because excessive acidity overstimulates salivary response and brings excessive protein into the mouth, leading to coarse mouthfeel.

These difficulties pale in comparison to the perils of overripeness. To work well in the cellar, the reactive potential of tannins and anthocyanins must be protected from field oxidation. We are trying to make a tannin soufflé, and if the eggs are already scrambled, there is nothing that can be done in the kitchen. The tannins that result from excessive hang time are not stable and will become grainy and dirty in short order, imparting neither antioxidative strength nor aromatic integration to the wine.

Field oxidation also robs musts of monomeric anthocyanins. It is not enough to have good color; the color must be unpolymerized so it is still reactive and able to fulfill its role as a cap on tannin chains. High pH associated with extended hang time will also suppress the rate of pigment stabilization through aldehyde bridging (which is mediated by its low-pH carbo-cation form), instead promoting browning.

Sugar metabolism and the vagaries of raisining and dilution from dew and rain have little to do with maturity, and brix is an unreliable maturity index. It is a reliable guide to eventual alcohol content, but as we shall see, elevated alcohol is an enemy of color extraction.

Coextraction

In 1974, Pascal Ribéreau-Gayon published a color plate that revealed a mysterious reality: by themselves, anthocyanins are not very soluble in 12% alcohol and confer only a light pink color.[3] If wine is a solution, red wine is not possible. He then showed how, in combination with tannins, the anthocyanins become deep red. Although no one knew what to make of this at the time, he was really demonstrating that color and tannin together form colloidal structures.

Recent enlightenments on the nature of extraction invite us to forget everything we thought we knew on the subject. Most winemakers concentrate on the methods of extraction: pumpover vs. punchdown vs. *délestage;* vigor and frequency of mixing; temperature; use of pectinolytic enzymes; and so forth.

In 2001, Roger Boulton published a review of a decade of research on copigmentation that revealed winemakers were barking up the wrong tree.[4] Unless a home is provided for anthocyanins to extract into, no amount of punching down, pumping over, enzyme treatment, or temperature adjustment will result in stable color extraction. Boulton's

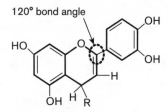

ANTHOCYANIN (color)

Apolar rings (sparingly soluble)

Positively charged (repel each other so cannot stack)

FLAVANOL (tannin building block)

Uncharged, but does not lie in a plane (functions as a poor cofactor)

120° bond angle

QUERCETIN SUPER-COFACTOR

Flavanols & Super-Cofactor Flavanol
(A_{280})   (A_{280}) & (A_{365})

Uncharged and planar (can stack between anthocyanins to create colloids)

FIGURE 4. Configuration of anthocyanin vs. catechin vs. quercetin. The four bonds of carbon atoms assume a tetrahedral arrangement in 3D space. If, however, one of the bonds for every carbon in the molecule is a double bond, molecular configurations such as anthocyanins can lie entirely in a plane, stacking tightly with other planar flavonoids. The common skin and seed flavonoids are not planar and make so-so cofactors. But the UV protectant quercetin is planar, thus empowering it as a "super-cofactor" for extracting color into copigmentation colloids.

revelations concerning the makeup of copigmentation colloids showed that a color molecule was not going anywhere unless it could pair with another similarly shaped but uncharged monomeric tannin molecule, a "cofactor." Anthocyanins can't form into colloids by themselves because they have a positive charge and repel one another (fig. 4).

Anthocyanins belong to a class of phenolics called flavonoids, which are composed of three six-member rings hooked together. The most abundant flavonoids in skins are called catechin and its isomer, epicat-echin. Unlike anthocyanins, however, these flavonoids aren't ideal cofactors because they don't lie flat. They're lumpy. When exposed to moderate sunlight early in the season, grapes produce a UV protectant called quercetin, which is a more planar "super cofactor." Boulton showed that these extractive "copigmentation colloid" intermediates are entirely composed of monomers. Oxidatively polymerized tannins resulting from extended hang time do not assist extraction, nor do most oak tannin products.

Boulton's findings elucidated the wisdom of the practice of field blending and cofermentation of varieties practiced in many European appellations, where tannic whites are included with well-colored, tannin-deficient reds: palomino with garnacha in the Rioja, viognier with syrah in the Rhone, trebbiano with sangiovese in Chianti, as well as the interplanting in old California vineyards of small amounts of petite sirah, carignane, or alicante bouschet with zinfandel, barbera, or mataro (known now as the uptown "mourvèdre").

In optimizing coextraction from other sources, gallic acid, a breakdown product of ellagitannins from oak, is an excellent cofactor. It is not available from the surface of toasted oak barrels, staves, chips, or dust but only from untoasted oak that has not been heated or sawn. But beware: untoasted oak typically contains the planky aromatic defect trans-2-nonenol. Unless carefully air cured in a manner that does not build up TCA (2,4,6-trichloroanisole, the moldy aroma also associated with corkiness), untoasted oak can ruin a fermentation. Thus it should only be purchased from a reputable supplier and used immediately.

Copigmentation colloids are not stable. If young reds are deprived of oxygen, they can lose their color almost overnight, and dry, grainy tannins will result. Since water polarity is the driving force holding the colloids together, copigmentation does not occur at all at 20% alcohol, and thus precipitation may even take place near the end of high-brix fermentations—another peril of extended maturity. Bitartrate crystals may also take up pigment and carry it into sediment.

If one follows a methodology to encourage vine balance, to harvest ripe but not overripe, and to provide material in the must for coextraction, the elements for graceful aging will be present in the young wine. We have bought ourselves a ticket, but we have not arrived. In fact, if the fruit is exceptional, we have now created a monster: aggressive, reductive, and quite unpleasant. Taming this beast, feeding its appetite for oxygen, will provide the driving force for our tannin soufflé. Judicious blending and proper oak choices are best made immediately. The ins and outs of élevage technique are the subject of the next chapter.

TAKE-HOME MESSAGES

- A fruit-forward impact wine compares to a reserve-style vin de garde as a pop fly compares to a line drive.

- Winemaking is a branch of cuisine—the ultimate slow food—and has much in common with the making of sauces, because the soulfulness of flavor integration is a result of refining its structure.

- Oxygenation at this early stage does not shorten the wine's life; paradoxically, it increases antioxidative power by stimulating latent phenolic reactivity.

- If one follows a methodology to encourage balance in the vine, harvests ripe but not overripe, and balances the must for coextraction, the elements for graceful aging will result.

3

Building Structure

The Basic Tool Kit

So now we're pregnant. We have just finished a discussion of bringing wine to the point of being ready to build structure, but we have not spoken of how to do it, only how to create the condition.

If you were making wine according to my recommendations, you would have taken certain leaps of faith and committed to a postmodern pathway, the details of which I have yet to explain. In the first two chapters, we touched on the basics of postmodern winemaking: its history, its general tenets, and its usefulness in growing and making age-worthy wines. I explored the role of good colloidal structure in aromatic integration, soulfulness, and longevity, and stated the principles necessary for obtaining the ideal building blocks for stable colloidal structure.

To prevent any confusion, I should pause at this juncture to clarify that when I employ the term *structure,* I intend it literally in reference to macromolecules such as tannins and proteins that form into colloids suspended in wine. There are many English-speaking connoisseurs, critics, and Masters of Wine who employ this term in a very different way. Their use does not address any physical arrangement in the wine itself but rather an aesthetic mapping of the measurable elements of balance, such as acidity, sugar, alcohol, and astringency, which work together in a pleasing and balanced manner. To them, a wine with good structure is one in which the elements together create a focused and harmonious whole, as might the characters in a well-spun narrative or the parts of a musical composition.

Tannins and other macromolecules that have an affinity for one another form into particles that can approach the size of a bacterial cell. Their size and shape affect wine's aroma and texture. Sugar, acids, and alcohol, by contrast, are small molecules that are a part of the solution in which the tannin and protein colloids are suspended, and thus are not a part of these physical macromolecular structures.

The French *oenologues* with whom I have worked use the term *structure* in my physical sense as described above (indeed, that's where I learned it), the other sense handled in French as *éléments qui supportent les arômes.* I suspect that along with many other imported terms such as *grappe* (bunch) and *raisin* (grape), Anglos long ago simply misapprehended their French acquaintances and gave birth to an English usage that differs in its particulars. I will argue for the predominance of my more literal usage, in which the structure exists in the wine itself and not as an aesthetic theoretical construct residing within human cognition.

If you got hooked by my advice, you're now well invested in exploring an entirely different wine style and way of working. In this chapter, I will detail the techniques developed by Oenodev to craft good wine structure. As I warned you, these practices result in wines that may at times be rather unpleasant in youth, exhibiting hardness and reduction. Accordingly, I will, as promised, chart a path out of those thick woods.

These techniques are not a recipe, nor do they constitute the only path to good structure. Years ago I was treated by winemaker Boris Champy to an in-depth look at the techniques used to obtain integrative structure at Christian Moueix's Dominus in Napa. Although their methodology did not, could not, touch on my system at any point, it was clear that our goals and our guiding aesthetic were the same. We had simply worked out different paths to similar ends.

My postmodern tool kit includes a suite of new membrane applications I helped develop over the past two decades. Reverse osmosis has proven a very handy asset in obtaining balanced wines of any desired ripeness, whether to remove diluting rainwater or to lower alcohol content in rainless climes like California. Its VA (volatile acidity) removal capability also provides a valuable safety net for low-sulfite wine production and in support of cellar strategies pursuing microbial balance. Ultrafiltration is a powerful new method for managing phenolics and for making concentrates useful for coextraction during fermentation.

These are potent tools, demanding elucidation. But not quite yet. I do not consider that my early work with reverse osmosis provided any clear window on the fundamental nature of wine, and a discussion of this and other membrane applications will have to wait for Part III, Technology, and chapter 18. For the most part, these weren't really winemaking advances at all; rather, they are tools to liberate our work in the vineyard from its focus on brix, allowing us to achieve proper maturity and balance. They also attracted the attention of some very hip Frenchmen engaged in far more fundamental winemaking exploration. In this chapter, therefore, I present Oenodev's élevage philosophy, which includes what I consider the core competencies of postmodern winemaking: oxygenation, lees work, and familiarity with the diverse functions of oak.

APOLOGIES AND EXCUSES

We are about to roll up our sleeves and sort through the nitty-gritty of the working model of postmodern winemaking. I invented almost none of this. My personal contribution is limited to having organized it into a useful construct.

Since I regard the working winemaker as my main audience, I am going to drag readers through some technical mud. I caution lay readers to hold your hopes of total comprehension lightly, as I intend to speak very specifically to a process that may be outside your experience—the actual making of wine. I will try to be as clear as I can, but if you fall off the hayride, just skip down and climb back on board.

Is the model precisely true? I doubt it. This is not a chapter full of facts, and I recommend the reader to approach it with an open mind and a large grain of salt. We are at a stage in understanding oxygen's role in winemaking that might be described as prescientific—if one were, erroneously, to view science as a collection of established learning. We are at a point in the discovery process where we can use technical-sounding language to present hypotheses, but these are far from verification. I sometimes picture us postmodern types as spouting technical poetry.

I hope that we are like the centuries of natural philosophers who followed Linnaeus's lead and compiled a biological taxonomy based on observable traits, long before there was any understanding of DNA or even genetics, or those generations of chemists who ordered the elements into a periodic table based on their behavior alone, in total absence of an atomic theory. In the early stages, ideas that later are commonly accepted may seem outlandish, even threatening.

Such ideas are, of course, mixed in among a lot of bushwah. In these circumstances, one tends to go with what works. What follows is a description of some winemaking procedures that work very effectively, together with some technical assertions that, even if untrue, provide a powerful predictive platform for working with structure.

Exploratory projects have a different feel from the scientific corroboration that comes later (see chapter 12, "Winemaking's Lunatic Heroes"). Research funding comes not from academic sources geared to verification but from commercial elements that are entirely results-oriented and have little patience with controlled experimental protocols, let alone with publishing for their competitors' eyes.

I hate to break it to you, but professional scientists are not generally equipped for discovery. Nobody sent Darwin to the Galápagos to investigate evolution. He earned his passage as a gentleman companion to the *Beagle*'s captain and, like Copernicus, withheld publication of his revolutionary ideas for decades.

I mention all this as a feeble excuse for the dearth of references that inform this important chapter. I do my best throughout the book to explain what led me to believe the assertions I make here. For now, though, it is enough of a challenge simply to articulate what they are.

"I WILL FEAR NO TANNIN"

I learned this mantra from Randall Grahm. In modern winemaking, excessive tannin is viewed as a problem best avoided by careful handling and sorting of fruit, use of gravity systems, gentle crushing, delicate cap management, and low-pressure pressing (if any). When these measures fail, the standard fix is a protein fining treatment (egg whites, gelatin, casein, and isinglass), which one hopes will relieve astringency without stripping too much flavor.

The postmodern view is, I believe, an older one in which tannin is an asset, not a defect. The more, the better. This outlook arises from awareness of structural refinement techniques. In other words, skill.

Say you wake up one morning, and someone has unloaded a huge pile of bricks on your front lawn. Not a good way to start the day, right? After you simmer down, you hire some guys to haul them to the dump.

Or, if you're a mason, you put an addition on your house.

Experience with élevage unlocks the possibility of harvesting at true ripeness, when tannins are at their meanest, and permits the winemaker to pursue full extraction and extended maceration without fear of bitterness or astringency. These are culinary skills, not far different from chocolate-making techniques.

TINY BUBBLES IN THE WINE

In the last chapter, I discussed the elements of vine balance, proper maturity, and good extraction necessary to imbue young red wines with the prerequisite materials for building a structure deep and fine enough to integrate aromatic elements such as oak, vegetal aspects, and microbial notes into a coherent, soulful "single voice" capable of imparting distinctive expression of the vineyard's unique characteristics.

Breaking that chapter as I did may conceal the fact that the copigmentation colloids are not the same colloids that bring about aromatic integration. The former have been shown by Roger Boulton to be composed entirely of anthocyanins and cofactors, both monomeric and present in a one-to-one ratio.[1] Cofactors are simply a means for extracting color and some other lovely flavor elements, such as, perhaps, the spicy cinnamic acid derivatives, which are otherwise insoluble.

Newly fermented red wines begin their lives with aggressive, coarsely particulate tannins (I believe these are the copigmentation colloids themselves), which are sensed forward in the mouth, just on the tip of the tongue. We call these "green" tannins in imitation of the French *tanin vert*. In addition, young red wines often exhibit closed fruit aromas and reductive off-odors. This is a *good* thing. Like an infant's temper tantrum, these disagreeable behaviors are signs of intense vitality that we can channel toward greatness.

Copigmentation colloids are unstable and do not remain in wine beyond the first year. Polymerization can occur in either of two directions, depending on the oxygen exposure the wine receives and the skill with which it is administered.

If kept away from oxygen, tannins will remain like cocoa powder—coarse, gritty, poorly formed aggregates that lack integrative properties and offend the entire palate, defects rather than assets. Such raw, undeveloped tannins are the hallmark of the reductive winemaking practices that modern winemaking ushered into France fifty years ago.

One of the worst offenders was the tannat of Madiran. Here in the late 1980s a desperate vigneron, Patrick Ducournau, in cooperation with Michel Moutounet at INRA Montpellier, worked out methods for harnessing tannat's reductive strength as a force for good. He named his invention *microbüllage* (literally, "micro-bubbling"), which has come into English as "micro-oxygenation."

By definition, MOx involves continuously dissolving pure oxygen gas into wine at a rate equal to or less than its uptake capacity. Yes, Virginia, wine gobbles up oxygen. Poof—gone! And in doing so, it can convert its vitality into structure the same way a wire whisk whips egg whites up into a meringue. Newborn reds can take up oxygen and build structure a thousand times faster than they will when they are old. It's not unusual for a new tannat to consume oxygen at one hundred times the rate a barrel supplies.

The main purpose in bringing oxygen to a new red wine is to stabilize color. The red anthocyanin pigments that give wine its hue also have the property of capping tannins, restricting their length by terminating their polymerization. Thanks to Dr. Vern Singleton of UC Davis, we have a pretty good understanding of how this works, and I have devoted the entirety of chapter 6 to his vicinal diphenol cascade reaction, a fascinating mechanism at the heart of wine aging.

It is essential for wine collectors to know the difference between the aggressive tannins that mark deteriorating wines from the equally aggressive tannins found in young wines that will improve.

Nonoxidative polymers are compact and regular but do not efficiently incorporate anthocyanins as "bookends," with the result that excessive tannin lengthening occurs, leading to aggressive cooperative binding to salivary protein, as depicted in chapter 2, figure 2. The mouthfeel of nonoxidative polymers is initially smooth and low in volume, but as they lengthen they become dry, grainy, and dirty, occurring all over the mouth, including the cheeks and under the tongue. This evolution is commonly associated with browning, oxidative aromas and precipitation. We call these "dry tannins," from the French *tanin sec*.

Instead of the long, dirty, dry tannins we get when we withhold oxygen, oxidative polymerization, done right, produces finer colloids composed ideally of short polymers (oligomers) of 5–7 units in length, daisy chains of phenolics with anthocyanins on both ends. Groups of perhaps fifty of these appear to come together to form stable colloids that don't progress further. These have a fine texture and excellent aromatic integration properties.

Oxidative polymers possess freely rotating linkages and are less compact than are nonoxidative ones, resulting in a larger perceived volume in the mouth and an aggressive hardness, a sheetlike grippiness, entirely on the top of the tongue, that causes it to stick to the roof of the palate (*tanin dur,* or hard tannin). Over time, as lees proteins and other side reactions coat the tannins, blocking salivary protein interactions, these hard, grippy tannins begin to melt at the back of the tongue, eventually softening completely, producing a velvety impression and a great deal of aromatic integration (*tanin fondu,* or melted tannin). This softening process may take quite a bit of time. Oxygenated wines are aggressively tannic in youth compared to their untreated counterparts, often coming to resemble them after about two years, after which the MOx wines steadily improve while untreated wines begin to dry out.

Blasting in oxygen in short bursts is not MOx, and actually has reverse effects, breaking down structure rather than building it, in the same way that blackening a steak is different from simmering a pot roast in a slow cooker.

MOx is the centerpiece of a whole system of élevage. This French term compares the "raising" of a wine to the active process of raising a child. The MOx approach to élevage includes a sophisticated knowledge of oak functionalities, press wine blending, lees timing, and temperature effects.

School of Hard MOx

Even for those with no love for MOx's creepy high-tech reputation in the Luddite press, or who simply prefer to stick to conventional techniques, experience with oxygenation is nevertheless essential to a full understanding of the bizarre, paradoxical nature of wine itself. Simultaneous with its structure-enhancing effects, MOx is, in essence, an oxidative titration: a snapshot of a given wine's reactive capacity. That's a very useful thing to know, and to know how to influence.

Antioxidative power is a rapidly moving target, different for every wine. A burly young Cabernet Sauvignon deprived of oxygen is a bull in a china shop; a tender young Sauvignon Blanc subjected to a young Cabernet's appetite for oxygen has as much chance as a toddler in an Ultimate octagon—yet a couple years after vintage, an extended-hangtime Cabernet may be just as feeble. Without a grasp of these disparate realms, well-considered cellar stewardship is an illusion at best. (See chapter 7 for the challenges of reductive vigor.)

Two decades after Ducournau's discovery, nobody doubts that micro-oxygenation is here to stay. Seemingly outrageous claims about taming tannins, integrating vegetal aromas, stabilizing color, controlling reduction, and replacing or outdoing barrels are now an accepted part of the winemaking fabric. Winemakers increasingly view oxygen the way a carpenter treats a power saw—as a dangerous but essential tool to be treated with care and respect.

The challenge is no longer to *prove* it but somehow to *do* it, and do it *right*. No small task. MOx provides a window onto the weirdness that is wine. Its implementation takes quite a bit of getting used to, almost like moving to some foreign land.

The Three Faces of MOx

Micro-oxygenation practices are divided into three phases, each with a different purpose (see table). Phase 1 work occurs when the wine is at its most responsive, and is the central focus of postmodern work because it takes advantage of the fleeting opportunity to harness the wine's youthful energy to transform its structure into something stable and refined. As I explained in the last chapter, oxygenation behaves homeopathically, initially *increasing* O_2 uptake capacity, paradoxical as that sounds.

Phase 1 is usually avoided altogether by conventional winemakers because it requires intensive training and involves substantial risks for the unschooled. It also ties up tanks, increases the time required for aging, and often causes young wines to show poorly for a time.

Phase 2 work is done post malolactic (ML), just after SO_2 addition, to refine and civilize tannins and partially quench reductive strength prior to barreling down. It is also effective for wines not destined for barrels, in conjunction with oak alternatives. This is the MOx most commonly employed in California, a far cry in its results from Phase 1. However much large wineries may wish to replace barrels with tanks by introducing oak alternatives and oxygen, tank-treated wines must also be given an opportunity to off-gas tanky aromas, a tricky problem that MOx does not address. It is my own custom to move wines to neutral cooperage after Phase 2 structuring.

Phase 3 is performed after barrel aging, when the wine may have become too delicate to continue in wood but still needs a tannin "haircut." Commonly, the pithy, untoasted oak tannins of new barrels take a year or two of wine penetration into the stave to begin to extract, and thus can disrupt a maturing wine's harmony at just the wrong time. A couple of months in tank receiving half or a quarter of a barrel equivalent can restore roundness and grace. Phase 3 is also employed to knock

MICRO-OXYGENATION'S THREE PHASES

	Definition	Purpose	Uptake Capacity (ml/L/mo.)
Phase 1	Immediately after dryness, pre ML	Color stability, structuring, and building reductive strength	10 (pinot noir) to 100 (big cabernet)
Phase 2	Post ML and SO$_2$ addition	Structural refinement, aromatic integration, redox balancing	1 to 10
Phase 3	Post barrel aging	Harmonization, quenching reductive strength	0.2 to 1.0

down reductive strength prior to bottling, particularly in preparation for bottling under screw caps, which do not supply a burst of oxygen as corks do by virtue of their compression when inserted.

Shopping Equipment

As with a kitchen appliance, picking out micro-oxygenation equipment begins with identifying your goals. The stove or food processor that's right for you depends on whether you are Masa's or McDonald's.

That said, as winery expenditures go, MOx equipment is quite a bargain, topping out at about $2,000 per tank system. My advice is to buy the best. High-performance MOx gear is one of the best deals of any capital investment you can make for increasing quality.

The original MOx units were stripped-down experimental prototypes. These have proven inadequate for serious full-plant installations, where pennies saved in investment can cost many dollars of inconvenience. Today's systems enable hyper-ox, macro-ox, micro-ox, cliqueage, and sulfide treatment, all from the same diffuser. Internet-based control panel displays can link to lab and sensory databases and fixed sensor inputs for temperature, dissolved oxygen (D.O.), and so forth, enabling adjustment and troubleshooting from any location, including your iPhone. That said, the wisest initial purchase is usually a high-end small unit on which you can build your skills.

Your key choice is the diffuser. For post-ML Phase 2 work, just to soften aggressive tannin for early release or to polish the rough edges imparted by an average-quality oak alternative, many wineries (foolishly, I think) choose a low-end model with a stainless diffuser. Bear in mind that this type of equipment is not suitable for pre-ML Phase 1 work for structure enhancement, color stabilization, and aromatic integration. For Phase 1 work, the tiniest possible bubble size is critically important. Membrane-type diffusers have the added benefit of providing a built-in continuous bubble-point integrity test.

Most large conventional wineries have already adopted Phase 2 MOx wholesale. If your intent is to produce clean, affordable wines in a factory setting, you probably know all you need to know about this primitive form of micro-oxygenation. Yes, tanks can replace barrels, and tannins can be softened using even the cheapest MOx equipment on the market. For you, the big news is that the experimental prototype systems of a decade ago have been replaced by professional plant-integrated systems that interface with your existing process control, lab, and sensory databases, placing the control panel on your browser instead of atop the catwalk.

But don't kid yourself that this type of work reveals anything about wine's nature. The skills involved in Phase 1 micro-oxygenation are entirely different from straightforward Phase 2 work. Thinking of MOx as a way to rush wines cheaply to market is like thinking of your Lamborghini as a really good flashlight. Which it is. But this misses the point of a high-performance vehicle.

Wineries that have turned the corner to postmodern methods generally place a premium on quality over image and are able to shift a few marketing dollars to skilled wine production labor to ensure that the winery's credibility resides in every bottle. Any size is possible, even large volumes. Rule One is stay close to the wine. Rethink your assumptions, trust your senses over your theories, and go with what works. Because MOx is weird and counterintuitive, smart wineries generally budget for a bit of coaching from an expert for the first couple of years at least.

THE DEVIL IN THE DETAILS

Setting up for Phase 1 micro-oxygenation involves a fair degree of prior planning and adjustment of standard crush protocols. Treatment is ineffective when wines are cloudy or cold. Suspended particulates such as yeast and grape solids are powerful oxygen scavengers. Fortunately, a good diffuser run at 60 ml/L/month will often clarify a burly young Cabernet in forty-eight hours. Not so for a wimpy Pinot Noir, however. The rich get rich and the poor get poorer. ML suppression is important

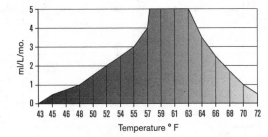

FIGURE 5. Empirical temperature dependence of oxygen uptake reactivity.

to maintaining clarity, so SO_2 at the crusher is commonly bumped to 45–50 parts per million (ppm) to slow its onset.

It is pointless and dangerous to run oxygen outside the ideal range of 59–65°F. The engine of oxygenative structuring I mentioned above (Singleton's vicinal diphenol cascade reaction, fully explored in chapter 6) is extremely temperature-sensitive, with reactivity plummeting by 70% at 50°F. That means a warm wine can absorb almost four times as much oxygen at 59°F as it can when chilled to 50°F (fig. 5). A single degree's difference changes everything in a cellar. Here again, oxygen trials dramatically reveal essential information for winemaking in general, explaining, for instance, the common occurrence of volatile acidity in the cold cellars of Burgundy and Oregon.

Unless you have heatable glycol, keeping your tanks in the proper range is a challenge. Pumping through heat exchangers doesn't work very well, as stirring up solids renders treatment ineffective. Drum heater belts are an inexpensive fix, able to hold a 4,000-gallon tank 15°F above ambient temperature with 1,000 watts of house current.

The lighter the wine and the farther the tannin/color ratio veers from 4 to 1, the trickier MOx treatment becomes. Big Cabernets and Petite Sirahs are easy to work, and often beg for it. Pinot Noirs should be avoided by beginners, and even Zinfandels tend to be very tricky. Blending in press wine is often very useful, and well-selected oak products can supplement deficient wines by providing cofactors as well as oxygenative phenolics (see chapter 4).

DRIVING WITH YOUR TONGUE

Ducournau developed a system for monitoring MOx treatment through frequent tasting. Sulfides or aldehyde are the primary indicators that the O_2 rate should be adjusted up or down, supplemented by the openness

| Wine Type: | Cabernet Sauvignon | | Blend No. | CS2000MV | | Tank No.: | S2003 |

Tasters' initials:	CS / TL	CS / TL	CS / GS	GS / TL	CS / TL	CS / TL	CS / TL
MONTH: DAY:							

ACETALDEHYDE INTENSITY

Score	C1	C2	C3	C4	C5	C6	C7
5							
4							
3							
2			X				X
1	X			X			
0		X			X	X	

SULFIDES INTENSITY

Score	C1	C2	C3	C4	C5	C6	C7
5							
4							
3							
2		X					
1					X		
0	X		X	X		X	X

FRUIT INTENSITY

Score	C1	C2	C3	C4	C5	C6	C7
5							
4							
3			X				X
2	X	X		X	X	X	
1							
0							

VEGETAL INTENSITY

Score	C1	C2	C3	C4	C5	C6	C7
5							
4		X					
3	X				X		
2				X		X	
1			X				X
0							

TANNIN EVOLUTION

	C1	C2	C3	C4	C5	C6	C7
Melted							
Round							X
Firm						X	
Hard		X	X	X	X		
Green	X						
Dry (!)							

	C1	C2	C3	C4	C5	C6	C7
Temperature:	60	62	57	61	61	60	60
pH:	3.5	3.5	3.5	3.5	3.5	3.5	3.6
Turbidity:	ckdy	OK	OK	OK	OK	dull	dull

| Present O2 rate: | 0 | 60 | 60 | 35 | 50 | 50 | 50 | 50 | 45 | 45 | 45 | 45 | 45 | 45 | 45 | 50 | 50 | 50 | 50 | 50 | 50 | 0 | 0 |

| Adjust O2 to: | 60 | 60 | 45 | 50 | | | | 45 | | | 45 | | | | 50 | | | 50 | | | 0 | | |

FIGURE 6. Example record of micro-oxygenation of a 2000 Cabernet Sauvignon. Each column represents a day of treatment. Along with treatment rates and changes, sensory scores are recorded on a five-point scale. Excessive aldehyde suggests reducing treatment rate, while the presence of sulfides indicates the rate can be increased. Tannins evolve from green to hard to firm to round to melted. Diminution of uptake capacity at Day 8 is caused by temperature drop below 59°F, causing temporary aldehyde production, which was absorbed once the wine was warmed. Onset of ML is indicated by an increase in turbidity and pH. Over the course of three weeks, this wine absorbed fifty times what a barrel would give it. Pronounced integration of vegetal aroma is typical.

of fruit expression. Tannin evolution is followed from green to hard to firm to round to melted.

I have encountered amazing resistance from Californians to piloting MOx by palate. They want numbers. But a wine's behavior cannot be reduced to a few instrumental parameters, any more than we would wish to navigate a car without being able to see out the windshield. I believe the source of this resistance is that palate training is sadly lacking in California's academic institutions.

In any case, instrumental parameters such as dissolved oxygen have yet to prove an acceptable substitute for the human palate. I think that's good news. Woody Allen said, "Ninety percent of life is just showing up." Oxygenation forces us to show up for our wines, learn their ways, and discuss and guide their evolution on a frequent, even daily basis, continually focusing on where the wine is and what our intentions are. Annoying as it is, this approach inevitably leads to better wines and better winemakers. Get over it.

I would love to include here complete instructions on how to drive the tannin bus, but the time is not ripe. In fact, MOx is really weird, and it will take seven more chapters before I am ready to present you with the terminological keys to the MOx city. Not until chapter 11 will I be able to provide a complete description of tannin sensory distinctions and their evolution. Meanwhile, figure 6 shows a typical MOx tracking sheet.

PLEASE LEES ME

Finally, I want to touch on the use of lees in building structure. Here again, timing is everything. In Phase 1 micro-oxygenation, lees gobble oxygen and suppress phenolic reactivity. They can also adsorb precious anthocyanins (the key to good structure) as well as promote their enzymatic destruction, with the result that wines dry out and fall apart.

I think of lees as being like egg yolks and tannins the egg whites from which we will make a soufflé. To begin with, the yolks must be separated out and set aside while we turn our attention to the whites, whisking them into a rich, light meringue. Once we have the structure built, we fold the yolks back in for a rich fatness. In the same way, we first oxygenate tannins into a mouth-filling, refined structure. Just as the presence of yolk prevents the formation of meringue, early lees stirring prevents oxidative tannin structuring and destroys color. Only after the structure is complete and the pigments have been incorporated may the lees be incorporated through frequent stirring. In big wines, this process may actually allow the wine to take up the entire mass of fine lees after two or three years in barrel.

After the gross lees have been discarded, fine lees may rest on the bottom of the tank or barrel, or they may be held in separate cooperage, where they are stirred and oxygenated to minimize the formation of sulfides until ready for use. Lees must be matched to the wine involved, as Cabernet lees will ruin a Pinot, while Pinot lees will deplete a Cab.

In wines that have dried out, oxygen will only make things worse, but lees can bring such wines back from the brink by coating coarse edges. Lees of the current vintage can prove useful for freshening and softening older wines on the verge of collapse.

LIFE IN MICRO-HELL

After two decades in the cellar, the controlled introduction of oxygen has taught us several lessons. First of all, *structural MOx work does not tend to hasten the bottling date.* In general, wines are strengthened and stabilized, often demanding extra age, but they are also more expressive and better balanced than the same wines untreated.

Plan on investing three to five years in full implementation of MOx. The first year, concentrate on developing your basic MOx technique, typically with a single unit, ideally guided by an experienced practitioner. In the second year, you can apply this technique to diverse wines and styles and begin to learn about early blending and the complexities of oak and lees management. Only after you've got all this down can your winery's physical transformation begin, as you grapple with vintage variations and follow bottle evolution over time.

MOx does not lessen a winemaker's workload. Instead, it pushes us to invest extra time but with generous dividends in wine quality and winemaking acumen. It was, to say the least, interesting for me to discover, thirty years into my career, that practically everything I thought I knew about red wine was wrong. Keeps you young, I guess. Learning high-performance MOx is such a pain in so many ways that you will certainly hate it. But you'll also love what it teaches you.

Part Two of this book includes portraits of two fully evolved postmodern winemakers, Gideon Beinstock (chapter 13) and Randall Grahm (chapter 14), both of whom have worked extensively with MOx—indeed, Randall was the first on this continent to work with it. Yet neither currently employs it, as I do, as a routine aspect of the yearly work. Their reasons contain wisdom and bear reflection. Gideon finds that while oxygen offers a tool for softening his relentless mountain tannins and rampant reduction, the palate architecture that oxygen produces restricts access to the depth of his Cabernets. Randall offers that while he may use it again, for now he wants to understand how his new grenache plantings will evolve on their own.

Neither of these giants has eschewed MOx because it interferes with his Natural Wine image. The technique, though, seems to appear on every blogger's hot list of forbidden manipulations. I think that's because winemakers use it but prefer not to talk about it. This disingenuous use of technologies lies at the heart of the Natural Wine movement's complaints. A key tenet of postmodern practice is this: *Never use a technique or additive that you aren't willing to disclose and defend.* Since this cannot be accomplished within the confines of a wine label, www.postmodernwinemaking.com provides links to websites that organize voluntary disclosure, discussion, and education regarding matters of concern to consumers. I encourage every reader to use the site to establish common ground.

TAKE-HOME MESSAGES

- I believe the postmodern view is an ancient one in which tannin is an asset, not a defect.
- Micro-oxygenation is, in essence, an oxidative titration: a snapshot of a given wine's reactive capacity.
- A wine can absorb almost four times as much oxygen at 59°F as it can at 50°F; a single degree's difference changes everything in a cellar.
- Wines vary three orders of magnitude in their antioxidative vigor. The same wine that in youth can absorb one hundred times the oxygen a barrel can give it will in a decade be capable of less than a tenth of a barrel's uptake.

4

The Seven Functions of Oak

When asked what I mean by postmodern winemaking, I settled, after much thought, on the following definition: the practical art of touching the human soul with the soul of a place by rendering its grapes into liquid music.

This apparently airy statement has proven its worth time and again as a practical working vision. In this chapter, I'd like to illustrate its use in working out a satisfying philosophical position in an area of great aesthetic turmoil for today's winemakers. Let me start the ball rolling by asking flat-out a very loaded question: If presenting authentic flavors of origin is our primary goal, what, if anything, is the proper role of oak in postmodern winemaking?

A growing number of Natural Wine advocates have a simple answer: Oak has no such role. But these purists include few actual winemakers. My favorite corollary of Murphy's law states that nothing is impossible for the man who doesn't have to do it himself. Indeed, when it comes time to actually do the job, ultratraditionalist Georgian winemakers fermenting their wines in buried clay vessels called *qvevris* often resort to wood to perfect their big reds. Even their legendary Friuli disciple, Josko Gravner, comes out of qvevri with his amazing whites and ages them for an additional six years in large neutral oak.

Even U.S. federal regulations, which are no treasure trove of wine-making wisdom and guidance, distinguish wine from beer and other beverages through the basic principle that wine has no ingredients—oak flavor being one legal exception. Barrels got grandfathered in as a container long before anybody paid attention to their role as a flavor source, and oak alternatives rode those coat tails.

Is this bald-faced hypocrisy, or the triumph of real human aesthetics over simplistic dogma? In Ernest Callenbach's novel *Ecotopia,* when Northern California and the Pacific Northwest secede from the Union, the new republic legalizes only local produce. Except for coffee. Who can imagine Seattle, Portland, and San Francisco absent their morning cup?

The great Thierry Lemaire of Oenodev taught me that oak is like cosmetics for wine. "When it is used properly," he said, "you can't tell she's wearing any." Jim Concannon likens oak to garlic in cooking: at best, it's invisible, lifting out flavors. "Of course," he adds, "some people just like to be hit over the head with it." If the winemaker's role is to present the grape's natural features, oak is a tool for making those features more presentable.

A purist might say that a self-respecting woman should wear no makeup. But in practice, most people prefer to look their best. Likewise, wine has to please its customers, and few brands will sacrifice fiscal viability for philosophical purity. Nor is unbalanced wine forgiven by anyone because of its purism.

"I first broached the idea of a postmodern Barolo with Giuseppe Vajra of the G. D. Vajra Winery in Vergne on the outskirts of the village of Barolo," says Henry Davar in the December 2011 issue of *Wines and Spirits* magazine, describing how Vajra had grown up in the middle of a war, a polarized modern versus classic debate, while his father sought a middle approach. "Compared to the winemakers of the 1970s and 1980s—the decades of the Barolo Boys, new barriques, and the rotofermenter—many of today's younger winemakers exhibit more sensitivity to the potential of the grapes, the nature of the vintage, and the personality of the cru." Davar goes on to explain that today the two factions are merging, borrowing from each other's tool kits and aesthetics.

Randall Grahm likes to talk about *vins d'effort* and *vins de terroir,* essentially wines that show their processing versus those that highlight natural aspects. There is a place for oak in the latter but as a supporting actor or even an extra with no lines. Oak isn't the enemy of *terroir* per se, any more than any other particular tool. But inept, clumsy winemaking certainly is. Over-oaked wine is just bad cooking.

Oak's proper use is to correct imperfections so the real wine can emerge. Any defense attorney makes sure the defendant is neatly groomed and attired before appearing before a jury. This isn't a charade; it's a convention that allows judgment of the real person rather than the unkempt trappings.

Complete wines do not need oak extractives. In 1986, I visited J.L. Chave just after his Hermitage had received 100 points from Robert Parker and asked him which coopers he used. "I honestly don't remember," he told me as we rooted through his cellar looking for markings. "My grandfather bought all these barrels." Big, dense wines like Chave's don't need the wood extractives new barrels provide, but they do crave the barrel's other features, and benefit greatly from time in old barrels, to out-gas off-odors and facilitate slow oxidative development. Barrels also create both oxidative zones above and reductive zones below, intermixing their reaction products.

It pays to consider what deficiencies a particular wine may possess in order to choose the right oak to supplement them. Wines like Pinot Noirs are likely to flag at their task of surviving a year or better of age, and benefit from substantial help in the form of oak antioxidants, color stabilizers, sweetness, and mouthfeel contributors.

Oak is not the only way to help a deficient wine. The aromatic contributions of complex indigenous yeast/bacteria fermentations are just another method, in no way philosophically superior, to introduce artificial supplements in character, complexity, and mouthfeel that the grapes themselves do not contain.

DISSECTING OAK'S FUNCTIONS

It is said that the Eskimos don't have a word for snow. Hey, up there, it's all snow. Instead they need dozens of distinctions for different kinds of snow, ranging from powder to slush to ice. In the same way, *oak* is not a useful term for winemakers. The postmodern approach identifies seven broad distinctions in oak extractives.

Novice winemakers look at wood first and foremost as a flavoring agent. This is a mistake. Oak has five primary functions that must be addressed before its aromatics can have any relevance.

1. Coextraction

As discussed in chapter 2, red wine is a lot like chocolate, containing tiny phenolic beads that contain tannin, color, and flavor. When we ferment crushed grapes on their skins, it is challenging to extract the anthocyanin pigments, which are not soluble in aqueous solution. Since anthocyanins are positively charged, they repel each other and won't aggregate into colloids. They can only be extracted if they are interspersed with uncharged phenolic cofactors, like a giant club sandwich.

Untoasted oak is a rich source of hydrolyzable tannins called ellagitannins, which break down in must to yield prodigious quantities of gallic acid, a powerful cofactor. Toasted wood does not enhance color extraction. The toasting process oxidatively polymerizes these small molecules into large chains that will not assist anthocyanins in forming colloids. Worse, the barbecue aromas of toasted wood are amplified by yeast action to produce a strong Worcestershire sauce aroma.

Green untoasted wood contains trans-2-nonenol, a nasty, planky sawdust aroma that persists in wine for years. To prevent this, oak needs curing outside in weather that will leach tannins and foster subtle microbial transformations. Curing wood is an art, and skill is required to avoid the formation of TCA, the corky aroma. Thus only highly reputable coopers should be entrusted with the production of untoasted chips or barrel heads.

2. Antioxidative Power

A common deficiency in musts is reductive strength, without which structural integrity, good texture, and graceful longevity are not possible. Besides its coextraction properties, gallic acid is also a wonderful antioxidant. As a vicinal triphenol (see chapter 6), it imparts supplemental reductive vigor to weak wines that are poorly concentrated or that have lost their energy to field oxidation during excessive hang time. In oxygen's absence, ellagitannins will lend a harsh crudeness, but proper exposure to oxygen will transform this to a fat, round texture. Oak plays a particularly important supporting role in Pinot Noirs, which often cannot support the extensive aging required to elaborate their flavors without supplemental antioxidative power.

3. Sweetness

As a general rule, the desired palate architecture for red wines is a sweet core of fruit contained by an angular frame of tannin. Some wines start off with excellent fruit core but lack definition—this is typically true of Barbera, Grenache, and some Merlots. Others have the frame but not the fruit, a common problem in Mourvèdre, Carignane, and Cabernet Franc.

Oak can be a source of a wide variety of sweet elements. Untoasted wood supplies a coconut influence (whiskey lactone), usually subliminal, which lifts out varietal fruit aromas. This compound is rich in French forests where sessile oak species (*Quercus petraea* or *Q. sessiliflora*) predominate, such as those of Alliers, Vosges, and Argonne. Alternatively, toasting can enrich vanilla, toffee, and sometimes sweet coffee elements. The flame converts cellulose to cellobiose, an exotic sugar that can feed *Brettanomyces*. It is important to match the wood you are using to the deficiency you are trying to address.

4. Framing

The oak selections that supply framing are opposite to those providing sweetness. Certain forests, particularly those of eastern Europe and Limousin, which favor the pedunculated species *Quercus robur,* supply wood containing the most tannin. Moderate toast can bring out spice elements that accent mouthfeel. Very heavy toast can produce deep espresso notes, which frame fruit well and enrich flavor persistence in the finish. As in the Hippocratic Oath, "First, do no harm," it is generally best to employ these influences with great restraint.

5. Structure for Aromatic Integration

Wines containing vegetal or microbial notes often benefit from enhanced structure, which can serve to integrate these aromas into the background, allowing them to merge with and support fruit character. Oak can assist this process indirectly in several ways already discussed, such as anthocyanin extraction and structural supplementation. Oak introduced during primary fermentation can also provide sacrificial tannins that remove protein and deactivate yeast enzymes destructive to color. Structural enhancements may call for extractives of gallic acid from wood, usually in the form of high-quality untoasted oak chips.

Aromatic integration should not be confused with aromatic masking. We are not trying to use oak aromas to cover up vegetal or microbial defects, but rather we seek help from oak supplements in creating a structure that incorporates them into an integrated whole. The goal is that all the wine's natural elements are clearly apparent but are incorporated into an aromatic whole such that they all make sense together, in the same way that a symphony conductor combines the sounds of a cornet, an oboe, and a violin into an integrated single voice.

6. Curing Aromatics; 7. Toasting Aromatics

Oak aromatics receive so much emphasis that little need be said here. A year of air curing is essential for degrading plankiness (trans-2-nonenol) and to enhance whiskey lactone. The longer subsequent curing occurs, the more ellagitannins are leached. High temperature is necessary to create clove spice, vanilla, caramelization, and espresso aromas.

I list these functions last because all too often the first five functions are ignored when choosing an oak regimen. Decisions based solely on aromatic embellishment result in unbalanced wines—cloyingly sweet or overly framed, with poor structure and problematic integration of aromas, tiring easily in the cellar.

SHIPS INTO CHIPS

The magical changes that occur in the maturation process in the barrel are not easily replicated. Barrels breathe. They inhale a small, steady dose of oxygen. More uniquely, they exhale, cleaning the wine of funky off-odors. They facilitate settling, good lees contact, and interaction between reductive and oxidative zones within a small space, with intriguing flavor benefits.

Old barrels do all these things quite as well. So we buy new barrels . . . why? New barrels as a source of barrel extractives are fiscally foolish and environmentally reprehensible. High-quality chips, when prepared with skill and care, provide these extractives much more reliably, responsibly, and economically.

French oak barrels are made from 200-year-old trees planted by Napoleon to build future navies. When bark is stripped away and heartwood removed, some 25% of the premium wood remaining yields staves for barrels (fig. 7). The rest, perfectly good wood, is generally discarded. Why? Because winemakers want to look cool.

For the past decade, I have completely separated in my own work the function of a neutral barrel from the use of extractives. I find it silly that we regularly purchase pieces of fine oak furniture for $1,200 each for use as flavoring agents. Fortunately, a postmodern sea change is under way. Talented coopers today take this precious wood resource, air cure

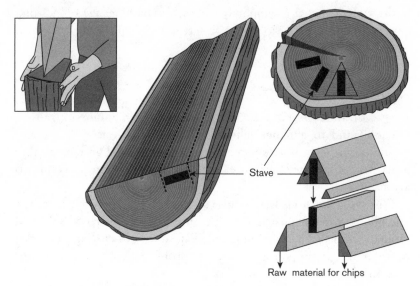

FIGURE 7. Oak waste in barrel production. French oak forests are two hundred years old when they are cut down for barrel production. Of the prime wood, 75% goes unused for wine simply because it cannot be employed in building barrels. Why cut these trees down at four times the necessary rate?

it, and custom toast chips according to a wide variety of regimens for specific uses. I haven't bought a new barrel since 1999, and likely never will.

SCORING THE SUBLIME

To paraphrase Forrest Gump, a barrel is like a box of chocolates: you just never know what you're gonna get. The innate variability in oak forests, even within a single tree (south side vs. north side, high vs. low), is staggering. An exhaustive French government-funded study by INRA in the mid '90s documented vast inconsistency in wood composition everywhere they looked.

The point was hammered home at a seminar on oak held at California State University Fresno in 2001. First, Jeff Cohen, then at Rosenblum Cellars, treated us to a book of splendid prose from his own hand, comprising one-page sensory descriptions of twenty-seven cooperage house styles, an extremely well articulated and perceptive guide.

The next talk featured Steve Pessagno, who stated disarmingly that he would be more comfortable with barrel alternatives if only he knew what he was doing. Meanwhile, he said, he could get all the complexity he desired from the variability in Seguin Moreau's medium toast. If he filled fifty barrels with Cabernet, he could expect after a year to select ten for reserve, ten to dump on the bulk market, and the rest would become his regular bottling, imbued with far more nuance and complexity than he could ever intentionally bring about.

This is not very good news for the guy who only has six barrels. And for the vast barrel warehouses at Mondavi Woodbridge, Bronco, and any number of other behemoths, averaging has taken the place of the human attention that might be given the same wine in tank. The barrel evokes a powerful symbol of artisanality for the wine lover, but in large operations, small cooperage utterly removes the winemaker from intimate knowledge of the wine that a tank would provide. But barrels look really cool.

THE GLORIOUS STAVE, THE HUMBLE CHIP

Full disclosure: I used to sell Oenodev's chips, and I still love them. But what I really longed for was to sell *staves*. So sexy. The oak alternatives halfway house, stacked inside a tank but otherwise just like barrels, right? I begged my French colleagues to make them. They would love to, they said, if not for the unfortunate fact (as they explained in that patient, diplomatic way all Frenchmen have) that staves are very stupid.

The biggest challenge confronting winemakers and oak vendors is the problem of reliable consistency. One sample won't tell you much, because products vary from lot to lot. Jeff Cohen's treatise is precious because it reflects decades of experience from which he extracted an average profile for each cooper, albeit an ideal to which no single barrel actually conforms.

A piece of wood as big as a stave, my French colleagues instructed me, can never be produced consistently. Sure enough, I remember once unloading a truckload of hundreds of staves, stacking them in two identical tanks, and filling each with the same Merlot for micro-oxygenation. One tank took 35 ml/L/month for three weeks; the other took 75 ml for six weeks. Subtracting whatever the oxygen uptake might have been from the Merlot's native tannin, that's a *lot* of difference. I saw their point.

Why *do* we use staves? Americans cling to several myths.

Myth #1: Staves are split along the grain and have no exposed end grain, which in chips imparts a planky harshness. But if you look at oak under a microscope, you can see that it has lots of rays—tubes that run perpendicular to the grain. Tannins are extracted much more readily through these rays than through endgrain. That planky dryness we want to avoid arises from poor wood selection, inadequate air drying, or inconsistent toasting, not from exposed end grain.

Myth #2: Staves, like barrels, have a toast gradient that adds complexity. The reality is that the untoasted interior of a stave imparts a green pithiness at just the wrong moment, just as occurs in barrels. It would be so much better if the toast were in the interior and the green wood on the inside surface, exposed to the young wine, which can better handle it. This isn't possible, so the best we can do is to use small chips and introduce the various toast levels in the order we desire rather than be restricted by considerations that dictate the building of a container.

Myth #3: Toast fixes color during fermentation. 'Taint so. Anthocyanins are not fixed by aldehydes unless oxygen is present, which is never the case during fermentation. If they were, the high concentration of aldehyde in fermentation would fix everything. But that doesn't happen. What fermentation *does* cause is an amplification of the barbecue furfurals to the level of Worcestershire sauce. Ugh. Toasted staves contribute no copigmentation cofactors or antioxidative ellagitannins to fermentations.

Myth #4: Staves replicate the complexity of cooperage at lower cost. In reality, when the cooper builds a fire inside the barrel to make the wood pliable for bending, barrel complexity arises from the differing heat zones that result from the varied distances from the fire that surfaces lie. The traditional use of untoasted heads adds sweetness and tannin. Stave manufacture, which is done in temperature-controlled ovens, in no way resembles coopering.

The lowly chip is the perfect format for blending to achieve consistency. It allows toasting in a rotating drum (similar to coffee beans), which produces even, predictable results, allowing precisely flavored products. Unlike dust, chips retain aromatics and do not surface-adsorb wine flavors. Any degree of complexity can be achieved by blending different chip products, and these can be easily experimented with in single-bottle trials, which take about two months to resolve. Staves, conversely, share the inconsistency, inconvenience, and expense of barrels and offer no technical advantage over chips.

To be sure, there are plenty of crappy chips on the market. My advice for starting down this path is to buy only the most expensive chips you can find and get your flavor from them instead of from new barrels.

Old barrels still provide essential functions, and should be treated reverently and preserved for one's grandchildren. It appears that there will always be enough lunkheads around who want to unload their once-used barrels at a small fraction of the cost of new. Barrel sterilization with ultrasound or microwave can alleviate even the most fastidious winemaker's microbial paranoid fantasies, and when they lie empty between fillings with wine, storage with a water solution containing citric acid and sodium bisulfite (a heaping cup of each) is preferable to the currently trendy SO_2 gassing when your goal is a fully leached barrel. Once they no longer leach out pithy green tannins, you will, like Chave, come to regard your oldest barrels as among your greatest assets.

Oaky dokie?

TAKE-HOME MESSAGES

- The bigger and more complete a wine, the less oak extraction and the more time in old barrels it needs.

- View your wine programs through the lens of what oak's seven functions can supply. When it fills in deficiencies, oak becomes invisible.

- Never buy another new barrel. But don't tell anybody, because barrel producers throw really great parties, invitation only. I hope you appreciate how many convention perks this advice is costing me.

5

Vineyard Enology

The Power of Showing Up

Things should be made as simple as possible, and no simpler.
—Albert Einstein

Humans are not well equipped to look beyond the simple. In his master-piece, *The Quark and the Jaguar,* Nobel laureate particle physicist Murray Gell-Mann examines the challenge of conceptualizing complex systems. It appears that one of the accomplishments of twenty-first-century science will be the development of tools for working with intricacies.

In the meantime, what we do instead is dissect complex reality into constituent parts that are easier to grasp, trying to manage the whole as the sum of the pieces. This is called reductionism. Though a poor sub-stitute for a true grasp of the whole, reductionist rationalism often mas-querades as the only legitimate form of scientific inquiry.

If we are honest with ourselves, rationalism must always be con-fessed a charade. When even a single atomic particle must be thought of as both a particle and a wave, and when hundreds of different dimers result from all the possible ways of linking just two identical tannin monomers, how can we hope ever to dissect the complexities that occur in a single glass of wine, let alone the natural chaos of a vineyard?

For the past half century, we have busied ourselves with the viticul-tural equivalent of ethnic cleansing. Our rational limitations manifest themselves in our cherished professional winegrowing practices, many of which are chosen primarily for their convenience to our way of think-ing rather than to further what is best for wine, environment, or health. It is easier to conceive of and control a vineyard monoculture than a full-blown ecological system, and as soon as petrochemical pesticides and herbicides hit the market in the 1950s, many growers took to simplifying their task by eliminating every weed and bug. We then went on to abandon the practice of mixed cultivar plantings and to heat treat for viruses, further dumbing down the system.

The pursuit of orderliness is not the true face of science. Rather than conduct an inquiry into the complexities of natural balance, we bought ourselves time by changing the question from "What is the nature of a farm ecology?" to "What simplifying steps can I take to rationalize farming?" Another tactic in excluding extraneous input was to divide winegrowing into two academic disciplines: viticulture (the growing of grapes) and enology (the organized study of the making of wine).

The viticulture classes I took at UC Davis in the '80s paid scant attention to wine grape quality. Our focus was on yields, pruning weights, acidity, and, above all, sugar (brix), all easily measured without resorting to the vagaries of aesthetics or sensory science. Often quoted in my UC Davis classes was Ray Kroc of McDonald's: "You cannot manage what you cannot measure." This training left viticulture graduates running commercial vineyards totally unprepared to debate quality with high-handed winemaker customers who want to drop half their crop to achieve flavor concentration.

I myself am a pitiful example of academic divide-and-conquer. In all candor, growing quality wine grapes requires all the attention a single individual can muster. You work it, breathe it, and dream it, awaking each morning with a new understanding. You can't just phone it in. Knowing that I could never devote that much dedicated attention in my daily work, it has been my strategy to forge strong and lasting relationships with dedicated growers, and to try to hold up my end of an intense and continuous conversation about a win-win focused on quality.

Having come clean on this, I am nevertheless obliged in this book to touch on this most important of winemaking topics. Fortunately, I can in good conscience address postmodern approaches to the vineyard by introducing you to someone who's really been there. While your typical winemaker will mouth the platitude that wine quality happens in the vineyard, Kay Bogart has actually walked the walk.

After fifteen years on the winemaking side at a string of gigs culminating at Opus One under Genevieve Janssens, in 1997 Kay approached the talented winemaker Mark Lyon of Sebastiani with a proposal to focus on vineyard work. But not as a viticulturalist. "Vineyard Enology," as she termed it, focuses not on growing grapes but rather on making sure they contain the right ingredients to make the intended wine. Spotlight on the purple stuff, not the green stuff. What follows is largely what Kay worked out at that time and built on with my kibitzing while she directed the Vineyard Enology (VE) program at Vinovation from 2000 to 2005.

VE isn't a prescribed methodology. It isn't dogmatic about how the work is done, and is equally comfortable around conventional and organic/biodynamic producers. It also recognizes that what works in one site may fail in another. The focus is on results, which have at their source unique flavors of place, informed through a familiarity with wine structure, which depends for flavor depth and profundity on rich active tannin and maximum monomeric color. "Tannin is almost never the limiting factor in structural and color considerations," opines Doug Adams of UC Davis, who has studied grape maturation for two decades. "The main issue to address is boosting color development so there is an optimal color to tannin ratio."

In keeping with the holistic balance sought in postmodern winemaking, VE works on enhancing positives rather than eliminating negatives. If a good structure can be created, then pyrazine aromas can be integrated. The very practices that increase color also serve to decrease veggie aromas. Pyrazines exist to repel birds, while color develops to attract them. Once the vine switches into seed-maturation mode, the flavors come into balance naturally.

The goal of VE is to exploit these natural processes to achieve wellness and balance rather than to eliminate isolated problems. In this regard, it has much in common with Eastern medicine, whose holistic approach is reflected in the principal tenets of Vineyard Enology:

1. Promote living soil.

2. Achieve vine balance.

3. Harvest at proper maturity.

LIVING THE DREAM

The term *living soil* is employed as a dodge around the "O" word, borrowing from the best intentions of the organic movement without drinking the Kool-Aid. It refers to the encouragement of a healthy soil ecology through minimal pesticide and herbicide use as well as promotion of an appropriate cover crop, minimally tilled. It does not necessarily go as far as the extreme and sometimes absurd practices required for organic certification.

We're really just talking about what was done in every vineyard until the mid-twentieth century, before which time all vineyards were essentially organic. "I've been an organic farmer for fifty-seven years," joked Charlie Barra of Redwood Valley Cellars in 2005. "But I only just found out about it twenty years ago. Before that, I thought I was just *cheap.*"

The best indicator that all is well is a healthy earthworm population. On my website, winesmithwines.com, I feature "dirty pictures" of growers holding up shovelfuls of soil perforated by earthworms. By processing organic matter into humus rather than glue, earthworms prevent concretion and produce an aerated, friable soil. The many advantages of this living soil include encouraging root depth, canopy control, and protection from hot weather spikes by providing both water tension and retention, a soil that is drier in wet years and wetter in dry years. Living soils enhance wine minerality (see chapter 8), thus increasing palate vibrancy and wine longevity.

BALANCING ACT

Viticulturist Diane Kenworthy, with over a quarter century managing the vineyards of Simi and Ravenswood, promotes vine balance as the economic meeting place for winemakers and growers. Vine balance involves optimizing color by hanging adequate crop to hold back canopy and provide flecked sunlight on the fruit. Rather than throw their weight around as buyers, Kenworthy observes, winemakers are better served by working with growers to find the right crop load.

Far more Napa vineyards are undercropped than overcropped, necessitating leaf pulling and other manipulations to manage the resulting vigor. Notwithstanding the acknowledged density of wines obtained from some low-yielding vineyards, the myth that low yields result in greater flavor concentration has little factual support. Drop crop on a vigorous site with available nutrition and water, and you're going to get leaves, shading, vegetal aromas, poor color, berry enlargement, diluted flavors, and increased rot. Yet many highly paid winemakers insist on this foolish practice.

An important aspect of light exposure is the formation of quercetin, a UV blocker that acts in grapes like suntan oil. Quercetin, which is formed in response to sun on the fruit early in the season post-bloom, has another important use in winemaking. Color molecules, as we have seen, are not very soluble and need to form colloids in order to be extracted into fermenting must. Unfortunately, they are also positively charged and repel each other, and thus cannot form into colloids by themselves. The formation of copigmentation colloids requires anthocyanins to be spaced apart by similarly shaped but uncharged phenols that can stack in between them and separate their charges. Quercetin's unique flat shape makes it a powerful pigment extraction cofactor.

THINKING LIKE A GRAPE

Grapes use birds to spread their seed. After spring bloom and fertilization ("set"), berries first enlarge to pea size through cellular division. At the end of Cycle One, the berry is about 12° brix—half again the sugar of a ripe tomato. To discourage premature consumption of the immature seed, grapes up to this point are hard, tart, harsh, low in fruit flavors, and high in vegetal flavors, while keeping their green color to camouflage them from birds looking for a meal.

Once seeds mature (that is, once they can germinate into viable plants), pigment and flavor elements quickly form to attract avian vectors. In the space of a few weeks during Cycle Two, berries color up, flavor up, sugar up, and become attractive to birds, which will swallow them and spread them around.

A concerted midseason shift in vine dynamics from vegetal growth to fruit maturation is vital to proper fruit development. Figure 8 shows the growth phases that vines undergo during the season—first shoots, then berry cellular division (Cycle One), followed by post-véraison fruit enlargement and maturation (Cycle Two), which transforms the grape into a visible and tasty snack. Fruit development takes a lot of vine energy to accomplish. To persuade the vine to devote its resources wholeheartedly, it needs some indications that reproduction would be a good move.

Grapevines evolved as a low bush in the dinosaur era amidst ferns and other low-lying flora. Current thinking is that this era came to an end about 63 million years ago when a meteor impact in the Yucatán Peninsula sent billions of tons of dust into the atmosphere, creating globally perhaps a decade of darkness in which the dominant gymnosperms (ferns) were replaced by angiosperms (flowering plants) due to their better seed longevity. Result: the Earth became rapidly enforested, with the consequence that *Vitis* was being choked out. The grape's adaptation was to invent the tendril, a climbing mechanism that is really a cluster with no berries, switched on by shade. Only when they receive direct sunlight do grape buds become fruitful, dif-

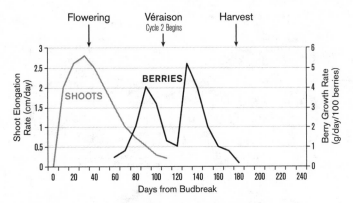

FIGURE 8. Shoot, root, and berry growth rate comparison.

ferentiating microscopic cluster primordia in the year previous to flowering and fruiting. Figure 9 shows how the wild grape reproductive cycle works.

Vines shift gears most enthusiastically under moderate stress. Figure 10 relates the Cycle Two shift to vineyard conditions—water availability, incident light, canopy temperature, air movement, and nutrient status, all of which must exert a moderating influence. For example, too little sunlight shuts down color and flavor development, but too much causes sunburn. Too little air movement leads to rot, but excessive wind results in stomatal closure and shutdown of sugar transport. Each of these aspects affects all the others, as shown. A shot of fertilizer results in more canopy, less light, higher temperatures, less air movement, and increased soil water depletion.

In the irrigated vineyards of the American West, the midseason steering wheel for vine balance is irrigation control. Leaf water potential (LWP) is a preferred tool for gauging water availability because it makes no assumptions about soil water tension and instead simply asks the vine itself. This technique is an equally valuable diagnostic tool in unirrigated vineyards in the American East and in Europe.

To measure LWP, a young leaf is taken at solar noon and placed in a pressure chamber with its petiole emerging through a gasket. Gas pressure is then applied until a sap bead appears, thus duplicating the force the vine required a moment before to draw water from the soil. Vines with access to free water read at –10 bars or less. A reading of –12 to –14 bars at véraison is desirable in promoting the transition to Cycle Two. The value of the instrument is that perfect water tension occurs

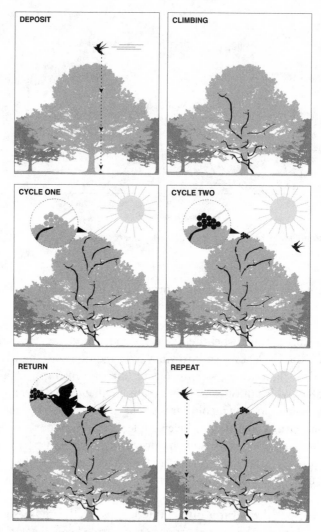

FIGURE 9. Grapevine life cycle in the wild. A viable grape seed exits the digestive system of a roving avian vector and is deposited in a nutritious plop of, well, bird shit. The resulting seedling finds no direct sun on the forest floor and thus produces no fruit but instead uses its tendrils to begin climbing the nearest tree. Years later, shoots emerge into the sun atop the forest canopy, and light cues stimulate the differentiation of grape clusters. A grape approaching véraison has considerable sugar, but until the seed is viable the vine must use a variety of tricks to repel birds and camouflage the cluster: hard texture, green color, bitter taste, high acidity, and vegetal aromatics. Once the seed is ready, Cycle Two quickly transforms nasty into nice: big, soft, sweet, highly colored, richly flavored berries, which are eaten and borne to another site where the cycle repeats.

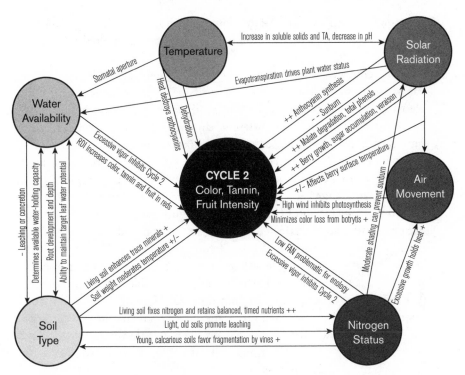

FIGURE 10. Vineyard influences on Cycle Two vigor.

before visible symptoms are exhibited. Dried tendril tips and other canopy indicators will show water stress signs at over −14 bars in most cultivars. A reading of −17 bars marks the permanent wilt point and is believed to trigger stomatal closure.

Water tension management has been shown most effective prior to véraison. Late-season water stress has little beneficial effect on color and flavor development and in addition can lead to stressed flavors such as black pepper and to field oxidation and fruit deterioration.

MARKS OF MATURITY

Until very recently, modern enology has made little attempt to teach any indicators of ripeness but brix, pH, and TA (titratable acidity). The implementation of true ripeness indicators has been particularly slow in California. Organized systems for looking at phenolic data developed by CASV in Bordeaux in the 1990s are still not in widespread use in California, and although Jacques Rousseau's *Winegrape Berry Sensory*

Assessment system was translated into English in Australia, it is taught domestically only in private seminars by the Italian enologist Gianni Trioli.

While convenient to measure, the sugar content of the berry (brix) has virtually nothing to do with maturity. The great vineyard of our planet Earth is a massive experiment in cultivar response to climate, and by comparing maturity in different climate zones and latitudes, we can learn a great deal about grape maturation mechanisms. A 1996 Australian Wine Industry Technical Conference about the reproductive biology of grapes determined that the primary metabolic changes occurring in berries (sugar and acid content) were unrelated to the evolution of secondary metabolites (color, flavor, tannin).

Sugar and acid are affected by heat summation and rain. Recently, John Gladstones's brilliant *Wine, Terroir, and Climate Change* added humidity and summer day length as important factors. Europe's greatest vineyards tend to be planted at the highest possible latitudes to ripen their respective *cépages,* and autumn rain will often dilute their musts. Thankfully, it turns out that a little rain often gets them into the correct zone. In California's dry climate, the problem is more vexing, since as a general rule we have no autumn rain at all, and brixes soar as we approach the desired ripeness.

Achieving flavor ripeness, by contrast, is simply a question of time. Riesling from Geisenheim on the 50th parallel is picked in the second week of October, when it is hoped to reach as much as 17° brix (10.2% alcohol), the legal minimum for *spätlese* (literally, "late picked"). Riesling in Sonoma's Alexander Valley (38th parallel) is also picked in mid-October, but there we hope for less than 25° brix (15% alcohol). Even on a single site, the cold vintages of 2010 and 2011 taught us that California vineyards that would not achieve flavor maturity until over 25° brix in warmer years were overripe in these cool years at 23° brix.

The inquiry into the true nature of ripeness has only just begun, because until very recently, New World winemakers had to pick everything at 23.5° brix to obtain "balanced" alcohol, whether or not the grapes had properly matured. When I attended UC Davis in the early 1980s, the question was never put on the table. In 1992, I was privileged to entertain Pascal Ribéreau-Gayon, then director of the Faculty of Oenology at the University of Bordeaux, with whom we were working on a project for an international claret blend in a global experiment of Bordeaux varieties for the Benziger Family. After tasting a wide variety of our wines on a visit to California, he expressed the (to me) shocking opinion that, despite their high sugars, our California grapes were more often than not simply unripe. "If it were left up to me," he said, "I would ripen to higher brix, looking for truly ripe flavor, color and tannin, and dilute the must back to normal alcohol potential."

This was before alcohol reduction technology appeared on the scene. But even then, Pascal knew that if brix is to be ignored in favor of other parameters, means must be found to achieve alcohol balance at the winery. The Old World has long applied corrective methods. Inventive styles like Champagne and Port easily achieve an artificial balance thanks to the strategically timed addition of alcohol and sugar. Napoleon's minister of the interior, Jean-Antoine Claude Chaptal, solved the problem for French table wines by legalizing and encouraging beet sugar additions, a practice still widely used for top Burgundies and Bordeaux. The French knew how to add sugar, but no process existed yet for removing it.

In the 1980s, juice evaporators became available, as well as hypertight reverse osmosis filters that could remove rainwater from must.

My personal contribution to Vineyard Enology was to develop a different use of reverse osmosis than the French had been using, this time to lower alcohol rather than to raise it (see chapters 16 and 18). My method, along with the competing Spinning Cone technology, created the possibility for an assessment of ripeness outside of brix in dry climes like California and Australia.

While we still don't have a means for removing sugar per se, these methods are employed after the sugar is converted to alcohol by yeast fermentation, and the net effect is the same: "reverse chaptalization." For the first time, Californians could uncouple the harvest decision from brix and concentrate on the elements of true ripeness: color, flavor, and tannin. The problem then was to get the winemakers to consider true ripeness independent of brix. I became notorious among my winegrowing clients for threatening to run over their refractometers with my car.

In assessing maturity, postmodern principles point to some very specific desired characteristics in red musts that are our goals. Flavor finesse is achieved through fineness of texture. The smaller the grain size of the colloids that make up the tannin structure, the greater their combined surface area and thus the greater their power to integrate aromas and their stability over time.

These colloidal structures are aggregates of dozens of polymerized tannins that form through the oxidative linking of a large variety of flavonoids, three-ringed compounds that are synthesized in skins and seeds during the season. The winemaker can control this polymerization in the cellar if anthocyanins arrive in the must as reactive monomers. These are present at ripeness but are converted to useless polymeric forms as a result of field oxidation associated with overripeness. We can't make a tannin soufflé if the eggs are already scrambled.

As we saw in chapter 2 (and will more thoroughly explore in chapter 6), oxidative polymerization requires a specific molecular constituent group called a vicinal diphenol, which has the ability, when activated by oxygen, to form a linkage and then re-create itself, cascading into a polyphenolic string. These daisy chains are terminated when a color monomer (anthocyanin) is added to the chain. Color molecules are the bookends on the polymer; the more color, the shorter the polymer, and the softer and more refined the texture. But this only works if the antho-cyanin is a free monomer, not already fallen victim to polymerization through field oxidation. Our goal is to time harvest in order to catch color development when the reactive monomer has hit maximum and before it is lost to polymerization—ripe but not overripe.

An additional consideration is to promote extraction in the fermenter. Since color is extracted from the inside surface of the skin, it is well to wait until the gelatinous pectin pulp begins to break down, as indicated by a colored "brush" when the pedicel is pulled away from the berry. In addition, copigmentation colloids are destabilized by high alcohol, so high brix musts lose much of their color at the end of fermentation.

STINKY IS GOOD

A challenging aspect of the postmodern approach is the proclivity of well-extracted, properly ripe musts grown in living soils to produce sul-fides. While disconcerting to the novice winemaker, these unpleasant but transitory compounds are actually a good thing, a sign of healthy life energy that can be utilized for building good structure and also indicative of good aging potential.

The postmodern winemaker's response to sulfides will vary accord-ing to the wine's intended style and aging curve, a topic addressed in chapter 7. Suffice it here to say that the postmodern tool kit contains plenty of options for dealing with sulfides, which unless present in quite gross amounts are almost never a real problem. Sulfides have been lik-ened to acne: if your teenage son doesn't have pimples, he's less likely to be happily married when he's sixty-five.

Intolerance of reductive behavior in highly concentrated wines like Cabernet and Syrah has prompted many winemakers to drive the life energy out of their grapes through excessive hang time and field oxidation. While this certainly results in well-behaved young musts that require little attention and are easily bottled in youth, the practice robs the wines of both longevity and distinctiveness, leaving pruny wines that taste alike and have little shelf life. Unfortunately, so many California winemakers have taken this road that many of the country's sommeliers now typecast us as producers of shallow, short-lived impact wines and do not take us as seriously as they once did.

Winemaking is empirical, succeeding through a long succession of failures. I am sorry to confess that having opened the door to the world above 23.5° brix, I have been personally responsible for an awful lot of terrible wine being made. Ideally, I would have begun by educating winemakers on ripeness assessment, the handling of reduction, and the perils of excessive time on the vine. As Søren Kierkegaard observed, "Life can only be understood backwards; but it must be lived forwards." My apologies.

INTEGRATED BRETT MANAGEMENT

The Integrated Pest Management (IPM) approach to vineyard ecology encourages beneficial organisms rather than simply wiping out pests. At one time considered risky and fairly wacky, IPM is now a mainstream viticultural practicum, and it is widely recognized that vineyards that foster beneficial organisms are far less prone to plagues like grape leaf skeletonizer and rampant leafhopper infestations. Most winemakers, however, have yet to transfer this wisdom to the cellar.

While the majority of winemakers are still trying to eradicate and suppress microbial growth, a new idea is emerging that the wine spoilage organism *Brettanomyces* yeast, or Brett, is really an opportunistic pathogen. As with certain hospital diseases, sanitation actually promotes its dominance, and its suppression in the cellar leads to problems in the bottle. The bleeding-edge practice known as Integrated Brett Management (IBM), which similarly promotes microbial balance in wine rather than draconian control, is the theme of chapters 9 and 10.

Why do postmodern winemakers take this apparently risky approach? For the same reason that there are no sterile filters in dairies. Dairies seek other means of stabilization because they realize that the physical properties of the structured food that is milk are disrupted by sub-micron filtration. In other words, sterile-filtered milk is no longer milk. Similarly, structured wines sacrifice their powers of aromatic integra-tion, flavor depth, and soulfulness when sterile filtered—something that never happened until the 1950s.

Once the decision is made to eschew sterile filtration, care must be taken to encourage whatever microbiological activity for which the wine is destined. The regimen involved in an IBM program is diametri-cally opposite to a control strategy, and the worst thing a winemaker can do is to dabble, to try being just a little bit pregnant. Einstein said, "It is impossible simultaneously to prevent and prepare for war." Half measures are hard to countenance, because the most dangerous situa-tion is to have only partial stability prior to bottling.

But isn't this a chapter on the vineyard? Yes and no. IBM provides a valuable illustration of the connectedness of the postmodern viewpoint. There you are in the vineyard at bloom, and you're thinking about what you can do to prevent the need for sterile bottling.

The three legs of the IBM stool are nutrient desert, integrative struc-ture, and microbial equilibrium. These goals are all vineyard-dependent. Creating the conditions for successful microbial balance starts in the vineyard, with nitrogen measurements of petioles or leaf samples at bloom. The purpose is to determine hot spots where supplemental soil fertilization is required to obtain a healthy must that does not require the addition of DAP (diammonium phosphate) to facilitate completion of fermentation.

A nutrient desert is created by promoting a healthy fermentation, with complete consumption not only of sugar but also of micronutri-ents. Brett is a fastidious organism that does not pack the genetic bag-gage to manufacture many of its essential nutrients. A grape containing a plentiful nutrient package is the ideal nutrient source, making fermen-ter additions such as DAP unnecessary.

DAP, which is just inorganic fertilizer, can cause runaway fermenta-tions that achieve sugar dryness without consuming micronutrients. If we feed them Twinkies, those yeasts just won't eat their oatmeal, and the result will be lots of leftover unconsumed micronutrients—like half-eaten pizzas left around to encourage the vermin.

These aspects of Brett control are an integral part of Vineyard Enol-ogy. Living soils supply plentiful and complete nutrition. Cover crops fix nitrogen, earthworms aerate soil and digest organics, and mycorrhi-zal fungi intercalate into grapevine root hair tissue, symbiotically trading for sugar rare trace minerals that grapes by themselves are incapable of taking up. Vine balance and proper harvest maturity encourage healthy, complete fermentations. Careful vine management results in the synthesis and extraction of the building blocks that enable a well-formed wine structure with integrative properties that can render Brett aromas into positive sensory elements.

AN OUNCE OF PREVENTION

Aristotle said, "The best manure is the master's footsteps." Woody Allen said it again: "Ninety percent of life is just showing up." It's impossible to overstate the advantages of the presence in the vineyard of someone who can be a bridge between the realities of grape growing and the intricate and often unique goals of a particular winemaking program. Never have I spent a day in a vineyard that failed to teach me something of value, and in general I provide my grower partners with some choice nugget to chew on as well.

You are constantly coming across things that you didn't know that you didn't know, whether it be a gopher hole, a broken drip head, or an insect pressure. This year I learned a lot about wind-induced systemic shatter in Cabernet Sauvignon, and I still can't imagine why it bloomed a month early, ahead of everything else. It also adds to your spiritual health, for there are no atheists in vineyards. From a pure marketing point of view, your genuine knowledge of your wine's source will inform your presentation of it to customers and enhance your image as the real deal.

A comprehensive glossary of grape terms can be found at http://eviticulture.org/glossary-of-grape-terms/.

TAKE-HOME MESSAGES

- A balanced vineyard ecology is the foundation of farming distinctive and age-worthy wines.
- The goal of harvest timing is to catch color development ripe but not overripe.
- Well-formed structure can render Brett aromas into positive sensory elements.
- Vine balance is the economic meeting place for winemakers and growers.

6

The Vicinal Diphenol Cascade

Red Wine's Defining Reaction

In this chapter, we finally confront the greatest fear of modern wine-makers. That would be chicken wire.

I'm sorry, but it has to be done. Yes, I will now attempt to render palatable the topic of phenolic chemistry, at least to open a door to its baffling collection of hexagonal pictograms guaranteed to drive the bravest enologist into fits of terror and ennui.

After five chapters of beating around the bush, it is time for my loyal readers to join with me to take on red wine's defining process, the peculiar and counterintuitive reaction with which red wine builds structure, in so doing elevating its soulful resonance and graceful longevity. To comprehend why, we must, Frodo-like, descend into the depths of enology's darkest recesses and attempt to drag its most daunting secrets into the light, hex signs and all.

Why have I suddenly turned so cruel? Because an appreciation of phenolic structure is essential to the postmodern view of wine. This journey will provide basic tools that will allow us to move beyond the modern approach we all learned in school. As we have seen, red wine is not a solution; moreover, the extent to which it deviates from solution behavior is a pretty good working definition of quality. Phenolics are the principal inhabitants of the nonsolution world, the world of structure, where soulfulness resides. A grasp of their behavior will empower us to steer the course of our wines' development.

Put another way, red wine–making is a type of cooking, related to sauce-making. Good béarnaise doesn't taste like its ingredients (tarragon, raw onion, vinegar, mint); it tastes like, well, béarnaise. The structure, not the composition, determines the flavor. Curdle the sauce, and it loses its integrative properties and tastes terrible. Likewise, the shape and size of suspended particles determine the wine's sensory characteristics and, more important, its aesthetic impact. (Hint: When I say "aesthetic impact," I'm talking about cash flow.)

A clear picture of how wine behaves benefits winemakers of every stripe. I'm not pushing here for micro-oxygenation, lees stirring, or any other winemaking technique. No recipes will be forthcoming. But to make wine is to choose a path. Increasingly, great winemakers elect, when they can, to do nothing, but even if the practitioner chooses to intervene in no way, that choice, together with its consequences for a wine's structure, remains central to the art.

The phenols in young wine resemble those of cocoa; they may continue dry and harsh, or they may transform into silky, visceral, flavor-carrying textures through pathways similar to those of chocolate-making. The engine of this transformation is that very reductive strength that modern enology calls a defect. This force may be harnessed by the winemaker who is familiar with wine's nature.

Are you with me? Then hang on tight, and let's get started.

WHAT'S A PHENOLIC?

All phenolics are simply derivatives of phenol itself, which is composed of a ring of six carbons with alternating double bonds (called a benzene ring) attached to an oxygen and hydrogen (-OH) (see fig. 11). This very stable structure lies in a flat plane, allowing many phenols to be stacked compactly like Ping-Pong paddles. Plants find phenols very handy as building materials, and grapes manufacture hundreds of different kinds for various purposes by attaching additional chemical groups to the ring.

No need to worry about understanding all the details of phenolics in wine. Nobody does. Take the dizzying array of thousands of different phenolic compounds, then start to tack these monomeric units together like Legos, and shortly you end up with many millions of combinations as unique as snowflakes. These polymers go on to form complicated structures in wine sometimes as big as a bacterial cell, no two alike.

If your eyes are beginning to cross, you're getting the picture. Wine structure does not lend itself to analysis. A full understanding of its

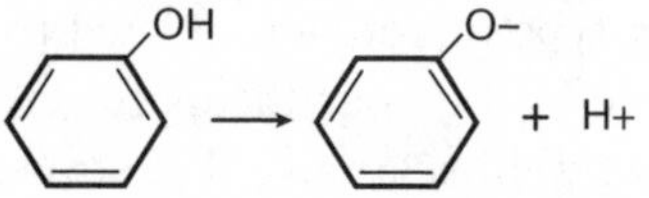

FIGURE 11. Phenol ionization.

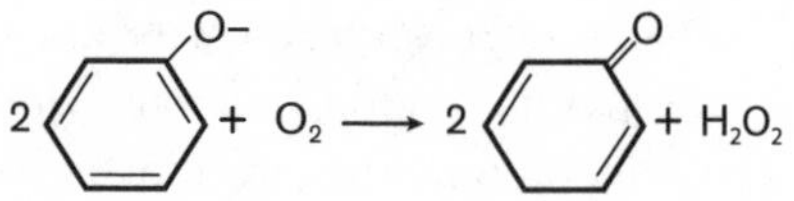

FIGURE 12. Quinone oxidation.

diversity is neither possible nor useful. What does prove handy is an overview of the parts of the process that we can measure and control. I will present here a model that, however true or false it may eventually turn out to be, has served postmodern winemakers well as a predictive tool.

The -OH group of phenol is mildly acidic and can be persuaded in basic solution (about pH 9) to ionize by giving up its H^+, resulting in a negatively charged $-O^-$ still attached to the benzene ring (shown in figure 11 as a hexagon, representing six carbon atoms bonded into a ring with three double bonds).

This ion on the right is called phenolate. Since wines are generally below 4.0 on the logarithmic pH scale, there is not much phenolate around; only about one phenol molecule in 100,000 is in the ionized state at any given time. Phenolate has the ability to react with oxygen to form a double-bond =O called a quinone (fig. 12).

Since there is so little phenolate around, the reaction with oxygen proceeds very slowly and isn't a very interesting reaction. Quinones absorb oxygen and bind SO_2, but that's about it. But a special case that is far more consequential is the subject of this chapter.

Phenols repel water and love to ring-stack. When placed in water, they try to get away, either by evaporating (many phenolic aromas are common in wine—vanilla, clove, menthol, and so on) or by aggregating, driven by water molecules into microscopic beads called colloids, herded like horses into tiny corrals.

If there are enough phenolic colloids around, volatile phenolic compounds will enter into them and ring-stack also, diminishing their aroma impact. This phenomenon is called "aromatic integration," and it explains why wines with good structure can contain large amounts of oak extractives, *Brettanomyces*-induced 4-ethyl phenol, or vegetal aromatics like methoxypyrazines without deleteriously affecting the wine's aroma.

Aromatic integration is a source of soulfulness in food, be it a béarnaise, a bisque, or a Bordeaux. When aromas are integrated into a single voice, the food speaks to the soul the way a symphony does when the entire orchestra plays as one.

Aromatic integration works better when the beads are very fine. This also gives a silky, refined texture to the palate. Smaller colloids mean more surface area of interface between the aqueous liquid surrounding the beads and the fatty or hydrophobic (water-hating) interior, be it a butter bead or a phenolic ring-stack. This is why textural fineness is related to aromatic finesse. The French use the same word for both.

THE CORE REACTION

One type of phenolic that plants find very useful in fruit is the vicinal (or *ortho*-) diphenol. This is simply a phenol with two -OH groups in adjacent positions on the ring. This molecule has the magical ability, in reaction with oxygen, to attach itself to another phenol and then to re-create its original reactive diphenol structure. This odd trait allows it to react over and over, daisy-chaining to create long polymers. The browning we see in freshly cut apples and bananas is polymerized diphenols, sealing the fruit in case of injury.

It was a bright feather in UC Davis's cap when Vernon Singleton in 1987 elucidated the mechanism of oxidative polymerization in all its bizarre aspects.[1] He explained quite clearly why, contrary to all common sense, a young wine challenged with oxygen behaves homeopathically, *increasing* its reductive strength. He also showed why oxygen uptake is so strongly temperature-dependent, a critical morsel of cellar knowledge.

THE BASICS

Grape skins are rich in a special type of phenols called flavonoids, whose triple-ringed shape appears so frequently in wine chemistry texts. Some of these are red-colored anthocyanins, but most are tannin building blocks that contain adjacent diphenols. When o-diphenols see oxygen, magic happens (fig. 13).

Without going into the details of Singleton's explanation, we can say that the phenolic ring basically goes Rambo, hungrily searching out a nearby molecule (generically designated "R" in the figure) to attach to the ring in any unoccupied position. Possible molecules that could so attach include another diphenol, an anthocyanin pigment, a sulfide, or a protein fragment, usually from lees. Once this bond is formed, the diphenol is re-created and can react again.

With one important difference. Since the R-substitution can help share the negative charge created by ionization, the phenolate is now

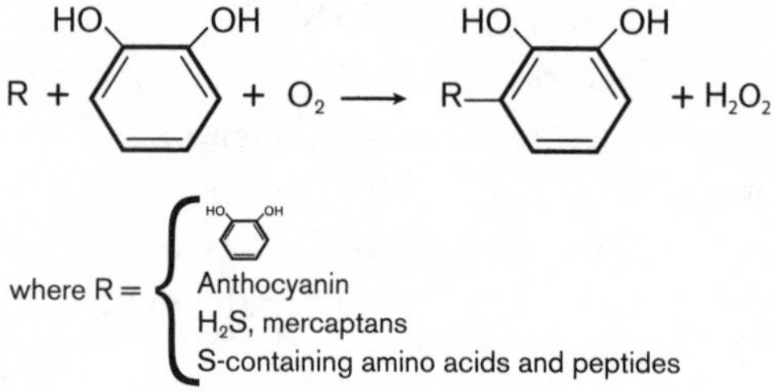

FIGURE 13. Vicinal diphenol oxidation.

more stable, thus more favored, and its equilibrium pH shifts from 9.0 to 8.5. As a result, there is now one phenolate molecule in 50,000 instead of 100,000, so the reaction occurs twice as fast. In effect, the introduction of oxygen has made the wine hungrier for oxygen. Instead of oxidation, we get increased reductive strength.[2]

For those who claim there is no scientific support for homeopathy, time to reconsider. More along these lines in chapter 21, "Science and Biodynamics." And with that little teaser, it's back to the chicken wire.

Since the re-created reactive diphenol now reacts faster, the cascade repeats again and again, resulting in a complex of random linkages. The shape of the resulting polymer is thus dependent on the concentration of the various reactants and their relative affinity for the reaction.

In effect, oxygen acts like a wire whisk, and the tannins, like egg whites, firm up into a rich, light structure similar to a meringue. In this way, the reductive strength of the wine is harnessed as an engine of finesse and soulfulness, like a churlish teenager who takes up the cello. Bottled poetry, indeed.

THE KEY ROLE OF COLOR

The anthocyanins responsible for red color (fig. 14) readily combine with tannins, which are similar in composition, with one key difference. Anthocyanins are not o-diphenols and cannot daisy-chain. Instead they act like bookends, terminating the polymer. The more anthocyanins, the shorter the resulting polymers and the finer the tannins. Heavily colored wines like Syrah tend to handle their tannins better than light wines like Pinot Noir, which have a tendency toward dryness.

As I said, the more anthocyanins we start with, the shorter the polymers we end up with. Smaller polymers aggregate into smaller colloids. Not only do these feel softer and finer, but they have a greater combined

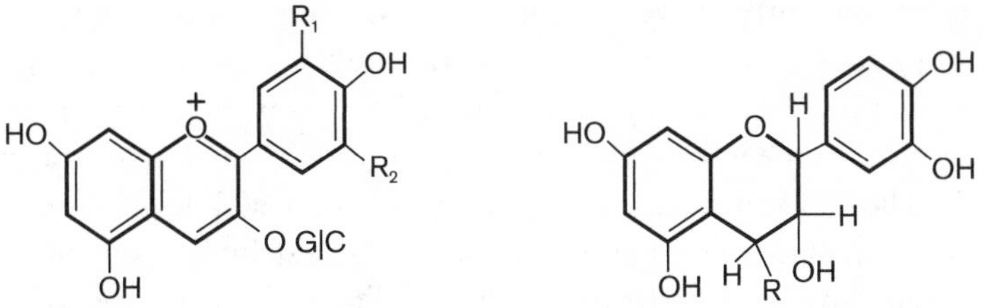

ANTHOCYANIN (color)
Contains no vicinal diphenol
(terminates polymer)

FLAVANOL (tannin)
Contains a vicinal diphenol
in the B ring to the right
(can oxidatively polymerize)

FIGURE 14. Building blocks of red wine structure.

surface area as well and impart greater aromatic integration. That's why the finer the texture of a sauce or a wine, the dreamier it tastes. In general, darker-colored wines have a quality edge (Pinot Noir being the exception, as always).

Measuring the monomeric anthocyanin concentration of a young red wine to gauge softness potential is quite useful but slightly tricky. Unfortunately for the amateur wine enthusiast with a cellar, red wine's darkness itself is not sufficient for determining monomeric anthocyanin concentration. Color density doesn't account for the degree to which field oxidation may have polymerized pigment, particularly in cases of long hang time. Wines that look very dark may actually be quite fragile. It helps to look for an overly amber edge—a bad sign.

For technical winemakers, there is more bad news. The standard Somers-Boulton spectrophotometric methods for assessing color aren't much better. They look at monomeric anthocyanins at pH 3.6, where only 15–30% of anthocyanins are in the colored form. In fact, young red wine color is mostly invisible. If you want a shock, pipette some strong acid into a young red, and watch the color quadruple. The invisible fraction varies widely according to the precise ratio of the five anthocyanin types as well as alcohol content and other factors. Fahgettaboudit.

The best available molar estimator for anthocyanins is an offshoot of the Adams astringency assay called BP (bleachable pigment).[3] It is easy to run (if you have the right centrifuge), and its LPP (long-chain polymeric pigment) is also a good analytical index of dryness. Problem solved.

Young pigments are very vulnerable and easily lost to adsorption by lees and attack by enzymes. Once incorporated into polymers, however, they are protected. Early stabilization of color through cascading polymerization benefits wine's appearance, texture, and aromatic properties. The diphenol cascade promotes color stabilization directly through polymerization but also indirectly by aldehyde bridging.

As you can see in figure 13, each turn of the diphenol cascade produces a molecule of hydrogen peroxide (H_2O_2), a highly reactive oxidant with a strong affinity for SO_2, with which it will combine to form sulfuric acid (H_2SO_4). Since we don't add SO_2 prior to the completion of malolactic fermentation, peroxide in young reds will instead oxidize ethanol to acetaldehyde, which forms bridges between tannins and anthocyanins to further stabilize color.

TIMING IS EVERYTHING

Aldehyde bridging is believed to be initiated by a low-pH form of acetaldehyde called a carbo-cation. The reaction thus goes faster at the lower pH that the wine has prior to the acid decrease brought about by malolactic fermentation. For all these reasons, red wines benefit most from early oxygen introduction, preferably the day of dryness. This is when oxygen reactivity is highest, anthocyanin concentration is highest and at its most vulnerable, and aldehyde is readily formed and consumed.

Conventional modern methods work very hard to do just the opposite—to exclude as much oxygen as possible. This is fine for Sauvignon Blanc and Riesling, but in the absence of oxygen, reds get into trouble. Nonoxidative polymerization is a different pathway that does not as readily protect anthocyanins, resulting in long polymers. These bind more aggressively to salivary protein, resulting in drier, harsher mouthfeel.

Besides the cellar choices that determine whether oxidative or nonoxidative polymerization will predominate, there are other timing issues. Chief among them are early blending for phenolic balance and the management of lees.

The early presence of lees in young reds is deleterious for two reasons. Lees react readily with oxygen, dampening phenolic activity and suppressing the cascade. Lees also adsorb anthocyanins and contain glycosidase enzymes which attack them. Just as egg yolks prevent the formation of a meringue structure, lees must be separated through clarification in young red wine. As with a soufflé, their later incorporation after the structure is formed can be beneficial for adding fatness and richness.

The tannins in big, concentrated reds will clarify themselves, so it is the small wines that require attention. The rich get rich and the poor get poorer. Centrifuging a young, delicate Pinot Noir takes guts, but this is not the time to hold back. Settle it out in an egg-shaped tank if you must, but clarify that wine in its first two weeks, or regret at your leisure.

Like General McClellan's conservative Civil War generalship that nearly destroyed our nation, many winemakers like to play wait-and-see. But keeping valuable press wines to themselves for years destroys both the press wine and the wine it could have helped. Early blending of press wines is a high art that is extremely time-sensitive. The goal is a balance between color and tannin, specifically a 4:1 ratio between total phenolics (A_{280} direct reading) and Adams bleachable pigment.

For you nongeeks (I assume that includes practically everybody), just try to balance the tannin and the color. Press wines are a wonderful source of color, but they are way too concentrated to survive on their own for years in the cellar in solitary confinement. Many other blends work best when the wines are young—Merlot and Cabernet Franc, Grenache, Syrah and Mourvèdre (fruit, color, and tannin), Barbera, and anything supplying tannin.

The vicinal diphenol cascade reaction is extremely temperature-dependent. Because it involves two reactions (one with each of the -OH groups), we label its kinetics of the second order, a fancy way of saying that its temperature dependence is squared. Patrick Ducournau determined empirically that red wines take up oxygen almost four times as fast at 59°F as at 50°F. This means that every 1°F drop in cellar temperature can reduce oxygen uptake substantially.

The strong dependency on temperature of red wine oxygen uptake has vast implications for cellar management. Red wines are not protected by SO_2 in the same way whites are. In 2000, Aline Lonvaud-Funel, a biochemist at the University of Bordeaux, reported that acetic acid bacteria in red wine are not inhibited by the pigment-bound SO_2.[4] Because it is in rapid equilibrium, our standard analyses report pigment-bound as free SO_2, but this is false. There is essential no truly free SO_2 unbound to pigments in young red wine. It is O_2 uptake by the vicinal diphenol cascade that protects the wine, and cold cellars suppress its action. This explains why the Pinots of Burgundy's and Oregon's cold cellars are prone to volatile acidity.

Overripe fruit, as a general rule, also has very low comparative phenolic vigor—often losing 90% of its reactivity in three weeks on the vine. North Coast Cabernets, which can at perfect ripeness absorb oxygen at a rate equal to 60 barrel equivalents over a month's time, will, if given an additional three weeks on the vine, be unable to absorb more than a tenth this amount and will fall apart in a handful of years.

It is possible to measure the phenolic O_2 uptake capacity of a wine. In 2011, I organized a collaborative study to reintroduce a brilliantly simple and inexplicably neglected eighty-year-old method for measuring this critical attribute, the subject of the next chapter.

TAKE-HOME MESSAGES

- Vern Singleton did a great job elucidating oxygen's role in red wine structure, and it is high time we digest his discovery.
- Study of the peculiar and counterintuitive details of phenolic reactivity provides insights that are well worth the headache.
- Cellar temperature, lees exposure, SO_2 management, and many other routine winemaking choices require a firm grasp of oxygen's impact on them.
- Because acetic acid bacteria are not inhibited by the pigment-bound SO_2, phenolic vigor is all that protects young red wine.

7

Redox Redux

Measuring Wine's Oxygen Uptake Capacity

Academically minded winemakers often encounter frustration while studying Ducournau's methodology in that suitable instrumental methods have yet to be developed to supply "hard numbers" and automate oxygenative wine treatments. Instead, sensory assessment of aldehyde, sulfides, and the openness or closedness of aromas has proven the simplest and most sensitive methods. I say it's a good thing that in order to run an operation with wine, one must actually be trained to taste the changes in tannin types and detect aroma variations. This is no less reasonable than to be expected to look out the windshield of a car when driving. Only the daffiest of experimenters would require a road test of a new car to be run on instruments only.

Any observant winemaker or attentive wine collector knows that young wines, especially tannic ones or minerally ones, exhibit aromas that are "closed." That is, they have less apparent fruity intensity than they develop later in their lives, and often, in youth, reveal greater flavor intensity on the palate than in the nose. They may even produce sulfides, which aging will dissipate.

In all fairness, while a windshield is well understood, we have not knit together a complete understanding of what causes the aromatic expression of wines to be open or closed relative to redox potential. One contributing cause for this phenomenon of "closedness" is undoubtedly the aromatic masking that occurs when such wines produce aromatic sulfides such as hydrogen sulfide (H_2S: rotten egg smell) and mercaptans (known outside the wine industry as thiols, and smelling like diesel fuel, onion, skunk, or canned asparagus). But in addition, wine fruitiness itself varies rapidly and reversibly from day to day according to the rate at which oxygen is introduced.

When produced from grapes containing raisining, wine has been shown to exhibit fruity elements resembling hazelnut, tawny port, and bacon, products of Maillard reactions between proteins and sugars. Since these compounds contain positively charged N^+ groups, they should at wine pH be ionized, and therefore nonvolatile. If the redox potential is high, however, such a compound might accept an electron (e^-) and become charge-neutral, thereby released from aqueous solution into the aroma. (See the discussion in chapter 18 on acidity and aroma.) We thus have a plausible basis for the observed sensory effects, even if wine redox measurement remains elusive.

PEERING INTO A WINE'S FUTURE

New techniques have brought terrific progress to wine production since World War II, resulting in increasingly sound wines. Yet modern practice has surprising blind spots. A compelling example lies in our shallow understanding of reductive strength. Stacked up against the routine measurements of pH, TA, alcohol, VA, and free SO_2, perhaps the single most important thing a winemaker can know about a wine is its antioxidative properties. These dictate a wine's resiliency to oxygen exposure, its aromatic openness, and its longevity potential—both how good it tastes right now and how well it will cellar.

What could be more important? Yet this characteristic is never measured and seldom even considered.

At UC Davis, Vern Singleton studied for decades a manometric method for measuring oxygen depletion. When I arrived at the Department of Viticulture and Enology in Wickson Hall in 1980, I discovered, parked under the first-floor stairs, an oxygen uptake analyzer that Singleton had abandoned in frustration after failing to interest students in its value.

Singleton's white elephant under those stairs was a Warburg (VAHR-boorg) apparatus. Warburg's device is used in biology to measure a sample's specific oxygen uptake rate (SOUR),[1] the speed at which the sample initially reacts with oxygen, by clocking vacuum buildup with a manometer and a stopwatch. Inside the enclosed Warburg flask, a vacuum is created by any chemical or biological activity that consumes oxygen over time. For wine, a Warburg device can also estimate a sample's total oxygen uptake potential.

The story of the rise and fall of the Warburg apparatus as an enological tool holds deep lessons for how science functions and how it sometimes inexplicably fails to progress. It is as if our access to knowledge, apparently ever expanding, is actually limited by our historical point of view: every time we gain new insights, we simultaneously leave behind some detail we aren't making use of, almost at random.

Our working knowledge is like that of a person touring a great mansion from room to room. The new wonders we behold in the room we have just entered are so much more apparent than the objects we can no longer see in the room we just left. The essence of the postmodern view is to try to sneak a peek back into that last room to see if we inadvertently left behind something important.

Otto Heinrich Warburg was a pioneering biochemist and one of the most remarkable men of the early twentieth century. Born in Germany in 1883 of Jewish descent, he nevertheless served as an officer in the Prussian elite cavalry in World War I and was awarded the Iron Cross. He won the Nobel Prize in 1931 and was even supported in his work throughout World War II by Hitler's regime.[2]

In an attempt to understand the fundamental causes of cancer, Warburg studied in great depth the effect of pH on aerobic metabolism. He developed a device to track the rate of oxygen uptake in tissue cultures. By the late 1920s, Warburg devices were commonplace laboratory equipment, and in 1933 a doctoral student of Louis Pasteur at the University of Bordeaux named Jean Ribéreau-Gayon published as his thesis a method utilizing this equipment to investigate the incredible appetite of red wines for oxygen.

Over their lives, red wines are capable of consuming several complete saturations of oxygen. As explained in chapter 6, the vicinal diphenol cascade proceeds slowly because the pKa (ionization pH) of phenolate is about 9, so that at wine pH (usually 3.0–4.0), only about one phenol in 100,000 is reactive. This combination of high capacity and slow reactivity allows wines to protect themselves from oxidation for decades.

Ribéreau-Gayon, who later became director of the Faculty of Enology at the University of Bordeaux prior to Peynaud, and who fathered Peynaud's successor (Pascal R.-G.), found that raising the wine's pH, as Warburg had been doing with tissues, caused the rate of oxygen uptake

FIGURE 15. Inexpensive vacuum apparatus for measuring reduction.

to accelerate dramatically. Because at pH 11 phenols are entirely in the phenolate form, they react thousands of times faster than at wine pH, thus allowing a reasonably accurate determination of their total reactivity potential in a single day.

Easy. Cheap. A sealable jar, a little lye, and a vacuum gauge (fig. 15). This all happened eighty years ago. Yet this method remains in obscurity today, despite its central importance to winemaking.

Reductive strength receives almost no attention in the modern winemaking community. Instead, longevity is linked at winemaker school to indirect measures like pH, without regard to differences in composition and style. A Sauvignon Blanc and a Cabernet Sauvignon with identical pH's will hardly age at the same rate, and even what we mean by successful aging will be entirely different for each.

While pH is certainly important in determining the speed of phenolic reactivity, many other factors are at work as well. The reactive chain of wine oxidation is complex and poorly understood, and the final evolution of a wine takes years to sort out. Reductionist logic has proven to be out of place in assessing age-worthiness. Ribéreau-Gayon's genius was to show us a simple way to query the whole wine's bottom line.

THE METHOD

As I write, an ongoing collaborative study is under way to modernize and standardize an up-to-date version of Ribéreau-Gayon's assay. To record here any detailed protocol would be pointless, for it is certain to be out of date by the time of publication. Instead I will summarize the general idea and direct interested readers to www.Winemaking411 .com/Products for an up-to-date protocol and a list of the collaborators and discussions to date.

Warburg's apparatus employed a mercury manometer in order to minimize systemic volume changes as vacuum was created. Mercury is expensive, toxic, and tricky to handle in the chaos of a typical winery lab, so the first step in modernizing the system, implemented by Nicolas Cantacuzene and John Ritchie of Emeritus Vineyards in 2010, was to substitute colored water. This necessarily made the apparatus less compact (760 mm of Hg, which is twelve times as heavy as water, corresponds to thirty-two feet of water column). Nicolas and John opted for a six-foot tube perched on a ladder and elected to run the analysis in the wine cellar to maintain a constant temperature. A video of their method can be viewed at www .youtube.com/winesmith1.

REVIEWING THE BASICS

Readers will be more familiar with the rudiments of the chemistry of acidity than the ins and outs of oxidation/reduction. For those familiar with neither, a quick read of the basics about acids in chapter 18 might be useful in digesting what follows.

Oxidizing agents take up electrons (e⁻), while reducing agents contribute them. This puts redox on a parallel footing with acid/base chemistry, an acid being a compound that contributes a proton (H⁺) while a base is a substance that can take up a proton. We have two ways of talking about acidity: pH and TA (titratable acidity). A wine's pH measures the concentration of free, dissociated protons, expressed as an inverse power of 10, wines running between $1/10^3$ (pH 3) and $1/10^4$ (pH 4). Free protons' importance is as a speedometer of aging, and pH has no direct impact on acid taste.

TA measures all the available acidic protons, whether free or bound. Think of free protons as being like cops on the beat, while TA is analogous to the total number of cops on the payroll. A high TA is associated with the sensation of tartness and crispness. TA and pH are only loosely related, and it is possible to have a wine with a high TA and also a high pH—lots of titratable protons but a low concentration of free protons, leading to a wine that tastes tart but spoils fast.

In the same way, we can talk about the redox state at any given time—that is, whether the wine is open or closed—as well as the total amount of oxidation a wine can withstand over its lifetime.

The wine's state of being, its momentary degree of reduction, can vary day to day depending on the concentration of readily available electrons, also known as its rH, or redox potential. But unlike pH meters, an rH meter has proven difficult or impossible to build for complex fluid systems like wine. At this moment, tasting the wine has proven the most useful method for determining redox state.

The analogy isn't perfect, because in acid-base chemistry things equilibrate essentially instantaneously. Not so for oxidation-reduction reactions. Redox equilibrium is often inhibited kinetically, so it takes time—sometimes lots of time—for the complex Rube Goldberg array of interrelated oxidation reactions to shake out.

To one extent or another, every wine gobbles up oxygen. But how fast? We are also interested in a second measure: the rate at which a given wine will take up oxygen.

In addition to redox state and oxygen uptake rate, Ribéreau-Gayon's analysis provides a third distinct measurement: the total amount of oxygen a wine can consume over its lifetime. This tells us the wine's aging potential and how fragile it is—matters of great interest to the winemaker and the collector.

To summarize, we can speak of (1) a wine's momentary oxidative state, (2) its current reductive rate, and (3) its total oxygen uptake potential over its lifetime.

Initial consumption rate and total uptake are only loosely related. In Bob Dylan's immortal words, "Just how much abuse will you be able to take? Well, there's no way to tell by that first kiss."[3]

In elaborate and cumbersome experiments in the 1970s, Singleton painstakingly showed that the accelerated reactions in a Warburg apparatus were not as complete as they would be if the reaction proceeded slowly at wine pH. That is, the total amount consumed in the accelerated conditions at high pH was never as much as the same wine would gobble up in its natural course over the years. But Singleton was able to confirm that as an index, measurements obtained by the method proved very useful when comparing one wine to another. The relative consumption of oxygen gives a useful indication of overall longevity and vulnerability to oxidation.

Despite the method's commercial utility as a quick-and-dirty bell-wether, a careful scientist like Vern Singleton was not enthusiastic about pushing it as a nonquantitative index. What was needed was for real-world winemakers to take Singleton's practical hint and incorporate the index into their own daily routines. Simply put, we coughed up the ball. Today it seems ludicrous to have ignored such an important aspect. But one must consider the context of those times. Californians had only just begun to make unfortified table wines and had not yet mastered the clinical competencies that today's cellars take for granted.

Before the 1976 Judgment of Paris, we were mostly making small wines, and before *60 Minutes'* "French Paradox" segment aired in 1991, we were mostly making whites. Americans were drinking Lancer's, Blue Nun, and Wente Grey Riesling. Grapes were picked at low ripeness and were by and large low in phenolic concentration. While oxidation was rampant in Cabernets, the reduction problems brought on by organic practices and screw-cap closures were in the far distant future.

Once these events occurred, we might have exhumed the Warburg apparatus to guide our struggles with reduction. But as it turned out, no dice, and here we are thirty years later, still without a clue as to what Singleton was driving at.

Forces are converging today—improved vineyard practices, the production of more concentrated wines, screw caps, organics, and the perplexing effects that oxygenation can produce—to engineer a global winemaking train wreck centered on our ignorance of reductive strength.

THE SECRET LIFE OF WINE

Due to complex electrode interactions, redox measurements of wine are notoriously difficult to obtain, and so far there is no standard method. The reactive redox ladder is subject to kinetic inhibition, easily disturbed by measuring devices, and numbers are never wholly reliable. Ask any enologist or collector the true test of age-worthiness: "Only time will tell."

Randall Grahm of Bonny Doon Vineyard in Santa Cruz, California, taught me how to speak about this plainly: Wine is a living thing. It has qi, the Chinese life energy. When it is young, it is best served to exchange qi with the world around it. When it is old, it must guard its qi. Life energy diminishes during aging, so starting out with an excess can be a good thing. It is like testosterone—if your fifteen-year-old son has no pimples, he may not be happily married at sixty-five.

That kind of talk will freak out academically trained enologists. Odd as it seems, I have found that wine aging is easier to explain to the novice than to the modern enologist.

When discussing "reductive strength" or the somewhat more digestible term *antioxidative power,* oxidation and reduction being opposite directions on the same street, it must be borne in mind that wines vary greatly in their fragility or robustness. As long as winemakers remain unaware that wine's ability to take up oxygen varies a thousandfold, there is no possibility of rational navigation through issues of ripeness, blending, barrel regimen, closure choice, and longevity.

Perhaps we should just stop thinking about "wine." Just as Eskimos instead of using the simple word *snow* employ finer distinctions—powder, slush, ice—we should try to avoid lumping together disparate styles as "wine," recognizing, for example, that the characteristics of fresh whites (and our goals for market acceptance) bear no resemblance to those of age-worthy reds.

The post–World War II revolution introduced reductive winemaking to Riesling, a set of practices vindicated in the brilliant system developed by Bordeaux oenologue Denis Dubourdieu and applied to the wonderful Sauvignon Blancs of New Zealand. But these same practices have brought disastrous results to Cabernet.

Tannins require oxygen for proper evolution. This is the basis of chocolate-making, where it is called "conching." That chocolate waterfall in Willy Wonka's Chocolate Factory really exists. Highly phenolic cocoa extract is pumped around and falls in sheets, exposing sufficient surface for continual O_2 saturation, feeding the building of structural colloids through controlled, limited oxidative polymerization that absorbs tremendous quantities of oxygen. The result is dark chocolate, which is profoundly flavorful, its texture hard rather than harsh. If milk protein is then added, it cooperatively binds to the polyphenols, reducing astringency and creating the soft mouthfeel we associate with milk chocolate.

Concomitant with its structure-building effects, precision micro-oxygenation allows winemakers to measure, without additional equipment, the speed with which oxygen is taken up. A wine that will consume 4 ml of O_2 per liter of wine per month (a barrel supplies about 1 ml/L/mo.) will drop its dissolved oxygen by 0.1 ppm per day. At the moment of dryness, a typical Cabernet will consume around sixty times this amount, which means it can deplete a saturation (about 8.5 ppm) in a few days and, if kept from oxygen, will become quite reductive.

The same wine, a few months later and after SO_2 addition, will have decreased its O_2 appetite by an order of magnitude. A couple of years later, it will reach a point where it cannot even consume what the barrel is giving it (1.0 barrel equivalent, or BEQ). If left *en barriques,* D.O. will then climb, and volatile acidity will begin to increase as *Acetobacter* is provided available oxygen to feed its metabolism.

Grapes submitted to extended hang time will behave entirely differently. When challenged with oxygen immediately post fermentation, rather than take 60 BEQ for a month, they might take 30 BEQ for three days. Thus 90% of a wine's reductive strength can be lost due to field oxidation, robbing a decade of cellaring longevity through three weeks of field oxidation on the vine.

In the absence of catalysts, oxygen is actually a very poor oxidizing agent in wine. It will raise redox levels but is not very reactive. In 1987, Singleton published the mechanism of phenolic reactivity, the famous vicinal diphenol cascade, the subject of chapter 6, which, in a nutshell, stimulates covalent bonding of an unoccupied position on an o-diphenol ring and spins off hydrogen peroxide as a side product. Species bonding to the ring include an anthocyanin, another diphenol, a sulfide such as H_2S, ethyl mercaptan, or a sulfur-containing peptide.

In each case the vicinal diphenol is re-created to react again, but then the alkyl substitution of the ring lowers the pKa (the pH at which ionization is 50%) of phenolate oxidation from about 9.0 to 8.5, effectively doubling reaction speed. This explains Ducournau's surprising early discovery that oxygenated wines at first increase in reductive strength. Feed a wine oxygen, and its appetite increases. It's like bodybuilding—do it right, and you get stronger, not weaker. Oxygenation is not oxidation.

By raising the wine's pH to 11, the Warburg apparatus simply accelerates this reaction. We can then determine the wine's entire phenolic uptake capacity, thus allowing us to tailor its cellar treatment and predict its longevity and its early behavior upon bottling. Almost.

NEEDED RESEARCH

Now the bad news.

Phenolic reactivity is not the only source of reductive reactivity. An active fermentation can consume an entire saturation within hours. But even after they die, postfermentation yeast cells break down into cell walls, fatty acids, and various proteins and peptides that gobble up oxygen. In practice, their effectiveness depends on how much is in suspension and how much cells have broken down. In the specialized wines of this type, which include *méthode champenoise* sparkling wines, Muscadets sur lie, and some Chardonnays, lees influence can be profound. White wines with nine months of *bâtonnage* (lees stirring) can take 5–10 years to come around in the bottle.

Our collaborative study, coordinated through the California Enological Research Association (CERA), has not yet determined whether these reactions are sufficiently accelerated at high pH to be included in the Warburg analysis. Most likely they are not.

A second difficulty, even more slippery, is the apparent reductive properties of minerality (see chapter 8). Here is enology's most unfortunate and yet most promising intellectual mud-wrestling arena. On the one hand, minerality is an obvious trait acknowledged by connoisseurs and the preponderance of winemakers. On the other hand, we have no idea what it is, and it retains the academic status of Bigfoot and flying saucers.

Let us split those hairs in the next chapter. For now, you have my testimony that a telltale buzz in the finish, apparently associated either with special bedrock or with living soils, seems to add reductive strength to wines when we MOx them.

Since we don't even know what it is, we have no way of determining whether reduction due to minerality is accelerated by pH shift. Lees and minerality as sources of reductive strength have never, to my knowledge, been investigated with a Warburg device, and it is not clear to me whether high pH conditions would accelerate these reactions in the same way phenolic oxidation is speeded up. If they aren't, we will not be able to measure them in the time frame of the Warburg analysis.

It's time we found out. For white wines, typically low in phenolic content, lees and minerality are probably more important contributors to reductive strength than phenolic oxidation. If we need another method for these wines, we had better start scratching our heads.

Trouble is brewing around these issues. As our best vineyards gain in vine age, as we learn how to pick grapes at proper maturity, we will intensify phenolic vigor. Add to this sophisticated lees-stirring techniques, increased minerality associated with minimum tillage, and other enlightened viticultural practices, throw in the trend toward screw-cap closures, and the likelihood of wines that do not show well in youth looms large.

Awareness of reductive strength, including perhaps a Warburg device in your winery lab, is a good way to start diagnosing problems before the marketplace does it for you.

TAKE-HOME MESSAGES

- Increased competency in both the vineyard and the winery is increasing the frequency with which we encounter reduction.
- Winemakers are obliged to gain awareness of a wine's momentary oxidative state, its reductive rate, and its lifetime oxygen uptake potential.
- The rebirth of a simple, inexpensive method shows promise for categorizing a wine's fragility or robustness. Sensory methods remain our best piloting tool.

8

Speculations on Minerality

Some of you are already wincing. No topic has wrought more confusion and ruffled more feathers among dedicated enophiles than the incessant bandying about of the lofty-sounding "M" word. For some (myself included), asking whether minerality exists is like asking whether we think the sky is blue. Yet for many, the term just isn't nailed down.

The current confusion over minerality is hardly surprising. The well-known sour/bitter confusion is another example of the poverty of linguistic palate training that most Americans receive in youth. Yet no one doubts the existence of these sensations. Why is this particular descriptor so elusive?

Uncertainty over wine sensory definitions is aggravated by trends in modern communication. We live in a crazy time for connoisseurs, because it is much easier today to e-chat about wine than to experience it jointly.

Wine just isn't cyber-friendly. The Internet has made it much more convenient to talk about wine in its absence, often with silly results, and the inane discussion about minerality is a great case in point. Research undertaken by Hildegarde Heymann's sensory group at UC Davis shows that the word is bandied about without consistent definition even among professionals.

This will probably continue to be the case until we become somehow better connected through shared experience. The trend toward online tastings is healthy enough, but participants have to lay their hands on the wines being discussed, and our wine distribution system has not caught up, particularly for small brands.

An additional source of bewilderment in this area is that, by and large, most widely distributed New World wines simply aren't very minerally. Such wines, in fact, are systematically eliminated from wide distribution.

Why is that? Paradoxically, they're not there because they're not there. Nonconformity is the kiss of death in the broad market. Safeway has no shelf space for weird-tasting "interesting" wine.

The three-tier distribution system carries at most 5% of the labels produced in America, primarily from giant industrial concerns with marketing muscle and mainstream styles in huge volumes. The remaining 95%, the wines outside the "McWine" industry, are difficult to obtain. Industrial wines farmed on rich, dead soils without cover crops—your typical $12 Merlot or Chardonnay—are likely to display little or no minerality. Santa Cruz Mountain Chardonnays are all pretty minerally, but when's the last time you saw one at Raley's? As a consequence, one can drink a lot of wine, particularly in the New World, and never have need for this distinction.

One more source of confusion is that there are at least three aspects of wine flavor for which some tasters can find no better term. Sometimes the word *minerality* refers for some people to the aroma of wet stone, for which I prefer the term *petrichor,* the smell of new rain as it liberates natural oils from rock in the desert. Second, flavors in the mouth can also resemble stone or well water, a common attribute of Semillon. My definition represents a third sense, which differs entirely.

Inconsistency of usage, however, can hardly be viewed as evidence that minerality does not exist. Science is supposed to embrace confusion and organize inquiry. That the existence of minerality is questioned in scientific circles says plenty about what passes for science today. In the quasi-scientific technocracy of today's winemaking priesthood, enthusiastic inquiry into such mysteries is often replaced by an authoritarian circling of the factual wagons.

In all fairness, I have to admit that the phenomenon hasn't yielded any easy answers to those of us who have been poking around its edges. Even I dance around the topic throughout this book. Here, though, I want to bring together in a single chapter my take, however incomplete, on this elusive phenomenon. Forgive me, therefore, when I repeat myself.

THE WORLD ACCORDING TO CLARK

If we were sitting in the same room, I would simply pop some corks and show you what I mean by minerality. What follows is my personal point of view on how that palate sensation connects to viticultural practices and behavior in the bottle, and I'll speculate on where it comes from.

Now, nobody has appointed me the new Noah Webster, but in my lexicon, minerality is not an aroma, nor is it a flavor by mouth, though it could be argued to be a taste. It is an energetic buzz in the wine's finish, almost like an electrical current running through the throat. It has a nervous raciness similar to acidity, with which it is often confused, but farther back in the mouth (fig. 16).

I got my definition originally from Randall Grahm, who once sat me down and showed me what a big difference a tiny drop of a soil amendment, mixed mineral tincture, could make in the finish of an otherwise ordinary glass of plonk. I developed an appreciation for minerality from my late wife, Susie, as well, since she was crazy about minerally wines. Once I got the hang of it, I found the trait easy to spot, and since I taste wines from a lot of different regions and circumstances, I've been able to observe tendencies in its source and behavior.

I hope it will not be considered crassly commercial for me to mention that I make some very minerally wines, particularly my WineSmith Faux Chablis and Diamond Ridge Vineyards Aspects, and you could try them. Other reliably minerally wines include Chardonnay from the Pinnacles or Santa Cruz Mountains, any Corton, and any Sercial from Madeira. Mosels usually have it, and California's Riesling counterparts usually don't. The varieties Cabernet Franc and Roussanne tend to be strong in this attribute if not overripe. You can compare true Portuguese ports, always from schist and always minerally, with just about any New World port (not). And despite the general dearth of examples among big brands, Blackstone Merlot is usually pretty minerally.

My French tutors at Oenodev, the cutting-edge winemaking pioneering firm, focused on this attribute as an indicator of longevity as well as its flip side—reductive problems in youth. It is found to be an attribute of wines grown in limestone, schist, slate, and decomposed granite. There is clearly something special about these soils. In 1756, when the Marquês de Pombal mapped the world's first delineated winegrowing region, he based the region's borders on schist, and went so far as to behead cheaters passing off grapes from adjacent terroirs as Douro. Soil matters. Even today, despite soaring prices for Côte

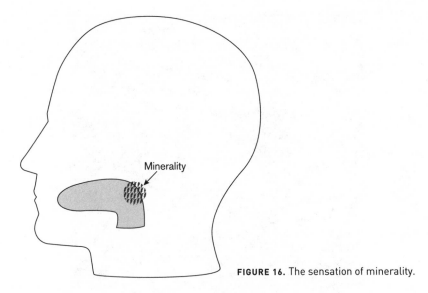

FIGURE 16. The sensation of minerality.

d'Or, potatoes are chosen over Pinot Noir on soils just a few meters off the limestone.

WORM'S-EYE VIEW

It turns out that excellent minerality can be obtained on any site if living soil principles are applied. According to French terroir expert Claude Bourguignon, the development of mycorrhizal fungi will facilitate trace mineral uptake by expanding the grape rootlet surface a hundredfold, facilitating a symbiotic exchange of minerals for sugar. Sure enough, when Dr. Stephen Krebs, ace viticulturist at Napa Valley College (fig. 17), worked with me on a project to make Chablis-style Chardonnay at their south Napa site, we worked by promoting a living soil through a no-till policy, and exceptionally minerally wines came into being from a Yolo sandy loam.

Mycorrhizal fungi are tricky to grow. Fastidious organisms sensitive to a wide variety of herbicides and pesticides, they depend on a complete, established soil ecosystem to flourish. According to Soil Food Web, a healthy earthworm population is the simplest reliable indicator of a balanced soil ecology.

Nobody has pinned down what exactly is happening in wine that leads to these sensations and effects. In his thesis at the University of

FIGURE 17. Steve Krebs with living soil at Napa Valley College. Photo courtesy of Napa Valley College staff photographer.

Bordeaux, Tuscan winemaker Paolo De Marchi of Isole e Olena measured high iron content in his very minerally Nebbiolos. But composition by itself doesn't explain things very well. I worked with Susan Rodriguez, director of CSU Fresno's Wine Sensory Lab, and famed analytical chemist Barry Gump to try to nail down what components might contribute to a minerally character. It was easy for Susan's tasting panel to differentiate the wines I supplied into minerally and nonminerally groups, but Barry's broad-spectrum atomic adsorption analysis, which scanned the entire periodic table, couldn't find any simple compositional driver.

Dr. Heymann at UC Davis has speculated that sulfur compounds cause minerality, but I believe this is backwards: minerality causes reduction, not the other way 'round.

WHAT'S IT ALL MEAN, MR. NATURAL?

It is possible that minerality is actually very similar to acidity. An acid is any compound containing hydrogen atoms that are easily detached as ions. Since a hydrogen ion (the atom minus its electron) is just a proton, we can as easily say that acids are substances that can contribute one or more protons to solution. Upon entering the mouth, those protons stimulate the flow of saliva, by which they are neutralized, and our taste buds tell us how much of this reaction is going on through the sensation of tartness. Acidity can thus be described as a flow of discharged protons sensed by the tongue.

Most of the protons in wine are bound to weak acids like tartaric, malic, and lactic, which are in equilibrium with the free protons. These act like a series of reservoirs of acidic protons that get depleted sequentially because the acids are of different strengths, thus forming a kind of ladder of buffer capacities. When wine enters the palate, the first to be depleted is the strongest acid, tartaric, which you taste on the tip of the tongue. Then malic ionizes in the midpalate, then lactic a little farther back, and last acetic (which clings to its protons most) is neutralized in the throat.

Just as titratable acidity is sensed on the palate as a flow of protons discharging from binding sites on weak acids, minerality may very well be a flow of electrons released from various metallic elements of the periodic table as they move to higher valences. Elements such as zinc, aluminum, magnesium, and many others have an oxidized state as well as a reduced state. They can move from the former to the latter by giving up an electron, for example, $Fe^{2+} \rightarrow Fe^{3+} + e^-$. This is the rust reaction, and also the main mechanism through which soils retain oxygenation after tilling.

There are dozens of important mineral redox couples, so you can have a series of electron reservoirs, just like acids except that they donate an electron instead of a proton. Acidic discharge of protons, however, occurs very rapidly, while oxidative discharge is likely to be kinetically inhibited and may occur very slowly in the bottle. That's a good thing, because it would allow minerals to oppose slow oxidation and confer the added longevity we actually observe in minerally wines.

Minerals can play a second role as well. Some minerals are present in large quantities, others little or none; but trace minerals may have an important catalytic role to play in overcoming kinetic barriers along the energy ladder in which redox reactions arrange themselves. We don't know all the ins and outs, but it's plausible that specific mineral mixes can essentially constitute a multistage battery in the wine. UC Davis phenolics expert Andy Waterhouse has shown the importance of iron in catalyzing the vicinal diphenol cascade.

But it appears that the right chemical composition is not enough. To get the electrons flowing, the battery needs to be charged. Reductive energy has a variety of sources, though we don't know which are strong enough to be effective at rendering the appropriate elements into a reduced state. Proper ripeness, which results in aggressive phenolic reductivity, is probably one such source. Oak tannins and lees stirring may also contribute to charging up the battery by moving the mineral redox pairs into the electron-loaded reductive state. Fermentation, which every winemaker knows has enough reductive strength to create sulfides, may not have the energy differential to reduce metals, for if it did, every wine would be minerally.

The analogy is clear: electron flow versus proton flow. It seems plausible that if we can sense one, we can sense the other. The minerality of which I speak is the same sensation you get when you lick a fresh battery—a static discharge.

I'm no taste physiologist, and I doubt that anyone really understands how acid perception in taste buds really works, let alone minerality. We do know that acid perception (i.e., tartness and salivary response) is related to titratable acidity, not pH—the free proton count—and not total acidity—the total anion count. Analogously, sensory minerality can be imagined to relate to mineral discharge rather than redox (sometimes called rH) or total mineral composition.

This is, of course, all speculation. It's the first step in the scientific method, not the last. A hypothesis that is not too outlandish provides some tangible theoretical basis for the phenomenon to be considered and tested. In the meantime, I hope we can all stretch our credibility toward an openness to the concept of minerality and a curiosity that can only be satisfied by tasting appropriate wines. Experience and training are our path toward a more unified use of the term.

The reason I focus on my particular definition of minerality, that of the electric buzz in the finish, is that it informs my daily work. Minerally wines are more reductive, misbehaving in youth but aging much longer. I am required to figure in this source of reduction during efforts to balance a wine's vigor with oxygen and in making such decisions as time in the barrel and closure selection.

FOREVER YOUNG

We may not know what causes minerality, but much can still be said about how it behaves. When wine is in this antioxidative condition, it will gobble up whatever oxygen gets to it but in the absence of oxygen will cause closing of aromas and formation of H_2S and other sulfur compounds that are favored in the reduced state. That's why it takes ten years for my Faux Chablis to come around and be drinkable.

If this picture is correct, we would predict a decrease in the minerality characteristic during aging, and this is exactly what we observe. Acidity does not diminish, but minerality does. Over time, the wines become flatter and less vibrant.

Bottom line: If a young white wine has less aroma than you think it should, is maybe even a little stinky, but you experience lots of flavor by mouth and it tingles in the finish, you might lay some of it down to see if it improves with age. In general, however, consumers are largely new to wine and don't have cellars, and thus are untrained in evaluating different wines' aging trajectories.

We have a problem, Houston. As we move toward curtailed petrochemicals, reduced tillage, deeper roots, cover crops, proper ripeness, and screw caps, we will need to do what we can to educate consumers that youthful reduction is a mark of quality.

By contrast, red grapes subjected to excessive hang time will have much lower reductive strength and will not appear minerally. Moreover, the bitterness of high alcohol will obscure the sensation even if it is present. These wines, which exemplify the current trend in Napa Cab top-end collectibles, will lack both phenolic vigor and mineral energy and will be short-lived. H.L. Mencken said, "Nobody ever went broke underestimating the intelligence of the American people." But is it wise to bet the farm that nobody will notice that the emperor has no clothes?

The advantages that California presents for growing grapes are innumerable. But we also have three major disadvantages. First, owing to our latitude, our days are relatively short, which inhibits the development of great Rieslings—not much to be done about that. Second is our lack of limestone, slate, and schist, although we do have granite.

Third, we lack rainfall, which limits us from dry farming and presents challenges to maintaining living soil.

There are many lovers of distinctive, terroir-driven wines who have quite simply given up on California wines. I believe their judgment is premature, and my WineSmith Faux Chablis, grown on sandy loam, proves that with living soil practices minerality can be obtained on any soil, just as Bourguignon said. As some of us begin to take more seriously the challenge to make interesting wines with vitality and life, bottled poetry is on the rise. Cracking the code on minerality is an essential milestone on that path.

TAKE-HOME MESSAGES

- Certain wines have an energetic buzz in the finish, almost like an electrical current—a nervous raciness similar to acidity, with which it is often confused.
- Element composition by itself doesn't explain minerality very well. The battery also needs to be charged.
- Current trends will compel us to educate consumers that youthful reduction is a mark of quality.

9

Winemaking at High pH

In this chapter, we consider the winemaking terrain above pH 3.6. Since the standards existing today (though not necessarily tomorrow) dictate freshness rather than aged characteristics in commercially acceptable white wines, this discussion is limited to red wine production. Consumer expectations for red wine differ from whites in several salient ways:

- More tolerance of browning
- Less emphasis on clarity
- Less emphasis on fresh fruitiness
- More value placed on complexity, less on cleanliness of aroma
- Greater longevity expectations

The dominant themes of low pH winemaking are prevention and control. In high pH winemaking, we often acknowledge that we have given up on prevention and try instead to steward the wine, directing its inevitable dramas toward a stable and agreeable resolution.

MICROBIAL EQUILIBRIUM

The microbiological triangle considers the three requirements of absence of inhibitors, nutrients, and inoculum. Any one of these elements may be addressed to control an organism's growth, as long as the ecology of the organism in question is understood. When blending, it is important to consider that two stable wines, when combined, may supply missing elements required for spoilage. The utility of these elements in the high pH realm is entirely different from that in the low pH environment.

Inhibitors

Sulfur Dioxide

Before getting started, I direct non-winemakers to Appendix 1, "Winemaking Basics," to review the use and properties of this widely used preservative (nearly universal in wines throughout the world), and in particular to distinguish sulfites from sulfides and sulfate.

In later chapters, I will address the groundbreaking work of Paul Frey, Tony Norskog, Gideon Beinstock, and other pioneers who are recapturing the skill of winemaking without SO_2. Having myself produced a series of quite good and remarkably age-worthy Syrahs without sulfites, I strongly support Frey's assertion that excellent wines, arguably superior to sulfited offerings, may reliably be made without the use of this additive, in the same way that unpasteurized cheeses are the world's best.

I disagree with Frey that it is easy. I rank this achievement among the postmodern winemaker's loftiest goals, akin to climbing Mount Everest without an oxygen mask.

Baby steps. In this chapter, I think it is enough to discuss the handling of sulfites at high pH without terrifying winemaker readers with the prospect of eliminating them altogether, a prospect most regard as commercially irresponsible if not unpardonably silly.

In a 1980 article, I stressed the role of *molecular* sulfur dioxide (the tiny proportion of free SO_2 that is not ionized) to control the growth of microorganisms in low pH winemaking.[1] Since the effectiveness of molecular SO_2 as an inhibitor is greatly lessened at high pH, it is more sensible to speak in terms of adjusting the overall free SO_2, which is substantially all in the ionic bisulfite form, for its action as a scavenger of peroxide, preventing aldehyde formation rather than acting as a microbial suppressant.

When oxygen enters a red wine, it reacts with phenolics and promotes their polymerization. A side product of this reaction is hydrogen peroxide, which may be damaging to wine flavor and can oxidize ethanol. Its reaction with SO_2, however, occurs much faster, so a small amount (say, 20 to 30 ppm) of bisulfite is extremely effective in scavenging peroxide. Since SO_2 is depleted by this action and by aldehyde binding, it must be measured by aeration/oxidation (never the iodine method) and maintained at a reasonable level throughout aging.

A desirable consequence of sulfite oxidation to sulfuric acid, which instantly ionizes to sulfate, is the liberation of a titratable proton, with the effect that high pH wines over time tend to experience slightly increased TA and substantially decreased pH. The rate of this reaction is proportional to the fraction present of the fully ionized sulfite (SO_3^{2-}), which, though tiny, is ten times greater at pH 4.0 than at pH 3.0. This reaction goes so slowly below pH 3.6 that it can be ignored, but at pH 3.9, during extended barrel aging, it can result in an increase of as much as 0.5 g/L in TA, accompanied by agreeable sulfate flavor effects and a reduction of 0.1 or more in pH. The reason the French express titratable acidity as sulfuric acid is that for many years this was the only legal way for them to add acid.

Total SO_2 should also be measured and, if possible, kept below 100 ppm, at which level it exhibits an inhibitory effect on malolactic bacteria. A soapy finish can also be detected at about 200 ppm total SO_2.

Addition of SO_2 to young wine will be observed to bleach monomeric pigment, a frequent source of heart failure for young winemakers. Calm down. This is a reversible reaction, and actually stabilizes red color by maintaining a pool of monomeric pigment that is restored to the wine as it ages and the pigments polymerize.

Temperature

Since at high pH, SO_2 is not very effective in inhibiting spoilage organisms, other means must be employed to prevent spoilage. A low-temperature cellar is one possibility, as many types of organisms such as *Brettanomyces* and film yeasts do not grow well at 55°F. Cool cellars are not, however, a good strategy if you do not intend to sterile filter prior to bottling, since activity in the bottle may ensue, resulting in unpredictable development and bottle variation.

My strategy is just the opposite: to build as stable and integrative a structure as possible, and to allow the wine to undergo at least one and preferably two summers at 60–65°F to allow microbial resolution. I will elaborate on this strategy in the next chapter, "Integrated *Brettanomyces* Management."

Alcohol

High-brix musts result in wines that make a powerful flavor impact when young but fail to age well. If grape maturity is extended in order to obtain flavor concentration and color with an eye to subsequent de-alcoholization (see chapters 16 and 18), the procedure is best performed early in the wine's life. Wine colloids are unstable at high alcohol content and tend to fall apart. Moreover, balancing alcohol opens the door to microbial equilibrium and, unless the wine is to be sterile filtered, should be begun at an early moment. My practice is to reduce wines immediately to approximately 13.2%, and later to balance them to an appropriate "sweet spot" (see chapter 11) by addition of clean high-proof wine spirits, thus tuning the final blend and increasing stability. For those of you utterly shocked by my candor concerning wine manipulation, please refer to chapter 20, "Spoofulated or Artisanal?"

Nutrients

Oxygen

Organisms such as film yeasts and *Acetobacter* that require oxygen for respiratory metabolism may be controlled by eliminating it from their environment through the use of inert gas and, preferably, by maintaining wine in full containers. Frequent topping, however, has been argued to introduce more oxygen than it prevents, since it breaks the vacuum that builds in a well-made barrel. Many winemakers therefore prefer to bung and roll wines that have completed fermentative activity.

Cool cellars inhibit the growth of many organisms, but they also increase the solubility of oxygen in wine. More important, the rate of phenolic reactivity with oxygen slows down tremendously below 59°F (at 50°F it is only 30% as fast, as discussed in chapter 6), so cold cellars such as those in Pinot Noir country tend to encourage vinegar spoilage. Oxygen control is not effective against fermentative organisms, including *Saccharomyces, Brettanomyces/Dekkera,* and malolactic bacteria.

Oxygen is not the enemy of all wine; as we have seen, wines have vastly differing requirements and aesthetic targets. Low-oxygen winemaking, while useful for microbial control, is not always desirable from the point of view of phenolic management. Young reds often benefit from large amounts of oxygen to facilitate color stability and the formation of structure. Older reds are generally fed oxygen in much lower levels to assist textural and aromatic refinement, without encouraging oxidative microbiology or tannic dryness.

Fermentable Sugar

Complete fermentation is an aid in the suppression of fermentative organisms such as *Brettanomyces/Dekkera*. Titration methods such as Lane-Eynon for residual sugar are not sensitive enough for the determination of completion, and enzymatic glucose + fructose is far superior. This assay, however, does not measure cellobiose, a sugar created by firing new wood and assimilable by *Brettanomyces*.

Malic Acid

Malic and lactic acids can be tracked nonquantitatively (i.e., as being either present or not present) by the simple and inexpensive method of paper chromatography to monitor the onset and finish of malolactic fermentation. Enzymatic malic analysis requires a spectrophotometer but is a wonderful method to monitor progress of malolactic and is one of many reasons for even small wineries to consider the purchase of a "spec," which has many other uses as well.

Because it is not microbially stable, I cannot conceive of a situation in which one would consider adding malic acid to high pH table wine.

Inoculum

Introduction of Commercial Organisms

I have already discussed the introduction of malolactic bacteria, so I want to confine my comments here to choices having to do with yeast.

Inoculation for primary fermentation with commercial organisms is widely though not universally practiced. Commercial yeasts vary greatly in their fermentation vigor. Slow fermenters such as Pasteur red are popular for red wines, since they allow prolonged fermentation on the skins at elevated temperature.

"Wild" or "natural" yeast fermentation simply means that we have not inoculated and do not know what characteristics the fermenting yeast may possess. Personally, I like the Australian term *feral ferments* because some wild fermentations are prone to foaming, sulfide production, vinegar production, high total SO_2 metabolism, and sticking. Ah, terroir. Advocates point to the advantages of sluggish fermentation and the complexity of flavors that occur in these wines.

An idea that has recently gained currency is that the advantages of both methods may be obtained by reducing the size of inoculum of commercial yeasts. The resulting delayed onset of fermentation allows natural non–alcohol tolerant yeasts such as *Hansenula* and *Kloeckera* to add complexity at the beginning of fermentation while still allowing the commercial yeast, with its predictable characteristics, to finish the fermentation. This strategy may be of particular interest to organic winemakers.

The growing voice in the Natural Wine community in favor of uninoculated fermentations is discussed in chapter 23, "Yeast Inoculation: Threat or Menace?" My favorite corollary to Murphy's Law is, "Nothing is impossible for the man who doesn't have to do it himself."

Sanitation

Wineries are not sterile environments. Spoilage cannot be prevented simply by maintaining an environment free of microbes. Most wineries of any age have indigenous populations of *Saccharomyces, Brettanomyces,* film yeast, malolactic bacteria, and vinegar bacteria, and there is growing evidence that many organisms inhabit wine that we do not know how to grow in pure culture and have thus never discovered. Taking care to minimize populations by reasonable sanitation procedures is nevertheless the policy of most California wineries. Less so in European cellars, where indigenous microbial populations have stabilized and a *goût de maison,* or house flavor profile, which has developed over centuries and whose evolution and control has been empirically incorporated into cellar practices, may be a valued element of the wine's distinctive character of place. Domaine Beaucastel in the Rhône and Château La Gaffelière in St. Emilion are examples of wines in which *Brettanomyces* plays a distinctive aromatic role without which the wine would be unrecognizable.

Since no human pathogen can live in wine, winemakers can afford to be much more blasé about sanitation than other food producers. In high pH winemaking, if the goal is often to allow the wine to undergo all potential microbial activity at the winery, sanitation should be considered in this context. For unfiltered products, a warm cellar (60–65°F) that promotes potential activity may be a wise choice.

Because of its alcohol and acidity, even high pH wine is an unusual environment, and most organisms cannot grow in it. Contact with sewage, for example, is less of a threat for wine spoilage than contact with pockets of spoiled wine. The importation of bulk wine, used barrels, and other wine-containing equipment should always be considered an event that might introduce a virulent strain of spoilage organism such as film yeast or *Lactobacillus*.

Filtration

I like to define winemaking as "the art of intelligent compromise." In the context of a particular wine, filtration and fining decisions balance flavor loss against in-bottle spoilage. Some California wineries, for example, filter their Cabernet but not their Pinot Noir. Some decisions, such as whether to filter table wines containing fermentable sugar, are pretty straightforward: filters are better than sorbate and cheaper than high-tech pasteurization.

In high pH winemaking, the key to bottling without filtration is to eliminate the nutrients listed above from the equation by provoking microbial activity at the winery. This means working counterintuitively— to encourage rather than suppress the wine's inevitable microbial destiny, controlling its extent early on through good must nutrient conditions resulting in complete fermentation.

Phenolic Chemistry

The first person ever to suggest to me that making red wine at high pH was a good idea was Pascal Ribéreau-Gayon, who when we met in 1991 was director of the Faculty of Oenology at the University of Bordeaux. He expressed delight over a 1990 Merlot he had been involved with that had a pH of 3.95 and a TA of 2.9 (though this joke was on me, because in the American convention expressed as tartaric instead of sulfuric, it was really 4.5, still low). I was shocked.

He explained to me that at that point in his career he had published 250 papers, half on phenolic chemistry and half on microbiology. The whole point of his life's work, he told me, was to elucidate the chemistry and microbiology of high pH red wines so they could be made responsibly. To be truly great, he felt, a red Bordeaux must have low titratable acidity.

Acidity, he pointed out, stimulates salivation, and no matter how refined the tannins are, they will always seem coarse when the mouth fills with salivary protein. Try it out by acidifying a bit of wine with a little citric acid—he's right.

Pascal told me that in two years the Merlot in question would have a pH of 3.85 and a TA (in U.S. terms) of 5 grams per liter, the result of sulfite oxidizing to sulfate. During that time, moreover, the high pH would help this concentrated, tannic Pomerol to protect itself through oxidative polymerization. That conversation was the beginning of my postmodern education.

Mentioned in chapter 6 but worth repeating here, University of Bordeaux biochemist Aline Lonvaud-Funel in 2000 reported that acetic acid bacteria in red wine are not inhibited by pigment-bound SO_2. Because it is in rapid equilibrium, our standard analyses (both iodine titration and aeration oxidation) report this type of bound SO_2 as free SO_2, but this is false. There is in fact essentially no truly free SO_2 unbound to pigments in young red wine. These wines are protected from oxidation only through O_2 uptake via the vicinal diphenol cascade that protects the wine. Cold cellars suppress this action, and long hang time destroys phenolic reactivity, leading to fragile wines.

Layers of soft tannins may be encouraged by blending and even by cofermentation of complementary varietals. The French notion of élevage (to "raise" the wine as one raises racehorses) embraces many approaches to enhancing tannin structure, including micro-oxygenation (to build structure, round tannins, integrate aromatics, and quench reductive proclivities), periodic macro-oxygenation (to open and advance the wine's aging), and lees contact. The timing and levels employed are critical to the success of these techniques.

The rich finish of a classic Bordeaux is not entirely attributable to phenols. Potassium and sulfate both contribute the back palate mouthfeel, and are natural by-products of high pH winemaking. Sulfate is the product of sulfite oxidation, which occurs much more rapidly at high pH. Potassium is the counter-ion in the highly buffered solutions typical of this genre, and confers richness and flavor persistence to the wine's finish. High pH wines are typically not cold stabilized, since this results in lowered potassium and higher pH.

Cold stabilization may be useful, however, to reduce high TA in red wines whose acid taste creates the impression of harsh mouthfeel. It should be kept in mind that while cold stabilization in low pH whites lowers pH, in the high pH realm above 3.65 it raises pH instead. In chapter 18, I discuss some new membrane methods that can decrease acidity and bring about bitartrate stability without harming structure.

In my system, fresh, unstructured whites are made below pH 3.6. Crisp dry wines such as Sauvignon Blancs and Pinot Grigios bottled at about 3.2, with TAs around 7 grams per liter, while fatter styles such as

California Chardonnays and Viogniers might push 3.4 pH and TAs in the low 6s. For big Cabernets and Syrahs, I favor a pH of 3.80–3.85 and TAs near 5, and for lighter reds such as Pinot Noir and Barbera, I'll shoot for bottling around pH 3.70 and TAs around 6 grams per liter.

All of these specifications come from fruit that is harvested at pH 3.4–3.5. If I am way over this zone, I'll acidify with tartaric acid. My non-ML whites drift naturally down to 3.2, while the ML+ chardonnays end up at 3.4 by themselves. The heavily extracted reds, following ML and skin contact, end up at around 3.8 after cellaring, and the lighter reds at 3.7. It's a nice system that in each case doesn't try to fight the wine's innate chemistry.

Under no circumstances will I bottle above pH 3.9, as this results in a soapy aroma and phenolic reactions that tend to crash and burn in the bottle. So when I say high pH, I'm saying it's okay to drive 70 or 75 mph on the freeway but not 100, okay?

TAKE-HOME MESSAGES

- The desirable target zone for bottling red wines intended for aging is pH 3.70–3.85, depending on tannin concentration, in order to obtain sufficiently low acidity for grace on the palate.
- Sulfur dioxide is managed completely differently in wines over pH 3.6.
- Microbial management employs knowledge of the ecology and nutritional needs of desirable and undesirable organisms, as well as inhibitory mechanisms.

10

Integrated *Brettanomyces* Management

One of the most controversial topics in winemaking is the role of the yeast *Brettanomyces* (together with its spore-producing twin, *Dekkera*). People's reactions to its peculiarly earthy, animalia aromas vary considerably, due in part to the widely varying mix of flavors that strain and substrate produce and in part to differences in personal sensitivities and interpretation (one man's "sexy" is another man's "disgusting"). With some exceptions, though, most connoisseurs have experienced on different occasions both faces of Brett: the sultry, profound earthiness and the repulsive barnyard stench.

There is a growing feeling that there is no close relationship between concentration in the liquid and aromatic expression in the nose. Pascal Chattonet in 1992 showed synergistic effects between Brett aroma compounds and declared "spoilage thresholds" for the organism's marker compounds (426 ppb for 4-ethyl phenol [4EP] and 4-ethyl guaiacol [4EG] together or 600 ppb for 4EP alone).[1]

Linda Bisson, who deserves praise for her flexible and evolving view of the organism, elaborated on this simplistic view in a January 2013 UC Davis seminar, "A New Look at an Old Problem." The situation is very complex. These are only two of perhaps a dozen compounds involved, which are not produced by all strains. These can both synergize and mask. Individuals vary tremendously in both sensitivity and preference. Most important, there is growing evidence that a good phenolic structure can reduce apparent aroma at least fivefold. "We had a

Napa Merlot that required us to add five times the Chatonnet threshold amounts just to demonstrate the aroma," Bisson said.

This is the postmodern view. We prefer to concentrate on local truth over universal truth, in that every individual is different and every wine behaves uniquely, owing to its ability to deviate from solution behavior and integrate aromas. What is required of the winemaker is to move beyond theory and attend to what is actually happening and how it relates to the winemaker's goals.

It's high time I stated my views concerning this beast and its handling, as usual somewhat at odds with modern enological thinking. For winemakers interested in bypassing sterile filtration when possible (count me in), Brett management is the central problem facing the making of serious wine.

The reason is simple. The focus of postmodern philosophy is the creation and preservation of beneficial macromolecular structure. This structure manifests in wine as colloidal particles sometimes nearly as large as a bacterial cell. The benefits of good structure—profundity, aromatic integration, and graceful longevity—appear to be lost in sterile filtration, despite the fact that no tannin material may be retained by the filter. While this lack of residue has convinced some of my colleagues that filtration cannot be harmful to wine structure, I do not concur. My hypothesis is that the action of tight filtration somehow disrupts rather than removes structure.

Integrated *Brettanomyces* Management advocates another approach, one that preserves and also takes advantage of the benefits of good wine structure, an element usually missing in the debate about Brett. It utilizes a three-legged stool approach:

1. Create a nutrient desert.
2. Foster microbial balance.
3. Achieve aromatic integration through good structure.

Microbial activity when properly husbanded can amplify distinctive terroir characteristics and soulful appeal. Wines lacking good structure, in contrast, fail to incorporate its influences properly, and the resulting perception of *Brettanomyces* as a defect has led to draconian control measures that produce wines of less interest.

Central to the conventional wisdom of Brett control is the maintenance of free SO_2 at a level of around 30 ppm at relatively low pH's in order to maximize its effectiveness by increasing the percentage of the free SO_2 that is in the un-ionized molecular form. Good studies have shown

***Brettanomyces* Ecology**

1. In an aerobic environment, Brett can utilize proline as a sole source of both C and N. This amino acid is available in high quantities in both wine and beer, and is not metabolized by *Saccharomyces*.

2. Brett employs a parasitic, secondary contaminant strategy, though it rarely takes over completely. It lacks the genetic capability to synthesize biotin, folic acid, and other essential micronutrients; instead it depends on other organisms to exude these compounds during their autolysis. Brett is well controlled to less than 500 cells per millileter by other organisms normally present in wines. Sterilized wines can reach 10,000,000 cells per ml.

3. Brett principally enters wineries from bees and is spread in barrels and bulk wines from other wineries. It establishes ubiquitous sequestered low populations in wineries that are extremely difficult to eradicate.

4. Brett can ferment cellobiose, a synthetic sugar produced by toasting of new wood.

5. Brett cannot grow below 59°F.

that this form greatly reduces the number of colonies of Brett that grow on a petri dish. However, 2012 studies by David Mills's group at UC Davis using quantitative PCR (polymerase chain reaction)–DNA amplification technology, which does not require culturing to detect viable cells, suggest that free SO_2's main effect may be to reduce culturability rather than actually kill cells. We may be simply treating the symptom.

When draconian control measures are incorporated into a general winery protocol, they harm the development of its wines generally. Paradoxically, not only do these wines incorporate Brett less well, but they are also more susceptible to it, which leads to a snowball effect in exactly the wrong direction. Due to its clever survival strategy (see sidebar), Brett in this environment outlasts other organisms whose competition normally controls it. Brett is like a hospital disease, fostered by the very sanitation measures designed to suppress it.

In the recent past, control practices have reached the level of academic dogma, with the consequence that *Brettanomyces* (together with its sexual spore-producing twin *Dekkera*) is now classified outright in many quarters as a spoilage organism. The intrusive aromas of unmanaged Brett include horse sweat, leather, shoe polish, salami, foie gras, truffle, dog doo, and (the late Ralph Kunkee's classic descriptor) "wet dog in a telephone booth."

Neurological studies in guinea pig brains have shown that sensory inputs associated with important events—for example, an A-flat played to signal feeding time—result in increased neural mapping for the stimulus. In the same way, expert wine tasters can become sensitized to aromas of oak, bell pepper, VA, and other "defects" such that they no longer experience them as untrained consumers do.

Nevertheless, only the most zealous of its critics fail to acknowledge "good Brett" at least occasionally. In his hilarious article "Attack of the Brett Nerds," wine importer Kermit Lynch issued a call to reason that has unfortunately been largely ignored.[2]

Why not simply eradicate this organism and make clean, sterile wines of appealing fruit character? Fresh, unstructured wines such as Rieslings are easily stabilized by modern technological tools (sanitation, fermentation with pure yeast strains, temperature control, pH adjustment, maintenance with inert gas and sulfites, and sterile bottling). But winemakers often find these tools are best placed aside in the development of fully evolved, structured wines for which profundity is the goal rather than purity of "varietal character," a concept invented by researchers at Gallo in the 1950s and later taken up as an experimental convenience at UC Davis.

A winemaker's personal discovery that profundity rather than purity is our objective is the beginning of the path to postmodernism. A fully evolved Brett strategy completes the journey.

THE EMERGENCE OF CONVENTIONAL WINE

I feel I must restate here that the modern technological system developed in Germany shortly after World War II brought into being a new kind of wine unseen in history. Without sterile filtration, the off-dry German wines we regard as "traditional" were impossible to make because they were unstable in the bottle.

Such wines, more properly called "conventional" wines, did not exist in commerce in the eight thousand years of truly traditional winemaking. Reductive winemaking methods are extremely effective for the production of aromatic white wines whose appeal is based on freshness, varietal purity, and crisp acidity.

No problem. I love a good modern Mosel. But take note: This style has in the past half century almost entirely eradicated the market presence of traditional white wines, which once shared the mature evolution, oxidative development, and microbial complexity that today is the exclusive province of red wines.

Fresh wines target aesthetic goals quite distinct from those of mature wines. Freshness, varietal simplicity, and crisp acidity are undesirable traits in reds, even today's conventional offerings. The point of most red wine (with exceptions such as nouveau Beaujolais) remains to evolve its initial simple aromas of berries and herbs into something richer and warmer that touches the soul more profoundly. Tannins must themselves evolve from a coarse astringency into a rich underlying structure that supports and integrates developing flavors into a coherent single voice.

Reductive winemaking has several disadvantages for wines intended for cellaring. These wines depend on properly formed phenolic colloids, wherein reside almost all red pigment and tannin, to provide a refined structure that does not interfere with fruit expression through harsh aggressivity. Aromatic products of microbial metabolism, oak influences, and vegetal characteristics are also integrated by good structure into a coherent background that is positive rather than interruptive. Modern oxygen-free practices suppress the development of good structure, and sterile filtration disrupts it. Low pH and high titratable acidity also present challenges for mature reds.

THE FALLACY OF ACIDITY AS A VIRTUE

As I discussed at the end of the previous chapter, high TA exacerbates tannic aggressivity by drawing excessive salivary protein into the mouth and coarsening the impression of tannin, thus counteracting the winemaker's efforts to achieve textural refinement. Low pH inhibits wine development and microbial stabilization, as do sulfites and cool cellars. Palate liveliness is to be prized, but its best source is not acidity but minerality (see chapter 8), which confers energy to the finish, though the sources and mechanisms of the latter are still poorly understood.

The mastery of winemaking at high pH is essential to postmodern work,[3] covered in the previous chapter as a necessary prerequisite to a specific discussion about our beast. The reaction speed necessary to useful phenolic development requires elevated pH. If pH is the gas pedal of aging, then pH 3.70–3.85 is analogous to freeway speeds of 55–70 mph, allowing us to cover some developmental distance in the cellar.

CREATING A NUTRIENT DESERT IN THE VINEYARD

The first steps toward microbial balance should be taken in the vineyard. The goal here is to encourage a vigorous fermentation that will consume not only all traces of sugar but also essential micronutrients, the absence of which can hold secondary growth of *Brettanomyces* in check. Paradoxically, the production of a wine poor in nutrients results from a must rich in nutrients to promote healthy yeast action.

Brett's strategy is insidious. Rather than compete with *Saccharomyces* (normal wine yeast) during primary fermentation, it emerges later, during aging. The nutrient status of wine in support of secondary microbial growth can be considered to have four aspects: fermentable sugars, nitrogen sources, micronutrients (vitamins and other cofactors), and oxygen. *Brettanomyces* growth must be suppressed in both of its modes—fermentative (requiring sugar) and respiratory (requiring oxygen).

We can assess the risk of Brett fermentation by measuring enzymatic glucose + fructose. Levels above 1,000 mg/L are unsafe, and we'd prefer to see < 500. The winemaker must determine empirically the best method for achieving sugar dryness. Considerations include the choice of commercial yeast inoculum vs. wild yeast, temperature of fermentation, avoidance of highly elevated sugar in the must, and a host of other factors.

Since oxygen is not necessary for later fermentative growth, we must depend on primary fermentation to reduce fermentable sugars. Even given good consumption of sugar, toasted wood contributes to wine the fermentable sugar cellobiose, which Brett can also utilize. Thus a secondary inhibitory strategy is advisable.

As part of its strategy as a secondary infectant, Brett is a nutritionally fastidious organism lacking the ability to synthesize for itself many micronutrients. In order to inhibit Brett in both of its growth modes, it is beneficial to encourage consumption of micronutrients during primary fermentation. To this end, vineyard conditions must be managed so as to deliver a healthy, nutrient-rich fruit to the crusher. Nitrogen measurements at bloom can be used to evaluate where fertilization might be needed, often in "hot spots" rather than throughout the field. Overfertilization, which results in excessive vigor and poor ripening, must be avoided through careful topological nutrient management.

In nutrient-deficient musts, the addition of simple refined chemicals such as diammonium phosphate should be minimized. This chemical is a favorite of modern enologists because it relieves yeast stress and brings about a vigorous, smooth fermentation without sulfide production. However, this mode of fermentation is not useful for consuming micronutrients. When the yeast is fat and happy, it does not need to make enzymes to digest micronutrients as a food source. If you feed them Twinkies, they won't eat their oatmeal.

Our primary ally in suppressing respiratory growth in the barrel is the wine's reductive strength. This is because it has been shown that *Brettanomyces* is able, in the presence of oxygen and ample micronutrients, to feed on ethanol as a carbon source. Unlike *Saccharomyces,* Brett can metabolize the amino acid proline, ubiquitous in wine, as a sole source of both carbon and nitrogen if oxygen is present. Primary fermentation inevitably leaves behind plentiful amounts of proline.

If it is to protect itself, the wine must maintain its ability to consume oxygen. In the vineyard, our goal is to maximize reductive vigor through good concentration of tannins and to avoid excessive maturity, which can damage reductive vigor.

MICROBIAL EQUILIBRIUM IN THE CELLAR

Exactly like Integrated Pest Management in the vineyard,[4] IBM seeks in the wine cellar to utilize the natural competitiveness of a complete ecology to maintain the activity of each type of microbe at an acceptable level. It seeks to play out in the cellar any metabolic conversions to which the wine is prone, so that sterile filtration is unnecessary. Any influence inhibitory to this goal should be dialed back to the point where microbial processes achieve completion. Among inhibitors to be considered are alcohol, temperature, sulfites, volatile acidity, and pH. Storage temperature must, for example, be held above 60°F for a sufficient period to permit activity to proceed—a couple of summers perhaps.

An elaborate experiment performed by Ducournau's group at Oenodev provided unexpected enlightenment on the subject of microbial control of Brett. The intention of the study, carried out on a young, sound French Merlot, was a thorough investigation of the effect of micro-oxygenation on *Brettanomyces* growth under various rates of oxygenation and temperatures. Accordingly, the wine was divided into twelve trials, of which six were inoculated with Brett. Prior to the inoculation, all but one of the trials were flash pasteurized to prevent any interference from preexisting organisms that might be present in the wine.

When plated onto petri dishes, the unpasteurized inoculated wine achieved the expected growth of about 500 CFUs (colony-forming units), a typical result. But all the pasteurized inoculation grew to 10^7 CFU, whether micro-oxygenated or not. That's 10,000,000 cells per ml. I had never seen this kind of growth, and I came to understand that our greatest ally in controlling Brett has been the presence of other microbes. Brett is an opportunistic pathogen; like a hospital disease, it can be promoted by excessive sterile practices. I have since seen this same effect in wines that were sterile filtered or treated with the chemical sterilant Velcorin and then barreled down.

Further evidence supporting the IBM approach is that sulfite-free producers report lower levels of *Brettanomyces* in their wines. In a 2004 panel discussion at Napa Valley College, Paul Frey (Frey Vineyards), Tony Norskog (Orleans Hill), and Gideon Beinstock (see chapter 13) all shook their heads when queried regarding Brett incidence. "We have lots of challenges," said Frey, "but runaway Brett just isn't one of them."

Just as the most flavorful and distinctive grapes derive from vineyards employing IPM rather than draconian pesticides, so a microbial equilibrium results in more interesting flavor development in the cellar. Like the great unpasteurized cheeses of Europe, wines permitted a natural microbial balance can achieve richness and profundity beyond comparison. Since many dangers await a wine or cheese so exposed, the transformation must be handled with great skill and attention through a carefully thought out program that considers application of postmodern principles to every facet of the wine's development.

Except in new cellars, *Brettanomyces* is a ubiquitous organism, a fact of life. Like athlete's foot, one usually cannot hope to eradicate it. Like keeping one's feet dry, control of this organism based on suppressing growth by denying it facile growth conditions is the most realistic solution. Keep in mind that the goal is to facilitate a truce with Brett so a stable condition exists at bottling. Through nutrient depletion and good reductive strength, we create the best environment to allow the wine time to play out its inevitable development. Any reductions in alcohol content and volatile acidity as well as exposure to new toasted wood should occur early, prior to the period when the wine is held above 60°F to resolve its development.

Final blends should be assembled well in advance to avoid the possibility that a blend may promote additional activity of which its parts were not capable. Different wines can hold back activity for different reasons. Blends tend to be less stable than their parts; one component may contain nutrients such as cellobiose (the sugar extracted from new wood) but lack the necessary vitamins contained in another component. Enzymatic hexoses should be as low as possible in unfiltered reds, and in no case should exceed 1.0 g/L.

An appreciation of the wine's reductive strength is critical to good cellar management and to the timing of bottling. Reductive strength is a function of phenolic reactivity, mineral composition, and lees contact. Late-harvest reds may appear heavy in tannin and color yet exhibit very little reductive strength. Sensory properties of reductive wines are vibrant purplish hues, a closed aromatic profile, and the presence of sulfides. Direct measurement of reductive strength is the subject of chapter 7.

AROMATIC INTEGRATION

The third "leg in the stool" of the IBM system is the aromatic integration that takes place in wines of refined, stable structure. The basic idea is that in wines of good structure, microbial aromas that otherwise would appear as spoilage elements can be integrated as elements of positive aromatic complexity. Just as in a good béarnaise sauce we cannot perceive distinct aromas of tarragon, fresh onion, vinegar, and mint but instead perceive a rich "single voice," so the aromas of varietal veggies, oak, and microbial activity become integrated into a proper phenolic structure.

In chapter 2, I presented the essentials for the creation of good structure. The finer the colloids in such a structure, the more surface area will be available for aromatic integration. Monomeric color is essential for building fine structure. Oxygen, properly applied to a balanced tannin/pigment phenolic blend, acts like a wire whisk in the creation of a rich, light tannin soufflé, and subsequent lees stirring can add fatness and refinement. These steps are also similar to chocolate-making, in which the conching process uses oxygen to convert cocoa powder into dark chocolate that milk protein softens to make milk chocolate.

Wines of proper ripeness and good extraction that are afforded early structural refinement can carry many times the supposed "threshold" of 400 ppb of the Brett metabolic marker 4EP without apparent aromatic expression. Indeed, the nuances imparted to the flavor impression in the nose and by mouth by a Brett manifestation in wines of good structure are likely to be absent of intrusive spoilage characteristics, resulting instead in greatly enhanced profundity and soulfulness.

Although presented here as a third element, the creation of good structure should be addressed quite early in the wine's life, creating the conditions for integrating subsequent microbial activity. Wines benefit most from oxygen immediately after completion of alcoholic fermentation. Since many aspects of Phase 1 oxygenative structuring (see chapter 3) are counterintuitive, it is best to work with someone skilled in the art. Properly administered, oxygenation is homeopathic, increasing rather than degrading the wine's reductive strength, bizarre as that sounds.

MAKE UP YOUR MIND

Thorough work by Ken Fugelsang and Bruce Zoecklein provides a cautionary tale against the idea of microbial equilibrium.[5] In laboratory studies, which consistently showed a double bloom of Brett in several strains (presumably the first fermentative and the second oxidative), 4EP continued to rise even after viable cells were no longer cultured. As a result of this finding, I have often seen judges at wine competitions condemn a wine in which they thought the current level was acceptable or even positive because they thought it might get worse—guilty until proven innocent.

In my own experience, I have not observed Brett increasing in the bottle if it has had a chance to do its thing in the cellar. By running 4EP assays on individual barrels, I have certainly observed that they do not march in step, but once having hit a maximum, each barrel tops out at the same level and ceases to produce subsequent quantities.

My conclusion is that most problems with Brett are a result of indecision. The organism is easily controlled in fresh, unevolved white wines by a combination of sanitation, low temperature, low pH, SO_2 maintenance, and sterile filtration. But because these conditions preclude microbial equilibrium, a strategy of moderate suppression in the cellar in the production of top reds destined to be bottled without sterile filtration can lead to completion in the bottle. The balanced ecological strategy advocated here cannot be implemented halfway. If you're making classic red wines, you're probably already a little bit pregnant, so maybe it's time to embrace the baby and take up responsible parenting.

LIVING PROOF

David Mills's use of Next Gen Sequencing (NGS) reveals a whole world of wine microbiology and may open the door for the balancing of a wine's microbial ecology to take the place of draconian eradication tactics.

Mills's studies of microbial populations in botrytized juices at Far Niente Winery abound with startling revelations.[6] The first was that a substantial portion of the fermentation was conducted by organisms other than the inoculated strain. Second, there was substantial cross-over between the microbial populations of these wines and those of dry wines made at the same winery, providing support for the role of indigenous microbial populations in flavors of terroir. Mills believes that a major thrust of coming research will be to understand how climate, soil, altitude, and other local factors influence microbial ecology and the characteristics of resulting wines.

Mills's research assistant Nicholas Bokulich and his colleagues published a paper titled "Next-Generation Sequencing Reveals Significant Bacterial Diversity in Botrytized Wines."[7] The NGS probe revealed the presence of a long string of genera that don't appear in my college notes: *Proteobacteria, Alphaproteobacteria, Rhodospirillales, Acetobacteraceae* (okay, that's no surprise), *Gluconobacter, Zymobacter* (previously only found in palm sap), *Oceanospirillales,* and *Dyella* spp. Bokulich was actually able to isolate and culture two species, *Methylobacterium populi* and *Sphingomonas pseudosanguinum,* not previously detected in wine.

NGS techniques are being refined and improved monthly. By the time you read this book, our understanding will be quite a bit more advanced. I predict that a year from now, the list of organisms known to inhabit wine will have more than doubled. Because developments are occurring too rapidly for print journals to keep up, events can best be followed online at www.PLoSOne.org or by checking Mills's Website at http://mills.ucdavis.edu/research-projects.

TAKE-HOME MESSAGES

- Brett management is the central problem in the making of serious wine. Modern enological practices cause Brett and exacerbate its effects.
- In the vineyard, our goal is to maximize reductive vigor. The action of tight filtration somehow disrupts structure.
- To master Brett management is to understand what red wine really is.

11

Harmony and Astringency

Nice and Rough

Just as the heart of rock and roll is the beat, the foundation of the soul of wine lies in its texture. In this book I have often discussed the connection between fine colloidal structure and the aromatic integration that leads to soulfulness. Beyond this physical feature, great wines are tuned into harmony, an illusion that we as humans hold in common. For the postmodern winemaker to work in this medium requires both technical expertise and artistic instincts.

Over the past two decades, researchers have developed a language for tannins and a road map for their evolution. Much technique lost in the modern era has been recaptured concerning the role of oxygen, lees, and oak, and additional tools such as membrane technologies have been added to the winemaker's kit. In the previous ten chapters, I laid out the resources now at the disposal of the postmodern winemaker and outlined their consequences for the promotion of integrative structure and graceful longevity.

No general dogma exists guiding the degree of refinement, edge, or rusticity a winemaker may deem appropriate. For style direction, the practitioner is well advised to consider traditions for which the local appellation has or could become known, with an eye to minimizing consumer confusion by delivering wines that support a consistent local expectation. Depending on the region's historical context, the winemaker's experimental latitude will vary. A winegrower in, say, Suisun, may be advised to swing out more creatively than might be stylistically appropriate in the more established neighboring Napa, and in ways that might even be contrary to local ordinance in the Médoc.

NATURE IN THE ROUGH

Why does astringency exist? Primarily, it is a way for plants to persuade us not to eat their children. Actually, they would be delighted for us (and birds) to swallow their children whole, but not to chew them up on the way down, and only when they are mature and ready for the voyage through our entrails and into fertile soil.

Astringency is a tactile sensation, not a taste. As hunter-gatherers, our forebears needed instantaneous, hard-wired sensory clues to phenolic content—astringency and its taste analog, bitterness—to distinguish nourishment from poison, determine ripeness, and so forth. Sensory stimuli from all five senses are directed to the thalamus in the midbrain, where snap decisions tell us whether to swallow or spit. The midbrain is like a security kiosk at the gateway to our cognition. Our job as winemakers, like any chef, is largely to get the thalamus to stamp our passport and send us up to the frontal lobes rather than down to the fight-or-flight centers of the reptilian limbic system.

Tannin can confer richness and satisfaction, and its integrative properties can enhance soulfulness, but excessive astringency is repulsive and hides the wine's charms. Threading this needle requires a depth of cellar skills. Since winemaking is a performance art, we must also know our audience and the extent to which they differ from us.

GROPING THE BEAST

Richard Gawel of the Australian Wine Research Institute's Tannin Project published in 1998 an excellent review of red wine astringency research.[1] Its physical basis is the natural affinity of salivary proteins for wine phenols, a combination of hydrogen bonding and hydrophobic interactions. These are weaker than true covalent bonds, so the longer a tannin polymer is, the stronger the cooperative binding to protein. Doug Adams's astringency assay shows that protein bonding begins with polymers about four units long.[2]

Postmodern winemaking makes use of these principles to shape polyphenols that are as small as possible, thus forming into small colloids that maximize surface area and promote hydrophilic/hydrophobic interaction. Incorporation of anthocyanins is thought to terminate polymerization—thus, the greater the color concentration, the finer the tannin. Harshness can be reduced by blocking interaction with salivary proteins through the incorporation of lees peptides and other sulfur-containing compounds as side chains on the polyphenols. With care, oxidative linkages can bind sulfides to tannins, converting stinkiness into softness.

DUEL OF THE TITANS

Astringency's physical causes have received much recent attention from various camps, with apparently contrary findings. At UC Davis, Ann Noble's long and impressive research on this topic[3] is unlike her aroma research, which resulted in the highly differentiated Aroma Wheel™. Noble did not distinguish different kinds of astringency but concentrated instead on exploring differences among tasters in the duration and intensity of astringency, which she and Uli Fischer linked to individual variations in salivary rate.[4] Likewise, Master of Wine Tim Hanni has used the variation in mapping of taste bud density among subjects to develop a theory predicting wine style preferences based on sensitivity.[5]

Richard Gawel's team, in contrast, produced a Mouth-Feel Wheel that distinguished seven primary and thirty-three secondary terms for astringency.[6] A greatly simplified version of tannin terminology that I use in my daily work with wine tannins employs just seven terms (five shown in fig. 18 and the rest explained below), pretty much stolen outright from standard French usage and reluctantly translated verbatim. (Don't blame me; I've never liked the term *green tannin*.) This scheme has proven valuable in predicting tannin progression over time as, hypothetically, phenols rearrange themselves into polymers and colloids during careful exposure to oxygen.

The findings of Noble and Hanni are important in liberating personal preference from the province of pundits. Good for them. Consumers are entitled to their own likes and dislikes, and ought to place no more faith in wine reviews than they do in critiques of films and restaurants.

Taken to the extreme, however, this disconnectedness leads to the death of art. How can I make delicious wine if my sensory apparatus bears no relationship to that of my customers? If we are all unknowable, then music and even good cooking is a pointless endeavor. But

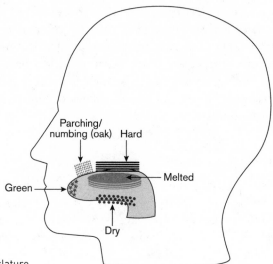

FIGURE 18. Tannin nomenclature.

experience clearly tells us otherwise. I cook, I sing, I make wine. When I get it wrong, I can tell; when I get it right, people not only respond positively, but in agreement with the exact nuances that I also perceive.

Fortunately, it is possible to reconcile these two, Noble/Hanni's more qualitative and Gawel's more quantitative perspective—how we are alike and how we differ—through an understanding of the stages of perception: what is actually there, what our senses tell us, what our brain makes of this information, and whether we like it. Let's call these four stages:

  I. Phenomenon

  II. Sensation

  III. Integration

  IV. Preference

Our two camps form a nice, orderly complementarity in this hierarchy. Research distinguishing how people are different concentrates on Stages II and IV: differences in sensory hardware and differences in preference. Research into shared apprehension of sensation concerns itself more with Stages I and III: correlating true differences that exist in nature with linguistic descriptions of the sensory impressions and additionally examining the compensating process contained in human software to realign our perceptions with actuality.

In the end, individual differences in sensory acuity do not divide us as much as they might. We all have different hearing sensitivities, but unless we are simply deaf, this doesn't alter our ability to draw emotional content from music. We all find a major chord cheerful and a minor chord melancholy.

The reason differing sensitivities don't necessarily preclude finely synchronized aesthetic experiences is that we all share sophisticated compensating software. Once our five senses have collected signals, a huge amount of processing takes place to correct for differences in environment and acuity. Our brains are highly skilled at extracting salient details held in common, compiling an integrated package through leaps and guesses. That's how, years later and from a different angle, we recognize a face. We are masters at filling in the gaps. This software is so powerful we don't even notice we're doing it.

The human software to fill in gaps is given us at birth, something deep in the DNA and strongly shared. This is the source of our sense of harmony and explains why fine nuances of discord and harmony, to which we relate without being told, show up in wines as they do in music. Wine's ability to communicate subtle emotional messages is its primary appeal, and accessing this mysterious language is the foundation of postmodern winemaking.

TALKING TANNIN

At the risk of being boringly repetitive, I'll summarize the postmodern picture of what's going on with tannins (refer to figs. 2 and 3 in chap. 2). Young red wines generally contain monomeric anthocyanins and unpolymerized tannin building blocks such as catechin, epicatechin, quercetin, and gallic acid from skins and seeds. These are not soluble but gather into copigmentation colloids,[7] tiny beads that are perceived as a graininess on the tip of the tongue—known as *tanin vert,* or "green" tannin (see fig. 18). There is, at this stage, little astringency elsewhere on the palate, even for big wines.

I just gotta throw in an aside here. Since I was taught at UC Davis the theory that only polymers are astringent, I asked Michel Moutounet why red wines, being entirely composed of monomers, are astringent and then smooth out as they polymerize. He offered the theory that cooperative binding of salivary proteins occurs along the surface of the copigmentation colloids into which the monomers are arranged, in other words, bundles of monomers functioning collectively like a polymer. Works for me.

Left undisturbed in a stainless steel tank capped by inert gas, these monomers undergo nonoxidative polymerization into regular chains (for you phenolic geeks, linking the 4 and 8 positions on the flavan-3-ol). The resulting polymers are compact and have relatively little mouthfeel and protein interaction. In these conditions, however, anthocyanins are not readily preserved, so the chains continue to elongate, becoming increasingly insoluble and drawn to salivary protein, so that the textural impression after a few years migrates from the tip of the tongue to a general dirty graininess throughout the tongue and cheeks, which we call *tanin sec,* or "dry" tannin, the only type of tannin that occurs under the tongue in the back of the mouth.

A small amount of oxygen early in the wine's life will send these phenols on a completely different course. Oxidative polymerization, which utilizes the vicinal diphenol cascade I described in chapter 6, efficiently captures and stabilizes anthocyanins and creates randomized, open, freely rotating polymers that interact strongly with saliva, creating an impression of increased volume and aggressivity. In a few days of micro-oxygenation, green tannin is transformed entirely to *tanin dur,* "hard" tannin, which sits entirely on the top of the tongue and moves back to create an angularity in the finish. The impression is not at all grainy but sheetlike and grippy, like peanut butter, causing the tongue to adhere to the top palate. The oxygen pickup from simply barreling down young red wine moves it in this direction.

Because the oxidative cascade increases oxidative reactivity, the formation of hard tannin is accompanied by an increase in reductive strength and often will induce formation of sulfides and decreased aromatics. In addition, the wine gets harder and harder for a bit. It's awful. Randall Grahm refers to this period as "the valley of the shadow of death," a frightening time for the novice practitioner.

After a week or three, however, the grip begins to abate, and the wine begins to open. We call this the "firm" stage. Further oxygenation will melt the tannins, beginning from the back palate, where angularity is replaced by velvety softness, while the front of the mouth remains grippy, a stage we call "round." If we are employing MOx, this is often a good place to stop, retaining enough reductive strength for subsequent barrel and bottle aging while ensuring both stability and longevity. For wines intended for early consumption, oxygen can be continued until the tannin is completely "melted" *(tanin fondu).* Melted tannin is quite stable in the bottle but has little antioxidative power and can fall apart if excessively exposed, leading to dryness and precipitation. Complete melting is a better idea in the case of wines destined for screw-cap bottles rather than other closures.

It's worth noting that these changes in texture occur without any alteration in the total phenol content of the wine. It's the way the tannins are assembled that determines their sensory properties (as well as the expression of other aromatics such as Brett and bell pepper). Choices concerning the degree and type of astringency are the responsibility of the winemaker, without which expression of natural terroir is often defeated.

Our seventh term refers to oak tannin and is borrowed not from the French but from Gawel's terminology. Located on the front part of the tongue just behind the tip, this type of tannin is very drying, but since that term is already in use for an entirely different type of tannin, here we use the term *parching*. Oak is also associated with eugenol, or oil of clove, a topical anesthetic that numbs this area, so we expand the term to *parching/numbing*. Oxygen can be used to soften this type of tannin, resulting in a slick and greasy mouthfeel.

Since there are often delays in the introduction and extraction of oak tannin into young reds, care should be taken to prevent delays in extraction treatment lest the wine's grape tannin profile be prematurely resolved while oak tannins still need smoothing. If oxygenation continues beyond when native grape tannins are properly formed, dryness may result. It's easy to slip up in terms of timing when introducing oak tannin; wine does not penetrate deep into oak barrels to extract pithy oak tannin until the later stages of oak cellaring.

THE MYSTERY DEEPENS

"Finally, a full understanding of astringency cannot be achieved without an appreciation that it is a perceptual phenomenon. The role of the perceiver cannot be discounted."[8] So Gawel ends his review.

In accord with Gawel's words, my work with alcohol sweet spots, with musical pairings, and with cork taint due to TCA has shown that there is another source of astringency that is not related to our theories of composition. "I wouldn't worry 'bout it none, though—them ole dreams is only in yer head," comforts Bob Dylan's shrink. Here we enter the deep end of postmodern thinking, where we have absolutely no rational handle on how to proceed except to trust our gut.

We have already discussed the role that differences in taste sensitivity, salivary rates, and past experience may play. But beyond these lie some very peculiar traits that give us a window on wine's true nature and on our own nature as humans. It's odd, for example, that a mere 4 parts per trillion of TCA can cause a wine to be astringent. The human nose is incredibly sensitive to this moldy aroma, which ruins the fruitiness of wine. Yet the physical phenomenon of tannin-based astringency occurs only above, say, 400 parts per *million*. At 4 parts per *trillion* (a hundred million times less), TCA cannot really be binding to salivary protein to any perceptible extent.

TCA smells nasty, like a moldy newspaper. Its effect on astringency demonstrates the role that fruit aromas play in creating the illusion of harmony. Consider for a moment the difference between music and noise. At the beginning of a symphony, the instruments quietly tune up—a most obnoxious sound. Then they strike up together, with much greater volume, and we are carried away by music, for which we have a very high decibel tolerance as long as we are emotionally taken up. One false note, though, and we wince.

There is a sweetness to music that is bestowed by the midbrain—a hall pass to cognition's upper floors: contemplation, emotion, sometimes ecstasy. Without this endorsement, it's just a lot of clatter. Good wine is granted similar privileges, and these can be revoked if a disharmony such as corkiness is introduced.

What forced me finally to grasp that wine is liquid music was the phenomenon of sweet spots.[9] When Vinovation started offering alcohol adjustment services, wineries came to us because at high alcohols their wines were hard to drink, excessively bitter and astringent. We noticed that if you take out too much alcohol—resulting in, say, less than 10%— you see another kind of harshness we called acid-based astringency.

At first we assumed that wines would become more balanced if we got anywhere in the 13–14% alcohol range—a preference bell curve. Not so. After thousands of blending trials, we finally had to admit the obvious—and it was the last thing we were expecting. Every wine has discrete balance points we all can identify where the astringency abates and the flavors are married and harmonious. In such a series, the wines adjacent to the harmonious spots taste especially disharmonious: 0.1% alcohol too high is hot and bitter, and 0.1% too low is harsh and sour (fig. 19). In a recent experiment on a 2008 Cabernet Sauvignon, we found sweet spots at 13.7% and 14.2% alcohol, which eighty-four judges rated an average 6.0 and 6.1 respectively on a ten-point scale for astringency, while the blend of the two at 13.95% alcohol was rated 25% more astringent, with an average rating of 7.5 (confidence level very highly significant at $\alpha < 0.1\%$).

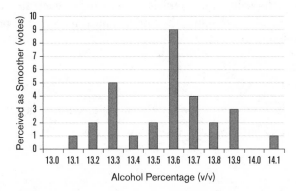

FIGURE 19. Sensory smoothness of Merlot rated at different alcohol levels.

Similar results have been obtained in thousands of alcohol reduction trials. Figure 19 shows a similar experiment where judges were asked to rate sensory smoothness of a Merlot at various alcohol percentages, showing the same familiar nonlinear pattern.

A key point is that this effect, which has nothing to do with phenolic content or structure, is very strongly shared. Something in the blend is perceived as on or off, in the same way that when the piano is out of tune, everybody leaves the bar without even knowing why.

Here's a fun experiment you can do at home. Open a nice big Cabernet Sauvignon, taste it, and take note of the level of astringency. Boot up iTunes, put on the Doors' "People Are Strange," and taste again. You'll feel the wine smooth out. Then put on "When the Saints Go Marchin' In" (Louis Armstrong's Golden Legends version will work). The wine will become almost undrinkably harsh. If you have a glass of white Zinfandel around, the effects will be the opposite. I play around much more with this in the final chapter.

What's going on here? My notion is that wines, like music, carry emotional modalities. Cabernet likes dark, sinister music because it resonates with its nature. White Zinfandel likes silly, positive party music. When the wine's emotional essence comes into conflict with its environment, the midbrain revokes access to its upper recesses and the stimulus, classified as noise, is sent to the brain's primitive limbic recesses, and harshness ensues.

Whether or not that makes sense, this experiment dramatically demonstrates the importance of context for astringency perception. In addition, it shows how strongly shared is our sense of harmony, however divided we are in our individual preferences. Holding these disparate concepts simultaneously in mind is a challenging exercise in mental gymnastics, good for building the philosophical muscle that postmodern winemaking requires.

TAKE-HOME MESSAGES

- Individual sensitivities and preferences for tannins vary.
- A sense of harmony and dissonance is strongly shared.
- There is a working language for tannins.

PART TWO

Practices

12

Winemaking's Lunatic Heroes

The human mind treats a new idea the same way the body
treats a strange protein; it rejects it.
—Peter B. Medawar, Nobel Prize–winning biologist (1915–1987)

The notoriety of California and its attempts to out-France France in the
1976 Judgment of Paris are paradoxical in view of the notion that wine
is, by its nature, a product of place. Our breeds are origin-driven, so to
judge a California Chardonnay superior to a white Burgundy makes as
much nonsense as to find that a Great Dane is superior to a schnauzer
or vice versa. What could this possibly mean?

I explore these inanities in more depth in chapter 24, where I advocate for judging reform. Placing these injustices to one side for the
moment, in the present chapter I have a different agenda. Here I will
labor to persuade every reader of the debt of honor we owe to winemaking's ill-advised, unhinged losers.

Much of the charm in a career making wine in America is the imperative for pioneering. This is in contrast to European oenologues, who
enter an industry hidebound in tradition, with winemaking procedures,
styles, and markets thoroughly entrenched for centuries. Their science,
though certainly scholarly, possesses a self-congratulatory tone, as if to
answer the question, "How can it be that our wines are just so damn
good?"

Not so in the New World. Here we grasp at straws, hopeful for any
handhold, some vineyard/varietal/style combination that can find
buyers. We often toil in obscure and uncelebrated hinterlands where
consumer recognition resides entirely in our imaginations. New acquaintances in a restaurant will readily discuss the selection of European

wines—Which is better with the fish course, a Muscadet or a Chablis?—but an Iowa La Crescent or a Santa Cruz Mountains Chardonnay is unlikely to receive parallel consideration.

"I refuse to join any club that would have me as a member," declared Groucho Marx. While there may be an element of self-loathing in our studied ignorance of American appellations, I believe that a growing appetite exists for the wines outside the mainstream, and that time is on our side, so that winemaking pioneers across the country will see their efforts vindicated throughout the coming decade.

European winemakers both envy our freedom and pity our floundering. Winemaking in the New World today is a process of continual discovery. It's an odd sort of team sport in that it takes a village, where advances are sparked by a peculiar mix of geniuses of differing stripes. The American winemaking scene is a fluid social organism in which diverse enterprises interrelate to advance our self-comprehension.

Wine's ongoing saga illustrates the interplay between science and human values in a mythos that holds profound lessons for how cultures learn and develop. We all were taught the scientific method in school, but too little was said about the origins of the hypotheses it tests. Where do theories come from? I want to argue here for honor and affection for the screwballs who at much personal sacrifice get the R&D ball rolling in critical new areas in our industry today.

Science is no longer the engine of progress it was in American winemaking forty years ago. The easily solvable problems that emerged in the late 1960s are yesterday's news. Clean and simple won't cut it anymore. The chief docket item in today's highly competent and competitive marketplace is the pursuit of greatness. Knockin' 'em dead. To delve into elusive goals like terroir, soulfulness, and somewhereness calls for out-of-the-box exploration that sometimes benefits more from originality than from solid grounding.

What we do, we wine producers, we divide the workload. Winemakers of every stripe work the discovery process together. Team America. Breaking and remaking the mold falls to men and women of iron constitution who lack better sense. On the flip side, the pick-and-shovel work of scientific verification goes to the careful, the impeccable, the credentialed.

It helps that in the wine industry, all factions are more broadly schooled than in most other fields. Every enologist is called upon to speak poetically, and even the most Luddite dreamweaver had better know how to titrate and run brixes. Enology's foundation is solid fundamentals, but at its core lurks a creative element that's a little bit crazy, just as baseball is mostly solid fielding but depends on a pitcher who can't bat worth a darn but can dream up and deliver the unexpected pitch.

MY FAIR LADY

The upstarts of Iowa, which has gone from six to nearly one hundred wineries in the past decade, can take heart that they are technically way ahead of where California was forty years ago. They have reached a level of wine industry penetration that is, by national standards, about the average, much like the situation in the Golden State in 1960, which didn't start out as that preeminent producer of big, bold table wines you're looking at today.

California rose to prominence in the 1940s by delivering inexpensive ports and sherries: high-sugar, high-alcohol wines that cost next to nothing to produce. These products dominated American wine production just after Prohibition when cheap land, cheap Dust Bowl labor, and WPA water projects perfectly aligned to enable its Central Valley to offer much lower prices than the established quality table wine– producing areas in Missouri and Ohio. Constituting nearly all California wine production from 1933 until 1960, these high-alcohol products were naturally sterile and required no microbiological expertise. Such wines actually benefited from oxidation and even steam heating. Back then, enologically speaking, we didn't know anything.

Up until 1960, 95% of California wine was port and sherry, with an average alcohol over 18%. The introduction of Blue Nun and other light, sweet table wines in the 1960s changed everything. The innovation of sterile filtration, a product of atomic energy,[1] caused a tsunami swing from fortified wine to table wine in one short decade. By 1970, the vast majority of California wine was less than 14% alcohol.

This meant big trouble for winemakers. Perhaps half the wine being bottled had some kind of classic defect—VA, aldehyde, geranium tone, heat or cold instability—you name it.

Brilliant work at UC Davis saved the day. Advances in our understanding of pH, SO_2 management, sanitation, oxidation prevention, temperature management, control of malolactic and other microbiological sophistication swept in an era of clean, competent table wine production that grew in scale a thousandfold by 1990. California's 1976 success in Paris shifted the focus from light European knockoffs to big Chardonnays and Cabernets that France couldn't match (see chapter 17, "Some Like It Hot").

As competent winemaking became commonplace, the goal of aesthetic excellence, steadfastly ignored by Davis as a matter of policy,[2] became the new Holy Grail for commercial wineries. This is the way of things. Science conquers problems within its grasp, leaving behind the less tractable hard-core problems, naturally selected Darwin-style.

ENTER THE DRAGONS

Stepping into this void have always come explorers who perceive the need for deeper work. It seems absurd that the classifications of Bordeaux were established in 1855 without the slightest inkling of how wine actually comes to be. Yet it is true. Not until 1857 did Louis Pasteur, a thirty-five-year-old chemist, disprove spontaneous generation and only decades hence elucidate the mechanism of fermentation and actually name yeasts as its agent.

Not only was this information unnecessary to winemaking in its first eight thousand years, but it was also steadfastly resisted by the rank and file. Fifteen years after Pasteur's gooseneck flask experiments, Pierre Pachet, the renowned professor of physiology at the University of Toulouse, still labeled his theory of germs "a ridiculous fiction." "My strength lies solely in my tenacity," reported Pasteur.

Thomas Jefferson foresaw the great potential of American wines in his Sangiovese plantings at Monticello. In 1840, the third largest winery *in the world* was in Hermann, Missouri, and Ohio led the country in wine production. These early dreams stumbled badly due to phylloxera, Pierce's disease, mildew pressures, and winter kill, and it has taken two centuries (minus a fifteen-year reset during Prohibition's "Noble Experiment") to work out all the angles, but the Monticello AVA today produces some of the nation's most profound Viogniers and Bordeaux-style blends, and Missouri's Nortons, Chambourcins, and Vignoles are national benchmarks.

Martin Ray's name appears early on anybody's list of American winemaking lunatics. Besides his odd penchant for varietal labeling and his madcap attachment to Santa Cruz Mountain Pinot Noir, Ray was crazy enough to advocate sur lie aging as well as bottling his Pinots unfined and unfiltered. We would welcome him as an early postmodernist except that he was premodern.

In 1965, another screwball named Robert Mondavi had the temerity to install the southernmost winery on Highway 29 in the supposedly frozen tundra of Oakville, despite the published conventional wisdom that grapes might not grow there. Still crazier was Richard Sommer, who in 1961 built the first post-Prohibition winery in Oregon, planting Hillcrest Vineyard in the Umpqua Valley. Neither of these men achieved quite the reputation as a simpleton that Dr. Konstantin Frank enjoyed for his imbecilic planting in 1962 of vinifera above Keuka Lake in New York, a vineyard that, now a half century old, is widely regarded as the source of the best Riesling in North America.

Dr. Frank's gamble could be called conservative compared to his disciple, Ohio madman Arne Esterer of Markko Vineyards, who in 1968 began decades of trial and error threading the needle to grow vinifera on the south shore of Lake Erie that today produces some of the densest and longest-lived Chardonnays in the United States. "Right down by the water is safest, but in summer it's too cold there to ripen," advises Esterer. "You need a well-drained site high enough above the lake to ripen but close enough for winter protection. You want to plant where you can just see the water." Weirder still, planting must be on north-facing slopes. Early bud push also exposes the warmer spots to more spring frost hazard, but worse is the increased danger of winter kill. The sunnier south-facing aspects will come out of dormancy if there's a week in February of warm weather and then get murdered when it turns cold again. One hundred years seems a minimum expectation to work out the best strategies in these climatically limited regions.

Elmer Swenson had a dream, too. An admirer of T.V. Munson, whose work in Dennison, Texas, on phylloxera-tolerant rootstocks was credited with saving the vineyards of Europe, Swenson had inherited a Wisconsin farm on which he foolishly decided to grow wine grapes. Since there existed no varieties suitable to his climate, Swenson simply began in 1943 to breed them. Sure, why not? His Edelweiss, La Crosse, St. Pepin, Brianna, Swenson Red, and St. Croix varieties read like a list of the Midwest's most popular wines, now appearing on the lists of thousands of midwestern wineries.

Innovation is not highly treasured in the wine industry. Most people get into the business to do something old, not something new. Many of the visionaries we admire today were considered by their contemporaries to be not so tightly wrapped. Sean Thackrey, a steadfast wine rebel since the early 1980s, is perhaps the New World's most enthusiastic student of ancient techniques, and his real contribution is to render what he reads into practice as if his winery were a test kitchen for alchemy. Another militant Luddite, Christian Mouiex, famously dumped an entire tank of Dominus Estate Cabernet after learning that it had been acidulated with tartaric acid.

Paul Frey, an unlikely prophet from Redwood Valley who presided over decades of really quite wretched sulfite-free wines while he patiently dialed in his now wonderfully successful methodology, approached me in 1997 with the peculiar notion that red wine phenolics had the capability to consume oxygen and incorporate aldehyde. I blew him off. Only much later did I realize that the 1987 Singleton paper he had been quoting actually embodied the essence of red wine evolution, structure, and aromatic integration described in chapter 6.

The Benziger Family's transformation from proprietors of the world's largest Chardonnay mega-boutique into a diminutive brand based on Biodynamics seemed almost suicidal. The list of big-time established savvy players also drinking the Kool-Aid of founder Rudolf Steiner includes Jim Fetzer and Paul Dolan, who managed, well before green was trendy, to cajole even Brown-Forman into sustainable practices for a decade, proving that environmental responsibility could indeed be practiced at the corporate level. Some winemakers become heroes just by breaking the wall of silence, by telling the truth. I take my hat off to Michael Havens, who in 2001 let the *New York Times* crucify him for micro-oxygenating his Merlots, and to Randy Dunn, who had the courage to admit in a 2004 *Wine Spectator* article that he embraced reverse osmosis for alcohol adjustment.

Always so far out there as to stay barely in view, Randall Grahm could make this list several times. Freakishly experimental in all things, he revolutionized California's varietal focus to include Rhône and Italian varietals, and led us out of the marketing Stone Age with innovative, playful, and intellectually challenging wine labels (a far cry from the "urine sample" labels of the 1970s) that dared his customers to smarten up. He was the first California winemaker to experiment with micro-oxygenation and the first to move beyond it. Now he's growing grapes from seed, an obviously foolish notion . . .

THE FOOL ON THE HILL

I've named some celebrated successes. But just as important are the numerous lunatics who miss the mark. We benefit just as much from failed concepts as from successes. The sacrifices of the luckless also-rans, driven by passion, also strengthen the community intelligence.

It's hard to estimate the fraction of zany ideas that succeed. Clearly, it's pretty small. Even big success stories like Henry Ford and Thomas Edison ran far more failed ventures than successes. Proctor and Gamble's R&D department budgets a 3% survival rate for new ideas.

With failure rates that high, progress requires a gigantic pool of courageous, visionary, obstinate, lunk-headed spendthrift whackos to keep up our momentum. Oh, and vast sums of money, most of it completely wasted. How do you prescreen out the bad ideas? Beats me. Who would predict that a forty-seven-pound chicken could resonate as a major national brand? Time seems the only dependable test, pluck and luck the surest keys.

Training in the scientific method leads to an orderly, logical approach to inquiry that is better suited to confirmation than to the creative leaps new discoveries often require. The current debate over Biodynamics, explored in chapter 21, illustrates well why the scientific process is constrained from much discovery. "Biodynamics is a make-believe world with no earthly connection to our functioning, real, material world," writes Stu Smith in his blog, biodynamicsisahoax.com. "I don't want to live in a society that can't tell the difference between fantasy and reality."

The bottom line is that to generate useful new ideas requires a very large number of independent, creative players driven by inspiration and unconstrained by common sense. Sounds like the wine industry to me.

THE MISSING LINK

I am, of course, leaving out a step.

The heroes of the exploratory phase do not speak the same English as the professional scientists who might later confirm their discoveries. Attempts to communicate holistic concepts often engender ridicule and frustration in a reductionist ear trained in Science-Speak. *Energy,* for instance, is not a good word to bandy about between these groups, because it has very different meanings and applications both groups think they own.

In *The Copernican Revolution,* Thomas Kuhn explains that in a worldview based on earth, water, air, and fire, these elements obviously arrange themselves in that order (that is, flame rises in air, air rises through water, while earth falls). In that context, the idea that the Earth was not at the center of the universe was not just blasphemy—it didn't even make sense.

Similarly, the postmodern view that wine's chemical composition does not determine its sensory properties seems obvious nonsense. But consider that the source of the differences in the sensory properties of a lump of coal, a graphite tennis racket, and a diamond is not compositional (all three, after all, are pure carbon) but entirely structural. Now we can talk. The first step in new thinking is to translate the new paradigm into old language that, however unlikely, is at least understood.

What is needed is a translator. Someone who speaks both languages and is slave to neither. Harvard ethnobotanist Mark Plotkin spends his time following tribal medicine men into the Amazon's deep forests to learn about the herbs and vines they use.[3] He takes their lore and presents it to the guys in the American Medical Association, packaged a little differently than he heard it in the bush.

This is the role to which I aspire, and why I write. Although I have done some pioneering, I lack the resources to explore a serious holistic winemaking system. Nor do I possess the credentials to perform a significant body of publishable scientific verification testing. It interests me to take on something that nobody else is doing. My screeds are in part love letters from the edge, written to enologists who may choose to play with them by applying scientific rigor to the hypotheses I've dragged back from the jungle.

IN A NUTSHELL

Discovery divides naturally into three sequential realms that call on very different skills and temperaments.

Phase I: Exploration, Observation, and Characterization of New Phenomena. The Explorer mentality is creative, nonjudgmental, even unhinged. Substantial resources are put at risk. Players are often not trained scientists, but a detailed record of observations is invaluable.

Phase II: Construction of Hypothetical Predictive Models. Dogmas, old wives' tales, apparent patterns, and beliefs are translated into testable hypotheses that saner minds might examine. Requires fluency in the languages of the Explorer and the Experimental Scientist, while slave to neither.

Phase III: The Scientific Method. The Experimental Scientist employs conventions of verification to test hypotheses, often by comparing double-blind randomized experimental design models against observed data. Exclusively the domain of the skeptical, meticulous, professionally trained scientist.

Now the bad news: Hypothesis testing is not a dependable tool.

Most scientific work is oriented toward preventing confirmation of incorrect hypotheses (Type One Errors), and "significant" findings must meet the standard of avoiding false confirmation 95% of the time. The tighter this standard, the more probable that real effects are missed. It is not uncommon that the chances of missing a real effect (Type Two Error) run 90%. This means that today's science misses all but the most obvious effects. Every practicing scientist should read Tom Siegfried's article "Odds Are, It's Wrong."[4]

Faced with these uncertainties, most of the time winemakers just go with what feels right. Then, long before academia can provide useful answers, the market decides the winners. What the heck. This is the same method through which genetic designs are naturally selected and species are improved. Nature just goes with what works. Science plays no important active role, and mostly just attempts to report what happened.

I'm doing what I can to stimulate interaction between our precious lunatics and our intrepid scientists. But by and large, it's likely that the postmodern winemaking revolution will not be televised. In the end, winemaking is really just the art of having the right superstitions.

TAKE-HOME MESSAGES

- Enology is no longer the engine of progress it was forty years ago.
- Courageous fools who perceive the need for deeper work are continually stepping into this void.
- Breaking new ground is risky behavior from which we all benefit.

Gideon Beinstock's Mountain Magic

Handling Extreme Terroir

If anyone deserves the title Terroir Extremist, it is surely Gideon Beinstock (fig. 20). After some thirty-five years with Renaissance Vineyard
and Winery, one of the state's highest and remotest sites, he has now
moved a mile down the road to his own certified organic home vineyard, Clos Saron, which turns out one of California's top Pinot Noirs in
absurdly tiny quantities from an unlikely mountain glen. Renaissance,
located in Yuba County in the Sierra foothills, has been declared
"California's best-kept Cabernet secret" by the likes of wine critic Matt
Kramer, and even the controversial writer Alice Feiring reserves praise
for Clos Saron wines.[1]

A conversation with Gideon is a thing to be savored. You never
know what he'll say. It's among my most cherished perversities to carry
into our discussions any preconceptions I can afford to part with, for
the sheer pleasure of watching him gnaw, chew, and occasionally tear
to bits my theoretical cornerstones with all the serious playfulness and
benign ferocity of a new puppy.

Though considered in the vanguard of the Natural Wine movement,
he never seems a fanatic of any stripe. He is instead a thoughtful and
attentive explorer, never willing to knock anything before he tries it.
His working method is refreshingly empirical. He is no slave to theory
but instead a constant student of the wine itself and of what techniques
may bring benefit. This pragmatism may be the trait that unites postmodern winemakers.

FIGURE 20. Gideon Beinstock at Renaissance Vineyard. Photo courtesy of Yotahm Beinstock.

He is equally gifted in the area of inventive articulation, dispensing fresh and tasty philosophical delicacies with dependable regularity. Increasingly, his method is simply to bide his time.

SKY PILOT

Gideon's vision isn't for everyone, nor are his challenges typical. Remote mountain winegrowing has unique aspects, some natural, some cultural. Thin air and fog-free conditions resulting from elevation and distance from maritime influence result in high incident light, which on well-exposed, thin, rocky, well-drained soils typical of altitude tends to encourage Cabernet Sauvignon and Syrah to produce massive quantities of remorselessly hard tannins. These impart so much antioxidative power that considerable reduction is present in youth.

Another consequence of the remote location is an absence of tourism. Combined, these factors impel production of distinctive wines capable of gaining attention on the world stage rather than the softer, more approachable styles typically found in tasting rooms along Gold Country's Highway 49.

Kramer refers to such wines as possessing "somewhereness," and this trait is amplified by natural winemaking practices. The energetic buzz in the finish that decomposed granite appears to impart is augmented by the organic practices employed at Renaissance and to an even greater extent at Clos Saron. The downside is that intense minerality imparts additional reductive strength, resulting in austere wines that require considerable cellaring. Beinstock's low-sulfite regimen encourages flavor dimensions that depart still further from the mainstream.

"I'm growing toward encouraging distinctive 'peculiarities,' the opposite direction of clean, standard wines in which abnormality is equated with flaw," he says. "Peynaud spoke of inhabitants of remote regions who became used to defects which with education they would eliminate. Today, it's more appropriate to encourage diversity."

BEAUTY AND THE BEAST

In the first two decades after its founding, in 1975, Renaissance was a bastion of conventional winemaking practices, with German-trained winemaker Karl Werner applying the full range of postwar technology to these grapes. Karl produced stunning Rieslings, to be sure, but also Cabernets with tannins so hard that few buyers appreciated them.

In Werner's defense, when I attended a recent vertical tasting of thirty vintages dating to the late '70s, there was little to complain about in any of them. Even Werner's earliest efforts had emerged with all the balance, complexity, and grace one could wish for. Nevertheless, I have seldom encountered a site that cried out more for application of the postmodern view, and in 1999 Gideon began experimenting with me to explore various techniques to tame the tannins.

ROCKS OF AGE

"Once you taste the soil in a wine, you know that's not something that happens by accident," Gideon says. "You have to choose your dream very carefully. But then you need to comply with the terroir, not the reverse. In the long term, you sort out empirically the best way of working. The original plantings of cabernet and riesling didn't take the soil and topography into account, and we've pulled 80% of it out, picking the spots that were working and paring our production down to the best wines.

"Working with oxygenation really taught me a lot. Oxygen is certainly the key to constraining and integrating tannin, and our wines have an unbelievable appetite for it when they are young. Newly made Cabernet is very dynamic, and can go from aldehydic to being full of sulfides in a day. The ability to measure the exact oxygenation level and observe wine response taught me a great deal about what to expect from different strategies and timing, much of it quite counterintuitive. It was also very valuable to acquire a language for tannins and to understand their progression.

"I discovered that the downside of MOx is an amplification of the middle palate, and I've moved away from the technique, because for our wines it creates a certain layer of fat that blocks rather than fills the wine's central expression. It does some good things, like adding richness and acting as a tool to balance reductive aspects. But gradually I have moved away from it even if that decision presents challenges.

"In many circumstances it is still the right tool. For Renaissance wines, a light touch can perhaps retain the essence of place without trade-off. A lot depends on who you are targeting in the market. Our wines can be very challenging to the novice consumer, and MOx can be a potent means to address that problem. It's a power tool, and you have to use it with great care and with specific goals in mind."

THE "M" WORD

In chapter 8, I explored the subject of minerality, by which I mean a lively tingle in the finish, often confused with acidity but farther back in the mouth. It is sometimes described as resembling an electric current running through the throat, and it's possible that's exactly what it is.

Just as titratable acidity is sensed on the palate as a flow of protons discharging from binding sites on weak acids, minerality may be a flow of electrons released from various elements of the periodic table as they move to higher valences, such as $Fe^{2+} \rightarrow Fe^{3+} + e^-$. This oxidative discharge may occur very slowly in the bottle, opposing oxidation and conferring the added longevity we observe in such wines.

If so, we would predict a decrease in the minerally characteristic during aging. Since his wines are so pronounced in this character, I ask Gideon whether the hypothesis has merit. "Over time, the wines certainly become flatter and less vibrant," he offers. "Minerality probably does diminish with age, but it can take a very long time. The type of soil seems paramount. I see big differences here from block to block. Organic practices, sun exposure, and ripeness are also related."

An independent phenomenon to which the term *minerality* is sometimes attached is the aroma of wet stone, for which I prefer the term *petrichor*, the smell of new rain as it liberates natural oils from rock in the desert. "For me, there's a whole vocabulary of soil aromatics," Gideon says. "Sometimes it's like chewing on dust, even in a white wine—not tactilely but aromatically. Other times it's more like wild mushrooms or wetted hot stone."

THE YEAST OF OUR WORRIES

"We stopped inoculating (except for stuck fermentations) in the early '90s and have become more and more convinced of its benefits," Gideon says. "There are drawbacks, too—less purity but more complexity, which combined with organic farming becomes more and more a signature of the place and gives you increasing consistency of expression.

"Grapes are the carriers of terroir, but they aren't the whole message. This is an extremely subjective area. A yeast definitely contributes its own distinct mouthfeel and aromatic profile. To select for strains that will produce a healthy fermentation is the main reason to use SO_2 at the crusher."

My consulting experience confirms these observations. Natural wine–makers all want to eliminate the practices of adding sulfites at the crusher, inoculating with commercial yeasts, and sterile filtration, but in reality you will rarely find a practitioner willing to eschew all three.

HOW LOW CAN YOU GO?

A fascinating artistic turn is Gideon's move away from sulfites. Following an initial add of 35–40 ppm at the crusher, nothing is added subsequently at any stage.

Before readers jump into these practices with both feet on their own homegrown fermentations, I will hasten to point out that Gideon has stacked the deck in his favor. These are not ordinary wines. Their intense minerality and highly reactive tannins impart tremendous anti-oxidative characteristics. Such wine is literally its own preservative. Moreover, their huge structure may be relied upon to integrate microbial aromatics that in another wine might express themselves unpleasantly. So if your vineyard is a bit more downslope, you might not want to try this at home.

"The phenolics, the minerality, the structural vigor we have permits us, even pushes us away from SO_2," says Gideon. "Initially, SO_2 purifies and creates more definition of flavors. But after some time, the unsulfited wine shows much more complexity, layering, and interest. It just has more depth and life. SO_2 removes the nuanced edges, which are replaced by clearly defined pure fruit, but you lose all those weird, distinctive, intriguing elements that make the wine worth making.

"The interaction of sulfur with phenols is a very complex effect. It tightens tannins and freezes their development, and creates an artificial layer which at first appears like structure, a kind of gloss. Our wines are plenty tight already, just as they are," he says. "Some elements of the retardation sulfited wines experience may be largely just temporary, but with our wines, it can take a very long time, sometimes decades, to resolve."

My own experiments with Renaissance syrah fruit made with a completely sulfite-free regimen showed the same phenomenon. In fact, after two years of side-by-side trials at WineSmith, we abandoned the sulfited control, which was simple, shallow, and boring by comparison.

Always amazing to me is how much the sulfites repress the vineyard's pure varietal flavors of place. As with a great unpasteurized cheese, the microbial action reveals wonderful depth. Though one might expect masking instead, the vineyard's characteristic bright cherry fruit expression is somehow dramatically enhanced.

Another surprising aspect of these wines is their incredible staying power after opening. I encourage customers to leave the half-full bottle in the trunk of their car for a week, and it's a lot of fun to receive the incredulous phone calls as they report back that the wine has only improved. My explanation is that, like the action of so many pharmaceuticals on the human body, sulfites actually short-circuit the wine's natural immune system.

Often these wines require of the winemaker the patience, faith, and stern constitution that parenting a prodigal teenager might demand. "Lactic acid bacteria will sometimes generate a mousy finish that you can dispel with a little SO_2. But I've learned that it's not permanent damage," says Gideon. "On the other hand, with sulfites, the retardation is just temporary, and it can return."

NATURAL DISASTERS

Retailers like Miami's Chip Cassidy have adopted a policy that shies away from sulfite-free wines. "The bottle I'm tasting may be great," he says, "but there's just too much bottle variation to recommend it to my customers."

How much of this is real bottle variation is a matter of heated debate, revealing much about wine's true nature. Any wine salesman will testify that the same bottle poured in a series of different environments throughout the day will taste entirely different with each customer. This adaptation to environment goes double for Natural Wines, which are extremely responsive to the context in which they are consumed.

Gideon has learned the hard way that these wines don't sit well alongside conventional wines. "At one comparative Pinot Noir tasting, my wine stuck out as edgy and unclean, with a touch of VA. The next day, by itself, the same wine was showing beautifully. It was a very disturbing experience and showed me the power of context.

"The better distinctive wines do their proper job, the less well they fit into the standard commercial mold. Fortunately, consumers don't race wines like horses but rather consume them one at a time."

The converse is also true. At a tasting of over two hundred wines in the late '90s, the '92 Ridge Lytton Springs Zinfandel was generally acclaimed as wine of the evening, and Gideon bought a case, only to be disappointed. "It was a great show wine, but it turned out it didn't stand by itself very well."

As British wine writer David Peppercorn observes, "Wine is about pleasure. If the wine gives pleasure, it isn't flawed. Sometimes this means creating interest through discord."

"If there's a clear flaw, I will solve it by interventionalist means," confesses Gideon. "You have to survive economically, and that means somebody has to buy the wine. I'm not St. Gideon of the Vine."

TAKE-HOME MESSAGES

- High-altitude conditions promote high tannin and reductive strength, which require special treatment.
- Production of distinctive wines of place may impel winemaking choices in the opposite direction from standard commercial practice.
- Low-sulfite winemaking is an emerging tool not for the timid.

14

Randall Grahm

California Dreamer in Search
of the Miraculous

Søren Kierkegaard famously observed that life must be lived forward
but can only be understood backward. If the past is any guide,
Randall Grahm's seeming oddball eccentricity has consistently
morphed into tomorrow's mainstream normality (fig. 21). His wacky
promotion of Rhône varietals in California turned out to be simple
common sense. His offbeat packaging and effetely clever newsletters
sired an entire generation of imitators. The rise of screw caps is
directly traceable to his wooing support in the media. There is no
denying his impressive nose for the next big thing, and I have little
doubt that a decade or two hence, Biodynamics (BD) will be considered standard fare.

His "vinothology," *Been Doon So Long,* a collection of reminis-
cences, poetry, and prose from Bonny Doon's twenty-seven-year history, contains running commentary from his current calmer voice,
allowing us to know the man more deeply than when cute witticisms
were a higher priority for him than transparency.[1] His discussion of
reduction, as simple and straightforward an explanation of the subject
as one could wish for, is a must-read for the inquiring enologist.[2]

His recent induction by the Culinary Institute of America into the
Vintners Hall of Fame, his 400,000 Twitter followers, and spots on
Oprah and Michael Krasny have turned RG's life into a reality show
with little opportunity for escape, save in a few private corners that he
sanely protects.

FIGURE 21. Randall Grahm. Photo courtesy of Bonny Doon staff photographer.

I wanted to understand how the public face connects with the thoughtful and experienced technical artisan I have worked with over the years. For me, Randall is a kind of periscope for looking into the future. So I invited myself down to his home where he honored me with a simmered lamb/preserved lemon invention that proved perfect for talking turkey.

POSTMODERN PRODIGY

Famous for his marketing genius and charismatic playfulness, Randall is less known as an early postmodern innovator. I find the man dearer than the myth, and in order to avoid another puff piece, we confined our discussion to the technical path this matured practitioner has lately chosen.

When I was first initiated into the rites of postmodern thinking in 1997, our hero already had a half decade under his belt working with oxygen, chips, lees, and the other tools of structural élevage. Terms like *reductive strength, minerality, fundamental mystery,* and *graceful longevity* pepper his conversation. Yet today, many of those tools lie discarded in his attic like so many toy soldiers.

Today, twenty years down the road, he views oxygen structuring differently. "The trouble with Phase 1 MOx is that you don't get to know the wine before you transform it," he says. "I may come back to it, but for now I need a keener sense of what my vineyard is giving me on its own."

Evoking Heidegger's hammer, he notes, "As winemakers, we're fundamentally engaged in doing rather than being, using tools without understanding them. We never really grasp what the hammer is until it breaks." (No way I'm going to try to cover it in these pages, but if you want a serious handle on the true nature of artisanality and our relationship to tools, Heidegger's hammer is postmodern philosophy ground zero and definitely worth Googling.)

"MOx is profoundly helpful in resolving underripeness issues in Europe, but I don't know if that tool is right for the cépages I'm making. Wine needs to pass through a reductive winter. My own experience is that here [in California] the wines don't have enough reductive resiliency, and they don't rebound from treatment."

Yet Randall considers his past work with oxygen an indispensible window on wine's reductive behavior, a central focus of his current work. "The longer a wine can age and develop, the greater it can ascend," he explains. "Anything that extends its trajectory is beneficial."

CAPPING THE CORK

The immediate logical extension of this philosophy is the screw cap, and Grahm has pursued the transition from corks with all the subtlety and diplomacy of Attila the Hun.

Do corks breathe? "I think they do," he says. "After the initial shot of the oxygen they contain, granted the very best corks behave like screw caps. They have a very low oxygen transmission rate, which a wine with some life energy can withstand and even benefit from."

If corks breathe, how does he account for Mosels with no tannin that last thirty years? "I believe the mineral uptake in those wines behaves like a multistage battery with incredible preservative properties. There's also glucose and gluconic acid, plus those Germans use lots of SO_2. These wines are definitely able to consume some oxygen.

"But even expensive corks have natural variability. I'm not against rolling the dice to achieve natural variability, for example in planting grapes from seed. But randomness in packaging, in the wine's life in bottle, is in no way charming. Add in the TCA problems, and it's clear that corks have to go.

"Unfortunately, synthetic closures have worse problems. They are unforgiving of bottle dimension variation, sometimes being impossible to get out and other times falling in with a thumb's pressure. Unlike screw caps and good corks, the material they are constructed of has a continual oxygen transmission rate that inevitably destroys wine. Their only reason to exist is to fool the consumer—a synthetic look-alike, like a plastic houseplant. Perfection would be a total seal, like a glass ampoule.

"Screw caps change everything. You have to adapt your practices, maybe intentionally bottling with 1.0 ppm or more of dissolved oxygen. I'm concentrating on timing of SO_2 addition, making big additions early on rather than regular small shots that maintain a level but disturb the wine's efforts to seek its own natural balance. We have a very cold cellar, and development happens very slowly."

GO EAST, YOUNG MAN

Been Doon So Long contains a list of thirty-two "things I wish somebody had taught me when I was at Davis."[3] Number 29: "Go spend some time in Europe before you get too tied down."

As he tells me, "They are just so damned concerned over every aspect of gastronomy, as if life depended on it. A French couple will spend two hours discussing the olive garnish. It forces you to wonder why. Villages all over Europe have taken thousands of years to find and develop very special vineyard sites producing utterly unique wines. The locals know *exactly* what to do with these wines because they have been fully incorporated into their cuisine and cultural rhythms."

Moreover, Europe is a huge library of varietals and clones, largely untapped. And gastronomic discourse has a frankness we don't see. "If the vintage is crap, they will say so. Food is sacred, and they take their essential pleasures seriously. You don't see that here, because the consumer doesn't know what to think, so [is] more easily bamboozled.

"In California we think we're clever when we make big, ripe wines. But we have the world's most benign climate—there's nothing original or interesting about those wines. It's too easy to make good wine here. We don't apply ourselves."

However, Randall also sees natural advantages in California growing conditions. "Grenache in Hecker Pass and even Soledad is just amazing, much superior to what you find in the southern Rhône. We have regions with an adequate growing season to develop deep aromatic expression but cool enough to retain finesse and acidity."

PUTTING DOWN ROOTS

Randall Grahm is raising the bar. "I don't want to be eclectic anymore. I just want to do one or two things extremely well." He has divested the lion's share of his vast product portfolio, and this severe pruning has left him with a tiny core of products that occupy his full attention (when he isn't signing books in Sheboygan).

His idea of making California winegrowing less easy is sustainable, biodynamic, ethical winegrowing, an extremely restrictive form of expression that, like the sonnet or the haiku, produces the highest art. When Randall speaks of the New World's cultural proclivities and natural foibles, he mostly means California. So what is he doing here? Why, in the midst of his vast self-makeover, does he choose to exert his last great store of will to the making of an original wine in a place he has often said is devoid of terroir, where it is unclear how to make a statement that improves the world, and where truly sustainable agriculture is nearly impossible?

"It's my karma," he answers. "I'm a Californian, born and bred. I cut my teeth in a Beverly Hills wine retail shop. I'm not a kid anymore. I have one good project left in me, and I'm going to do it here."

Over the past decade, Randall has worked hard to rehabilitate his Soledad vineyard, which he openly admits may never be truly sustainable (if there turns out not to be enough rainfall to dry farm). Yet he has managed after much struggle to begin producing Albariño that I find extremely charming. Doesn't that deserve a tip of the hat?

"Succeeding in that vineyard is like winning the Special Olympics. Sure, we're proud of what we've accomplished. But we wouldn't have a chance in the real Olympics. If I'm going to take that on, I need a site with all the natural advantages I can find."

The site he has chosen is in the obscure region of San Juan Bautista. A host of technical experts, biodynamic gurus, and a geomancer have visited it and offered impressions, opinions, and cautions.

"The most important thing," he says, "is that the site is capable of producing wine with a distinctive, discernible terroir. It must have the right natural attributes, a genuine distinctiveness, and also inspire others. I have to bear in mind that I won't live to see a project like this through. The legacy needs to be picked up by the next generation.

"So first I had to make sure the site made basic sense. The soils and topography are interesting, and dry farming is perhaps feasible. But a stable family situation and proximity to a great town like Santa Cruz are just as crucial. Also, the wildness of the site captivates the spirit, and its history as a worship place for the Native Americans and later the mission fathers [it's near the site of the fifteenth California mission] is easy to relate to."

Is he convinced he can make wine of the stature he's shooting for? "It's way too early to tell. I wish I could say that we [will] have these great vins de terroir, but we're not there yet. In all candor, the going is the goal. If I can spend three days a week in that vineyard, that's a home run with the bases loaded."

DANCING TO DEMETER

When I check in with Randall on how his Biodynamics experiment is going, I find him enthusiastic about the results but tenuous as to how it all works. Who can say if the horn silica preparation 501 is stimulating photosynthesis and decreasing water requirements? It's an experiment, but it's not, in fact cannot be, controlled, so he is without persuasive evidence. "You really have to take the whole biodynamic practice and observe its effects over a reasonable length of time to get a sense of its efficacy," he says. "Vines farmed biodynamically have generally appeared much healthier—apart from the years when they haven't."

He does not rule out the possibility that in some circumstances, certified organic practices may be more appropriate than Biodynamics, perhaps because of how well balanced the soils are to begin with. If you begin with things in reasonable balance, you are free to use BD's lighter hand. "You can't serve two masters. Terroir is my one unshakable belief. The biodynamic practice for me needs to serve terroir, not the other way around. In Soledad, for instance, there are some compaction issues which seem to be working against what we are accomplishing with biodynamic practice. Aubert de Villaine[4] seems to feel that for some of his vineyards that need more intervention, organic works better than BD.

"Biodynamics is really a spiritual journey which focuses on the practitioner himself. To be totally honest, I have not myself been sufficiently involved in our farming practice to consider myself personally transformed, except at a certain intellectual remove. I am hoping to remedy that with the new property. Subordinating my ego to a larger ideal is not something that comes particularly easy to me. If I am not out myself stirring the preps, I will be deeply disappointed in myself."

I asked Randall to talk about the biodynamic practice of the interpretation of sensitive crystallizations. (Wine and calcium salts are evaporated in a petri dish and the resulting patterns are read like chicken entrails.) He is clearly still in the fake-it-till-you-make-it stage. "It's very arcane, and I have a lot to learn. At this stage, I can at least recognize when the wine just won't coalesce into a harmonious pattern, which tells me something isn't right with the blend. We also show the crystallization portraits on the label as a new aspect of full disclosure."

THE BULLSHIT METER

The life of Randall Grahm is a living inquiry into the relationship of the artist to his audience. Frankly, I'm suspicious whether his positions originate in well-considered values or merely from what sounds good, in an effort to surf the wave of public approval.

What is the proper relationship of the winemaker to the consumer? Winemaking is a performance art: it doesn't exist without its audience. To what extent should our production choices, such as what is "hands-off winemaking," be defined by what can be floated past critics and consumers?

Some of the first words out of Randall's mouth in many press interviews distinguish between vins d'effort and vins de terroir. While this strikes me as a useful dichotomy, it bothers me that the concept disrespects the epic efforts that winemakers expend, not for profit, but to please the consumer. Are vins de terroir without effort?

"What I'm really trying to say," Randall says, "is that in an original wine, one tries very hard to stay out of the way, so the winemaking does not leave a distinct stylized imprint and has a very discreet impact."

We discussed the phenomenon of Josko Gravner, a Friuli celebrity winemaker who makes hundred-dollar sulfite-free whites fermented in clay vessels buried in the ground, reportedly full of aldehyde, VA, and browning. Like Jackson Pollock, he has attracted a ravenous following as well as a healthy collection of skeptics. Neither of us is ready to make up our minds about this fellow.

I ask Randall outright: is he a visionary or a charlatan? "In a quantum universe," he says, "you can be both. Like the L.A. waiter who says he's an actor. He's a total fraud, right? Then later on, he turns out to be Sean Penn."

In his full disclosure on his 2006 Syrah, he reveals the use of chips, but he's also quick to add, "We don't do that anymore." Chips reduce fourfold the deforestation of two-hundred-year-old oak trees. "Chips are the environmentally sensible way to go, something I really want to work. But so far, they just don't," he says. "I haven't found products I can incorporate into my process. On the other hand, I must also admit that half the barrels I buy make the wine worse."

Does the choice to defend screw caps but to distance himself from chips really derive from forecasting which waves of public opinion to surf?

Randall is very firm that the making of great wine can't be viewed as a profit proposition. A shrewd compromise is still a compromise. In the short or even in the medium term, it is pointless to think in a context of commercial viability. You just have to stay alive, keeping your eye on the prize, impelled instead by legacy. "Particularly at this moment," he points out, "nobody is selling anything. It's impossible to be interesting enough for people to want to buy your wine. It's like somebody flipped a switch and suddenly nothing works."

His pronouncement sounds morose, but there is an underlying glee-fulness in him, which I share. If the magical persona of Randall Grahm can't make wine move, what chance do the rest of us have? It means you might as *well* follow your bliss.

"Artists live in two universes: the theoretical, quixotic world and the commercial reality. It is vital that these remain separate but equally important that there is a connection between them. The wormhole between these realms is marketing."

Grahm has certainly mastered that connection. On the downside, this mastery, and not the quality of his wines, is his current claim to fame. "If I died today," he admits, "they'd write on my tombstone, 'He was a great marketer.'"

What is the difference between selling and selling out? "It's terrible when you don't like your own wine. In a perfect world, we all find a niche that works both for us and for the consumer. I've set out to make an original wine that improves the world and that inspires others."

WHAT'S IT ALL MEAN, MR. NATURAL?

"There is too much conversation about what the making of Natural Wine *isn't*," Randall says. "We should be talking more about what it *is*. One mark of a great site is that it finds its own natural harmony which is beyond our capability to improve upon. You can try to balance it, but the wine goes its own way through the natural telos of the site."

When I contend that the most interesting wine in the U.S. is being produced outside of California, Randall isn't moved. "That may well be the case. For a Californian, however, it's, 'If a Missouri wine is poured in the forest . . . '" In other words, if no appreciative audience exists, can wine still be great? He seems to be saying that outside of following one's own bliss, nothing can be said to be innately interesting.

Grahm's dilemma is that he has firmly planted his magnum opus project in California but doesn't like anything about it. "In the New World, there's no guide. In making an original wine, what star do you steer towards, and how do you make midcourse corrections? You're on your own, Bub."

In his rock star days, it was hard to identify with Randall. Now he smacks less of Mick Jagger and more of Woody Allen. He's one of my favorite Tweeters, with his self-outed addictions to caffeine and Sunday crosswords, seeking at last to be Everyman.

I like this new guy—less awesome and more sympathetic, his daily doings peppered and salted with self-doubt and affection for life. For winemakers, his journey offers up a possibility for the rest of us—to be known, appreciated, even cherished for our real selves.

Epilogue

In 2012, I attended a City Arts and Lectures gathering in San Francisco, where wine critic Karen MacNeil interviewed Randall alongside East Bay wine importer Kermit Lynch, a good-natured proponent of Natural Wine. The event was given the unfortunate title, "The Science of Wine," a subject in no way addressed by any of the speakers.

No problem—I wasn't expecting them to do so. But I *was* eager to hear from Randall something beyond the aw-shucks distinction between vins d'effort and vins de terroir, perhaps a little something concerning the degree of effort it takes to succeed in producing a wine that speaks eloquently of its place of origin.

But no. To my vast disappointment, Randall was still kicking the same tired old horse. He spoke of the evils of the popular over-oaked, overextracted global fruit bombs that line the shelves at Dean and DeLuca versus wines that express a sense of place.

My main concern is that winemakers in this incredibly competitive market are trying to distinguish themselves from their colleagues through an "I-do-the-minimum" one-downsmanship instead of talking about their real work and respecting one another. To make wines of place that are also balanced and sellable—that is, to become invisible—takes enormous effort.

To be sure, Randall is up to something purer than your basic corporate winery, but so are 98% of the wineries on the D list that have no three-tier distribution. Sense of place is the game almost all small wineries are playing, and it's not clear whether Randall's biodynamic version is fundamentally any purer or crazier or more spiritual than an Iowa Mom-and-Pop feeding their family and their community by growing Brianna. Let's not diss ourselves by supporting the myth that neglect is the highest professionalism.

The Real Mr. Natural

Then I went to visit Josko Gravner in Friuli, who turned out to be a delight—calm, meticulous, self-effacing, yet quietly proud and softly defiant. We tasted twenty wines, superb without exception and all quite unique, though thematically very much of a piece. He really knows his stuff.

Gravner is a sweet and humble man. He claims to know nothing and to do nothing, and is proud that he knows none of the analytics on his wines. However, when I suggested that it takes a lot of talent to do nothing, he blushed and smiled and did not disagree.

Though I found him open-minded regarding technology, his goal is to work without it and unmindful of it. The management of volatile acidity is his greatest fear, and he works meticulously in the vineyard and the cellar to avoid conditions that promote it. He is using very small amounts of SO_2 at certain points for this purpose, which he says is unavoidable.

His philosophy put me in mind of a picture I got from Joel Peterson, founder of Ravenswood wines: the winemaker as tightrope walker. You focus best on your work if you do not consider that you have a net. This lends a positive perspective to the discussion, and for the first time gives the winemaker a path rather than an admonishment. There's a fine line between earnest dedication and boastful hypocrisy. Pride goeth before a fall, and Josko's humility exceeds that of Randall, but in both men the commitment to their philosophies goes well beyond appearances. Josko's mysticism has won him great commercial success, but he simply lets the wines do the talking. Paradoxically, he won me over with his disarming stance that, in the end, he really doesn't care what people think.

All that said, I wish somebody would give me a guiding principle for what's "legit" in terms of tools. Why, for example, is electricity okay? What about stainless steel, inert gas, plastic hose? Are harvesting, crushing, and pressing manipulations?

Together with Natural Wine advocate Isabelle Legeron, MW (That CrazyFrenchWoman.com), I have proposed a definition for manipulation. Manipulation is any winemaking practice that you as a winemaker, or your marketing department, are not willing to confess to your customers or the press. Voluntary disclosure is the winemaker's passport to getting right with the far left. As I write this, I am bravely at work with these folks to create a centralized website where conscientious winemakers might disclose all and discuss why. First we will have to convince them that it's good business to do so, which might entice the Natural Wine advocates to make nice with the industry for a change—and vice versa.

It seems that every time I ascend one of these philosophical mountains, I find RG's initials carved into a tree at the summit. Our hero was advocating ingredient labeling long before anyone else in the industry had a clue why that might be a good idea. In this regard as in so many others, Randall has been a visionary leader, the rest of us merely dogging his tracks.

TAKE-HOME MESSAGES

- In a perfect world, we all find a niche that works both for us and for the consumer.
- "You really have to take the whole biodynamic practice and observe its effects over a reasonable length of time to get a sense of its efficacy."
- "Go spend some time in Europe before you get too tied down."

Bob Wample

Thinking Like a Grape

Robert L. Wample is a get-'er-done kind of scientist. After reaching the summit of his academic career as chair of California State University Fresno's Department of Enology and Viticulture, he shocked the industry by leaving his seat to jump into private practice. "I saw an entirely new level of thinking about vineyards," he explained, "and simply needed to dedicate myself to implementing it instead of just talking about it."

Dr. Wample now serves as a plant physiologist for STI (Soil and Topography Information, Inc.),[1] a Madison, Wisconsin–based high-tech agricultural start-up firm that he is assisting in penetrating the wine industry.

At the origin of this radical move lies a fascinating series of events leading to a fundamental breakthrough in winegrowing with far-reaching consequences for the mainstream varietal conformist as well as the fringe *terroiriste*. In retracing Wample's steps, we will need to visit vineyards both vast and tiny in California's most and least chic regions, employing heady statistical methodology to merge high-tech farming with the purest winemaking art.

There are a lot of precision viticulture systems in place today. GPS-located, time-stamped maps linked to sophisticated plant sensors represent today's most rapidly growing agricultural innovations. Knowing exactly where and when a measurement was taken adds tremendous power to data interpretation, charting out vineyard variability to guide the grower's hand.

But Wample has gone beyond measurement. The model he is working on seeks to predict grapevine response to actual conditions, and to link it to metrics we can actually record and, more important, control. His work with Ridge Vineyards now challenges him to take that capability a big step further, moving beyond color, total phenols, and other specific measurable improvements and into the mysterious holistic realm of great wine, to bring his influence to matters of balance, harmony, and longevity. In a sense, Wample is orchestrating a Vulcan mind meld between man and grape.

SELECTIVE HARVEST

To understand this progression, let's go back to the 2005 vintage, in which Wample first applied some revolutionary ideas to differential harvesting. Wample's radical yet disarmingly simple idea was to set up a mechanical harvesting system that could field-sort two lots based on fruit quality.

In a couple of acres of merlot at the Wagner Trust Vineyard in Madera, California's Central Valley, near-infrared spectroscopy (NIS) was used to assess the brix and anthocyanin contents of fruit samples, which values were then mapped into high and low areas using geographic information system (GIS) technology, so that choosing a cut-off between high and low groupings would result in volumes of regular and reserve harvest lots in any proportion desired.

Step 1 was to choose an index of quality. When the color and brix maps did not match, Wample chose simply to ignore the brix maps, feeding only the anthocyanin data into his differential harvest system—a savvy postmodern move, as color is the key to structure, while brix is virtually unrelated to ripeness. Wample's rationale for favoring color as a quality index was twofold. Deeper color signals quality to consumers. But high anthocyanin content not only increases wine scores directly, it also leads to finer, softer tannins and prolongs ageability, as we saw in chapter 2.

Next, the machine to do the job was called into play, a GIS-enabled Korvan harvester with a reversible belt that could sort fruit into left and right gondolas, shifting belt direction as it crossed over mapped boundaries between low- and high-anthocyanin areas (fig. 22). The strategy worked, producing wines that sensory analysis was able to significantly differentiate. It also got Wample thinking about why the color showed up where it did. A predictive model would save the substantial expense of creating an anthocyanin density map.

FIGURE 22. Korvan Model 3016 selective harvester. Photo courtesy of Oxbo International Corp.

To get there, though, would require a lot more analysis. In 2006, Wample got funding for a larger project, this time looking at cabernet sauvignon. At Constellation Wines' Twin Creeks Vineyard in Lodi, thirty-five acres were measured for anthocyanin, brix, and berry weights on a grid of ten manually collected samples per acre, in late August and again in early September, just prior to harvest. By comparing these maps, which correlated well, Wample found that the earlier mapping appeared to be good enough that a color map might not need to be generated at the last minute, though further testing was needed.

When data values were mapped by GPS, variation across the field was again apparent. Differential harvesting of forty-ton lots resulted in 30% increases in both total phenols and anthocyanins, and a fourteen-member panel significantly preferred the high-anthocyanin lot.

While significant differences between the lots were promising, no easy causal pattern was discernible. Not only did brix fail once again to match up with anthocyanin, but maps of Normalized Differential Vegetation Index (based on chlorophyll reflectivity) were also completely

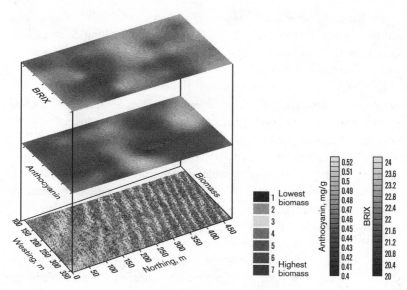

FIGURE 23. Merjan data plots. Mismatch of brix, anthocyanins, and biomass in the Merjan Vineyard.

unrelated. Wample had found a useful harvest tool but still no underlying causality (fig. 23).

Enter the Draggin'

Wample had so far failed to find an easily measurable parameter that could assess where the good stuff might be found without resorting to the expense and tedium of mapping berry composition. If, however, he could identify the underlying sources of variability, he might be able to go a step further, enabling the grower to improve problem areas and increase uniformity.

Wample went looking for this Holy Grail in an area that California viticulturalists have long pooh-poohed: soil variability. As late as the 1980s, New World viticulturalists at UC Davis and in Australia were still in denial about the European concept of terroir, scoffing at any direct connection between soil composition and grape composition. While technically correct, this hard-liner position diverted academic attention from the critical influence of soil on flavor expression. But in 2001, famed Down Under grape guru Richard Smart finally pronounced, "I give up. I was wrong. Terroir differences really do exist."

But practical application is another story. Vineyards are generally laid out in blocks according to property lines and tilling convenience. Since wire trellises favor linear layouts, soil variability is almost never considered, or even known.

The prospects for guiding viticultural practices according to soil variability were improved considerably in 2007 when STI launched its Soil Information System (SIS).[2] Thanks to a fleet of towed detection toys, including a conductivity sled "Surfer" and a penetrometer drilling "Diver," with moisture, resistivity, color sensors, and soil core sampling capability, the SIS was capable of collecting sixty-five data dimensions that were then digested by sophisticated fuzzy-logic software, rendering the complex dataset into three-dimensional vineyard maps.

At the request of Constellation, in 2007 Wample's project shifted to the Merjan Vineyard, eighty acres of cab sauv in Madera, a mechanically pruned, drip-irrigated vineyard on a variable mix of sand and clay that STI had already mapped.[3] Wample's data collection was astonishingly thorough and elaborate. In all, 1,360 ten-cluster samples were taken (650 on August 24 and another 698 on September 8), demonstrating, happily, that early-season sampling matched midseason sampling, validating the reliability of the more practical preharvest determinations.

Once again, GIS maps controlled the harvester conveyor belt based on GPS coordinates. The difference between the lots was such a steep curve that Wample discovered that because tiny differences in the chosen cut-off point for anthocyanins altered tremendously the amount available for the high-quality lot, he could dial in the volume ratio between regular and reserve lots.

Wample was later happily to learn that his sampling procedure was major overkill. Through statistical analysis of the robustness of the dataset, William Browning of Applied Mathematics, Inc., Gales Ferry, Connecticut, showed that the actual sampling necessary could be cut dramatically from ten per acre to as few as two, resulting in a cost of around $50 per acre, relatively trivial considering that, in one client's estimate, the resulting reserve lot sells for an additional $10 per bottle.

STI generates over sixty soil characteristics in addition to elevation, slope, aspect, and other topological data. At first, no obvious patterns were discerned between the soil maps STI generated and the grape composition data. Then Wample realized that the soil itself did not determine vine behavior but rather its interaction with weather and cultural practices. What was missing was a synthesis of the various metrics into a sort of dashboard that growers could understand and, ideally, take action to influence.

Cabernet's Five Principal Components

Principal component analysis (PCA) has become a powerful mathematical tool for digesting complex datasets. By extracting patterns, it often identifies the simpler forces that underlie large numbers of measurements.

When STI's gigantic SIS dataset was tossed into a PCA along with geo-located anthocyanin and brix data, five significant dimensions emerged. "We derived five drivers for influencing distribution of root system based on holding capacity, when water is applied, and how it moves through the profile," says Wample. At this point, the seasoned viticulturist's ability to think like a grape began to merge the data with an artistic sense of vine response. "We could finally ask, 'Where did the vines have a chance to develop a root system?' and 'How big a water bank account have we got?'"

Deriving names for the principal components was Wample's real accomplishment. "The statisticians looked at the data and couldn't make any sense of it. But with twenty years of grape irrigation studies under my belt, I could see meso-climatic variability sources within the data." STI data showed that the Merjan property's surface and subsurface texture profiles varied by percent clay versus sand. Higher brix was associated with five soil characteristics:

- shallower soil
- thicker subsurface layer
- thin surface layer
- higher early-season soil moisture throughout the soil profile
- higher level of compaction

A radically different set of parameters drove higher anthocyanins. These were associated with

- deeper soil profile
- thick subsurface layer
- slightly thicker surface layer
- decreased soil moisture throughout the profile preceding véraison
- compaction at deeper depths

But did these derived parameters constitute true grape behavior drivers, or were they merely descriptive of a particular situation? The first step in testing their predictive power was to alter conditions within the Merjan Vineyard the following year. "I figured that we should be able to improve the bad areas and make the good areas worse," says Wample. In 2008, alterations in the irrigation regimen did just that.

Surprised at the success of this experiment, Wample next decided on a rigorous acid test. If his parameters were really a deep look into the psyche of Cabernet Sauvignon, what would happen if he applied them in completely different vineyard conditions?

Wample took this model, derived in two hot-climate Region V Central Valley vineyards, to the chilly, windswept, highly celebrated terroir of Ridge's Montebello Vineyard, high in the Santa Cruz Mountains above Saratoga. Since STI had already done soils mapping for them, Wample boldly approached Ridge with the idea of a double-blind predictive study to see if he could establish correlation, despite its completely different conditions and its high degree of hands-on vineyard care.

Unlike Marjan's sand and clay textures, Ridge's soils are a mix of limestone and greenstone, a compressed mudstone muck high in problematic magnesium. "We were able to get a very high predictive correlation within zones at Ridge, over 90%," Wample reports.

Always a practical industry guy, Bob is greatly enjoying his move to the private sector. "After just a year, I have hundreds of clients interested in my work." But in the lofty philosophical firmament inhabited by California's top Cabernets, his quest for the Grail presents one more river to cross.

HOLISTIC CHALLENGES

At Ridge Vineyards, connecting the dots between what he sees in the vineyard and the artistic goals of winemaker Paul Draper is the work of ace viticulturalist David Gates. "Our goals are not always the same," he says; "they vary for each vineyard block. I've worked with these vineyards for many years and I know what each one is capable of, what Paul depends on from each.

"My main job is to permit each individual vineyard to express its distinctive terroir signature. Paul Draper isn't interested in high extraction. He's looking for a different kind of intensity linked to correct ripeness, terroir expression, and longevity. That's a lot different from just, say, trying to amp up color and tannin across the board."

Gates's goal is to maximize the percentage of each year's crop that makes the Montebello blend. In seeking the focused intensity seen in lots that make the cut, Gates tries to prevent both the overly green, herbaceous notes associated with excessive vigor and the clumsiness of overconcentration. "Good wine balance derives from good vine balance."

"In the greenstone areas, we see more seed tannin if we're not careful. These are much harder to manage. Paradoxically, our best blocks are the easiest to work. Where we have limestone, we naturally get a minerally characteristic that tickles your palate."

Because of his site's windswept, well-drained soils, spot irrigation is an important tool in Gates's kit. Water is, however, in extremely short supply. By filtering data from on-site information systems through vine response parameters, Gates gets a real-time edge about where his limited water will do the most good through his work with Fruition Sciences' sap flow monitoring system.[4]

"Late in the season, I can see, when sap flow decreases, whether the vine response is linked to water vapor pressure deficit—air dryness—or whether it has decoupled, a sign that the vines are shutting down, either due to excessive stress or physiological programming to day length and other natural programming," explains Gates.

Linking sap flow feedback to Wample's soil conditions parameters has the potential to provide Gates with a vine balance dashboard that allows him to react optimally and quickly. This will be particularly handy as Ridge completes the process of moving to organic practices over 65% of its acreage.

Recognizing the limitations of modeling is just as important as tapping into its power. "I'm very traditional, and I like to take a look at actual conditions with my backhoe," says Gates. "Data modeling is no substitute for pits. But it does tell you where to dig."

Wample agrees. "As we explore the characteristics that apply to other varietals, we need to keep an open mind. If you think about the evolution of Cabernet Sauvignon, could we anticipate a similar response from Cab Franc? How much of a rootstock effect should be explored? What about clones? I was pretty surprised that these characteristics seemed to hold up. When you have those extreme clonal variations, you have to be very careful. This is just the beginning."

TAKE-HOME MESSAGES

- Differential mechanical harvesting via GPS is a powerful new tool.
- Five soil behaviors have been linked to anthocyanin production in Cabernet.
- Today's challenge is to link reductionist science to holistic winemaking goals.

PART THREE

Technology

16

Pressing Matters

A Postmodern Tale

The sweeping changes in method and perspective that our industry has experienced since World War II call for a careful reexamination of our current position in order to ensure that what was gained outweighs what was lost. Since wine's innate impermanence precludes direct comparison with earlier eras, however, evaluating changes is a dodgy endeavor.

More generally, it's always difficult to assess how much true progress is occurring. The abandonment of knowledge goes unheralded, while the new and improved is proclaimed. Absent eternal vigilance, gains reliably upstage losses.

Of all we have learned in the past hundred years, what will our descendants value? Ideas more than things, I imagine, and tools, however simple, over toys, however big and shiny.

Many twentieth-century changes in practices were made possible by suddenly abundant resources such as inexpensive energy, stainless steel, aluminum, copper, and so on—all possibly quite fleeting. What acumen have we traded away for our modern conveniences? The calculator replaced the slide rule because it was faster, easier, and more precise. But in that shift, we lost a certain familiarity with how numbers work. Our GPS navigators are robbing us of the skill of map reading and our whole spatial sense of the communities we inhabit.

Often we are so quick to throw technology at a problem that we lose track of the benefits of the old ways and inadvertently fail to keep our options open. Adaptation to changing local conditions does not necessarily qualify as progress, for if those conditions do not persist, we may wish we still had the old knowledge. In the agricultural realm, the genetic advantages of GMO corn ought properly to be weighed against the value of the genetic diversity it is so aggressively replacing. The genetically robust wild types of many crops are now extinct, leaving us with high-performing but overspecialized derivatives incapable of adaptation to future contingencies.

We know our reliance on fossil fuels is not sustainable. Oil is nothing more than ancient plant material rendered into a combustible liquid over the eons. An ideal solution to skyrocketing agricultural energy costs would be a mechanism to convert cellulose (a cheap and abundant product of solar energy) directly into motion on site.

Such a device actually exists, and it creates a high-grade fertilizer as an artifact. It's called a horse. Unfortunately, except among a few blessed Amish, the nitty-gritty details of horse-based farming have largely disappeared. But I bet L. L. Bean's team is already gearing up Gore-Tex saddles for the coming boom in high-tech tack.

Nowhere is our break with the past more acute than in modern winemaking. With its pumps, lighting, and refrigeration, electricity ushered out the millennia-old system of traditional winemaking entirely, at who knows what cost? In an era of vastly greater fermentation-tank volumes made possible by electrical pumpover capability, the late Don Blackburn, founding winemaker for Emeritus Vineyards, argued strongly that the ancient method of *pigeage* (managing the cap with one's legs and feet) was essential to understanding how a fermentation is going.

A fine case in point is the hilarious story of the development of the modern wine press. In this rich tale we will find a useful allegory for the thrust of modern winemaking innovation and its inevitable reexamination under postmodern scrutiny.

In 1940, there were only two choices for a wine press: continuous screw and vertical basket. Large wineries used the former, small wineries the latter. Screw presses were disdained for their high tannin extraction, and since Roman times the vertical basket was the press of choice for fine wine because of its gentle action.

Then in 1950, vertical basket presses somehow stopped working. Five minutes' reflection at that point might have saved us half a century of wandering through the technological wilderness. But no. Instead, we threw electricity at the problem and sent equipment manufacturers on an odyssey of invention and reinvention, only to return to the source fifty years later, when vertical baskets are once again all the rage.

Basket Press Suppliers

AWS/Prospero Equipment	www.wineryequipment.com
Bucher Vaslin North America	www.buchervaslin.com
Carlsen & Associates	www.carlsenassociates.com
ColloPack Solutions	www.collopack.com
ConeTech	www.conetech.com
Criveller Company	www.criveller.com
EuroMachines, Inc.	www.euromachinesusa.com
KLR Machines, Inc.	www.klrmachines.com
Les Pressoirs Coquard (France)	www.coquardpresses.com
Mori	www.tcw-web.com
Napa Fermentation Supplies	www.napafermentation.com
St. Patrick's of Texas	www.stpats.com

After decades of banishment from commercial cellars, basket presses are making a comeback. More than a dozen suppliers have models on the market (see sidebar), and tony producers like Jordan and Opus One have jumped enthusiastically on board. UC Davis's new pressing system, developed and donated by the clever and generous Silicon Valley inventor T. J. Rodgers, is a modernized basket design that presses experimental lots right in the fermenter, employing hydraulics underneath that lift the fermenter itself against a fixed head.

What caused basket presses to fall from favor just after the war? And why are they on the rebound? In his 2005 article on the basket press renaissance,[1] Curtis Phillips reported that every winemaker he questioned cited press wine quality as their primary criterion for opting into a modern basket press.

Phillips's description of traditional press design reads: "The design tends to be inefficient for press yields and cycle time. . . . The juice or wine is expelled out the sides of the basket in a direction perpendicular to the force applied to the press cake. The pressure of the ram on the pomace press cake tends to close off the channels that allow the juice to be expelled from the press."

Few winemakers would disagree with this description, yet it is completely incorrect. In its simple misconception lies the seed of a half century of pointless technological meandering in the name of progress. The entire history of wine press evolution in the second half of the twentieth century can be seen as stepwise attempts to modernize the basket press. At each step, problems arose that led to the next generation, and eventually back to where we started.

In the 1950s, French manufacturer Vaslin was the first to apply electricity to the suddenly dysfunctional traditional device. The basket was flipped on its side and motorized so the heads (first just one, later both) moved into the center. This didn't work very well, because the resulting cake was thick and compact. When chains were added to break up and redistribute the cake, a series of pressing cycles could produce good yields but only at the cost of high solids and high phenols.

Then in 1955, Wilmes introduced the bladder press, a modification of the Vaslin press that also employed a horizontal basket, but in place of movable heads it employed an inflatable rubber bladder that pushed the cake away from the central spindle and against the drain surface of the cylinder. This thin pomace cake reduced press pressures, resulting in lower tannins and solids. It would have been ideal except that it was a nightmare to clean. Bladder presses were also restricted in size due to the limitations of the rubber bladder's elasticity.

Tank presses were a simple next step, replacing the bladder with an inelastic plastic membrane (essentially a tarp) and eliminating the central spindle. Tank presses could be built at any scale, and could be fully enclosed, eliminating oxygen pickup. Their low pressures permitted minimal tannin extraction, and rapid cycling was allowed by their open design, which permitted relatively easy cleaning if you were courageous enough to enter the enclosed space of the inverted press and didn't mind getting wet. CIP (clean-in-place) systems finally automated this unpleasant task, and the industrial wine press seemed as perfected as it was going to be.

TANKS BUT NO TANKS

Today's problems are actually the solutions we found to the problems we had yesterday. The new presses gave rise to a host of problems never before seen. Hard to load, they made whole-cluster pressing extremely laborious and time consuming. Their multiple motors, computer programs, axial feed designs, and CIP systems turned pressing into a high-ticket affair better adapted to large sizes, normally in tandem. With complexity came a proneness to breakdown, doubling budgets to accommodate redundant systems.

For ultrapremium artisanal production, the main difficulties with a tank press are the impracticality of pressing small, individual lots and the turbidity of press wine. Through initial static draining, tank presses can give free-run juice with low to moderate suspended solids, but their rotating action throughout multiple press cycles produces press fractions high in suspended solids.

Their fully enclosed architecture allows complete exclusion of oxygen. But that is not such a good thing.

"A basket press gives great aeration at the moment when reds are at their most reductive," reports Michael Silacci of Opus One. "A basket press puts you in much closer contact with the wine you're making. Compared to the rotation and mixing of a tank press, its continuous static pressure produces press wine more consistently high in quality, with a low solids content that makes it easier to taste what you've got. It's also cleaner and simpler to operate and unload, and gives you a nice, neat press cake you can forklift rather than an augered mess."

"I love my basket press," says Rob Davis of Jordan. "It's so much more fun to work with! You get your hands on the material, up close and personal, so you know what's going on. The pomace isn't as beaten up as with rotary designs, so you get less bitter tannins. Sure, you have lower yields, but you can use everything you get. There really isn't any true hard-press wine."

Traditional juicing of white musts results in at least one saturation of oxygen, a minimum essential for yeast alcohol tolerance to prevent stuck fermentations. With tank presses, oxygenation is a separate, counterintuitive step foreign to standard cellar procedure and thus often overlooked.

We can thank tank press technology for revealing another enological problem never before seen: pinking. The first commercial white wine in history to turn pink on retail shelves was a 1970 Gewurztraminer, followed by many thousands of Sauvignon Blancs, Chardonnays, and, well, you name it. Pinking is a skin extractive that occurs only in the reductive conditions tank presses make possible.

Unknown in traditional vinification, pinking is an endemic problem in modern winemaking that necessitates the universal addition of GAF Corporation's PVPP, a modified nylon powder, as a prophylactic. Since pinking is believed to be an intermediate form in an oxidative pathway, the vastly greater oxygen pickup built into basket press design avoids this problem by moving the offending compounds past pinking into a yellow form.

FIGURE 24. Marzolla basket press at Opus One, showing slotted floor. Photo courtesy of Michael Silacci.

BACK TO BASICS

What changed just after World War II is that we started making presses out of steel. Simple as that. Steel had the advantage of durability and was considered more sanitary. The steel bottom of the new presses also didn't leak. What escaped everyone's attention was that the bottom of a basket press is *supposed* to leak!

Here's the revelation: the primary drain surface of a basket press is *not the sides but the bottom* (fig. 24).

In 1982, the first modern winemaker to see the light was Harold Osborn of Maison Deutz. He realized what had eluded everyone before him—that the juice channels are properly located *below* the pomace, not in the sides. When he built a ten-foot-diameter basket press for sparkling wine production, he placed drain channels right into the floor of his press. This design made it child's play to load and unload whole clusters for the low-tannin style he desired.

The basket press achieves low solids in the press fraction as a result of its static design. Similar to the lauter tun in brewing, it has thin (0.7– 1.1 mm) slits to hold back the solids and allow liquids to pass through. The false bottom of a proper wine press provides an even, low-pressure drain surface that retains the pomace, and the structure of the pomace cake filters particulates.

In brewing, the grain solids, not the false bottom, form a filtration medium that allows the otherwise cloudy mash to exit as a clear liquid. Because brewers made the transition from wood to steel without changing the false bottom, the static lauter tun has remained for centuries essentially unchanged.

This realization allows existing basket presses to be easily fitted with a draining floor insert by your local welder. JohnsonScreens .com, for one, provides a wide variety of screen designs. Brewing systems manufacturers can easily shore up lauter tun false bottom designs to accommodate wine press pressures.

A false bottom allows basket presses of any size to be built. The huge and ancient rectangular basket press displayed for many years outside Domaine Chandon's tasting room measured 2 by 4 m but was only 50 cm tall, resulting in a press cake of 20 cm, exactly like a modern tank press, and in its era of human power it was much easier to load and unload by hand. Taller presses can be renovated by inserting draining disks at 50 cm intervals.

Another modern invention that ruined the basket press for whites, particularly for champagne production, was the crusher destemmer. Basket presses work well when whole clusters are loaded and then the gentle action of the human foot is used to "trample out the vintage." The cluster stem (rachis) provides channels for juice to exit the mass at low pressure. In destemmed musts, the pectin sliminess of unfermented white grapes blocks the flow of juice, resulting in sloppy cakes and low yields unless stems and/or rice hulls are mixed into the must.

FORM FOLLOWS FUNCTION

Finally, let us ask what we should have asked first. What is a wine press for?

The modern view, which rejected the basket press for its low yields and labor inefficiency, has also jettisoned the convenient, economical screw press for its rough action and high tannin extraction and the equally efficient belt press for its high suspended solids. We can conclude that the purpose of the press in modern winemaking is high yields, low tannin, and low solids.

Postmodern winemaking takes a different view of the function of the wine press. Our growing awareness of the positive role oxygen plays in healthy fermentations reveals the importance of the press as a juice aeration device. For reds (and for sur lie whites where structure is a goal), our increasing skill in building integrative tannin structure that supports distinctive terroir expression also causes us to look askance at pressing systems that minimize tannin.

The most desirable press is one that allows us to include all our press wine in the main lot. This ideal depends on the character of the material, our skill in working with tannins, and the style of wine we wish to produce. Second choice is a pressing system that allows us to taste clean press cuts. By minimizing and filtering out yeast solids that can obscure the sensory perception of tannins, basket presses qualify for high marks on both counts.

"With a basket press, after the first squeeze, the wine is very clear, and much easier to do sensory evaluation on," says Joseph Phelps winemaker Damien Parker.

EXTRACTING THE ESSENCE

The wine industry is chock-full of dedicated, intelligent people. Why, then, did we overlook the simple basics of press design and charge off in a technological direction?

In the early years of modernization, a break occurred between winemakers young and old. The substantial gap in technical knowledge of chemistry and microbiology between the upstart technologists and their empiricist predecessors led to a disrespect for the old ways.

Electricity changed everything. Wineries were rapidly transformed beyond recognition in areas such as lighting, refrigeration, and pumps, to say nothing of advances in laboratory methods and other technical metrics. While our formulas were improving, our disconnection with past wisdom meant that our appreciation of artistic subtleties was at an all-time low. The increasing winery scale and centralization that electrical power made possible placed a premium on efficiency and yields, areas in which benefits were easier to see and control than nuances of quality.

Since I entered the industry in 1972, most of this foolishness happened on my watch, and I too missed its import. If I look at my own early motivations, I see a faith in progress and a disdain for antiquity. It wasn't that I believed our predecessors were foolish, only that they lacked modern capabilities and limped along as best they could, right? I failed to appreciate technological conveniences such as electricity for the two-edged sword they really are.

This mind-set is part of what makes America a uniquely inventive country. Our loose bonds to the past permit us to experiment and advance much more aggressively than other cultures. Long may it wave. Postmodernism doesn't oppose progress. It does, however, advocate for careful examination of the consequences of innovation and thoughtful auditing for what may have gotten lost in the shuffle aesthetically.

In our headlong race for technical improvement, we moderns are disinclined to respect that the ancients may have had good reasons for the designs they worked out. In the rarified engineering circles where

R&D actually takes place, we are well advised to question our own preconceptions before we set out to reinvent the wheel. The postmodern movement was founded to reconsider modern innovations whose implementers haven't taken time to do so.

TAKE-HOME MESSAGES

- Press designs have come full circle in the past half century.
- A close look at modern wine press development holds rich lessons for how we think and act as an industry.
- The postmodern skill set changes our imperatives for pressing.

17

Some Like It Hot

It's all about integrity. Once you can fake that, the rest is a
piece of cake.

—Larry Hagman as J. R. Ewing, TV's *Dallas*

Wine alcohol levels have certainly climbed. Elin McCoy's survey of
Napa wine labels indicated a rise from an average of 12.5% in 1971 to
14.8% in 2001. Australian Wine Research Institute figures show the
same trend for Australian wines based on actual analysis, from 12.8%
in 1975 to 14.5% in 2005.

Mind you, in the '70s, common practice was to take advantage of the
federal leeway of 1.5% to allow vintners to print labels covering multiple years (with a vintage neck strap) for wines that had not even been
made yet, so the label declaration was in many cases meaningless. But
today the trend is to understate high alcohols, and often 14.8% is really
15.8%.

The trend toward riper fruit is even more drastic than the true alcohols indicate, since alcohol adjustment technologies now decrease 45%
of California wines by an average of 1%, often to avoid the fifty-cent
tax bump at levels above 14%.

TAKING ON THE CHAMP

What brought about this sea change in California's alcohols? To begin
with the obvious, the kind of wine California has come to specialize in
today is hardly the low-alcohol Euro-style quaffables, the Rhine wine,
Chablis, and rosé its wineries were dishing up in 1971, when our principal wine grape was Thompson seedless.

High alcohols from California aren't a new thing. In 1950, the average alcohol was over 18% in both California and Australia, when we drank almost entirely port, sherry, and muscatel, in tiny quantities at home and in church. The few drinkers of European table wines didn't believe domestic stuff was worth considering. Few remember that today's light, off-dry table wines did not exist, because the technology to make them was a product of the Manhattan Project.

Blue Nun and its ilk created in the early '60s an utterly new style of white wine. The post–World War II technological revolution supplied bubble-pointable sterile filters, inert gas, and other innovations that opened for the very first time the possibility for fresh, low-alcohol sweet wines to be commercially available, igniting a table wine fever that spread throughout the world, dominated by European brands that made them well, with American imitators clinging to their coattails.

Throughout the early '70s, the principal grape used in California wines was Thompson seedless, and the largest-selling table wines in the U.S. during that period were

1970	Lancer's Rosé
1971	Mateus Rosé
1972	Blue Nun
1973	Wente Grey Riesling
1974	Riunite Lambrusco
1975	Bolla Soave
1976	Fontana Candida Frascati

All low-alcohol European or Euro-style quaffables. Over the next thirty years, the wine Americans drank shifted toward California, while simultaneously the state's production boosted the wallop it packs. But to chalk up the change in table wine alcohol content to shifts in stylistic preference is a circular argument. Wines got bigger because they got bigger?

In the late '60s, a handful of pioneers, encouraged by the minuscule but consistent success of BV, Inglenook, Louis Martini, and Charles Krug with serious table wines, began to plant fuller-bodied varieties in tiny quantities. Small plots of Cabernet Sauvignon now appeared all over Napa plus a microscopic bit of Chardonnay here and there. By the early '70s there were dozens of wineries producing serious wines. American drinking habits were moving away from hard spirits, and baby boomer consumers began opening their wallets to the affordable luxury these wines provided.

But California needed a stroke of luck to get the luxury consumer's attention. That happened in Paris in 1976 at the famous Académie du Vin tasting when Stag's Leap Cabernet and Chateau Montelena Chardonnay shocked the world by swiping top honors from the established elite in Bordeaux and Burgundy.

It didn't take Napa producers long to figure out where their edge lay: The Big Wine. The hapless French, long since establishing Chardonnay at the top of the varietal pecking order and anointing the weighty Le Montrachet as the best of the best, had left the door wide open to New World producers. Considerations of finesse and terroir were on nobody's radar. To Chardonnay lovers of the '70s, bigger was better. End of story.

The Judgment of Paris led to the replacement of chenin blanc, grey riesling, and other light-wine grapes with cabernet sauvignon and chardonnay plantings as changes in winemaking style and practice moved toward Big. By 1980, cheap Chablis was "Out" throughout the nation and the noble fighting varietal Chardonnay was "In," with Delta Force–style wine marketer Bruno Benziger flogging Glen Ellen Proprietor's Reserve Chardonnay at two for $7 at Safeway. If the best is that cheap, why not buy the best?

NEW TARIFF IN TOWN

Thanks to the efforts of the World Health Organization, Americans decreased their per capita alcohol beverage consumption by over 20% between 1980 and 2000. This was largely accomplished in a single stroke.

When the federal wine tax soared in 1984 from 17¢ to $1.07 a gallon, jug prices tripled overnight, from $2 to $6. The big gallon bottles immediately disappeared from the shelves as consumers shifted en masse to 750 ml bottles, while wine consumption plunged from 12 liters per capita to 8 liters the following year.

We began drinking less and enjoying it more. How? We compensated by buying stronger stuff. In the 1980s, cabernet and chardonnay were generally picked at 23.5° brix, resulting in wines around 13.5%. We had already bumped the octane in a glass of white wine by a point or better.

STRAW MEN

The shift from light German-style wines to big French varietals is only half the answer to our puzzle. Today the average alcohol nudges 15% in the premium sector. Where is this alcohol coming from? Countless articles have recently emerged on this topic, each with its own novel slant. Let's look over some reasons offered up in the popular press for this trend, and then I'll take us behind the scenes into the minds of today's winemakers.

In a December 2006 article, "The Future of Napa Cabernet," in a discussion about the emerging Tulucay AVA (later to be christened "Coombsville"), *Wine and Spirits* magazine implicates global warming in the rise of Howell Mountain alcohols and the rush to the cool end of Napa. But studies at the Scripps Institute suggest the contrary: as interior valleys become warmer, southern Napa is actually cooling thanks to the influence of fog from the Pacific.[1] In reality, Tulucay wines are improving because of clonal research. As experimental plantings by Steve Krebs at Napa Valley College revealed, Clone 337 cabernet loves the cold, ripening readily and delivering huge tannins and great color in spots where standard up-valley clones like Clone 7 won't ripen at all.

Are the new super-yeasts to blame? Yes and no. Yeast strains can't change the conversion ratio of sugar to alcohol, at least not very much. The six carbon atoms in a sugar molecule have to go somewhere. Two atoms end up as carbon dioxide. The other four go to ethyl alcohol plus minuscule amounts of other flavors like glycerol and to the growth of the yeasts themselves. To change alcohol by 1% would mean 17 grams per liter of sugar were diverted to other by-products—an enormous amount. And super-yeasts make more cell mass, not less, thus lowering alcohol.

However, these ultravigorous yeasts do permit us to ferment to dryness musts that in the old days would have stuck sweet. So the new strains have indeed opened up the door for harvesting grapes with very high sugar content. But why would we wish to do that? Super-yeasts enable this misbehavior, but we need to look elsewhere for the cause.

Some say today's vines are grown so artificially that they fail to achieve the natural balance required to get ripe flavors at normal alcohols, and that our wines won't reflect balance until we embrace organics. In his 2003 talk at the American Society for Enology and Viticulture (ASEV) titled "Science of Sustainable Viticulture," John Williams of Frog's Leap reported that balancing soil fertility and abandoning inorganic fertilizers and excessive irrigation now gives him flavors at 23.5° brix that he previously didn't see until 28° brix.[2]

I have no doubt that John is exactly right. But the unsustainable practices that he decries were even more rampant in the '70s than today. I'm afraid that at its root, ripeness mania is more a mental disease than a reaction to some physical disorder. Like alcohol dependency itself, it is a good thing pushed too far.

SILICONE INJECTIONS BECOME THE RAGE

Pardon me for this heading, but the analogy is all too obvious. Winemakers went looking for tricks to amplify volume. Early offerings such as the lean, non-ML 1975 Spring Mountain and Freemark Abbey Chardonnays were superstars in their day, but the taut elegance they represented soon began to be replaced by heavier styles.

By the end of the '80s, the genius of Jed Steele, through brilliant vineyard selection, consummate blending skill, and pumping up the wines with oak, malolactic butteriness, and residual sugar, had established Kendall-Jackson Vintner's Reserve as the state's benchmark Chardonnay. His stormy divorce from his employer left his replacement, John Hawley, with big shoes to fill. The secret weapon that John presented to Jess Jackson to add still more richness was—you guessed it—extended hang time.

Richness through hang time was an appealing formula for a corporate don trying to build an industrial machine independent of temperamental artistic genius. And as grower advocate Andy Beckstoffer has often pointed out, since most grapes are sold by the ton, there was the added advantage to wineries that the shrinkage that bestowed extra richness came out of the grower's pocket.

THE RIPENESS ENIGMA

In chasing the classics, you can't just do what the French do. Emulating Bordeaux in sunnier climes has always been a brainy endeavor. It's tricky to distill the right lesson out of their experience. When we fail to connect the dots properly, it's often highly comic.

By Napoleon's time, vignerons in Burgundy and Bordeaux began boosting their modest brixes with beet sugar to about 13% alcohol potential to improve balance. In France, you pick on flavor and color, then fix the brix. Nearly half of the classified growths in Burgundy and Bordeaux routinely contain extra alcohol derived from 10 to 20 grams per liter of added beet sugar.

California's grapes sugar up much more readily, and standard practice until the '90s was to pick our chardonnays and serious reds at 23.5° brix. Period. Nobody really picked on flavor and color. The possibilities of enhanced ripeness were largely unexplored, with the exception of a few late-harvest Zinfandels, often as not products of stuck fermentations with residual sugar. We didn't have any notion, and no way of knowing, that at 23.5%, sugar, our grapes were often not really ripe.

France is cold, and it rains in the fall. Napa is considered a paradise for the vine because it's dry. Besides presenting a hostile climate to many pests and diseases, Napa's climate assures reliable alcohol in nine years out of ten. That's not the case in France, where good years are the minority and a great vintage is hoped for once a decade. Grapes obtain the same maturity at around 22° brix that California only achieves above 25°.

John Gladstones's brilliant new book, *Wine, Terroir, and Climate Change*,[3] offers an additional perspective on why other climes mature grapes at lower brix. At the risk of oversimplifying a lengthy and insightful discussion, Gladstones points to the notion, rather obvious in retrospect, that grapes are impeded in photosynthesis when highly humid conditions inhibit the evaporation of water.

This factor alone might account for the low brixes one sees in ripe fruit in many high-latitude areas, where diurnal summer temperature swings are moderated by longer day length. Absent botrytis, it is rare to see 20° brix in any variety in Germany, and low sugars also abound in humid areas in the upper midwestern and northeastern U.S. Even low-latitude areas such as the southeastern U.S. where weather patterns create high humidity are similarly characterized by low harvest brixes. But in California, where 40°F daily swings are typical, dew points, which correspond to the nightly low temperature, are consequently quite low and daytime air quite dry, and no such inhibition occurs, so fruit sugars up well in advance of ripeness.

In the early '90s, Conetech and my own company, Vinovation, introduced technologies for de-alcoholizing wine. Suddenly everybody could explore true ripeness and then readjust their alcohols to normal levels, taking advantage of improved yeast strains that made stuck fermentations less likely. It worked! California soon discovered that an extra week or two on the vine produced rich "dark fruit" aromas and concentrated, extractable color and tannins at 25° brix or so.

Now the bad news. These massive, vigorous young wines misbehaved badly. These were big wines prone to aggressive, grippy tannins and closed-up, stinky aromatics that masked fruit and accentuated green, veggie smells. Our wines were bigger, richer, and truer, but they tasted terrible.

French-trained transplants like Bernard Portet and Christian Moueix were quite familiar with these behaviors and knew them as marks of potential greatness. Reductive energy is strongest in the best wines, and the traditional cure has always been to age them. But the new wave of red consumers didn't recognize these virtues. And our winemakers did not exit academic institutions trained in the suite of postmodern élevage tools they needed to manage properly ripe fruit in the cellar.

HEART-SMART REDS

Throughout the '80s, white wines led the market and little red wine was consumed. That all changed on November 17, 1991, when CBS's *60 Minutes* aired a segment called "The French Paradox" suggesting that red wine helps prevent heart disease. Hey, worth a try! Red wine sales increased 39% overnight. The swing to reds was cemented in 1995 when *60 Minutes* covered a Copenhagen heart disease study that estimated optimum healthy consumption at three to five glasses per day. Yippee! Trouble was, trend-following novices couldn't stomach the kind of wines that won at Paris.

The market that emerged as a result of the French Paradox wanted big, drinkable wines *now*! They wanted rich, yummy reds with loads of heart-smart bioflavonoids and luscious fruit. Today, please.

Cabernet of normal ripeness is a bit on the chewy side for even the most health-motivated wine initiate. Do you have something a little softer? Every retailer's answer: Merlot. Ah, that's better. But does it have to smell so funny?

THE ROOTS OF PYRA-NOIA

When land prices on the North Coast of California began to skyrocket in the 1980s, producers looked south to Monterey and eventually the Central Coast for new vineyard sites for premium wines. Monterey County's Salinas Valley, salad bowl of the western U.S., was unlike anything California viticulturalists had seen before—a cold, sunny, windy desert with sandy soils in which the dreaded root louse *Phylloxera* could not thrive. To this they brought their new scientific marvel: the first large-scale planting of disease-free, own-rooted vines.

This scientifically purified master race of cabernet and merlot vines was incredibly vigorous, making lots of leaves, and the resulting fruit shading played perverse genetic flavor tricks, compelling grapes to express strong bell pepper flavors called pyrazines, which grapes in the wild use to repel birds from fruit containing immature seeds. The disaster that ensued left a "pyra-noid" imprint on California's winemakers that persists to this day. Veg is bad. Like, don't even go there.

UNLEASH THE FLYING MONKEYS

In the late '80s, wineries in California, Chile, and the South of France turned to Australian expertise, which, by virtue of their global marketing success and advanced scientific approach, they believed held the key to marketable styles. Their technique was simple: push for even greater maturity. "Field oxidation" refers to the Australian practice of resolving tannin prior to harvest. Crop left long enough on the vine loses its reductive strength and mean-spiritedness and softens into fruit-forward, user-friendly wine that "makes itself" in the fermenter.

This practice gave rise to the "flying winemakers," who revolutionized winemaking in the value segment. While it requires genuine expertise in the vineyard, it's well suited to industrial winemaking, as it leaves little to do at the winery; instead, wines can be made in massive factories by minimum wage labor with a limited enological staff overseeing thousands of tanks without the necessity of daily intervention.

Recent UC Davis studies indicate that hang time has no effect on pyrazines. Yet in a sense, the fix works, because raisiny aromas mask other flavors, including, unfortunately, varietal and terroir expression, making Cabernet, Zinfandel, Syrah, what-have-you, taste pretty much alike.

Excessive ripeness deprives the wine of depth, energy, soulfulness, and longevity in favor of early drinkability. These wines fit the bill precisely for a rapidly growing, unsophisticated market interested in rich, fruity wines for immediate consumption with no surprises under the cork.

Though their reign was short-lived, the stamp of "flying winemaker" techniques became indelibly imprinted on the philosophy of emerging regions for decades to come. Pretty soon, cult producers in Napa were hanging their cabernets left and right.

The hang time cure is a way to quench the reductive vigor of a red so it behaves like a white wine: simple, fruity, easy drinking, and pointless to age. But by the late '90s, the practice had spread to the ultrapremium segment, and moneyed consumers were paying $100+ price tags as long as the wines delivered a big initial punch. Critics were no wiser than winemakers, and the '97 Bordeaux, Barolos, and Napa Cabernets created some scandal by receiving high initial scores and then quickly falling apart in the cellar. But so what? With each successive vintage, size became more and more important (remember the silicone analogy?). Typecast as a game about blockbusters, California winemaking became a wet T-shirt contest, the wines eventually morphing into freakishly overendowed cartoon caricatures of their well-balanced progenitors. Today's blowsy, forward Napa cult Cabernets often weigh in at over 17%, and when I encounter them, I'm often reminded of Jack Nicholson's choice to risk his reputation as a serious dramatic actor while enhancing his bad boy image by accepting casting as the Joker.

CURDLED COLLOIDS

In chapters 2 and 3, I discussed the essential role of unpolymerized color in structure, texture, and longevity. Ripeness is valuable in optimizing production of anthocyanins and the cofactors that help extract them into colloids, as well as aiding extraction by liquefying pectins. Unfortunately, unpolymerized (monomeric) anthocyanins helpful to structure *decrease* during later stages of maturation, while high alcohol destabilizes copigmentation colloids, thus inhibiting extraction. The field oxidation associated with extended hang time thus deprives wine of depth, energy, soulfulness, and longevity in favor of early drinkability.

Even for wines of identical ripeness, elevated alcohol levels accelerate aging, promote oxidation, and both mask and diminish volatility of fruit aromas. Carol Shelton's experimental trials with the same Zinfandel barrel-aged at different alcohols showed that higher-alcohol lots lost freshness and developed raisiny aromas faster. The lower dielectric constant of high-alcohol solutions destabilizes tannin complexes, leading to graininess, precipitation, and accelerated browning.[4]

At first it seems reasonable to say, "What the heck. Let the lovers of minerality and terroir drink French and continue to ignore the New World." But the emergence of California as the source of Big Wine has a downside. We are not really making Le Montrachet. The greatest French wines combine *both* styles: incredibly broad *and* deep.

Californians are impressed by those who bulk up—we even elected one governor. But it didn't hurt Schwarzenegger's popularity when he turned up as an articulate spokesman for his odd but intriguing point of view. We can make big wines that have something to say. I just hope consumers won't write California wines off before we get around to it, though I'm afraid the really shrewd ones already have.

The evolution of wine styles in California parallels the genesis of decent coffee. In the Beginning, it was all dishwater. And the spirit of the marketplace said, "Let there be flavor!" And he separated the light from the darkness and the light he called Colombia Supremo and the darkness he called Heavy French Roast. And some folks looked upon the Heavy French Roast and for a time it was Good. But on the sixth day, a scowl lay upon the face of the consumer and he spake, "Enough is too much!" And on the seventh day the Starbucks roasters laid off the crude carbon, and it was Good.

JUDGE NOT, THAT YE BE NOT JUDGED

For those who love balance, I'm calling for both patience and enthusiastic support of wineries that dial it in. There's no question that winemakers the world over have been experimenting with extended maturity in the past decade or two, and we are learning. It's what we do. The lovers of Big Wine vote with their wallets, and vote they do.

If there is no appreciation of depth, longevity, and balance, we winemakers simply won't seek it. Alcoholic toasty butterbombs may be the destiny corporate wineries have chosen for us, but that's certainly not the limitation of our styles, and such wine speaks absolutely nothing about our terroir. But I fear we are creating the opposite impression among consumers, and losing the best of them. If California is not to be doomed to typecasting as devolved Muscle Wine, winemakers must redouble their efforts to explore alternative styles outside the mainstream and recapture the magic that our wine carried before bulking it up actually dumbed it down.

Pleasing the critics has certainly played a role. Robert Parker has become the standard punching bag for his supposed bias toward overblown styles, but in my view the Emperor of Wine is not entirely without clothes, as his detractors claim. Parker does indeed love big wines, but he loves other styles too and, more to the point, seldom has he dished out 90+ to wines that lack depth and soulfulness. The Pontet-Canet incident wouldn't have been news if it weren't the exception.

There *are* problems surrounding slavish consumer obedience to Parker that really aren't his fault. As an articulate, honest, and outspoken authority, he has attracted so much loyalty that he influences spending habits at the top end more than any other critic. Second in influence is the *Wine Spectator,* which also certainly favors size over elegance. But the real bad actors in this drama are the winery marketing departments, which, in search of easy answers, try to reverse-engineer high scores. Consulting firms like Enologix, Tragon, and Flavorsense, eager to supply simplistic "quality drivers" for big bucks, dominate the winemaking process at the expense of traditional values like balance, depth, and longevity.

NAMING THE DEVIL

So there you have it. The real root cause of increasing alcohol is the consumer appetites we seek to serve. "We have met the enemy, and he is us," quoth Walt Kelly. Just like Colombian coke dealers, we make high-alcohol wines because our customers have communicated with cash that that's what they want.

But hold on. Is this situation really the calamity it's portrayed as? Most writers on this subject indict these changes in California wine as some kind of scandal. Wine is the second sexiest of businesses, and exposés sell lots of magazines. But rising alcohols are almost entirely good news.

California is crowding the shelves with more and better wine than ever before. The Grey Rieslings and cheap Chablis of the '70s simply weren't as good as today's offerings. We've gained incalculable knowledge since then on what to make and how to make it, finding our best niche in a global marketplace. Dialing in proper maturity has been a key field of inquiry.

Are we there yet? Not on your life. But you can bet that every producer will keep dialing until its own tiny viable niche gets formulated. Initially, I quite liked the first few oaky butterbombs I tasted decades ago, but after a while I just got bored, and I'm confident that American consumers will follow suit as their palates mature.

It is possible to make wines that offer both richness and finesse, with profundity as well as the power to lift you off your feet. California winemakers have recently begun to get smarter at romancing their tannins while protecting depth and integrity.

A month on the vine doesn't substitute for a decade in the cave—what did you think? This is where the French have us: the understated, intricate creations of their talented wine jewelers. But we can make those wines too, and some of us will, because ultimately they will offer the best expression of our terroir.

TAKE-HOME MESSAGES

- Ripeness mania is more a mentality than a physical disorder.
- We have met the enemy, and he is us. Today's styles reflect an inexperienced market that wants big, drinkable wines *now*!
- Prevailing trends promise to support a widening variety of styles as the market matures.

18

The New Filtrations

Winemaking's Power Tools

When the water of a place is bad, it is safest to drink none
that has not been filtered through the berry of a grape or the
tub of a malt. These are the most reliable filters yet invented.
—Samuel Butler (1835–1902)

Twenty years ago, any winemaker you asked about the purpose of filtration (myself included) would have named clarification and microbial
stability. This twentieth-century view of wine filtration contains the
embedded notion that wine is a liquid, so anything suspended in wine is
an impurity, the removal of which can only increase its purity. The
postmodern view is that the suspended structures in fact contain wine's
essence, and that their exact nature determines wine's ability to touch
us in a special, soulful way.

As postmodern ideas catch on, membrane clarification and sterile
filtration may become as unknown in future wineries as they are today
in dairies. Milk, like wine, is a structured food, essentially an emulsion
composed of tiny beads of butter surrounded by clear whey. You can't
filter it without altering its nature any more than you can strain a stew.
Any attempt to force milk through a sterile filter has the effect of de-
homogenizing it, separating out the cream. In wine, sterile filtration
may also cause colloids to aggregate irreversibly into much larger ones
that, lacking the surface area to integrate effectively, tend then to precipitate out.

Not every winemaker agrees that sterile filtration, done right, harms
red wine. In fact, I'd have to say I'm in the minority on this point.

Whether or not good wine structure can reassemble properly post-
filtration will remain a matter for conjecture and debate until we get
tools to actually look at structure. It has been my observation that some-

times wines rebound in their integrating powers within a few months, but often they don't.

Since wines are generally sterile-filtered as part of bottling, observation is confounded by the phenomenon of bottle shock, which does seem to abate over time. I suspect that an awful lot of wishful thinking is also at play, for without sterile filtration, winemakers need to consider options like Integrated Brett Management (see chapter 10), a brave new world that understandably gives them the willies.

One thing's for sure, though. Just as dairies have done, wineries will use membranes for a host of tasks unimagined a decade ago.

WHAT'S NEW IN THE FILTRATION ZOO?

Today, reverse osmosis (RO) can remove rainwater, alcohol, vinegar, smoke taint, and Brett flavors. Ultrafiltration (UF) reclaims free run from press wines, pulls out browning without harming flavor, moves color and tannin from wines in which it is excessive to wines that need it, and helps build colloids in fermentations rich in flavor but deficient in colloidal building blocks. Through electrodialysis (ED), tartrates can now be removed without stripping flavor or structure while saving 90% of the energy cost. Each year, exotic new membrane processes present new options for selective removal, including a host of new approaches to acidity adjustment, a key to opening up much of America to winemaking.

The Holy Grail of tangential filtrations is to be able to clarify wine without harming its structure, and crossflow clarification (erroneously abbreviated as simply "crossflow") continues to gain steam. In my opinion, this technology works very well for unstructured whites, where a little tannin and color stripping is a good thing, but can prove disastrous for structured reds. Many disagree with me. For sure, the key to reasonable operation is to use a machine with a small enough dead volume that every drop of fluid flow gets through the membrane. The final few percent is phenolic "black gold."

Meanwhile, in the realm of microbial stability, the quest continues for alternatives to sterile filtration. Many winemakers are already using Velcorin to suppress Brett, and the future may see commercialization of many other methods not involving filtration. Ultimately, we may learn how to do nothing at all. The pinnacle of postmodern winemaking is to resolve microbial balance prior to bottling so sterility is unnecessary— the subject of chapter 10.

IT'S WEIRD WHAT WE THINK IS WEIRD

Any good craftsman will use only tools that he knows and respects. Many winemakers and consumers have regarded trends toward membrane applications with suspicion. Good for them. The postmodern view is that this distrust of technology is late in coming. Most of us are comfortable with electric lighting, refrigeration, packaged yeast, and stainless steel because we grew up with them in our homes. But in the context of eight thousand years of winemaking, these are utterly new.

My advice: don't fully trust anything with a power cord. The products of electricity have never undergone proper scrutiny, introduced as they were in an era when all progress was deemed good and corporate boardrooms sported portraits of smoke-belching factories. It is not too late to question what we may have lost.

It might be argued that the electric lightbulb has altered the human psyche more radically than any other invention in history. The Romans divided experience into Apollonian and Dionysian: the analytical mind of daylight versus the mood-oriented mind of firelight, starlight, and moonlight. By replacing fire in our homes as the primary light source, we have deprived our whole race of half our consciousness. In addition, the necessity of wiring our homes now surrounds us constantly with a nervous 60 Hz buzz from which we are only free out-of-doors.

If we can agree that an expanded inquiry into the downside of technology is long overdue, then I would invite readers to hear me out concerning some newer technologies that I hope are not especially more heinous than the devils we know. I'll proceed here to pass on the familiarity I have gained from twenty years of playing around with novel applications of membranes.

Full disclosure: I hold U.S. patents on RO processes for VA and alcohol adjustment, and collected small residual royalties until they expired at the end of 2012, though I have no direct commercial involvement in any of the technologies I'll discuss (fig. 25). In all modesty, however, I probably have greater breadth of experience in this area than anyone else on the planet. From this vantage point, I intend here to clear up some misconceptions and offer my personal beliefs and concerns regarding these tools.

WHO'S WHO IN THE MEMBRANE ZOO

Modern winemaking got under way in post–World War II Germany with the advent of bubble-pointable sterile membranes made from

FIGURE 25. The author delivering a Vinovation reverse osmosis unit.

plastic sheets etched in atomic piles. It is hard for today's connoisseur who enjoys mostly dry table wines to conceive that prior to this, off-dry wines did not exist and were the hot new thing. The world had never seen anything like these light, fresh, sweet wines, and the Liebfraumilch boom took the world by storm just like the Beatles.

Sterile filtration's vast ripples have profoundly transformed industries as diverse as pharmaceuticals, electronics, and biotech. For white wines, freshness has become the prime directive worldwide, showing the door to many serious traditional styles and ushering in New Zealand's Sauvignon Blancs and Italy's Pinot Grigios. In chapter 1, "The Solution Problem," I relate how this revolution also derailed red wine–making for half a century by replacing the centrality of structure and soulfulness with a culture of squeaky-clean fruit bombs.

UPTIGHT AND OUT OF SIGHT

From the onset, controlling the pore size of sterile filters was easy. First produced in atomic piles, radiation particles drilled a path through plastic sheets, with the subsequent dwell time in an etching solution determining how large the holes became. There was no limit to the tightness you could get—just reduce the time in the bath. But below 0.1 micron, the filters didn't seem to work. Perfectly clear solutions wouldn't filter because dissolved molecules instantly fouled the membranes.

The vital hints on how to prevent fouling came from the human body. Medical researchers looking to replace the function of failed kidneys created dialysis membranes that mimicked human tissue. But they didn't work. The researchers at last realized that blood flow through our capillaries was keeping human membranes clean. They dubbed this scrubbing innovation "tangential flow" or "crossflow." The filtrate is called "permeate" and makes up only a small fraction of the volume pumped into the capillary. The remainder, whatever does not pass through the filter, is called "retentate" and may be recirculated back to the initial tank.

The U.S. Navy enthusiastically picked up the new membranes to solve the vexing problem of producing drinkable water at sea by filtering out the salt. When you do so, a curious thing happens: the purified water tries to flow backward into the salt water. If you salt a cucumber slice, you'll see the salt draw water beads from its tissues; that's called osmosis. The pump pressure necessary to overcome this osmotic tendency gave the process its name: reverse osmosis.

The tighter the membrane is, the purer the permeate. Tight RO gives high salt rejection and purer water, but it also requires higher pressures for the same flow. While sterile membranes are measured by the diameter of the pore size (commonly 0.45 micron for sterile bottling), that's hard to measure for tighter membranes, so crossflow membranes are measured by the mass of a molecule that just fits through the pore. Large molecules don't pass at all, and small ones pass readily. The porosity is rated by the formula weight of a molecule that is found in the permeate at 50% of the concentration present in the retentate.

The formula weight of a molecule is just the sum of the weights of its constituent atoms. An atom's mass is essentially the sum of its protons and neutrons, each weighing one dalton. H_2O weighs 18 daltons: oxygen's 16 daltons plus the 2 hydrogens at one dalton apiece.

Sometimes dissolved substances form structures in liquids, a particularly common occurrence in wine. Filters can tell us a great deal about wine structures. Molecules sometimes form clumps whose functional weights are much larger than their formula weights. Water has positive and negative poles like a magnet, so although an atom of hydrogen weighs only one dalton, the charge on the ion H^+ attracts water to hydrate it to a functional weight of 900 daltons! Molecules can also aggregate into colloids many times their size, such as those that tannins and anthocyanins form in red wine. Proteins can assume shapes that are either loose or compact, greatly affecting their filterability in ways not predicted by formula weight.

RO was first commercially applied in the wine industry in the 1980s when European wineries seeking enhanced maturity in rainy climates opted to extend hang time into the rain and used RO to remove the rainwater. Grape juice permeate from a good tight RO (porosity = 80 daltons) contains only water, thus the sugar, flavor, and color are retained in their undiluted form and returned to the concentration present before the rain but with added flavor ripeness. In California, Barry Gnekow at Jerry Lohr's Ariel Winery began to use these membranes, which also pass ethanol (MW = 46 daltons), to make nonalcoholic wine by discarding the alcohol-containing permeate and replacing it with purified water.

To get proper ripeness in California, winemakers had to overcome an opposite problem from the French: we don't receive enough rain, so our brixes get too high. Gnekow's process used RO to remove a permeate containing a small amount of alcohol, actually less concentrated than the level in the wine, and replace it with make-up water containing no alcohol at all. This was fine for Gnekow's nonalcoholic wine, but for standard wine, by law, we couldn't use make-up water, so in 1992 I hit on and patented the idea of distilling the alcohol out of the wine-derived permeate, yielding pure water that was returned to the wine (fig. 26). This turned out to be a really good idea that is now used by over a thousand wineries to uncouple the harvest decision from brix and to fine-tune alcohol "sweet spots," the precise points of harmonious balance that every wine contains (see chapters 11 and 25).

A second innovation in the same patent was the capability to lower volatile acidity, a fancy winemaker code for vinegar. Acetic acid (MW = 60 daltons) and ethyl acetate (MW = 88 daltons) are the only other wine constituents that appear in significant quantity in tight RO permeate (passage is about 60% and 40%, respectively). Unlike water and ethanol, acetic acid will ionize and can be removed by a resin similar to that used in a water softener (fig. 27). This solved a problem created by extended maturity: birds attracted to the new ripe fruit caused damage that fostered bacterial growth, leading to acetic acid spoilage during primary fermentation. Since birds love rich, flavorful fruit, this tended to affect the winery's best lots, which were otherwise very good. We have been able to rescue many thousands of such wines over the years.

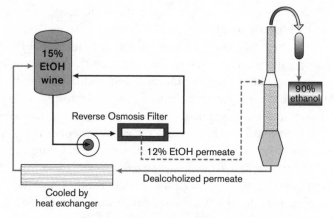

FIGURE 26. RO membranes are so tight that wine color, flavor, and tannin cannot pass through. RO permeate has the appearance of water but also contains dilute alcohol that can be concentrated in a still. If the de-alcoholized water is continuously returned to the wine, its alcohol content can be adjusted to any level without damage to its character. This process is the subject of the author's U.S. patent 08/218920; it allows wines without excessive alcohol to be made from grapes harvested at full maturity.

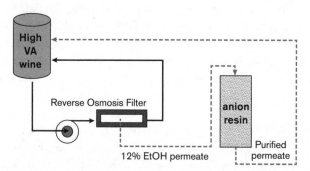

FIGURE 27. In another embodiment of the author's U.S. patent 08/218920, permeate from a wine containing acetic acid (vinegar) is passed through a water softener and recombined, thus reducing its VA level. It is a myth that VA is caused by negligence. Most is created during fermentation by the action of bacteria borne on attractive fruit that has been damaged by birds. Since 1992 dozens of VA-reduced wines have appeared on the *Wine Spectator*'s Top 100 Wines of the World.

FEDERAL STUFF AND NONSENSE

There are a variety of compliance hurdles to the implementation of membrane technologies. Simply put, the regulations often don't address what is actually happening. Despite the fact that RO permeate has a *lower* alcohol content than wine, it is bizarrely deemed by U.S. federal regs as a distillate and can only come into inventory on a licensed distilled spirits plant (DSP). The Australian Memstar system employs a second membrane on the permeate to migrate its alcohol to "strip water," which can be shipped offsite. This opens the door to alcohol adjustment at the winery without the necessity of an on-site still. But in the U.S., you still need a DSP.

Since applications like VA work by returning the treated permeate back into the wine, a DSP is not required to run them. Looser RO membranes are also employed to permit more efficient passage of larger molecular weight defects such as smoke taint and Brett flavors. Some providers even try to reduce the cost of VA removal (and skirt my patent) by employing loose RO, but the trade-off with looser membranes is flavor loss, and porosities over 150 daltons are wisely forbidden by law.

The advantage of RO is that wine character stays in the tank. True nanofiltration, which separates ions with one versus two charges (K^+ from Ca^{++}, for example, or nitrate from sulfate), encompasses the MW range from around 400 to 1,000 daltons. Since such separations are right in the middle of the wine flavor range, no use has yet been found for this type of separation, and it is not legal. However, the prefix *nano*- has great marketing appeal and appears in the product designations of many loose RO filters. The resulting confusion has led the Alcohol and Tobacco Tax and Trade Bureau (TTB) to approve nanofiltration in name only, yet restricting its use to porosities below 150 daltons and pressures below 250 psi, a virtual impossibility.

ULTRAFILTRATION NATION

In the postmodern view, wine is a solution containing suspended colloids that are the source of texture, soulfulness, and aromatic integration. Ultrafilters, which range from 1,000 to 250,000 daltons, allow the solution part to pass completely and hold back the structural portion— large polymers and colloids of various sizes.

UF is a playground for exploring how structured wine behaves. Porosities below 10,000 MW are used to remove browning and astringency from white wines. They are proof that red pigments exist in wine as colloids; regardless of their 450 dalton MW, monomeric phenols such as anthocyanins and other flavonoids will not pass through membranes in this range. Filtrates from even the most open UF membranes (200K MW range) have a lighter hue for most of the filtration, and tend to concentrate as anthocyanin-rich "black gold" at the end of the run.

This behavior can be exploited in reclaiming useful fractions from press wines. The first ~95% of the filtrate comprises a richly aromatic free-run quality. The last 3%, usually recovered using 25K membranes, is a cofactor concentrate composed of the monomeric proto-tannins that hold color colloids together and is extremely useful to add to fermentations to aid extraction of color and flavor depth. The remaining retentate (1–4%) is a polymeric tannin concentrate that is far more effective and well structured than powdered tannins for framing wines in the cellar that are too feminine or too vegetal in aroma, hence the need for framing or aromatic integration.

Ultrafiltration is thus an amazingly versatile tool for softening press wines without aroma loss, thereby eliminating waste, and for producing concentrates for blending and balancing without the use of nonwine materials such as powdered wood tannins and animal-based fining agents.

One smart ruling involved the way the Feds chose to differentiate ultrafiltration from tighter filtrations. This is a critical watershed, because RO permeates ideally don't have any flavor and therefore are not wines; instead, the wine character remains in the retentate, the part that is not filtered. Conversely, the goal of ultrafiltration is to create permeates that have the maximum of wine flavor. UF does not create an osmotic differential pressure, so it can run at low pressure. By setting a 200 psi maximum on UF operation, very close to the osmotic backpressure of wine under RO, the Feds effectively barred the door to membranes that retain aromatics, thus excluding, quite wisely, the destructive middle ground of nanofiltration from approved winemaking practice.

ADJUSTING ACIDITY WITH MEMBRANES

In 2011 California survived its most challenging vintage in decades — almost as difficult as a typical vintage anywhere else. We are so spoiled. Until recently, acid adjustment in West Coast wines consisted of deciding whether to add to the must one gram per liter of tartaric acid or two. Even our high-pH/high-TA challenges were mostly high-potassium problems, overcome by the nervewracking but effective practice of lowering pH with even more massive tartaric bumps, followed by precipitation of a blizzard of cream of tartar at pH 3.6.

The cool, rainy vintages of 2010 and 2011 have resulted in a comic assortment of pH/TA conditions that have sent winemakers back to their schoolbooks to relearn the basics. When pH wanders into the 4s in a cool, long season, sometimes the culprit is high malic (underripeness), sometimes high K^+ (overripeness). Treatments differ entirely. In 2011, it wasn't unknown to get both conditions in the same must.

In this we have joined the ranks of our east-of-the-Rockies winemaker brethren, now representing fully half the wineries in North America, whose expertise in this field is their chief employment qualification in the chilly northern climes of the Midwest.

The winery front office may sing love songs of nonintervention, but every winemaker knows that a dry white with 12 g/L of titratable acidity, or a brown, tired, dried-up Pinot, will fight an uphill battle to please even the most Luddite consumer. Sure, people want natural, and we want to give it to them. But above all, they want tasty wines and won't settle for less.

Fortunately, today's winemaker is blessed with a broad and rapidly expanding array of choices for bringing wines into acid balance, many of them using membranes in place of additives. The downside is that unless you have easy access to equipment, contracting with a mobile service involves some trouble and expense. Choosing among the dizzying array of techniques requires a firm grasp of acid-base chemistry.

THE BASICS ABOUT ACIDS

An acid is just a dissolved substance that can slough off a hydrogen ion (H^+), really just a proton. Because the acids in wine are "weak," some portion of the acidic hydrogen ions (protons) remains bound to them, dynamically coming and going in a constant dance.

To figure when to pull the trigger on harvesting a block, winemakers look at both titratable acidity and pH. A glance at 2011's must chemistry will convince even the most unschooled winemaker that pH and TA are not very closely related.

Both are measures of acidity (high TAs and low pHs denote lots of acidity), but TA is the sour taste, in contrast to pH, which is the amount of free, dissociated protons that are controlling the wine's chemistry and microbiology. TA is like the cops on the payroll, while pH is like the cops on the beat fighting crime. Or if you like, TA is like the number of women at a party, while pH measures how many of them are unattached. TA numbers make sense: TA is higher in tart wines. The pH scale, though, is counterintuitive: low pH means high free acidity.

In normal maturation, grapes get the energy to concentrate sugar into the berry by burning malic acid, lowering TA in the process. While TA is dropping, pH is rising from below 3.0 to approaching 4.0.

The strength of an acid is determined by its pKa (acid dissociation constant)—that is, the pH at which half of the acid is ionized. Lactic acid, for example, has a pKa of 3.8: above pH 3.8, it's mostly ionized (or in geekspeak, "dissociated"), and below 3.8, it's mostly not (you guessed it, it's "undissociated").

Some acids have multiple pKa's. Grape juice contains a couple of diprotic acids that have two acidic protons on offer, the stronger tartaric acid (symbolized as H_2Ta), with pKa's of 3.0 and 4.2, and the weaker malic acid (H_2Ma), with pKa's of 3.5 and 5.0. Big difference. At wine pH (3.0–4.0), tartaric acid is always a lot more ionized than malic acid is. Malic acid is like a really good donut shop where the proton cops like to hang out instead of patrolling the wine. Bottom line, the solution is heavily buffered, which is to say that wine works to maintain its pH the same way buffered aspirin works to quiet an acid stomach.

A lovely characteristic of tartaric acid is that its bitartrate form precipitates with potassium to form potassium bitartrate (KHTa) crystals that reduce TA. Very handy. This effect is maximized at pH 3.6, the peak of the bitartrate curve. This turns out to be a big deal: the natural Great Divide for winemaking.

Here's something weird. Above 3.6, KHTa precipitation lowers TA and raises pH, just as you'd expect. Below 3.6, however, TA is lowered, but so is pH. The acid goes down, but it also goes up. Softer taste, but more stability and freshness. Not too shabby.

Because of this effect, it is often possible to deacidify low-pH wines by adding potassium carbonate (K_2CO_3). This is always Plan A. Here's how it works. First, as the compound dissolves, it ionizes into potassium cations and carbonate anions:

$$K_2CO_3 \rightarrow 2K^+ + CO_3^{2-}$$

Next, the carbonate neutralizes some protons, benignly turning that nasty acid taste into carbon dioxide bubbles and water:

$$CO_3^{2-} + 2H^+ \rightarrow H_2O \text{ (water)} + CO_2 \text{ (bubbles)}$$

Since it removes free protons, this reaction does raise the pH; but the K^+ ions will also enhance bitartrate precipitation, and as long as this happens below pH 3.6, this precipitation will lower both TA and pH, moving us back in the direction of the original low pH. A wine with a TA of 10 g/L and a pH of 3.1 can emerge with a TA of 7.5 g/L and a pH of 3.3 at negligible cost. Hot stuff, but only if we begin from a low pH starting point.

BAD ACID TRIPS

If we have a lot of tartness in a wine, we might expect a nice low pH. In fact, lots of critics and Master Sommeliers think that tart wines age longer. 'Taint necessarily so.

The wrong mix of acids can lead to very tart wines with very poor shelf life. Grapes can get out of sync, giving you really high pHs when you still have high TAs. A high TA means the juice has lots of protons and a sour taste, but the high pH means they aren't free and available—that is, your protons are tied up somewhere. To revisit the police analogy, you have a lot of cops off duty, or in donut shops.

In a typical case, a juice may have a TA of 10 g/L and a pH of 3.9. Normally in California, the culprit is a high amount of potassium and tartrate. Tartrate is not a very good donut shop, but it will do the job if there's enough of it around.

In such a wine, we have lots of K^+ and lots of tartrate, so we might expect a big precipitation of potassium bitartrate. But if the pH is too far above 3.6, most will be in the fully deprotonated tartrate form, so the percentage bitartrate will be low and KHTa crystals will not readily form.

The other way juice can have high pH and high TA is if malate content is high. This happens all too often in Europe and North America but is rare in California except in chilly years like 2010 and 2011, when it's anybody's guess. Since malic acid is not easily removed, the first step is to determine whether that's our problem at all.

Lab analysis for potassium and malate is expensive and time consuming, but there's a simpler way. To test for this condition on site, dissolve some tartaric acid in a small amount of warm water and simply acidify a sample of the juice to exactly pH 3.6.

Now freeze the sample overnight (allowing for ice expansion), then thaw it out in the morning. Hopefully you'll see lots of white crystalline powder in the bottle. Either centrifuge, filter, or settle the sample out in the fridge, then run a TA. If the problem was high potassium, the resulting juice will have a big drop in TA to perhaps 8.5 g/L and a pH still at 3.6. If it works, go and do thou likewise to the big tank. If not, read on.

GETTING THE BUGS OUT

Before we move on to high-tech membrane solutions to an excessive malic acid problem, let's discuss biological solutions. Organisms that eat acid appeal greatly to our inner cheapskate. I will only speak generally here, because yearly advances in our knowledge promise to invalidate any specific information I might offer in this area.

Historically, biological deacidification has been fraught with hidden costs and dangers. Thanks to the beloved Ralph Kunkee's work in the '70s, malolactic fermentation is a big success story, and today few winemakers are daunted by the prospect of pushing a wine through ML. But malolactic has huge impacts on style and is thus tricky to use to reduce acidity without harming fruit aromas. Most other biological solutions also create by-products that alter style, so biological deacidification methods must be evaluated with extreme care.

All *Saccharomyces cerevisiae* yeasts consume some malic acid (generally around 10%) during primary fermentation without undesirable flavor production. Recently, strains like Lallemand's 71B have received favorable marks in reducing as much as one-third of malic acid.

PASS THE DOUBLE SALT

Were it not for the fuss and bother it entails, double-salt deacidification would be the standard treatment to reduce malic acid. It takes advantage of the precipitation of calcium malate that occurs at high pH. A portion of the juice, usually 20–30%, is drawn off and treated with an excess of calcium carbonate ($CaCO_3$). The carbonate reacts with 100% of available protons, both free and bound, completely neutralizing the juice to pH 7, while the TA drops to zero. Under these conditions, calcium precipitates both tartrate (CaTa) and malate (CaMa) in proportion to what is present, as well as calcium's namesake "double salt" (Ca_2TaMa).

When recombined into the main lot, a wine with a TA of 10 g/L will be reduced to 7 g/L, with also 30% of its buffer capacity removed. The wine can then be re-acidified with tartaric if needed, restoring acid balance. The process does not create calcium instability because the final wine has only 30% of calcium saturation.

Sounds good. The only trouble is, before recombining the treated portion, it is essential to filter it to remove all crystals and excess $CaCO_3$, to say nothing of pulp solids—a slow, messy proposition. To the rescue: crossflow clarification. The new tangential-flow filters making their appearance all over the country to replace diatomaceous earth (DE) filtration seem tailor-made for double-salt filtration. Time to start sucking up to your neighbor who has one.

Double salt must be done prior to malolactic, and preferably at the juice stage, due to the hazards of taking a wine to such a high pH even for a short time.

CHOOSE YOUR WEAPON

Reverse osmosis, discussed previously as a tool for removing rainwater from juice as well as for adjusting wine alcohol and VA content, has interesting prospects for deacidification.

In acetic acid removal, the un-ionized acetic acid at 60 daltons will pass easily through an RO filter with an 80 dalton porosity, but its ionized acetate counterpart with a functional molecular weight (FMW) of 600 daltons doesn't pass through at all.

A precisely identical method may be used in deacidification of excessively tart wines by employing looser RO membranes (near the 150 dalton legal limit) to pass malic acid at 134 MW. With a 150 dalton porosity, more flavor will be lost, but useful amounts of lactic and malic acids (pKa of 3.8 and 3.5, respectively) can be removed if the pH is not too high.

A new generation of membranes focuses on membrane selectivity. Although the wine industry is tiny by global industrial standards, we are beginning to receive trickle-down benefits from other industries, and off-the-rack technologies frequently appear that improve our options.

While RO membranes are impervious to ions, membranes have been developed that do just the opposite—ion-selective membranes that pass only the ions. Electrodialysis, patented by Eurodia and marketed in the United States as STARS (Selective Tartrate Removal System), was perfected some twenty years ago in France for economical, gentle, cold stabilization and has been increasingly employed to great advantage for deacidification.

In ED, wine is pumped between two membranes, a cation-permeable one that will only pass H^+, K^+, and Ca^{2+} and an anion-permeable one that passes tartrate and malate ions. A low-voltage DC current propels ions through these membranes, cations gravitating to the negative pole and anions attracted to the positive pole. In effect, KHTa is drawn into a brine that is then either discarded or sold.

In deacidifying the high-TA wines of recent cool years, neutralization with potassium or calcium carbonate is limited by rising pH. If followed by ED, pH can be brought back down while simultaneously removing K^+ and Ca^{2+} to prevent instability.

The beauty of the ED method is that, unlike conventional cold stabilization, it protects the colloidal structure of the wine, and also saves a lot of energy. ED can remove KHTa without the entrainment of colloids that accompanies crystal precipitation, resulting in very little flavor stripping. As a consequence, the method has been highly preferred to chilling by trained sensory panels.

When used in concert with tartaric acid addition, ED can often give you virtually any pH and TA you want. Since it requires high clarity, ED runs on finished wine, even post-ML. Besides producing superior wines, ED can trim a winery's energy bill by over 25%. A system with an output of 200 gallons per hour costs upwards of $200,000. Because of its high capital cost, ED systems are usually accessed as a service except in the case of large wineries.

Because it is less ionized due to its higher pKa, malic acid is removed by loose RO preferentially over tartaric. For the same reason, ED, which removes only ions, is not very effective in removing malic acid. This is its Achilles' heel: it is not the tool of choice for those overly crisp midwestern whites.

An additional alternative selective membrane technology is currently being marketed by Mavrik Industries. CEO Bob Kreisher is frank about its proprietary nature: "We want winemakers to feel comfortable with what our process does, but we worked hard on developing a system that works well, and we don't want to give away essential information to our competitors." Mavrik was nonetheless quite open to my observing what their system does, and I got a firsthand look at the deacidification of a 2010 Cabernet.

Mavrik's technology is reportedly based on an acid-selective membrane that passes *both* molecular and ionized species. This is big news, greatly simplifying our lives because we would no longer need to pay attention to ionization pH and malolactic status. Colorless, flavorless permeate from this membrane is passed through a weak anion exchange resin where malic, tartaric, and lactic acids are retained. A cation exchange column can also be employed to exchange potassium for H^+, with the effect of re-acidifying the permeate prior to recombination.

In this way, buffer capacity is removed, and pH and TA can be adjusted more or less at will. Although I cannot claim to fully grasp the details of Mavrik's proprietary magic, I can at least attest that the Cabernet came through it with flying colors and no discernible aroma loss. As Mavrik refines this technology, it may very well be the toy of choice in regions plagued by high malic acid.

Back in sunny California, extended hang time often results in high-potassium wines that resist pH adjustment with tartaric acid. A new approach to acidification of high-pH wines and musts now being pioneered by Eurodia uses a bipolar membrane on the cation side to exchange potassium ions for protons, thus raising the TA. Unlike tartaric acid addition, this lowers pH without increasing buffer capacity. The membrane works much like a cation exchange resin, removing potassium ions in trade for H^+, but without the stripping of flavor elements that occurs during direct contact of wine and resin. Bipolar anion applications may also be on the horizon.

THE BOTTOM LINE ON THE NEW ACID MEMBRANES

Any writer loves a scoop. In preparing this chapter, I was treated to a generous handful of new technologies that promise to transform American winemaking in an era of climate change, upending modern winemaking precepts and rendering current teachings obsolete.

Yet there is no bottom line to report. To a man, technology developers waffled and temporized concerning release dates, performance, efficiencies, and capital costs of their new darlings. The complex and peculiar machinations of TTB approval are an additional uncharted minefield through which wineries must walk with care and do their own homework.

We are smack in the middle of an era much like the 1960s when a tsunami shift to new kinds of table wines left us in total ignorance, walking a technical tightrope without a net. We are today completely unprepared for the impact of deacidification capabilities that even their providers have yet to fathom but that could potentially open up the possibilities of untapped winegrowing regions. Smart postmodern winemakers throughout the U.S., together with their state-sponsored academic partners, are well advised to place a high priority on understanding and evaluating the diverse menu of options that are soon to be thrown on our plate.

This chapter provides no dependable *Consumer Reports* purchase guide to deacidification. In its stead, I have sought to lay the groundwork for such an evaluation by outlining the options we all need immediately to get smart about.

DEVIL OR ANGEL?

Postmodern winemaking takes no ethical position on the methods I've discussed here. I have been very privileged to work with this diverse tool kit over the past two decades, and have found the experience invaluable for exploring wine's true nature and the possibilities that exist for working with it. Comfortable as I am with how they work, I may make use of these tools with greater ease than most winemakers, but concerning certain of them, such as sterile filtration and crossflow clarification of structured wines, I remain more skeptical than many. It is up to each winemaker to assess what works, and while I recommend distrust of anything with a power cord, I also believe the old adage, "Don't knock it till you've tried it."

TAKE-HOME MESSAGES

- With reverse osmosis, contrary to other filtrations, the wine's character doesn't pass through the filter.
- Ultrafiltration is a playground for exploring how structured wine behaves.
- Climate change and the conquering of new cold-climate regions demands that winemakers get smarter about acidity and the emerging techniques that address it.
- Choosing among options requires a firm grasp of the technical functionality, cost benefits, and legal factors involved in each.

19

Flash Détente

Winemaking Game Changer

Seldom appears a new winemaking technology with benefits so compelling that it promises to shift the entire industry.

The advent of electricity and refrigeration in the early twentieth century and the widespread use of stainless steel, inert gas, and sterile filtration just after World War II changed the winemaking world forever in a very short time. These technologies created new wines we could sell, increased the practical scale of our operations, shifting the economics of production, the architecture of wineries, the expectations of consumers, and the working notions of winemakers.

Sweeping consequences ensued for vineyards, the workforce, and the global marketplace. The wines we drink today, particularly white wines, have little in common with traditional wines one hundred years ago.

Flash Détente (FD), a process newly arrived from Europe, Australia, and South America, where it has been well entrenched for a decade, is now rapidly reshuffling the California wine industry's deck of cards and dealing whole new hands for all players.

"It's a gift from the gods," beams savvy Monterey grape kingpin Steve McIntyre, who installed a Pera unit in 2010 at the Monterey Wine Company. "A real game changer for growers. Now we've got people interested in merlot blocks we thought we'd have to graft over."

"I must admit, I was surprised. I didn't know pinot juice could be so luscious," says UC Davis enologist Kay Bogart. "If you can keep the Knott's Berry Farm boysenberry pie aromas, you'll make a killing.

Amazing." Kay is describing the aggressively fruity aromas that the French refer to as "amylic," also a marked quality of carbonic maceration. Amylic aromas are particularly pronounced in wine made by fermentation of the liquid phase of the Flash Détente process, when skins and seeds are removed prior to fermentation.

"There are so many different variables to consider," says longtime technology guru Barry Gnekow, who works with a Della Toffola Flash Détente unit parked at Lodi Vintners alongside my former partner Rick Jones. "Once you understand all the different ways to adjust the process, it becomes apparent that you can produce a very wide range of styles."

EXTRACTION IN A FLASH

Developed by European fruit processor Aurore and adapted to winemaking by the French research powerhouse INRA in 1993, Flash Détente combines thermo-vinification with flash evaporation (fig. 28). Grape must is heated to 160°–190°F and pumped into a vacuum chamber, which explodes the skins (*détente* means "release"), drawing off vapor and fully extracting skin color, tannin, and flavor while the evaporation cools the must back to ambient temperature. Since 8–12% water is flashed off as steam, musts are concentrated and elevated by about 2° brix if the strip water is not recombined.

Must can then be pressed immediately and fermented as juice ("liquid phase") or, alternatively, fermented on skins and seeds as with traditional reds. Liquid phase reds are easily barrel-fermented, obtaining the same enhancements to body and complexity we are accustomed to seeing in Chardonnays, as well as stabilization of color due to beneficial effects of oak extractives, if the correct wood is chosen (see chapter 4). Other options include prior dejuicing, dwell time at high temperature (controlled by speed of throughput) and cofermentation with unflashed must.

Strip water—the recondensed steam that is drawn off the hot must by vacuum to cool it, comprising 8–12% of the volume—can be recombined or discarded. Any highly volatile odors are stripped out by the steam. Amazingly, with the exception of aromatic varieties, strip water generally does not include much in the way of fruitiness.

For those who want to get just a little bit pregnant, "demi-flash," which uses lower temperatures and less evaporative cooling, is sometimes chosen by novitiates. But when it comes to heat-induced

FIGURE 28. Della Toffola Flash Détente installation capable of processing one truckload per hour.

oxidation, less is more. Since the optimum-activity temperature range for browning enzymes is 110–120°F and formation of the oxidized aroma hydroxyl-methyl furfural maxes at 140°F, the best way to dodge these reactions is to speed through the moderate zone to hot temperatures as quickly as possible. Don't be cool.

LOVE TO WATCH THEM STRIP

Barry and Rick treated me to a range of strip water samples from a wide variety of sources all over California in the 2010 vintage. This was perhaps the most eye-opening tasting of my thirty-eight-year career in wine, for it revealed hidden "terroir" components about which I had previously only speculated. In small wooded vineyards such as those of the Santa Cruz Mountains, for example, I have often sensed aromas of local plants—a topic of open debate on the Internet.

Speculate no more: it's happening. "We call it *air-oir*," says Gnekow. "Eucalyptus, smoke taint, tarweed—we see it all." The amaretto tones from a vineyard adjacent to an almond orchard were unmistakable.

Air-oir sounds utterly charming, and I imagine most winemakers would love to smell the ambient-air contribution that exists in their wines. Indeed, they should be beating down the doors. The shocking news, though, is that much of what's happening is not so good. In one Pinot Noir vineyard located along Highway 12 in Carneros, the diesel exhaust was overwhelming, leading me to speculate about the boutique Cabernet vineyards lining Highway 29 that drink up the fumes from millions of vehicles every year. The renowned austerity of Napa terroir may be nothing more than tourist smog.

"One vineyard behind a truck stop smelled of cooking grease," says Gnekow. "In another, we swore we smelled manure, and sure enough, it was adjacent to a cow pasture. Pure Angus butt—disgusting."

The biggest reason Monterey grower Steve McIntyre loves the Flash? Pyrazine content is lowered to near zero, with concentrated bell pepper aromas appearing in the strip water. If total removal seems extreme, the winemaker has the option of adding back as much as desired. "But they never do," says Gnekow.

WHAT ELSE IS NEW?

Once you get a hammer, everything starts to look like a nail, and Monterey Wine Company has found plenty of other uses for their new darling. In the cold, rainy vintages of 2010 and 2011, having the Flash in place saved the winery's bacon by providing remedies for two additional headaches: underripeness and rot.

Monterey's normally cool climate became in both years impossibly chilly, pushing harvest into a rainy October and November, fighting rot pressures to get anywhere near ripe. But with Flash, even with low-ripeness fruit, it was possible to fully extract anthocyanins normally blocked by pectin, while pyrazines were discarded along with extracted rainwater, with the result of a reconcentration of flavor and color and a substantial brix bump. "Pretty decent wines can be made from marginally ripe Bordeaux varieties," confides Steve.

For grapes suffering from botrytis attack, laccase enzymes, which otherwise would cause uncontrollable browning and destroy anthocyanin pigments, were instantly denatured. Moldy aromas were vacuumed away and unwelcome spoilage organisms pasteurized by heat. But for the Flash, Monterey was headed for an economic disaster, and instead dodged the bullet. Thank you, Santa.

WOULD YOU LIKE TO HEAR OUR MENU SPECIALS?

The biggest choice winemakers should consider is whether, post-Flash, to ferment on the pomace. Although Flashed skins are translucent ghosts, their physical properties make a difference. But more important, seed tannin is not extracted at all into liquid phase fermentations, giving the wines a creepy hollowness that challenges us tradition-steeped old codgers to keep an open mind.

Ferment this same wine on the pomace, however, and the hollowness doesn't happen. The wine is fruity, to be sure, but it possesses a traditional mouthfeel and the fruit is much restrained, a classic demonstration of the postmodern principle of aromatic integration through structure.

For my money, the variety that benefits the most from Flash is syrah. Although well loved by winemakers, growers, and critics for its rich color, complex aromas, ample structure, and soft tannins, Syrah has never made it to prime time with consumers for one simple reason.

It doesn't taste very good.

Syrah does not generally possess a sweet core of fruit. It's a movie with a brilliant cast of supporting actors but no lead character. Flash fixes that by dragging a nice plummy aroma out of the skins and dropping it squarely into the center of the palate. DEE-lish!

SAME OLD SAME OLD

Does Flash, as UC Davis authority Roger Boulton asserts, make all wines taste the same?

Well, yes and no. "An experienced taster can spot a Flash wine easily," says Jones. "There is a characteristic stamp." The earmarks of the process include clean, frankly fruity aromas, absence of vegetal aromas and *airoir* oddities, rich color, fine, soft tannins, and generous mouthfeel. Within the world that Flash creates, however, I believe there is as much interesting variation and probably more diverse regional grape expression than can be achieved with conventional winemaking techniques.

Flash wines *are* very distinctive. The amylic fruitiness they bring forth is not a standard note, as the *nouveau* analogy implies. Nonetheless, in my view, the aromas of Flash wines, while quite a bit more fruity, are not all alike but are instead drawn from a complex orchestra of possibilities every bit as diverse as their conventional counterparts.

When we travel to another country, at first the people seem all the same. But after we linger a while, we see that they are as different from one another as are our neighbors back home, with both groups of people marked by the stamp of their place. In this same way, Flash wines are all marked by certain common characteristics that enable them to reveal differing terroir characteristics with more purity, with or without the optional add-back of *air-oir* aromas.

"Flash wines are cleaner and require less fixing," says Gnekow. "Winemakers are more inclined to let the fruit speak for itself rather than supplementing and masking with oak and other tricks."

Flash is expensive when performed on a small scale. Combine that disincentive with the general anti-manipulation angst felt by small wineries, and the result is a big fat "Only if I have to." As large wineries adopt Flash and small ones do not, the marketplace will experience an acceleration of the division between these two winemaking universes as consumers are offered expanded choices. No doubt much electronic ink will be spilled as the moral imperatives are sorted out in cyberspace.

UNKNOWN COUNTRY

Rick Jones proposes to hand out T-shirts that say on the front, "Yes, we have the Flash," and on the back, "No, we don't have the answers." Guy Noir of our industry, he articulates some of Flash's persistent questions:

1. In healthy musts, how much juice should a winemaker pull off with a dejuicing screen and leave untreated? Are enzymes added back beneficial for hyperoxygenation in whites?
2. What are the effects of high- and low-temperature maceration and of dwell time prior to flashing?
3. Since no method is available for separating skins from seeds, we don't know how important skins are in the fermentation. It may be possible that mechanical seed extraction or pomace milling could provide an add-back material that would replace solids in the fermenter.
4. Absent fermentation on seeds, liquid phase wine color is curiously unstable. No doubt a magical solution will be found, but at present the problem remains unsolved.

TRANSCENDING TRADITION

In 2008, my Appellation America survey of Monterey was titled "That Ain't No Termato—That's My Wine!" I was poking fun at the

Monterey "pyra-noia" because we had just tasted 126 Monterey wines, not a single one of which had a textbook case of the veggies.

But we did see something else. In examining the winegrowing and winemaking practices of Monterey wineries, we saw a preponderance of long hang time, whole berry fermentation, oak chip additions, and other techniques aimed specifically at combating veg.

Like a refugee from a bad marriage, Monterey winegrowers have fixed their focus on a single target for thirty years. Enough, already! If Flash Détente is the magic wand that frees them to explore the positive nuances of their region instead of fighting their own identity, I can't wait.

Flash enables large wineries to provide a rich, generous, fruit-driven style of wine with soft, plush tannins, totally lacking in harshness or vegetal aromas. To the classically trained palate, these are not complete wines. But Steve McIntyre sees possibilities for the emergence of a whole new wine product category to emerge.

There is every reason to believe that a hugely fruit, well-colored, soft, drinkable quaff is precisely what Americans of the Pepsi generations are looking for. Think Arbor Mist Blackberry Merlot, only without the added flavors and sugar. Merlot that tastes like Nouveau Beaujolais on steroids.

"Liquid phase Flash wine," says McIntyre, "represents an opportunity for a whole new kind of wine style that sells at the $12 level." I think he's right. It would not shock me if a decade hence, half the wine we sell is like that.

The advent of Flash Détente is a shot across the bow of the increasingly dysfunctional three-tier system. I anticipate that soft, delicious, generously fruity Flash reds will soon begin to take Safeway by storm. In all probability, a backlash against this trend may increase the American consumer's appetite and political will to get access to the wines of small producers who make "real wine." If one result of this transformational technology is an increased appetite for undoctored wines produced by the large number of small wineries now struggling to gain adherents, then God bless the Flash.

SIZE MATTERS

Della Toffola's 30 tons per hour unit has a minimum lot size of one truckload, and serious price breaks are offered for multiple truck quantities. Not only are small lots more expensive, but they preclude style choices such as partial lot processing. A pilot unit, also by Della

Toffola, can process as little as 1.5 tons, but as with any industrial process, the most reliable results are obtained with full-scale equipment.

Successful, growing mega-wineries throughout the world are implementing Flash for one primary reason: fermentation tank turnover. When you can get maximum extraction in forty-eight hours, capital for tank farm expansion can be delayed and efficiency increased substantially without a hit to product quality.

Flash turns winemaking on its head because a bit of extra tannin is always welcome. I predict that the screw press will make a major comeback in large wineries as a perfect partner for Flash, and we may even see continuous systems for seed tannin extraction to enable liquid phase fermentations that result in wines with more conventional palate framing.

Iconic of the growing division between industrial and artisanal winemaking, Flash Détente currently excludes the small guy and widens the gap between vins d'effort and vins de terroir. A small winery simply can't produce the lip-smackin' delicious product an FD unit cranks out by the carload, any more than a microbrewery can duplicate Budweiser or a small creamery can make Velveeta.

There do exist three- to five-ton commercial units that may take by storm the regions outside California where ripeness, extraction, and rot are the norm and well-funded state programs charged with solving foul weather problems could provide a single machine for their whole region. The development of a three-ton system for midwestern wineries is a high R&D priority for Della Toffola, and their partnership with the Midwest may shortly change the face of winemaking prospects in Middle America.

OF THEE I SING

We Americans should be ashamed of ourselves. Flash Détente has been around for twenty years, and we're just finding out about it. With a table wine industry less than fifty years old, we have become awfully complacent in our old age, and the universities we depend on have lost their gumption.

The U.S. departure from the OIV (Office International de la Vigne et du Vin) was a bonehead move that took us away from the table where technologies are shared. Our universities make little attempt to interface internationally. There is little foreign language literacy among our professors, and even less interest in the practical problems of commercial wineries.

Well, lesson learned. Now that Flash has hit our shores, we may have a lot fewer problems to grouse to the academics about, anyhow.

TAKE-HOME MESSAGES

- Proven technology is recently arrived in California that gives complete control over pyrazines, rot, and color extraction.
- A matrix of winemaking options enables a wide variety of styles, including some novel and compelling ones that may open up large new groups of consumers.
- Tasting strip water reveals a disturbing gallery of aroma defects adsorbed on grapes that end up present in conventional wine.

PART FOUR

Philosophy

Spoofulated or Artisanal?

The faster the scientific advances, the greater the risk of
widening the gap between what we know and what we do.
—Emile Peynaud, 1984

Whatever people in general do not understand, they are
always prepared to dislike; the incomprehensible is always
the obnoxious.
—Letitia E. Landon, *Romance and Reality* (1831)

With some consternation, I have devoted here a chapter to clearing the
air concerning the tired old topic of wine manipulation. This issue
began to be raised in 2000 in a string of articles in which I was interviewed about wine technology. Prior to this, I had found that the few
visitors I received to my remote eyrie were deferential and well behaved.
These folks were different. I found that in their interviews, they were
not particularly good listeners. Many who had come seeking a thirty-
second quote on wine technology were so frustrated by my unexpect-
edly complex point of view that they sometimes lingered for several
days waiting for a line they could snatch out of context and insert in
their preconceived stories.

Because winemakers have a certain celebrity status, our industry, like
Hollywood, is inhabited by two types of scribes, those I call "journalists"—earnest reporters interested in getting at the facts and presenting
a balanced view—and "paparazzi"—sensationalists with little regard
for the facts who don't care if they harm their subject as long as they
can create a media buzz. In Hollywood, maybe this is the price of fame,
but in the wine industry, where we do not seek the limelight and nobody
is in it for the money, I feel that winemakers, all of whom work

extremely hard solely for the love of wine, deserve more respect than these muckrakers customarily dish out.

In this discussion, I don't intend to call anybody out. I'll mention by name only those who have conducted themselves with honor in this debate and deserve mention for it. To aid discussion of this complex and highly charged subject, I'm going to use some analogies with other creative realms: classic cuisine, musicianship, even women's cosmetics.

The articles that resulted from these interviews seemed to me so self-serving and shallow that I simply posted a dozen or so on www .winecrimes.com, a site intended to enable real journalists to read through what the paparazzi had to say. This worked pretty well, and I was able to post alongside them some thoughtful, balanced pieces from several quarters. Little by little, the calls subsided.

Yet nothing persists in America like a terse, provocative sound byte, and I still find myself being asked by consumers, when I describe my work, how I feel about wine manipulation. Apparently, if I'm to be of any use to readers as a window onto the winemaker's perspective, I need to address the reality that a lot of people are not pleased about the winemaking technologies I have introduced and promoted.

Often I read comments on the Internet that wine lovers want to see on wine labels what is being done so they can avoid manipulated wines. Since there is not enough room on a label for such intricate information, certification marks provide such assurances for organic, biodynamic, and kosher wine by proscribing specific practices, but no such mark has ever been proposed for Natural Wine. This peculiar situation, I believe, is related to the large number of disparate factions the movement contains, so that the movement's leaders are unwilling to articulate what it wants for fear of shattering solidarity (see chapter 22). The "M" word by itself is problematic because it has two meanings:

ma·nip·u·la·tion \mə-,nĭp-yə'lā-shən\ *n*. 1 : treatment or operation with or as if with the hands or by mechanical means, especially in a skillful manner. 2 : Shrewd or devious management by artful, unfair, or insidious means, especially to one's own advantage.

I'm going to assume that readers are all in favor of wines made according to definition 1, to wit, handcrafting. Those are not grapes in that glass. As everyone knows, wine is perhaps the most manipulated of all foods, and that's just what we want. Pick 'em, crush 'em, ferment 'em, press 'em, age 'em, bottle 'em, and nobody minds. Those aren't, it seems, offending manipulations.

Indeed, this first definition summons to mind the method that Georgian winemakers have used for thousands of years, in which, still today, a wine is painstakingly racked by hand from one buried clay vessel (qvevri) to another using a long-handled ladle, to the applause and cheers of Natural Wine advocates, for such personal attention is the very essence of the artisanality they worship so lustily.

So I don't think I am going out on a limb when I interpret the desire to avoid manipulation as somehow connected to the moralistic accusations embodied in definition 2. Defensive? Moi? More like puzzled. Like any other winemaking instructor, the point of my writing, teaching, and consulting concerns working with wine in a skillful manner. What, exactly, is unfair or insidious about trying to make wine skillfully? What are the rules I ought not break?

The vitriol that characterizes this debate has the taste of betrayal and broken agreements. I'm going to try to get to the bottom of what those are. I'm confident that we can put enmity behind us once we realize that all the players are good guys who want the same things. Critics and winemakers have hit a stormy patch in a great marriage, and we need to talk before we drive the kids crazy.

In an honest, open debate, this topic would have been well settled years ago. Proponents of the new techniques would present their wines and skeptics would taste them and discuss their reactions. That's what Wolfgang Puck does on TV when he demonstrates *sous vide* technology or freezes cheese with liquid nitrogen. It's fun. But in winemaking, none of this is happening. Unlike the free and open '70s and '80s, today's winemakers are lying low and keeping mum while paparazzi fire live ammo over their heads. Meanwhile, the gap between producers and the most serious wine lovers is widening, because consumers can smell the inauthenticity a mile away.

Before I launch into a discussion of modern winemaking tools, I should, for those who do not know me, articulate my bias. Actually, I have two. The first is as an owner of Vinovation, Inc., a wine production consulting firm I founded in 1992 that until 2008 sold goods, services, machines, and consulting to 1,200 wineries worldwide. Having dedicated myself to improving winemaking, I'm inclined to argue in defense of my approach.

As I explained in chapter 16, I bear some responsibility for the shift in attitude connected with the general rise in alcohol levels in this country. As Tom Wark rightly observed in his daily wine blog *Fermentation*, I have been at the center of the move toward the Big Wine.[1] I certainly don't apologize for my contribution, but it's fair to say that plenty of terrible wines have been made as we flailed around trying to perfect this newly born long suit for New World wines.

Second, I make and sell wine. Since my training is largely French, the niche I've chosen is stylistically Old World. I make Eurocentric, balanced, distinctive, somewhat offbeat wines that share the purpose of presenting alternative styles for California. They are not impact wines. They are, if I may say so, skillfully crafted wines of balance and harmony, each a unique expression of terroir. They age well—perhaps too well, as they take quite some time to come around in the bottle. I enjoy offering wines that show possibilities for California outside the mainstream: Chablis-style Chardonnays, racy Cab Francs, and Loire-style Chenin Blancs aged sur lie. That's pretty confusing to the marketplace, so I'm not likely to grow much. I'd be very pleased if readers of this book decided to try my experiments and judge my success for themselves.

British wine writer Jaime Goode went through my wines in November 2006 and came up with an article that I thought articulated my struggle well. Its title: "The Surprising Juxtaposition of Wine Technology and Natural Wines."[2]

A TIME FOR HEROES

There are plenty of heroes in this story. One is Randy Dunn, who is open in his praise of RO and his condemnation of overripe fruit.[3] Another is Michael Havens, who agreed in 2001, in the interest of consumer education, to have his face plastered all over the *New York Times* as an "outed" micro-ox practitioner.[4] There are some journalist heroes out there, too. Some, such as Jamie Goode, Patrick Matthews, Derrick Schneider, and Pamela Heiligenthal, have supported the politically incorrect view that good wine is good wine and that those who can enhance distinctive terroir expression are welcome to their tools. Others lean toward the conservative view but are tireless, rigorous, and open; here, Eric Asimov and winemaker/blogger Adam Lee of Siduri Wines come to mind.

There are villains as well. Some writers continue to widen the information disconnect between winemakers and wine buffs with all the good-hearted integrity of a Beverly Hills divorce attorney. These writers love to coax winemakers to be open—then nail them. When I started posting the particulars of techniques used for specific wines, it proved helpful in convincing Vinovation's winery clients to explore style options outside the lockstep mainstream, but that openness often made me a target among the media. No points for honesty from this bunch. Since I consider inauthenticity the very heart of the problem, it's ironic to watch critics go for the throat when a winemaker tells the truth.

Likewise, some retailers who have jumped on the bandwagon, dropping wines they liked and that sold well when they discovered they were made by someone willing to be honest about their production methods. More dupes than villains, I guess.

I don't know if the writer for the *Wine Spectator* who started it all in 2001[5]—and continues to rail against technology—has ever tasted my wines, though I sent him a flight. He hasn't returned my calls.

It is time for all players to start being straight. In my opinion, many journalists are disinclined to put their weapons on safety and venture out from their entrenched positions. Ye passionate scribes: I implore you to make a rigorous accounting of your politics, and consider if the wine world might be better off if winemakers could speak freely of their work without attracting fragging from those who claim to revere their craft.

IT'S ALWAYS SUMPIN'

It's the downside of bounty. Unlike in my salad days, a flat-out crappy bottle of wine today is quite rare. The problems that haunted wine lists twenty years ago—wines that were oxidized, sour, vinegary, or just incredibly funky—are scarce today. But the science and practical expertise that eradicated these problems sowed their own generation of complaints.

It's a timeless irony. The problems we complain of today are actually children of the solutions we found to yesterday's problems. Our *malaise du jour:* much of today's good clean wine is pretty doggone boring.

The Good, the Bad, and the Funky

No doubt about it: 95% of the wine we drink today is supplied by 2% of wineries—mostly big corporate outfits, commodity McWine in a dozen expected styles—with scientific precision and industrial efficiency. For the most part, large-winery marketing departments and winemakers who work for them are astoundingly responsive to market demands. Most wine is a commodity that sells based on very specific parameters that have been honed over the past couple of decades. The simple fact is that unusual wines, wines of distinction, don't sell very easily, so the mega-boutiques don't waste time and money making them. For them, producing "interesting" wine equals fiscal suicide.

The remaining 5% of sales is divided among thousands of small niche producers—we're talking about 98% of wineries, whose main marketing challenge is just the opposite, to create an honest point of distinction. It may be an extrinsic strategy: what's on the bottle—a cute dog on the label, a memorable tasting room experience, a tony pedigree, or some other distinction unrelated to the bottle's contents. But often as not, it's intrinsic: what's in the bottle—a distinctive style that builds a following over time. In terms of label count, wine in America is almost entirely composed of distinctive wines of place. But these do not appear at your local Safeway.

Anyone who hasn't tried it can't possibly imagine how much work is required to establish a new brand in national distribution today. In truth, there is almost no receptivity for a new player outside the norm. You would think that all that web-kvetching about terroir would show up in the marketplace in a way a guy could use to build a brand.

In your dreams, maybe. It's strange to spend all day trying to shoehorn a damned good Eurocentric Cabernet Franc or Chablis-styled Chardonnay onto crowded retail shelves and then come home to an Internet forever moaning about sameness and "anywhereness." We small winery guys keep wondering, when are you terroiristes gonna quit yer yackin' and start spending some money?

Selling Your Vision

What most small producers long for is instant celebrity. A 90+ Parker score is like winning the lottery. Like actors, musicians, and pro baseball pitchers, a select few are chosen for stardom. But as with ghetto kids desperately honing their hiphop routines or their three-point shots, very few who bank on being "discovered" avoid disappointment.

What's left is, to me, the fun part of the industry. Life on the D list is where most actors, musicians, and small wineries scratch out a living. We do it by making wines that are always more interesting than those of our corporate counterparts. It's a people business. I gain my clientele one person at a time. It's about relationships and shoe leather.

When you make your living one-on-one, you mustn't fib to folks. They can tell, and that means you're wasting your time. These days, consumers are assaulted by a constant barrage of hype, and only genuine, authentic passion can break through. To create a lasting loyalty, you gotta come from the heart.

But nowadays, being straight with wine lovers has become a dicey proposition.

In the '70s, the entire California wine industry (less than a tenth its current numbers) was famous for its spirit of openness and collaboration, with winemakers forever swapping brix and pH data and even consumers helping us unravel Bacchus's secrets. Since nobody really knew what they were doing, we were all actively engaged in learning from one another.

That openness substantially subsided the day in 1992 that Jess Jackson successfully sued his own departing winemaker, Jed Steele, for breach of confidentiality. Today's small guys, artisans of every conceivable stripe packed in cheek by jowl, live in a tougher town. None of them are in it for the money. For ego, for adventure, for artistic or financial freedom, sure, but nobody is getting rich. Staying alive is more like it. Making the best wine you can and staying out of trouble. Shrewd but hardly insidious.

Trouble in Paradise

Is it all good wine? Not on your life. But the proliferation of well-made wines is broader than ever before. Like books, like music, there is something for everybody, though nothing suited to all. Widespread experimentation with new styles and techniques means some wrong turns, for sure, but that's part of the fun. If they're smart, John and Jane Consumer will draw on a passionate and dedicated retailer to sort through this huge and complex menu through a personalized dialogue tailored to their tastes and budget. With the broadest availability and the highest quality standard of all time, any consumer or critic who complains about the current state of the wine market is pretty darned hard to please.

Beleaguered Buyers

Retailing, on the other hand, isn't an easy job. The average small wine shop carries between two hundred and a thousand wines. That's less than one percent of the market. It's hard work to taste and reject ninety-nine wines out of a hundred. For sommeliers with a list of thirty wines, it's worse: you get to pick maybe one wine in a thousand. I've been at this game full-out since '72, and I still can't order wine intelligently in a restaurant. It's simply impossible keep up.

COOKING UP GOODNESS

In today's ridiculously competitive marketplace, winemakers are squeezed hard to come up with stand-out, knock-your-socks-off, fall-out-of-your-chair-good wines. In pursuit of this laudable goal, some go too far and offer wines that shout a bit too loudly for attention.

Somebody recently coined a word for this kind of wine: "spoofulated." Overmanipulation. Fiddling around with a wine to pump it up, score ratings, and wow consumers at the expense of its natural terroir expression. The issue at hand is the extent to which winemakers, or any other chefs, are entrusted to protect the natural experience of place and lay aside cheap thrills.

Winemaking isn't a science. It's just a branch of cooking where we use a calendar instead of a timer—the ultimate slow food. Putting something distinctive and visceral on the table is the challenge that every chef deals with daily. As in all cooking, distinctive terroir expression suffers from overspicing. That doesn't mean all cooking is bad. You just need to have respect for the native flavors of your raw materials.

But what does all this have to do with tools? A recurring theme in the complaints about spoofulation has to do with recently devised, weird-sounding technologies that are somehow connected to this overmanipulation syndrome. Practices like micro-oxygenation (see chapter 3) and reverse osmosis (see chapters 16 and 18) are clearly under suspicion, though just why remains a mystery. From a health point of view, the careful exposure of wine to air seems about as harmless a treatment as one can imagine in a world where nobody seems to mind that French Bordeaux and Burgundies are routinely spiked with beet sugar. Why should they? It works.

When perfectly sound wines are deemed deficient because they don't fit our statistical consumer profile or lack sufficient impact, then the nip and tuck is as tragic as breast implants. Doctoring supposed defects by sneaking in mega-purple, residual sugar, or gobs of oak certainly robs wine of its distinctive characters.

Are these fiddlings detectable by the consumer or even the expert critic? Well, sometimes. I remember my first great wine love, the 1970 Clerc Milon. I snagged two cases and set into a bottle every month or so. By the twenty-fourth cork I couldn't bear the stuff, and that's how I learned about the excess of the barrel. Everybody loves vanilla—that's deep in our DNA—but eventually you gag on it. I came to realize that I'd fallen for all flash and no substance.

It's a well-known cheap trick. Good critics and retailers try to save their vulnerable clients from such blunders. But what about the truly artful dodge that fools the pros? It's not nice to fool Mother Nature, and I suspect that the invisible fake is the most irksome to our intrepid wine police.

HONESTY MATTERS MORE THAN PROCESS

Somehow the myth has gotten circulated that less is more. But the paradox is that sometimes doing "nothing" requires a lot of manipulation and technology. Sushi is a case in point. What could be a purer expression of raw materials? Yet to deliver fresh, unspoiled fish to your plate takes considerable art, skill, and technology. Does exposing wine to oxygen involve more or less manipulation than keeping it in stainless steel and blanketing it with inert gas?

Put yourself in the winemaker's shoes. Winemakers are under tremendous pressure to perform unrealistic feats, and they want a complete set of tools to please consumers every time. Aren't you just supposed to make delicious, wholesome, interesting wine?

Apparently not. Very vocal elements of the gatekeeper community want also to control the means by which we achieve that goal. It's not what's in the bottle that matters, it seems, but whether it got there by methods a wine critic or retailer approves of.

Actually, that doesn't sound unreasonable. More than ever, consumers need professional guidance if they're to make sense of the dizzying array of wines available in today's market. Real pros study tirelessly to develop palate training for the baffling assortment of genres against which all wine is judged.

When winemaking practices change, there can be trouble. Hidebound traditionalism is useful to critics in sorting the good from the great, but it's hard to keep score when the rules keep changing. Oh please, Lord, not a new playbook! It's only fair that any new technique needs to pass the test of time. Extended hang time, a new experiment of the past two decades, is an example of a technique that has revealed its downside in the cellar: it may bring out the fruitiness in young wines, but it also causes them to fall apart early.

Nevertheless, we are able often to move ahead together. When gate-keepers support change in the wine industry, it can happen quickly and smoothly. The transition to screw caps, as untraditional a transformation as one could name, is going swimmingly because the press has made sure that every retailer and sommelier understands the need and there is no opposition except among consumers who miss the "pop." Done deal.

But faced with increasing pressure to garner scores and maintain consistency, wine production in the past twenty years has responded by developing a great number of new tools and tricks that have not been so graciously received. Winemaking is just a form of cooking, the ultimate slow food, and one could point to precisely similar innovations in restaurants, where sous vide, foam technology, and liquid nitrogen are now the rage. But a crucial difference is that in winemaking, we left the media out of the loop. Wines got way better, thanks very much. By magic, folks are left to suppose.

As a result of this disconnect, some critics find these new methods irritating. I think they're mostly annoyed that recent technical progress wasn't done more openly. I don't blame them. The industry's character has become much more secretive over the past couple of decades for a number of reasons that I'll explore below. In the past two decades, the policy has been don't ask, don't tell. Now a cycle of distrust has driven innovative winemakers farther underground as critics' complaints become more shrill.

CHANGES

Much of this discord can be attributed to a series of sweeping transitions occurring simultaneously, altering winemaking's context utterly. Here are six.

1. Increased Competition

In California like nowhere else, winemaking innovations and philosophies can take root very rapidly, manifesting themselves in successful brands that can come into being and gain global acceptance almost overnight. The technical and economic aspects of style pioneering are inseparable, and their interplay is the essence of winemaking. Particularly in the New World, the struggle to establish new brands and vineyards depends on rapid quality development in order to compete against long-established European benchmarks.

When I was retailing in the 1970s, there were fewer than two hundred wineries in California, and Jackson's Wines and Spirits, an East Bay chain where I cut my teeth, carried just about everything there was. Today that's impossible. There are now almost four thousand wineries in California, as many outside the state, and tens of thousands of imports. In 2012, the Federal Label Approval count topped 160,000. Even the largest selections can include only one wine in fifty available. The great Jack Davies of Schramsberg told me back in 1980, "Clark, knockin' 'em dead is a dyin' art." I don't care if you're the top cult Cab in Napa—now you sweat for every advantage you can scrape up.

Paradoxically, more choices for retailers means *less* diversity on the shelf. That's what I said. In the 1970s, if you wanted a thousand domestic offerings on your shelf, you simply bought everything there was. Today you can pick and choose to hit a narrow taste profile that you think your customers are looking for: the expected Chardonnay, the expected Merlot, and so on. This is analogous to the AM radio dial; whereas in the past one station carried the full range of popular music in all styles, today each one specializes in a single genre. This is possible because there is so much to choose from. This "diversity paradox," and not wine technology, is the principal source of sameness in stores. The proof is that much greater diversity is out there than ever before, but you have to go find it.

2. Technological Revolution

Intense competition has created an eager audience among winemakers for new quality improvement capabilities. Coincidentally, rapid technical advances in medicine, food engineering, and other fields have provided new tools at a rapid rate. Just like doctors, who must study hard to keep apace of the underlying functions, benefits, and risks associated with emerging advances, winemakers can sometimes barely keep up, let alone school the press.

3. Paradigm Shift in Enology

This technical avalanche hit the industry just when a conceptual revolution was taking place within enology from modern to postmodern. The increasing sophistication and competitiveness of the twenty-first-century wine marketplace imposes demands on our winemaking skills well beyond those of cleanliness and drinkability. The soulfulness of *grands vins de garde* derives from the structure of the wine more than its composition. The capability of fine tannin colloids to integrate aromatic components of vegetal, oak, and microbial sources in defiance of dilute aqueous predictions is now being recognized.

In addition, oxygenation's capacity to refine structure as well as to measure and to alter wines' reductive strength has revealed its central role in enology, with tremendous implications for grape growing and wine aging. It has turned out that reductive phenomena cannot be fully explained without also taking into account the effect of viticultural principles, including phenolic transformations during ripening and the effect of organic farming practices on wine's natural immune system.

The conceptual shift that is the subject of this book makes things all the more confusing and difficult to explain when winemakers are barely able to grasp the new conceptual framework and incorporate it into their work.

4. The New Consumerism: A Social Revolution in Ethics

The Internet, with its unparalleled access to information, has enabled a whole generation of aficionados to engage in an intensive discussion on every aspect of wine. In their wonderful book *Wikinomics: How Mass Collaboration Changes Everything,* Don Tapscott and Anthony Williams characterize the imperatives of the new consumer. "Rather than being passive recipients of mass consumer culture, the Net Gen spend time searching, reading, scrutinizing, authenticating, collaborating and organizing," they write. "They typically can't imagine a life where citizens didn't have the tools to think critically, exchange views, challenge, authenticate, verify or debunk."[6] They tend to value openness, collaboration, and collective social responsibility. Not a good crowd to try to hide from. And they matter. Unlike Generation X, the Millennium Generation is discovering and buying a lot of wine. The blogger penchant for openness and frank, passionate discussion has led them to focus on good guys and bad guys. This is a disaster for old-school obfuscation but an opportunity for winemakers willing to talk straight.

5. Failure Rate for Technology

In contrast to a century ago, when people of all ages were gung-ho for "progress," today folks are increasingly suspicious of new technologies. You can't blame them. There's plenty of evidence in our culture that technology corrupts natural beauty. Don't get me started. Our lives are continuously violated by automated telemarketing, junk e-mail, and cable TV pop-up ads. Our quaint old downtown shops are now almost entirely replaced by cookie-cutter strip malls, identical the world over. And there's not much room for a Fred Astaire or Noel Coward in today's Hollywood, which has pretty much settled on the high-tech Big Film as its specialty, the same old retooled plot featuring explosions and mayhem having proved a more reliable box office draw than virtuosity, original dialogue, and story line. California's pursuit of Big Wine (see chapter 16) seems to follow suit.

It makes me mad. Let's beat up the next winemaker we come across. After all, wine should be the One Pure Thing, stomped by virgins and untouched by science. Osmosis-shmozmosis. Micro-ox my wine, I rearrange yo' face. These are the innocent passions of the media-spawned wine newbies, and God love them for it.

But the problem isn't the tools we use. The ticky-tacky houses in Pete Seeger's song don't all look just the same because of the hammers and saws used to build them but because they were banged out fast and cheap for a one-size-fits-all market mentality. Tools aren't the issue. Who hasn't ruined breakfast with a microwave? But does that mean Thomas Heller at the French Laundry shouldn't be allowed to own one? Countless great films attest to the value of video cameras, yet cable is mostly junk, because junk is cheap to make and it sells.

6. Critiquing the Critics

Critical wine review has also undergone a metamorphosis since the days of openness. The old guard critics were friends to the industry and played an important role as popularist connectors, a role that I have tried to emulate in my own reviews at Appellation America. Sadly symptomatic of the distrust that has infected wine journalism in our times, their friendliness became a source of scandal when consumers were made aware that these ambassadors accepted the odd lunch from wineries they reviewed.

The 1980s saw the introduction of a more lucrative business model, one in which Robert Parker, the *Wine Spectator,* and the *Connoisseur's Guide* established their credibility by peppering their issues with the occasional damning score or downturned glass. Violence sells, be it pro sports, prime-time TV, or wine reviews.

Thrashing and bashing has long been the province of food and theater critics. It is a peculiar imbecility of our culture that the willingness to go for the kill shot is somehow perceived as a hallmark of objectivity. In point of fact, mean-spirited sensationalism carries a bias far more insidious than the patronization of yore, because like a good attorney, the journalist-provocateur sees no obligation to present facts inconvenient to his case. Like the nightly news, today's wine blasts seek more to alarm than to inform.

SAMENESS

A common claim among today's scribes is that technology makes wines taste the same. Wine technology fall guy that I am, I can scarcely have a conversation with anybody in the trade without this issue emerging. I think my own wines prove otherwise. But when I'm open about the new tools I've employed, concerns immediately surface about eradicating distinctive terroir expression.

In a way, they are right. Technology has certainly robbed us of the spoiled wines we regularly encountered in the '70s. These were certainly (gag) more distinctive and varied: high VA, stuck fermentations, malolactic in the bottle, geranium tone, and aldehydes were well-known benchmarks we almost never see today. Darn.

Believe it or not, there are some very vocal proponents of imbalance in the name of naturalness. Alice Feiring comments in a recent *New York Times* post, "Call me a silly girl, but if it was a hot year I want to taste the heat. A wet one? I want to taste it. High acidity? Low acidity? Give me the best a winemaker can do. A fine winemaker can always make something fascinating. Vintage subtleties are part of the wine passion. I do not want 'corrected' wine."[7]

I ran into Alice recently at the First Annual Qvevri Symposium in the Khakheti region of Georgia, and I asked what she thought of a particular Chinuri done in qvevri. She said she found it "a little hot." She was right, but the observation surprised me. If you advocate for, say, no pesticides, you need to go beyond ignoring the apples with spots; you need to actively look for them at the store, pick them out, buy and eat them, leaving the more perfect ones for others less enlightened. If you advocate against smoothing vintage to vintage and claim to want to taste what nature provides, then you should overlook, even treasure, minor imperfections of balance.

In the real world, of course, this doesn't happen. Quality in the bottle comes first, Natural comes second. Any winemaker needing to feed her family had better do both. In practice, this means that uncompromising

Natural Wine is made mostly by trust-funders, and in tiny quantities. The way to support wine diversity is to get in your Prius and go find your local vintner, whether you're in Sandusky, Ithaca, Charlottesville, or Des Moines. I'm afraid that more the norm is to hit the organic section at Dean and Deluca, then go home and grouse about sameness on the Internet.

Eric Asimov also takes it for granted that less is more when it comes to artisanal wines. As he puts it, "The conflict . . . comes with winemakers who claim to believe that their wares are art, who say they believe in terroir and all the associations that go along with wines that convey a sense of place. These wines ought to be made naturally, without major technological reshaping. They are not intended to appeal to the broad populace, but to be distinctive."[8]

My favorite corollary of Murphy's Law states that "nothing is impossible for the man who doesn't have to do it himself." The real truth is that wines, and I mean all wines, become distinctive through artifice. That's what winemakers do, don't you know. Asimov's words simply have no meaning for a winemaker. How are we to know what constitutes Natural Wine–making and what qualifies as "major technological reshaping"?

Winemakers must not abandon the moral high ground to nonpractitioners. Rules from the uninitiated are more cynical than reverent. These men and women who actually give their lives to making wine are my colleagues, my clients, and my friends, and they deserve more respect from their supposed fans. They generally agonize, quite privately, a lot more about process than armchair critics are in any position to appreciate.

Like a pop singer, you gotta balance self-expression against what sells. Screwballs like me buck the system, trying to make a go of it with fringe experiments like Faux Chablis and sulfite-free Roman Syrah— fortunately not my day job. Winemakers are not acquisitive souls, but they do have bills to pay, and generally have dug themselves sizable financial holes. How to make a small fortune in the wine business? Start with a large one.

To some extent, we all end up chickening out. Just to pay the bills, we are sometimes reduced to kicking out on the side a White Zinfandel or the Basic Napa Cabernet that tastes just like the rest. The reality is that winemaking choices are ruled by a democracy in which people vote with dollars.

Heads up, ye geeks: hard-core wine buffs are disadvantaged in this contest because they have no product loyalty. They like to sample a different wine every day, so they don't support brands very well even when they love them. I am one of those people, so I speak from experience. Sip, smile, and on to the next thing. If you want your voice to count, you must enroll your less adventuresome friends who just want to buy good wine by the case.

Even at its leanest, the transformation from grapes to grand vin is hands down the most manipulative of cooking processes. Like any chef, the artisanal winemaker is charged with transforming raw groceries into an offering that displays their special attributes to best advantage. Distinctive flavor expression comes first, but the outcome, not the tools, are the issue, provided the winemaker knows what he's doing.

In my view, until we focus on ends instead of means, we won't make much progress toward naturalness. Banning the steady-cam won't make film more artistic. In fact, somebody please send one to Jon Nossiter—I'm still a little seasick from Mondovino. Banning black mascara from the shelves at Walgreen's wouldn't convince women to present their natural, unpainted selves in public. The real enemy is artlessness, not evil machines and methods. Lackluster wine is just bad cooking.

When Alan Goldfarb came to interview me,[9] he articulated an interesting distinction. I showed him my Faux Chablis, a French-style Chardonnay bottled at 12.9% alcohol with good minerality and distinctive aromatic expression. I also showed him the wine prior to alcohol adjustment at 14.8% alcohol—bitter, hot, and aromatically *null*. He remarked quite rightly that the alcohol-reduced wine had truer terroir expression but that the unadjusted wine, which he did not prefer (few do), was more authentic. Bingo.

This is the heart of the Natural Wine quandary. What matters most, terroir expression or authenticity? If authentic wines were actually jumping off the shelves, winemakers would be more inclined to sleep in and let the wine make itself. But artlessness is not, by itself, a turn-on. I find for the most part that consumers are more concerned with what's in the bottle than with the winemaker's methods. But okay, there is an element that does care about process, and these folks deserve the facts.

RULING ON THE RULES

Whatever importance the niche currently has, winemakers would love to tap into the Natural Wine movement as a game with rules—a specialty like certified organic or kosher wine. Right now everybody's saying, "Yeah, sure, I'm natural, I do the minimum," but there are no standards, no teeth. Kosher rules may be completely nuts, but by God, they are written down, right there in the Torah: goyim may not look upon the wine. Working with two rabbis on a kosher project was a laugh riot as I wrapped duct tape around those clear plastic hoses to prevent my infidel eyes from seeing the wine. But hey—it's in the book.

Natural Wine doesn't have this clarity of definition, and that has turned every producer into a bullshit artist.

Alice Feiring had the grace to supply me with her tentative personal list of proscriptions for Natural Wine–making, which I think reasonably represents the position of many concerned citizens. In "AF-approved" wines, these are the elements that matter:

- Wines made from grapes planted on interesting soils and climates, not farmed chemically, irrigated, or picked at over ripeness
- No added yeast or nutrients
- No enzymes
- No bacteria
- No added tannin
- No added chemicals
- No wood "product" (wood is used for *élevage,* NOT for flavor)
- No acidification
- No chaptalization
- No alcohol adjustment
- NOTHING should be added that is not from the grape itself
- No texture manipulation (MOX)
- No reverse osmosis (unless needed to 'save' a vintage)
- Sulfur used in the minimum, preferably from natural sources [I assume she means sulfur dioxide]

Given the financial crunch, there are surely some winemakers who would live with these rules, though I will not be among them. Let's work toward a certification mark for Alice's fellow travelers. Then we could get some economics going. Do X, get money Y. This formula, winemakers understand.

The notion that restricting winemakers' options will force them to make better wine certainly seems silly on its face. Yet consider the sonnet and the haiku, two of the most restrictive, and highest, forms of poetry.

FAMILIARITY BREEDS COMPLACENCY

The strange thing about Alice's list is the omissions: electricity, stainless steel, refrigeration, inert gas, sterile filtration. None of them traditional; post–World War II innovations all. Nobody argues that pumping over is better than punching down, or that pumped transfers are superior to gravity feed. These are conveniences, not quality improvements. Why isn't the Internet full of criticism of these powerful and dangerous technologies?

The reason is simple: it's because they're familiar. New tools are always obnoxious, while the familiar always seems safe. Then you find out that margarine is poison and butter is good for you. We all grew up with electricity, and we've lost touch with how truly weird it really is. Yet it changed every aspect of winemaking and empowered many truly ill-considered practices that persist today. Our kitchens are full of stainless steel, and we think of it as inert, harmless. But it's an absolute barrier to oxygen and to microbial equilibrium. Does this protect wine or stifle its development? It sure as heck isn't traditional!

After a while we get used to things. What could have been scarier in nineteenth-century France than the introduction of isinglass? *Sacrebleu*—throw fish bladders in the wine? But today this practice is considered *très chic*—isinglass is the finest of fining agents, reserved for those who care enough to spend the very most. Then again, in the past ten years we've begun to question the whole notion of fining with animal products. A skillful winemaker looks for more tannin, not less; more bricks to build the structure. As Randall Grahm reports his mantra: "I will fear no tannin."

The weirdness factor is a lousy yardstick. We live in very odd times, and the things we consider normal today are pretty damn peculiar by any traditional standard. And not necessarily for the better. Personally, I don't think it's healthy that we spend all our waking hours in bright spaces, be it sunlight or electric light. I believe the mind needs the restful moodiness that firelight and starlight offer and that all humans enjoyed in their evening hours until a hundred years ago. Weirdness is a slippery slope: faxes, CDs, laptops, and iPods have gone from weird to familiar to boring in a brief moment. Today's winemaking innovations will do the same. Indeed, for the lion's share of winemakers, that transition is already complete, so we simply don't share the consumer's panic about them.

The information gap between winemakers and critics is not a bad thing. Critics are not supposed to have the depth of winemaking expertise required of practitioners. They couldn't do their job well if they did. Instead, they are supposed to represent the consumer and approach wines with a beginner's mind. But they need to realize that this leaves them in a tenuous position to pass judgment on techniques.

WHERE'S THE BEEF?

In an information vacuum, you'd think the press would reserve judgment. Inflammatory rhetoric ain't helping the situation, because winemakers just duck and cover. Me, I'm on trial on two counts: alcohol adjustment (via reverse osmosis) with malice aforethought and microoxygenation in the first degree.

Charitably, I could opine that Ms. Feiring's characterization of reverse osmosis filtration as producing "sludge" simply reveals that she doesn't understand what RO does.[10] Think it through. Wineries pay Vinovation to turn 2,500 wines a year into sludge? Not. RO simply relieves their wines of obnoxious levels of alcohol. Where's my Medal of Honor? In this same information vacuum, Alice's beloved "natural" Burgundies are routinely beet-sugared to the same 13+ % alcohol balance, without obligation to report it to her. Would you?

This situation is no scandal. I am here to tell you that the adjustment of alcohol is as valuable and as trivial as adjusting the salt in a soup. Winemakers have a right, and perhaps an obligation, to make use of this tool when it makes for better wine. When the French add beet sugar for this purpose, which they do in approximately 40% of classified Bordeaux and Burgundy wines, they are not excoriated, and neither should we be for practicing filtration to harmlessly remove alcohol. In this, surely, we are on higher ethical terroir than Dr. Chaptal with his secret additive. Given the four-figure market for First Growths and Grand Crus, there is little chance that French wines will ever be required to come clean on their labels by stating, "Contains Beet Sugar."

And that's okay. Chaptal was no devil, and French wines are better because of him. Similarly in the New World, I believe that most consumers are quite happy to have properly ripe flavors with balanced alcohol. So are most winemakers. So shoot me.

PUTTING IT ALL IN CONTEXT

Randall Grahm in Jamie Goode's *The Science of Wine* makes a distinction between the moral imperatives of the Old and New Worlds: "If a producer makes a *vin d'appellation* then there is an implicit contract that he or she enters into, effectively promising to produce a wine of some degree of *typicité*, which I suppose would also include the characteristics of the vintage. If that producer utilizes certain techniques to wipe out vintage characteristics, even though he or she is perhaps producing a wine that most punters would prefer, I believe that winemaker is acting in bad faith. In the New World, where experimentation is encouraged and expected, the prime directive is to make the best wine."[11]

There was a time, now long past, when Europe was a laboratory chock-full of experimentation with new styles. The result was a whole series of extreme spoofulations such as concentration through hang time and rot, barrel aging (with its triple threat of foreign flavoring, oxygenation, and reverse osmosis concentration, for the skin of a barrel is an RO filter), spirits fortification, fining with animal products, lees contact, in-bottle fermentation, chaptalization, and on and on. The traditional wines we now venerate were yesterday's high-tech shockers: Amarone, Sauternes, Port, Sherry, Bordeaux, Champagne. Good for them. God save us, for one example, from the grapes of Champagne vinified *au naturel*.

Now it's the New World's turn to contribute some innovations, which so far are very modest by comparison. And yes, we're making some blunders in our first days—petroleum agriculture, excessive hang time, getting lost in theories and numbers—which the market will sort out. But mostly we're making such good wine that there is little of substance to complain about. What has not manifested itself is a distribution system to connect unusual and interesting wines, distinctive wines of place, to interested buyers. Nor has an interest in local wines developed in the U.S. such as has long been established in Europe.

THE POLITICS OF COSMETICS

A shockingly good read that bears on our subject is *Beauty Secrets: Women and the Politics of Appearance,* by Wendy Chapkis.[12] In this insightful collection, women of every description—from glam girls to bikers to dwarves to mastectomy survivors—grapple with what they can show and what the world will accept, just as we do with our wines. "Mommy, why do you have a mustache?"

I think I speak for most men that, on the one hand, we are philosophically on the side of come-as-you-are. Still, for myself, I not only support a woman's right to choose her looks, but I'm also aware of the public pressures to conform that the female gender experiences. If cosmetics are to be used, I'd say the prime directive is invisibility. And that's the principle that guides my winemaking. But more often than I comfortably admit, I really enjoy the outwardly spoofulated bustière and spiked heels of an overripe Amador Zin on steroids.

I think there is room in this world for all these choices to make an appearance. Natural Wine lovers have no cause to fear that centrism will eradicate their world. Nobody is dying out there because of wine manipulation. What's missing is honesty, and I assure you that a lot more of that would emerge if we would all just relax.

Full disclosure has until quite recently been a difficult thing for even the most sincere winemaker to manage within the space limitations of a backlabel. But technology has newly born solutions for this, too, and as we shall see in chapter 22, I have a plan.

TAKE-HOME MESSAGES

- Recent circumstances have conspired to cast winemakers in a more insidious light than they deserve concerning new technologies.
- Critics have ignored the real problems associated with less recent innovations.
- To restore our tradition of candor and openness, consumers will need to be brought up to speed on recent changes in winemaking philosophy.
- A certification mark for Natural Wine can provide the assurances its advocates desire.

Science and Biodynamics

The Limits of Rationalism

Louis Pasteur's theory of germs is a ridiculous fiction.
—Pierre Pachet, professor of physiology,
University of Toulouse, 1872

The same modern science that ushered in an era of sound winemaking has left us in the tall grass when it comes to producing soulful, transformative wine styles to excite today's competitive market. Modern agriculture has also left many winegrowers dissatisfied regarding the dangers that chemicals may present to the worker and the environment.

Postmodern winemaking respects the fundamental mysteries of nature and the human soul. Excellence sometimes requires us to operate outside the shallow waters currently illuminated by science, leading us into territory where formulas fail.

Varietal purity and sterile bottling may be fine for a Riesling, but you need more game than that to play in the Cabernet big leagues. We move into the shadows in three degrees. Some phenomena are merely obscure; we know the questions but not the answers. In other areas, we have not developed language to articulate the right questions. Finally, in some important areas, there may be no answers; organized knowledge may be fundamentally unobtainable.

We feel our way along. Newcomers to postmodern methods are often disturbed by our high reliance on the human palate over lab-generated numbers. Because we lack the tools to measure aspects that loom large for us—reductive strength, minerality, or colloid shapes, for example—a strictly analytical approach cannot today succeed. We know what the issues are. We just haven't conquered them.

In other cases, entire fields of scientific study are yet to be developed. Examples include the geometry of emotion,[1] the study of interactions within complex systems,[2] the nonanalytical chemistry necessary to investigate the diversity created by phenolic polymerization (see chapter 6), and the study of wine cognition.

Finally, I for one believe that there exist areas of fundamental mystery for which science can never provide useful answers. Theory can prescribe musical chords but cannot explain why a major chord is cheerful and a minor chord is melancholy. Yet we all agree that it is obviously so.

Every high school student knows the historical roots of science's battle against superstition and mythology. Ever since Galileo we have grown increasingly suspicious of myth and accustomed instead to testable, verifiable assertions.

But we are kidding ourselves. The slice of experience within our grasp is small. Winemakers need daily to delve into the shadowy realms where soulfulness hangs out, and a reliance on rationality bars access to much of our gut experience. We do our best artistic work when we are able to perceive without understanding.

Isaac Newton himself said, "I do not know what I may appear to the world, but to myself I seem to have been only like a boy playing on the sea-shore, and diverting myself in now and then finding a smoother pebble or a prettier shell than ordinary, whilst the great ocean of truth lay all undiscovered before me."[3]

Instinct, patient observation, and pragmatic trial and error have always guided pioneers in both science and art. Theory comes later, and is really just a device for organizing our findings, masquerading as explanation. To navigate uncharted realms, we must often let go of the comforting props of plausibility, theory, and statistical testing.

The advent of Biodynamics is a great case in point. It is plain from Stuart Smith's lively online forum, BiodynamicsIsaHoax.com, that the subject boils a lot of blood on both sides.[4] Just as the ACLU saw fit to defend the rights of skinheads to march and as flag burners challenge Americans' depth of commitment to the principle of free speech, so Biodynamics tests our true mettle as trained scientists.

A disturbing number of great minds representing some of our most established wine brands appear to have, well, totally lost it. Never mind Tony Coturri and Randall Grahm and other fringe elements. What has possessed sane businesspeople such as Maison Chapoutier, the Benziger Family, and Jim Fetzer to bury the horn?

In any scientific inquiry, the first step is the hardest: admitting that we don't know what's going on. As Einstein put it, "If we knew what it was we were doing, it would not be called research, would it?"

My goal in this chapter is not to defend Biodynamics. It sounds nuts to me. But so does string theory in particle physics. Instead, I'd like to talk about what it means to behave like a real scientist in any time of uncertainty.

Several approaches to validating or debunking Biodynamics seem worth looking at:

1. Assessing its historical foundations
2. Conducting controlled comparative experiments
3. Evaluating product quality
4. Assessing long-term survivability

In addition to empirical testing, science has always relied heavily on the credentials and integrity of researchers. Heavy hitters are always taken more seriously. When Nobel Prize–winning chemist Linus Pauling told us to take more vitamin C, we did—simply taking his word for it. But what of Rudolph Steiner's credentials?

DUBIOUS ORIGINS

Maybe Biodynamics' short-term survival doesn't really count as evidence of its validity. After all, winegrowing is more fertile ground for extreme experimentation than most other realms of agriculture. Not only does an interesting story boost marketing, but any actual quality improvements easily compensate for yield reductions.

Biodynamics founder Rudolf Steiner does have a track record that can be examined: he started the Waldorf Schools. Whether you like the approach or not, the Waldorf system has withstood the test of time. Critics of Biodynamics usually prefer to attack Steiner's specific credentials as an agronomist. This doesn't take much effort, since he had no farming experience, and there is no evidence that he conducted experiments to back up his theory and methodology.

But that doesn't prove that his system doesn't work. Steiner's ideas did not grow and thrive based on their innate sensibility. Biodynamic viticulture got started well after World War II, some fifty years after Steiner's death, and I think it is fair to say that their reinsertion was more romantic than scientific.

But this means nothing. It's not as if any truly rational system of farming exists today. The sustainability of conventional farming is in serious question, and the motives and methodologies of Monsanto and Dow scarcely bear close scrutiny.

Let's take a look at conventional petrochemical agriculture's supposedly rational approach. While the efficacy of sprayed agents to target specific pests and of fertilizers to increase plant size is well tested through experiment, what is missing is the consequence, both direct and indirect, on the whole ecology as well as for the resulting wine's quality. We just don't know anything. Modern science simply isn't very good at modeling complex systems.

More fundamentally, systems don't need to be rationally derived to allow us to work within them. Former Federal Reserve chairman Alan Greenspan's defense of Adam Smith's "invisible hand," which places laissez-faire capitalism above communism's central planning systems as a preferred organizing principle, stands today as prevailing economic theory. It guided the Fed through two decades of economic prosperity, but that doesn't make it true, and today its proponents have that feeling that Tom Lehrer described as akin to "a Christian Scientist with appendicitis." Still, whatever economic theory comes along to replace it is likely to be equally faith-based.

Darwin's vision of life itself as arising purely by natural selection from chance events was initially proposed as an argument against the Lamarckian theory of the inheritance of acquired traits. Darwin argued that innovations are generated *entirely at random* and survive if and only if they provide benefit. Origins don't relate to results in the development of species, and I see no reason why they necessarily should in a farming system either. If it works, and with a little luck, it may survive, even if it was generated without credible intention.

Ken Wilber offers an analysis that evolution proceeds naturally through transformative processes that transcend Darwinian evolution. For example, the intricate simultaneous genetic steps from a foreleg to a wing seem to demonstrate some kind of cooperative force at work that nobody understands but everyone acknowledges.

Similarly, I have found that many scientists find quite alien the unimportance of origins. When Newton spoke of standing on the shoulders of giants, he was articulating the sentiments of every scientist. Nobody can be expected to derive, let alone validate, all of the scientific work that forms the foundation of his own occupations. Just as he owes his personal existence to many thousands of successive couplings in an unbroken descendant line including both kings and crooks, so the scientific enterprise owes its existence to a specific chain of contingent events, not all of them savory or pristine.

But the state of science today simply is what it is, and cannot fall back on its genesis for validation. Its tenets are true and useful, or they are not. It is equally irrelevant that Biodynamics practitioners may stand on the shoulders of midgets.

In any case, there is no great likelihood that we will ever reduce agronomy to testable first principles. À la Darwin, all Biodynamics needs to do in order to be valid is to survive and thrive.

DIFFERENT LANGUAGE, SAME WORDS

Steiner's language, with its leaf days and root days, its quartz preparations and sensitive crystallizations, is part of what drives Davis-trained enologists crazy. Although the words are English, the system they construct addresses an entirely different view of reality.

The Chinese system of medicine sounds peculiar to Western ears, but its empirical holistic approach is far older and is increasingly respected by American physicians as a valuable supplement to conventional medicine. Eastern medical language does not translate easily, often reflecting a point of view entirely opposite that of the West, which concerns itself with reductionist simplification in order to treat disease.

For the Chinese, the focus is on holistic meridians. *Liver* is not the name of a discrete organ; rather, it denotes a whole system within a web of systems comprising a whole organism that can be nudged toward wellness. Chinese theory does not directly address disease; instead of trying to fix specific pieces, it centers on correcting overall imbalances.

Meridians and acupressure points cannot be said to exist or not to exist, any more than a chromatic scale exists in music, except in the musician's mind and soul. The question is whether this way of thinking and working produces useful results for artful expression between humans—not whether it exists, but whether it communicates.

The poetic language that Biodynamics practitioners employ sounds quasi-scientific. "The preps impact the energy force," says Oregon Biodynamics farming consultant Philippe Armenier. "They impact the soil and change the energy field of the plant."

Armenier's energy isn't the stuff of Maxwell's equations. Word confusion is the common stamp of paradigm shifts. It took physics most of the 1920s to figure out that Bohr's and Schroedinger's disparate theories of the electron were really just metaphorical attempts to use Newton's particle and wave concepts in a realm where they don't quite apply.

The affront that scientists feel when alternative philosophies co-opt their language ignores the reality that many terms were actually recently stolen and altered by modern science. *Energy* is a very old word that was synonymous with *vigor*, until Newtonians got their hands on it in the late nineteenth century. The terms *significant* and *ideal* are other examples. Don't get me started on a similar recent language heist around the word *planet*.[5]

DO YOU BELIEVE IN MAGIC?

Biodynamic viticulture did not begin until after World War II, and today's practice bears as much resemblance to its Steinerian origins as our modern tongue does to the Old English of *Beowulf*. Biodynamics consultant Alan York hardly seems like a crackpot when he presents Biodynamics' four principles:[6]

1. Create a *closed system* of nutrients and natural resources base to the greatest practical extent. Become aware of the waste stream, and capture and transform it into a fertility stream.

2. Creating *biodiversity* on the property. Monoculture undermines a property's ability to resist adversity. Balance the success of various life forms in an ecosystem so outbreaks of disease are generally held in check.

3. The *preparations,* two field sprays (one on the soil and one foliar) and six compost preps. These support and maintain life forces. Life comes from life. However life loses vitality and loses the ability to bring life forth. The preps aren't fertilizers but they are supportive of life processes such as sprouting, growing, flowering and fruiting.

4. Promotion of a *holistic system* which focuses on the interaction of all living things. We try to avoid acting against a specific problem, because when we do so, we produce unintended consequences. Instead, we try to work towards enhancing the robustness and health of the whole environment for the benefit of the whole ecology.

This is mostly good common sense. The problematic, emblematic aspects of Biodynamics are those darned preparations. Think about it. Without them, Demeter certification is not attainable. It's an open question how much certified Biodynamics growers really believe in the preps. By analogy, full admission to the Catholic Church may require you, in the words of Tom Lehrer, to "drink the wine and chew the wafer," but does that guarantee a firm belief in transubstantiation?

Longtime practitioner Tony Coturri thinks Steiner reestablished for us an intuitive relation to agriculture by articulating his clairvoyance of our deep connection to Nature. "The horn ceremony reminds us of that connection," says Coturri. "We often forget that farming is really a lifestyle choice, and place all our valuation on the almighty dollar instead of the spiritual quality of our lives."

I am willing to give the benefit of the doubt to Matthieu Chapoutier when he says, "Where the biodynamic method is innovative is in its use of scientific knowledge to reach the best quality by knowing when the vine needs something, and what it needs." Sooner or later, Matt needs to put up or shut up. But perhaps we owe him a decade or two of experience in the system. In the meantime, I appreciate his commitment to some sort of standard of proof.

BEYOND THE ALMIGHTY CONSUMER

If you've read this far into the book, you may have figured out that, pretty much without exception, I adore winemakers. This is a special industry. Nobody with a lick of sense is in this game for the money. Our individual visions lead us all down different paths, and the consequences of each dream get shaken out in the marketplace, Darwin-style.

Putting it that way makes our passions sound saner than they are. Yet as George Bernard Shaw told us, "Nothing is ever accomplished by a reasonable man," and our industry seems bent on proving it. Something about winemaking encourages exploration, and our knowledge progresses largely through risky, outrageous experiments, as we saw in chapter 12. In part, that's just good business. Wineries are constantly called upon to generate new media hype.

But there's more to the story. Much of the incentive to undertake Biodynamics or organics involves lifestyle. "If every California grower were required to live with their family in the middle of their vineyard, you'd see a lot more organic farming," says Tony Norskog of Orleans Hill Winery. Or as Biodynamics newcomer Randall Grahm puts it, "Biodynamics is really a spiritual journey which focuses on the practitioner himself. If I am not out myself stirring the preps, I will be deeply disappointed in myself."

SCORING STEINER

A report card on biodynamic winegrowing is pretty hard to come by. It would be difficult to invent a methodology more zany than the 501 prep in which cow manure is buried in a horn between the autumnal and vernal equinoxes and subsequently applied in minute dilution to foliage. A conventional double-blind controlled experiment might test its efficacy by measuring pruning weights, anthocyanin production, and insect populations.

But enthusiasts like Grahm caution against that approach: "You have to look within the whole system implemented over several seasons. It requires a leap of faith. Vines farmed biodynamically have generally appeared much healthier (apart from the years when they haven't)." It's fair to say that we would not try to test, say, a new carburetor design disconnected from the rest of the engine. The same goes for biodynamic practices separated out from the whole.

Are the wines any good? That's surprisingly difficult to say, because it depends on your definition of "good." In surveying thousands of wines at AppellationAmerica.com, I find that biodynamic wines operate under different quality rules, and just as label information like appellation or varietal is useful when tasting, it is helpful to know that the wine is biodynamic before judging it.

Personally, I like these wines. The biodynamic flavor profile has a higher tolerance for microbial defects such as VA and aldehyde but holds the wine to a much higher standard in terms of flavor interest, distinctive character, and minerality (see chapter 8). A perfect 10 for a conventional Merlot destined for Safeway might be denied typicity status as a Bio wine.

LONG-TERM PROSPECTS

Given a couple decades of practice, we might begin to ask if biodynamic vineyards have achieved commercial viability. What irks Stu Smith and others is that consumer curiosity is buoying up these experiments, giving them a competitive edge. In my view, this only partially levels the playing field for brave souls such as Randall and the Benzigers, who are diving out of an economic airplane hoping to knit together a functioning parachute on the way down, and I wish them all the publicity updraft they can conjure.

We never ask an existing life-form whether it is valid. If it exists, it must be viable, at least for now. One compelling reason Biodynamics is succeeding is that its restrictions and mysteries appeal to the consumer.

The test of viability often defies logic. Michael Pollan's beautiful book *The Botany of Desire* chronicles the peculiar relationships between agriculture and human caprice. The evolution of marijuana, for example, has been vastly accelerated by the War on Drugs.[7]

California's most widely planted grape, the Thompson seedless, is propagated because of its convenience for eating: no messy seeds. Think about it: this organism survives and thrives precisely because of its inability to reproduce. Indeed, no grape variety breeds true, so all wine grapes depend on humans for survival through vegetative cuttings.

Monsanto's petrochemical farming probably isn't viable in the long term either, but nobody is calling it a hoax. There is a faith that should problems arise, we will have the wit to deal with them. This has proven to be the case, except when it hasn't. The built-in difficulty is that through a kind of natural selection, we are left with just the unsolvable problems. The biodynamic practitioners have simply gotten off the petrochemical bus a little earlier than the rest of us.

HOW LITTLE WE UNDERSTAND HOW LITTLE WE KNOW

Do not condemn the judgment of another because it differs from your own. You may both be wrong.

—Dandemis

Any honest appraisal of scientific endeavor reveals that faith-based intuitions guide research at every turn. In his famous argument against quantum physics, Einstein insisted that "God does not play dice." We tend to discount statements of faith by famous scientists as demeaning to the speaker, imagining that religious window dressing was merely lip service to an anachronistic time when coded messages were required of sages.

If we examine the writings of Isaac Newton, we find a religious tone that we generally place to one side: "The most beautiful system of the Sun, Planets and Comets could only proceed from the counsel and dominion of an intelligent being." He also stated, flat out: "Atheism is so senseless & odious to mankind that it never had many professors."[8]

We believe in inferential statistics, randomized block experimental designs, and medical risk factors, and we worship rationalism like a deity. In the clash of Biodynamics and science, there is plenty of faith-based adherence to doctrine on both sides.

In such circumstances, my position is to advocate for humility and religious tolerance and an appreciation that diversity benefits the whole community by making us all smarter, a point I endeavored to reinforce in chapter 12.

In 2010, we were confronted in California with unprecedented mildew pressure that challenged the Biodynamics farmer. I find it rather creepy that the so-called scientific crowd on Stu's blog was cheering for a Biodynamics disaster. Sorry, boys, but a real scientist doesn't take sides, and doesn't delight in the misfortunes of those of a differing point of view who pursue the road less traveled.

Stu Smith's blogged response to one commenter's olive branch was, "What's the harm and who gets hurt? Well, for one, you do, if you accept the fantasy called Biodynamics, which is a make-believe world with no earthly connection to our functioning, real, material world. I don't want to live in a society that can't tell the difference between fantasy and reality."

Who does? But here we are anyhow. Objective truth is a child's myth, and the nature of reality is a question the profs will always dodge. Science isn't much of a security blanket. The more it illuminates, the more darkness is revealed. We hope gaining expertise in our chosen field will give us comfort, but the opposite occurs as we realize our ignorance in ever greater depth. It makes us humble, not smug.

In *The Open Door* (1957), Helen Keller wrote, "Security is mostly a superstition. It does not exist in nature, nor do the children of men as a whole experience it." Or as the late American poet John Ciardi put it, "Show me a man who is not confused and I will show you a man who has not been thinking."[9]

At the core of true science is a sense of awe and wonder. Besides the apparently benevolent intentions of its participants, I am attracted to the experiment of Biodynamics because of its impenetrability to conventional scientific investigatory practices. In coming together, Biodynamics will benefit from scientific scrutiny, but more important, science itself may be induced to learn how to ask better questions.

TAKE-HOME MESSAGES

- Biodynamics sounds nuts to me. But so does string theory. Its existence offers a delicious opportunity for scientists to test their true mettle.
- Something about winemaking encourages exploration, and our knowledge progresses largely through risky, outrageous experiments.
- Science isn't much of a security blanket. Objective truth is a child's myth.

Natural Wine Nonsense

I am not a member of any organized political party. I am a
Democrat.

—Will Rogers

The consumer has never had it so good. We have twenty times the
choices we had two decades ago, and poor wines have nearly vanished
from the shelves. If what you are after is drinkable quaff, you will find
it more consistently and cheaply than ever before.

But there is growing discontent with fruit-forward styles that die
young and global monster wines that are hard to tell apart. The Internet
now resounds with voices demanding "somewhereness." Many critics,
newly aware of the recent technological revolution in winemaking, have
sought to demonize new winemaking techniques as sources of shallow-
ness and sameness.

The rapidly expanding availability of new winemaking tools coupled
with a decreased willingness to share knowledge has led to a substantial
information gap between winemakers and their customers that I've discussed throughout this volume, and particularly in chapter 20. A sud-
den sense of betrayal has emerged, leaving wine lovers with a desire to
get back to basics.

Certification programs that have laid down strict rules for organic
and biodynamic wine have left many consumers unsatisfied, whether by
sins of commission or omission. This malaise has coalesced into a movement for Natural Wine. But what exactly is that?

In recent years, I have attempted to convince Natural Wine proponents such as wine writer Alice Feiring to create a Natural Wine certification mark, but without success. Clearly, these leaders want to foment

discontent and sell books—but do they want to solve the problems that support their activities?

Ms. Feiring was at least good enough to supply me with her own list of what constitutes a Natural Wine (see chapter 20). But why, after a decade of harangue, has the movement failed to formalize standards? My belief is that it isn't a movement at all. The Natural Wine "movement" is instead an uneasy coalition of strange bedfellows whose agendas can't all be satisfied by a single set of winemaking rules.

THE PLAYERS

As demonstrated in the Will Rogers quip that begins this chapter, a political faction comes of age when it learns to mock itself. The late, great Joe Dressner wrote in his "2010 Official Fourteen-Point Manifesto on Natural Wine," "The problem is that there was never an official faith and never a doctrine. The blogosphere and media created a construct, milked it for publicity and then deconstructed an 'ideology' that they had helped to define and promote."[1]

Joe advocated well for the Natural Wine movement in the context that it was, by his own admission, mostly a disorganized movement against things, not an advocacy for anything in particular. His "Manifesto" is a remarkable defense of a movement in which he claims it doesn't matter (though he seems later to have changed his mind).

Below are the eight constituencies of the Natural Wine movement as I see them, each with a few words describing its motivations. See which you identify with personally.

Non-Interventionist. Wine should not be casually fooled around with. Traditional winemaking is fine, but techniques that cheat or hide flaws are to be avoided if possible. "The best wine makes itself."

Environmentalist. Winemaking should not damage the environment. Concerns include erosion, petrochemicals, deforestation caused by barrel production, carbon footprint, and recycling.

Conventionalist. "I don't want to drink anything I can't pronounce. Give me standard winemaking without all the weird stuff."

Traditionalist. Prefers time-tested methods, the older the better. Suspicious of all recent technological innovations, including use of chemistry, microbiology, genetic manipulation, and petrochemical agriculture. Older manipulations like refrigeration, isinglass fining, or chaptalization are acceptable because they have withstood the test of time.

Health-Conscious. Wants to control food sources and protect the health of winery personnel as well. In addition to restricting the use of chemicals in vineyards and in wine, prefers moderate-alcohol wines and requires full disclosure of potential allergens and carcinogens. May have an aversion to the use of animal products in wine production.

Collector. Serious investment in age-worthy wine requires dependable microbial stability. Passionate about great wine that improves with time. "Don't take chances on my nickel." Nervous about experimental techniques and changes in processing, especially among established houses and wines intended for extended cellaring.

Authenticity Purist. Wine should be made from grapes alone, with as little addition and manipulation as possible in order to present a distinctive expression. More extreme than the Non-Interventionist: "If Nature gave us a difficult vintage, let's taste it!"

Terroiriste. Passionate about the unique flavors of a place. "Please don't obscure the wine's distinctive expression with excessive alcohol or wood, or employ practices that make wines all taste the same." May consider native microbiology as important to terroir as grape character.

THE ISSUES

Winemakers have been marching for naturalness a lot longer than consumers. Indeed, even the generally unenlightened federal regulations, though full of loopholes, take as their starting point the idea that wine should contain no additives not derived from grapes. Additions of water, natural and artificial flavors, sweeteners, mineral acids, grain spirits, starches, thickeners, glycerol, and many other additives commonplace in beer, distilled spirits, and almost all foodstuffs are forbidden for wine, albeit with specific exceptions.

Adherents to the movement seem to think that *natural* conveys something obvious, along with terms like *human rights* and *social justice.* But there are a lot of things that might bother people in the Natural Wine movement that apparently don't, such as the use of inert gas, refrigeration, stainless steel, motorized vineyard and winery equipment, half-million-gallon fermenters one hundred feet tall, and vineyard smog due to proximity to freeways. Then again, the movement seems perplexingly fixated on issues such as yeast inoculation (see chapter 23), which seemed to take winemakers by surprise. Don't these people eat bread? In short, where exactly is the beef? A clear set of guidelines would be useful.

The movement's tacit assumption—that traditional winemaking is in sync with the agendas of environmentalists, the health conscious, and terroiristes—is quite simply false. These groups are all demanding radical change in the way winemaking is done, not more of the same.

Nothing divides the Natural Wine movement more sharply than the issue of sulfite-free wines. The requirement, imposed by the Organic Food Production Act, written into federal requirements for the Organic Wine designation in 1990, and reaffirmed in 2012, resulted in excluding mainstream production of organic wine and confining it to well less than 1% of producers. The category is generally avoided by connoisseurs and collectors because of its reputation for inconsistency and poor shelf life. The result: a schism between connoisseurs and health activists, and a distinction in the marketplace between wines made from organically grown grapes (good) and organic wines (bad).

We do have a short list of things the eight constituencies could agree on, though nothing to build a movement around. Reduction or elimination of chemical herbicide and pesticide sprays and encouragement of cover crops are good both for the environment and for wine balance. Use of GMOs goes against tradition and also raises environmental and perhaps human health issues. Additives such as tannins, enzymes, and mega-purple, though commonplace conventional tools, are outside the scope of traditional winemaking and provide no environmental or health benefits.

But there is room for lively debate among these groups. Using the eight constituencies I named above, I prepared the table shown here, which lists all the issues I could think of (working mainly from Alice Feiring's list in chapter 20) and estimates the preference an informed member of each group would have on a scale of +10 to −10. Let's touch on a few of these points of difference.

Chaptalization and Acidulation

Corrections of deficiencies in musts (sugar in France and tartaric acid in the United States) have been commonplace for hundreds of years.

THE SUNDRY ELEMENTS OF NATURAL WINE PERCEPTION

	Non-Interventionist	Environmentalist	Conventionalist	Traditionalist	Health-Conscious	Collector	Authenticity Enthusiast	Terroir Enthusiast
Vineyard								
Organic Certification	+5	+10	-5	+5	+10	0	+10	+5
Biodynamic	+10	+5	-5	0	+5	+5	+10	+10
No tillage	+5	+10	-5	+5	0	0	+5	+10
No pesticides	+10	+10	0	+5	+10	0	+3	+5
No herbicides	+10	+10	0	+5	+10	0	+3	+5
Irrigation	-5	-3	+3	-2	0	0	-3	-4
Soil Food Web score	0	0	0	0	+5	0	0	+10
Extended hang time	0	0	+5	-5	-5	-10	-10	-10
Additions								
Acidification	-4	0	0	+2	0	+5	+4	0
Amelioration (water addition)	-4	0	0	-2	0	-5	-7	-5
Enzymes	-5	0	-2	-5	-2	0	-5	0
Fortification	-5	-1	+5	+5	0	+8	-5	0
Sulfites	0	-5	+5	0	-10	+10	0	+5
Chaptalization	-8	0	+5	0	-2	0	-5	0
GMOs	-8	-10	-5	-10	-10	0	-8	-5
Yeast inoculum	-5	0	+5	-5	-2	0	-3	+3
Diammonium phosphate	-3	-3	+3	-3	-2	0	-3	-3
Copper	-4	0	0	0	-4	-3	-3	0
Bacteria inoculum	-4	0	+3	-2	0	+3	-2	-3
Bentonite	-3	0	+5	0	+3	+5	0	-1
Tannin	-5	0	-2	-3	-3	0	-5	-8

Animal products	-4	0	0	-8	0	-3	-3
Color concentrate	-10	-3	-7	0	0	-7	-7
Velcorin	-10	-10	-10	-5	+10	-5	+5
Inert gas	-3	+8	-5	0	+5	+5	+5
Oxygen	-5	-8	-5	+5	0	-10	+10
New barrel %	-5	+5	+5	0	0	-10	-10
Non-barrel oak adjuncts	-2	-10	-10	+5	-5	-5	-5
Barrel wheat paste contact	-1	0	0	-8	0	0	0
Treatments and Practices							
Organic Certified Winery	+5	-2	0	+10	-2	+2	+1
Stainless steel only	0	0	-5	+5	-5	0	+5
Suppressed malolactic	-5	-2	-5	+2	-5	0	+5
Varietal purity	0	+7	0	0	+5	+8	+8
Residual sugar ("dry" styles)	-5	+4	-5	-2	-5	-5	-5
Non-gravity (powered) racking	-3	0	+5	0	+2	+2	+2
Alcohol adjustment	-5	-5	-8	+5	+5	-10	+5
Micro-oxygenation	-10	-5	-5	+5	-5	-8	+3
Centrifugation	-2	0	-5	+2	+2	-2	0
Diatomaceous earth filtration	-2	+5	+5	+5	0	-3	0
Microfiltration	-5	-5	-5	+5	+5	-5	0
Sterile filtration	-5	+10	-5	0	+5	-3	-5
Packaging							
Recycled glass	+5	0	0	+2	-5	0	0
Recycled paper labels	+5	0	+2	+2	0	0	0

Traditionalists forget that the Bordeaux first growths really should sport a "Contains Beet Sugar" ingredient label in most years. Without this adjustment, much great French wine would be thin and sour. Although collectors wouldn't have it any other way, purists understandably balk.

Similarly, consumers of New World wines interested in balanced alcohol and rich terroir expression will prefer the removal of excessive alcohol via technology. Something like 40% of French Appellation d'Origine Contrôlée (AOC) wines and a like percentage of California wines are alcohol-adjusted to the 13–14% range. The French wines are corrected up by chaptalization with beet sugar, while California wine is corrected down through RO membrane and Spinning Cone technologies.

Balanced wines not only taste better, they better reflect their place of origin as well. As journalist Alan Goldfarb commented upon comparing my 12.9% Faux Chablis (alcohol-adjusted with reverse osmosis) against the original 14.8% version, "The unadjusted is more authentic, but the 12.9 has more terroir expression."

Barrels versus Alternatives

For the traditionalist, French oak barrels symbolize the epitome of artisanality, separating the sacred chapels of the boutique North Coast elite from the immense tank farms of the typical Central Valley industrial mega-producer. For the purist and the terroiriste, however, they are winemaking's worst scourge.

To the informed environmentalist, using a new French oak barrel as a flavoring device represents the grossest form of wastefulness and affluent display. The trees from which French oak barrels are made are two hundred years old, and 75% of the prime wood of these venerable trees is discarded because it cannot be fashioned into a piece of watertight fine furniture, as discussed in chapter 4. Yet if chips and other barrel alternatives were used instead as sources of oak extractives, this carnage could be reduced fourfold.

Today, it is no longer small wineries that are the primary consumers of barrels. Decades ago, Robert Mondavi installed a hundred thousand barrels to distinguish his infant Woodbridge Winery from other behemoth facilities in the Big Valley. Not to be outdone, Bronco and other competitors followed in short order with six-figure installations of their own. Today, the lion's share of barrels purchased by California are housed in vast Central Valley warehouses, resulting in deforestation of France's precious resource on a scale never before seen.

Gluten-allergic consumers have raised questions about wheat paste commonly used in repairing barrel leaks. Barrel alternatives (chips, staves, and so forth) avoid this issue and, coupled with oxygenation, permit winemaking in neutral tanks on any desired scale.

Micro-oxygenation

A technique that in 2001 led to a headline on an Alice Feiring article that read, "Wine Is Made in the Lab, Not the Vineyard," micro-oxygenation poses a conundrum of equal depth. On the one hand, what additive could be more natural than the air we breathe? On the other, making wine in stainless steel under blankets of inert gas has permitted modern facilities to exclude oxygen in ways unavailable to traditional winemakers. With MOx, postmodern winemakers who understand the folly of this have a practical tool for reestablishing traditional winemaking techniques even in wineries built on industrial principles.

For purists and terroiristes, skillful introduction of oxygen is an essential tool in fighting reduction, particularly in red wines and those grown in soils that enhance both minerality (chapter 8) and reduction (chapter 7). On the other hand, early oxygenation amplifies structure and body, which may be undesirable for these groups.

It is also reasonable for collectors to be suspicious of the prospects for longevity of wines subjected to an experimental technique, and for purists to oppose the restructuring of tannins. In chapter 13, Gideon Beinstock talked about moving away from the technique in the context of his aesthetic goals in an aggressive mountain terroir, and Randall Grahm in chapter 14 explained how, at least for a time, he wishes to work with his new vineyard's fruit without such aids in order to get to know its proclivities. Both men understand that oxygen is essential to red wine evolution and have benefited from the surprising revelations the technique provided concerning wine's true nature.

If I can get a little angry just for a moment, in including MOx on their death lists, do non-winemaker critics really presume to pass judgment on the exquisitely earnest inquiries of actual practitioners of considerable skill and experience who have boots on the ground?

Sorry, lost my head. Must be the Jersey in me. California mellow—breeeeeathe. Okay, I'm fine.

Aside from the arguments I've advanced for structure-derived soulfulness, terroir expression, environmental benefits (in resolving oak chip tannins), and the balancing of reduction born of organic vineyard practices and screw caps, the most important benefits of MOx are for health. Conventional tannin management strips excessive astringency employing as fining agents animal proteins from milk, chicken eggs, sturgeon, and beef tendon, all possible allergens for sensitive individuals.

Although any winemaker will tell you that stripping wine of tannin with fining agents is detrimental to terroir expression and robs wine of soulfulness by deleting the tannin structure responsible for aromatic integration, all these problems are averted if the tannins are refined with oxygen by a skilled hand.

Indigenous Yeast

There is surprising fervor, which I explore in more depth in the next chapter, surrounding the desire to skip inoculating with packaged yeast cultures in the name of naturalness. The catalogs of yeast companies, with their outrageous claims of enhanced aromatics, do sound scary. Consider, for example, these excerpts from the website of Lallemand, the world's most important supplier, describing the flavors imparted by some of their yeast products:

> Lalvin ICV-D80: "characterized by ripe fruit, smoke and a licorice finish."
>
> Lalvin ICV-D47: "When left on lees, ripe spicy aromas with tropical and citrus notes are developed."
>
> Lalvin RA17®: "will liberate cherry and fruit aromas."
>
> Lalvin V1116 (K1)™: "flowery ester producers (isoamyl acetate, hexyl acetate and phenyl ethyl acetate). These esters bring fresh floral aromas to neutral varieties or high-yield grapes."

Don't count on it. Winemakers know by experience that these catalog promises are like TV hype, and we try not to take them seriously. As with a magazine ad for a new car, we might be swayed by a product that promises us hot chicks, but we're really focused on our basic transportation needs.

Here's how winemakers look at it. First and foremost, they want a clean fermentation that goes to completion. Next, they're interested in how to get the best extraction, which may mean that the most vigorous yeast isn't best, because it ferments too fast and robs the opportunity for slow extrraction. Yeasts have physical properties such as low alcohol tolerance, which slows fermentation at high temperature; low foaming, which is handy in allowing higher filling in barrel fermentations; and enzymes, which help break down pectins and sugar-bound flavors in the grapes themselves, seldom contributing any flavors of their own. Try it yourself sometime. Make some wine and learn.

Enlightened winemakers also try to be proactive in the areas of biogenic amines and precursors of the carcinogen ethyl carbamate, which can form if the wine gets heated.[2]

Now, I'm a high-risk eater. I love sushi, half-shell oysters, and unpasteurized cheeses, and I'm willing to risk gastrointestinal distress for their glories. But I don't try to hoodwink my friends into following suit, and I find it disingenuous for the leaders of the Natural Wine movement to soft-pedal the consequences of their simplistic natural yeast agenda for the rather large portion of their constituency that's in it (or so they imagine) for their health.

The levels of allergens, carcinogens, and other toxins typically run ten times higher in uninoculated wines (so-called natural fermentations). Much of the problem stems from all the non-wine yeasts and bacteria that have their way with the juice before it gains any alcohol. Inoculation with a dependable strain speeds the fermentation through this perilous time with good manners regarding undesired aromas, toxin production, and prompt and dependable completion, lest an arrested fermentation lie vulnerable to Brett and vinegar infestations that can feast on tiny amounts of residual sugar and leftover nutrients resulting from incompletion.

It is astonishing to many winemakers that the choice to inoculate is held in such low esteem by an ignorant and vociferous press. Frankly, I sometimes feel we industry types deserve all the crap the press dishes out for our failure in the past two decades to be straight with consumers about what we really do. The tragedy is, the public now trusts a bunch of Natural Wine zealots with their lives and health in preference to an industry that is much more aligned with their interests.

Indigenous yeasts and bacteria can be permitted to flourish prior to the onset of fermentation being carried to completion by a commercial yeast that is introduced late or in low numbers. This is a tough choice and should be left to the winemaker, as it is to the brewer and the baker. Wine critics are in no position to evaluate the economic damage that would result from a misguided fermentation or to ensure against it. A healthy fermentation that produces wine that sells is a natural miracle akin to natural childbirth, but in such cases the invested parties often have an ambulance at the ready.

In some wines, I inoculate because I prefer to avoid sulfites at the crusher. If I allow grapes to sit the required two to four days until indigenous *Saccharomyces* arise, a host of other yeasts and bacteria will produce dominant fruity ester characters that overpower the grape's aromatic expression. But hey, that's just me. Notwithstanding the argument that this microbial picnic constitutes some kind of terroir expression in and of itself, such wines all taste the same to me.

Glass Alternatives

Perhaps the widest schism looming in the Natural Wine movement has to do with packaging. The carbon footprint around the manufacture and transport of glass bottles outweighs all other wine industry inputs combined. Yet no collector wants to cellar plastic bottles, however ecological. And show me one ultrapremium cult producer who is ready to switch to bag-in-box, no matter how hermetic the seal. As a rule, small artisans gravitate toward heavy bottles, which have been conclusively shown to subliminally enhance value perception.

GETTING BACK TOGETHER

With their focus on recent technologies such as reverse osmosis and micro-ox, Natural Wine advocates seem less concerned with the much more sweeping changes of the mid–twentieth century with which this book is concerned, when traditional winemaking disappeared entirely, to be replaced by conventional winemaking with its electric pumps and sterile filtration, inert gas and stainless steel. Conventional winemaking is no more traditional than conventional farming is.

If I were not an optimist at heart, I would never have written this book. It's clear to me that greater openness can reunite winemakers and consumers. The Natural Wine movement coalesced around two sources of consumer dissatisfaction: frustration with sameness and suspicion of winemaker honesty. These are reasonable concerns, and ought to be addressed through dialogue with professionals who have dedicated their lives to enriching the dinner tables of these same wine lovers.

Consumers can only make informed choices if winemakers will be frank with them about their methods and their thinking. Winemakers are a sincere and introspective bunch, with very few bad apples. They choose their techniques for good reasons, ones that often run far deeper than the critics report. Once consumers begin to learn the trade-offs involved in the art and practice of winemaking, every strategy that winemakers employ can develop its own following based on the particular goals being pursued.

SAME OLD SAME OLD

The real culprit in sameness is that most consumers want predictability, not uniqueness. Paradoxically, more diversity in product offerings leads to less diversity in the stores. While the U.S. now produces over one hundred times as many wines as it did thirty years ago, this allows Safeway to pick and choose to create a very tight competitive cluster: the expected Merlot, Chardonnay, and Cabernet Sauvignon. In this hotly competitive world, any stylistic wandering is a death sentence.

American wine production has exploded from 200 wineries in 1975 to 8,000 or more today, and greater diversity exists today than ever before, with craft wines in fact comprising 98% of our domestic labels that, in very small lots, dare to be different. Meanwhile, however, the number of retail shelf positions has remained stagnant, and distributors have collapsed from 3,500 to 700 nationwide. Of today's 100,000 domestic wines, less than 2,000 have much play in the three-tier distribution network.

All wine lovers share discontent with the homogeneity on today's retail shelves. Although there is little hope for finding distinctive wines of place in general distribution, the good news is that distinctive wines of place lie right under our noses. Americans have little notion of the diversity and majesty of wines that lie undiscovered within range of their suburban van. Check out AppellationAmerica. com, a 20,000-page website that endeavors to record every winery, every wine, every appellation, and every grape variety that appears on a wine label.

Okay, you say, that's a lot of wine. But is it any good? Having run the Best-of-Appellation panel for three years now and sampled what is now out there, it is my finding that for many palates, California now produces our country's worst wines—boring, overripe, low-acid, and overembellished with oak, butter, and other cheap tricks. The general improvement in wine quality in the rest of the country (and in many less explored regions in the Golden State as well) is unbelievable, and with a little asking about, you will have no trouble connecting with practitioners who will far exceed your expectations in practically every new region.

This quality explosion exactly parallels the growth of gourmet dining in America. Thirty years ago, your chances of finding a decent Cobb salad or crab bisque in the Heartland were pretty much nil, but now great food experiences abound throughout the country. So it is with local wine as well.

The diversity and terroir expression the Natural Wine movement seeks is readily to be found in the burgeoning American wine movement. You've got two choices, and you probably want to go for both. One is to get in your car and visit your local vintner, and the other is to fight like hell for your right to buy wine from anywhere in this supposedly free country.

OCCUPY AMERICA

The lack of diversity in retail wine offerings in the United States is a political dysfunction, not a technological one.

If you are compelled to reach beyond local offerings, I wish you well. Fat cat distributors in many states have imposed clever boundaries that make it impossible for me as a California vintner to do legal business with you unless I pay an annual license fee (fifty of them) and file monthly reports of sales tax (also fifty monthly reports, usually all zeros), a basic expense for all fifty states of about $75,000, counting the labor to do it all. If I'm to justify that expense at 20% of my gross revenues, I need to sell $300,000 of wine on the Internet. That's completely impossible for the small wineries whose wines you want to get your hands on.

I suppose I am the only person in the wine industry who does not support the fight against House Resolution 1161, a draconian measure to make direct shipping illegal nationwide. Why on earth are we trying to defend our right to a system that renders distribution of small producers economically unworkable? Let's burn it down! Perhaps this will enrage consumers and vitalize them to demand action.

Hey, I'm sitting here aching to tell you about Virginia wines, New York wines, and even exceptional offerings from Iowa, Ohio, Michigan, and Idaho. But if there's no real access to those wines, why should I waste your time?

Dear reader, want to do something really valuable? The Achilles' heel of the state-based distributor monopoly is the simple extension to Internet retailers of the 2005 *Granholm v. Heald* decision, in which the U.S. Supreme Court established reciprocal rights for wineries in and out of any state. Although this decision caused states to license and tax out-of-state wineries, single wineries cannot afford the permits and administrative costs that have been imposed as trade barriers. But retailers can.

The Court never ruled one way or the other on retailers. The simple solution is to establish, through Congress or the courts, that Internet retailers like K & L in San Francisco and Zachy's in New York have the right to distribute wines across state lines, as do local retailers within the states. This is where consumer activists and wineries should concentrate their combined efforts. Everybody wins. In the end, I believe that in-state distributors and retailers would benefit as well from the increased wine consciousness that this would open up, because the three-tier system will always be a more efficient way to deliver wine than UPS.

THE WINERY SILENT MAJORITY

Like many of his ilk, Joe Dressner questioned whether Natural Wine can be made in the New World. I am here to tell you that it can indeed, and that exploring that possibility is the most fun any wine lover can have in this new Golden Age during which you are privileged to be alive.

Like the Natural Wines of France and Italy, America's fascinating diversity is not to be found on the supermarket shelves. You have to go to the source. I will venture a guess that Joe never tried a Snake River Viognier, an Iowa Brianna, a Conneaut Chardonnay, a Lehigh Valley Grüner Veltliner, a Long Island Merlot, a Monticello Petit Verdot, or a Wisconsin Pinot Blanc, to name a few categories that include some of America's greatest wines.

California itself abounds with unsung excellence: Santa Cruz Mountains Chardonnay, San Antonio Valley Cabernet Sauvignon, Temecula Sangiovese, Suisun Valley Sauvignon Blanc, and Fairplay Syrah, wines that put their mainstream counterparts to shame.

American wines got way better when we weren't paying attention. The best have been tearing up the few competitions that will allow them to enter. The cure I recommend for the Natural Whine movement is to load up the minivan and discover America.

TAKE-HOME MESSAGES

- The Natural Wine movement has proven incapable of articulating its beliefs.
- The Luddite agenda of traditionalists and collectors is not compatible with the radical change called for by the agendas of the health conscious and the environmentally concerned.
- While market forces have created an appearance of sameness among mainstream New World offerings, more diversity exists today than ever before. But don't look for it at Dean & DeLuca.

23

Yeast Inoculation

Threat or Menace?

Report from the field. Heads up, ye vintners. A panel discussion I participated in at the Portland Indie Wine Festival in 2009 called "Natural Wine in the Age of Technology" was a shocking reality check, at least for me. It underlined, much to my surprise, the truly scary disconnect that has emerged between conventional winemakers and their formerly doting groupies.

It was great to be invited by Alice Feiring to bat around ideas with Natural Wine folks. My hope was to arrive at a definition for that concept, perhaps even a certification mark. If a list of Natural Winemaking practices could be codified that has commercial practical appeal to producers (unlike the ridiculous constraints of organic certification), I figured that many winery players would choose to participate. Win win.

It's not as easy as it sounds. As I discussed in chapter 22, several consumer groups with different agendas are rallying under the Natural Wine flag. These groups do not want the same things. As at any political convention, careful thought and open discussion are needed to determine which mountains the movement as a whole is willing to die on.

We made progress. On some issues there is sensible consensus. No Mega Purple, no Velcorin.[1] Gotcha. Other arenas are too subjective to be readily certifiable. You just can't regulate bad winemaking due to excessive oak or excessive hang time.

On other issues, there may be internal division within the party. Barrel alternatives have environmental and health advantages, and micro-oxygenation, though despised by many, can replace animal-based fining agents and may represent a return to classical practices from the days before stainless steel and inert gas disrupted red winemaking tradition. So far, so good.

Reverse osmosis has also gained acceptance in these ranks as a way to support sulfite-free winemaking, despite its negative reputation. Wines with more terroir expression and less alcohol were well appreciated, but the unnaturalness of "deconstructing" wine came up. (Why bleeding seigné for rosé isn't also deconstruction remains unclear to me.) Natural or not, the inconvenient truth is that winemakers do a lot more RO than they generally admit, because it's a powerful tool for quality improvement.

In the end, Natural Winemakers need to choose some rules and let us know. Just spell out the guidelines, and some wineries will show up for it, the Feds will police the certification mark's rules as part of their charge to ensure truth in labeling, and consumers will know what they are getting.

STOP THE PRESSES

So, we were cruising through the issues when suddenly we hit a wall. Strong, very strong feeling welled up in the room against, of all things, yeast inoculation. Really? I was, in fact, caught completely flat-footed. Flummoxed, I responded incorrectly when asked whether my Wine-Smith 2004 Roman Syrah was inoculated, at which point it was embarrassingly pointed out that my own tech sheet specifies Pasteur Red yeast rather than wild fermentation.

Okay, my bad. But so what? This was, to me, a trivial detail, one of a thousand choices every winemaking project strings together, and it simply slipped my mind. My thinking in choosing a yeast was simply that without any sulfite addition, I wanted a reliable yeast working to avoid sticking or spoilage. (I generally do inoculate for yeast but not for malolactic.) Shoot me. I had absolutely no clue that this issue would loom so large for the natural whiners.

But when the moderator dragged out a catalog description from a yeast company, I suddenly understood. Naturally, the extravagant product claims of the corporate yeast titans like Lallemand and Anchor could lead any concerned wine lover to panic. "My God," I thought, "she actually *believes* that tripe."

Then it hit me. Oh dear. This is not good. For someone who has never made wine, catalog claims like "encourages the fresh fruit aromas of orange blossom, pineapple and apricot"; or "believed to enhance aromas such as fresh butter, honey, bright floral and pineapple"; or "flavor attributes are often described as ripe fruit, jam, hazelnut, and dried plums on the finish" are bound to drive any purist, anyone interested in true grape flavor expression, completely crazy.

A LARGE GRAIN OF SALT

Any experienced winemaker will tell you that yeast companies' flavor claims are regarded with about as much credibility as a Louisiana campaign promise. First-year enology students conduct fermentation trials on different yeast strains, and yes, there are big initial differences. All yeasts produce esters—banana, pineapple, and other fruity aromas—and the strains vary. The freshmen all go crazy, while the rest of us just laugh, because these esters are quite unstable, and a year later the differences have disappeared, in no way affecting most wines in commerce, particularly the mature reds.

Do yeast choices matter in these wines? You bet they do. But they do not, for the most part, impart extraneous flavors. They are products of the chosen strain's physical characteristics, like the texture and flavor artifacts that result from the baker's choice of a glass or metal pie pan—everything and nothing, a subtle choice of vehicle reserved for the skilled artisan in her efforts to bring forth her notion of the best expression of ingredients.

In contrast, uninoculated grape juice is attacked prior to the actual wine yeast fermentation *(Saccharomyces)* by a whole host of yeasts and bacteria, including *Candida, Brettanomyces, Metchnikovia, Pichia, Kloeckera,* to say nothing of bacteria such as *Acetobacter* (vinegar), *Pediococcus* (sweat socks),and *Lactobacillus* (PineSol and mouse urine), all of which may leave lasting microbial flavor profiles that permanently obscure grape expression to an uncontrollable extent.

It's not black and white. Clean wines can be made without inoculation, though less dependably. And the extra flavors from "natural fermentation" can certainly be positive for some styles. As long as there's not too much wine at stake, "feral ferments" (as Australians more precisely dub the practice) are actually kind of fun. Although my friend Carole Shelton uses commercial yeasts for most of her Zinfandels to ensure that the different vineyard sources show their grape flavor differences more purely, one of her most popular products is her Wild Thing, a distinctive wine if ever there was. It's wonderfully consistent from vintage to vintage, dependent as it is on microbiology rather than on the imponderabilities of place and seasonal weather that her more conventional offerings express. Mat Goddard's groundbreaking research at the University of Auckland reveals how little we actually know about the interactions of commercial and wild strains. It turns out that an inoculated strain is rarely the one that alone finishes the fermentation.[2] As a winemaker, I feel the style choice is simply part of my prerogative. I see no right answer, no moral good that is served either way.

WHERE'S THE BEEF?

As far as I can tell, detractors of commercial yeast have two concerns. One is that commercial wine yeasts might be genetically modified. But they are not. 'Taint legal. They are simply "wild" yeasts that have been studied, selected for beneficial properties, grown in large quantities, dried, and bagged up.

Second is the concern about flavors that are imparted by packaged yeast. As I have explained, not only is this concern naively overstated, but in my experience, uninoculated wines are more prone to microbial flavor intrusions than commercial yeast fermentations. What I personally most despise in fresh whites is the strong butter note that malolactic bacteria impart, a hallmark of the enormously popular Kendall-Jackson Vintner's Reserve Chardonnay. This same element cannot be reliably prevented in uncontrolled fermentations. If I were required to produce New Zealand–style Sauvignon Blanc, with its delicate purity of grape aromas, according to Natural Wine principles, I would start smashing windows.

One can argue that this intrusive, complex microbiology is natural. Certainly it was traditional standard practice until a scant fifty years ago, throughout eight thousand years of winemaking. Amazing as it seems, Louis Pasteur only elucidated the actual mechanism of fermentation in 1857, two years after the famous 1855 Paris Exposition that established the pecking order of Bordeaux châteaux's *grands crus*.

This doesn't mean there was no inoculation. The passing down of "mother" for wine, for vinegar, and for baking goes back to ancient times. Inoculation was all art and no science then, and the winemaker was more a steward of unexplained mysteries than a competent engineer managing the known, more shaman than scientist. The postmodern view is that we still don't really know much of anything, and I am cool with that.

STICKING WITH THE HORSE YOU RODE IN ON

But here's the thing. It is one thing to assert the unfortunate consequences of scientific arrogance and quite another to propose that the way out of the forest is to simply let nature take its course, come what may. The middle path through these trees is that of the artisan hero, armed with skills, humility, a suspicion of theory, and an open eye to detail.

Sure, you can simply crush the grapes, stand back, and hope for the best. That's what Georgians do and have done for millennia with their qvevris, taking care—and I mean exquisite care—that their whites receive six months on the skins, seeds, and stems. Fair enough. Enjoy. Myself, I like these wines and find their emerging notoriety both hilarious and encouraging. But unless indoctrinated and seduced in advance, critics despise these wines. They are amber in the glass, and their tannin is off the charts. Traditional Georgian qvevri wines, though fascinating and groovy for geeks, are just terrible for contemporary Western palates used to conventionally vinified whites.

But you don't need to go back millennia to find such disparities. Wines that were drunk before World War II, particularly white wines, would have almost no commercial viability today, short of curiosity value. Conventional winemakers use commercial yeasts to protect the purity of grape expression. Vigorous, predictable yeasts also make it much less risky for winemakers wishing to work without sulfites or to avoid sterile filtration because these yeasts dependably gobble up sugar and nutrients during primary fermentation and create a nutrient desert, a fundamental leg of the stool of Integrated Brett Management, elaborated in chapter 10.

In their ignorance of the artistic issues underlying real-world winemaking, how many of those who wish to restrict Natural Wine makers from the tool of yeast selection will be happy if the critical response to such wines is that they all taste the same?

Like any master baker, a winemaker spends a lifetime experimenting to find the perfect yeast, optimizing the extraction of grape characteristics for the specific set of fermentation circumstances to be carried out. Most winemakers are skittish about rolling the dice during fermentation. An uninoculated must is like Forrest Gump's box of chocolates: you never know what you're gonna get.

A package of commercial yeast, in contrast, is like a vineyard, containing as it does only identical copies of the same organism. Genetic purity is basic to wine commerce. The seeds in a Pinot Noir tank are not pinot noir. They are sexual recombinants and, if planted, would not produce pinot noir vines, any more than your children exactly match you. By law, varietally labeled wines are produced from clonal cuttings, faithful copies of the same known entity. Nonsexual perfect copies are sold in the New World under varietal labels and in the Old World are strictly regulated within appellations.

Randall Grahm's current San Juan Bautista project delving into sexual crosses of grenache through the planting of seeds (see chapter 14) is as interesting a proposition enologically as it is legally. Under the existing purity-based regulations, there is no reason to believe that Randall will be permitted to sell these wines. Any new variety has to be approved by the Feds, and here Randall wants to plant a whole vineyard full of unnamed individuals. He needs a lawyer.

So far I haven't heard any Natural Wine folks insisting that we grow our grapes from seed. Natural or not, if Randall's latest vision catches on as so many of his have, it would signify the end of the tyranny of the obsolete concept of varietal winemaking and the sales of wines in categories as now understood by the marketplace. In my opinion, it is already true that wines vary more by viticultural region than by varietal.

Extremism seems to mark and marginalize organic wines, whose practitioners, clinging steadfastly to a sulfite-free fundamental belief, now enjoy a rarified exclusivity. Almost every producer and retailer has simply taken a pass. What I find laudable, even tragically compelling, is the manner in which organic wine certification advocates such as Paul Frey of Frey Vineyards, who knew what they were talking about, marshaled their forces and took a hard stand against allowing sulfites for organic wine.

I dislike this outcome because I think sulfite-free winemaking is not so easy and because I don't mind a lowering of the bar, at least temporarily, to get more folks to jump into the pool. But that's just politics. Paul and I share the same goals, and although I disappointed him in this fight, he knows that we're on the same side. I know Paul cares about the planet. He is no pirate intent on sequestering a market position, though I have no such trust in the motives behind the exclusionary practices of the California Certified Organic Farmers (CCOF) . . . well, never mind.

WHY BLOW THE DOUGH?

The main reason winemakers inoculate is cleanness. Second is stability: a vigorous yeast is more likely not to stick its fermentation. Third is their physical properties, tailored to the intended fermentation regimen: tolerance of hot or cold temperatures, low foaming, osmotic pressure tolerance, alcohol tolerance, low sulfide production, and so forth.

White wines retain their fresh aromatics at low temperatures, which prevent them from being boiled off, but ironically they also produce fewer esters at lower temperature. Matching fermentation temperature to yeast strain is a balancing exercise, an exploration that can easily take decades in the context of vintage variation. Interactions with grape source and clone, impacts on body and mouthfeel, response to oxygen or its absence, optimum fermentation rate for the desired time on the skins, flocculation characteristics, and rate of breakdown during sur lie aging are among the varied considerations any decent winemaker evaluates for each wine style in a given year. This exploration is impossible if the strain one is dealing with is not defined.

Beyond these, health considerations deserve some attention. Since the 1980s, when the carcinogen ethyl carbamate was discovered in some wines,[3] the Wine Institute and UC Davis have recommended that wineries favor inoculation with Lalvin EC-1118, or Prise de Mousse, a champagne yeast with high enzyme activity that degrades the compound's precursor, urea.

Recently, concerns with red wine headache and other previously intractable health phenomena have implicated the allergenic properties of biogenic amines derived from nonspecific biological sources, principally wild bacteria. Many winemakers feel that opening up the fermentation process to just any old microbe does a disservice to sensitive individuals. It is likely that many wine drinkers who report sulfite allergies (a medical impossibility, since the body produces a gram per day and the compound is too small to be an antigen) are actually reacting to biogenic amines, which are commonly ten times higher in uninoculated "natural" fermentations.

WHO'S KIDDING WHOM?

Is the indigenous yeast part of terroir? Depends on what you think the "T" word means. We all worship at the altar of terroir, but we really don't agree on what it is. For many winemakers, terroir expression equals presentation of the unique grape flavors that the climate and soil of a place produce. Travel in Burgundy, and it becomes obvious: Fixin is Fixin and Santenay is Santenay, no matter which house makes it. Many winemakers believe a predictable commercial yeast accentuates these differences. Wild yeast doesn't result in more unique flavor expression of place but less. In my view, ferally fermented wines taste more of their microbes than their grapes.

The terroiriste faction argues instead that the native yeast is part of the land's expression. Some even oppose the old practice of "mothering," because they think the seasonal climate variations in a specific vintage are reflected in the populations that show up in the fermenter. It's a weird position, because rather than explore the distinctive taste of the place as expressed in the grape, they want (or so they claim) to taste variations within an appellation as the highest expression of terroir. Product inconsistency is what they are demanding. Okay, but show me the money. Much as we may appreciate the passion, talk is cheap. I want to see their personal credit card purchases in vintages when this didn't work out so well.

But that's not what appellations are for. They are simply consumer guides. We want to buy Côte-Rôtie, Sancerre, or St. Emilion knowing we can serve up our duck, mussels, or Époisses cheese to go with it. Here and there in the New World, such identities are also emerging—Napa Cab with steak, Amador Zin with barbecue. Once experimentation has evolved them, the main job of appellations is to provide dependability, courtesy of a winemaking tradition associated with that place.

The essence of appellation is the predictable expectation of flavors and style. If there's no mold, it just ain't Roquefort. To whatever degree soil and climate may contribute special properties to the cheeses of Parma or Cheshire, and assuredly they do, it's still largely the choices of the artisan, guided by tradition, that determine style, championed by admiring retailers for their glories and spurned when nature fails to cooperate.

SHOW ME THE MONEY

I think the yeast choice, with all its consequences, is properly the province of the winemaker. Most winemakers choose the predictability and pure grape expression that yeast inoculation affords. It is a rare bird indeed who will taste a wine and say, "Wow, this tastes completely unlike anything I've ever tasted. How delightful. I'll take a case." That's just not what happens in the marketplace, even in the hangouts of the ultra-natural.

Confronted with something that tastes odd, the impulse to chew and not to swallow goes way back to our hunter-gatherer days and resides deep in our shared DNA. Our brains are open to seduction. The earthiness of a paté, the sour sting of a pickle, or the honeyed aromas of a kick-ass Viognier charm us by presenting to our midbrains credentials that pass scrutiny.

In the final chapter of this book, "Liquid Music," I explore the risky philosophical ground that surrounds the thrilling moment that unpredictably occurs when tasting a great wine. I have many times been privileged to experience such moments, but I make no claim to understand them. The orchestration of such events is, nevertheless, central to the work of winemakers.

So we try. My own WineSmith Cabernet Franc, Faux Chablis, and Roman Syrah, the wines that interest me the most, certainly don't run with the traffic. That's why I can count the barrels on one hand. Mainstream Cabernet Sauvignon and Pinot Noir pay my bills, and with a truckload at stake, you can bet I inoculate.

For mainstream consumers to evaluate commercially complex trade-offs is too much to ask. Passionate wine lovers can certainly help out, though, if they can develop a distaste for the pat answers that armchair pundits offer up. My advice is to find wineries you like and leave the driving to the pros.

TAKE-HOME MESSAGE

We didn't complete our list at the festival. We ran out of time, but there was another reason as well. Once we listed all the things a Natural Wine consumer might want, we couldn't find a sensible formula. No winemaker on our Natural Wine panel was willing to abandon yeast inoculation *and* sulfites *and* sterile filtration. If there is to be a certification mark, it needs some flexibility, or there will be no takers. In an ideal future, winemakers will be open about the technical combinations they choose, even the weird-sounding ones, and they will explain their rationale as we did twenty years ago.

Active dialogue would be much more productive than the endless parade of winemakers claiming nebulously to "do the minimum." If Natural Wine fans want to make that dialogue happen, they need to practice sympathetic active listening. A respectful ear combined with some actual wine purchases will get a winemaker's attention every time, and can lead to increased experimentation with wild yeasts. Meanwhile, talk is cheap for the critic who doesn't have to live with the consequences.

New World Identity and Judging Reform

Your Honor, . . . how can they pass judgment on it if they
don't know what it's all about?

—Henry Drummond, in *Inherit the Wind*

We've all seen it coming. European wines are sold on place, the fledgling New World wines on grape variety. As a result, Europe's designations are more consumer-friendly, while America remains a confusing
science project. The time is approaching to convert our industry into a
real business by identifying and promoting just what our regions offer.

The prime directive of postmodern winemaking is to present in our
wines distinctive terroir expression. This means the winemaker is
encouraged to remain as invisible as possible, assisting the character of
place in its best expression.

Today, varietal New World wines from a growing multiplicity of
origins are having more and more trouble fitting the simplistic expectation of varietal norms. Commercializing regional character at Safeway
is tricky. If native regional influences won't cooperate with efforts to
make wines blend in with the lowest-common-denominator-style profiles for the expected Merlot or Chardonnay, shelf positions will be
hard to come by. On the other hand, those influences can, with time
and effort, become the very reason your wines are sought out, just as
Beaujolais and Chianti are.

Postmodern philosophy concerns itself very much with art and language.[1] Novice wine drinkers begin with a different, one might say
purer, sensory experience, one that is not forced through a screen of
expectation. As they taste more and more wines, they are taught
and invent for themselves expectations of perfection and meanings of

flavors. For example, they may initially fall in love with the smell of oak but, coming to see it for the cheap trick that it is, eventually come to wish for restraint in its use. In this way, a rich body of distinctions about wine style and function connects colors, flavors, and textures to their sources such as varietal character, climate, and winemaking practices.In the modern view, such distinctions converge with the experiences of others, leading to the possibility of quality judgments in reviews and competitions. Often European styles, which are more firmly established and regulated, are used as touchstones for New World wines of the same grape varieties. Next thing you know, we are dishing out hundred-point scores and gold medals as if they mean something.

The fly in this ointment is that these interpretive systems are human constructs that quickly come to dominate perception itself. In established areas, universal standards are meaningless because wines are experienced entirely through the lens of local custom. The locals in New Joisey or the Highland Scots do not perceive themselves as speaking with an accent, because the familiar becomes invisible. To outsiders, however, local dialects seem peculiar and quaint, while television-speak is perceived as accentless. Just so for the globally distributed styles of Chardonnay and Merlot, which relegate the offerings of small local producers to the D list despite their great charm and vast numbers.

Competitions today are places of considerable conflict between modernists arguing for consistency and conformity and postmodernists stumping for diversity and distinction. Time was, these factions were able to coexist because there were far fewer wines and a much higher percentage of defects, such as volatile acidity, oxidation, and sulfides, both groups could agree to disregard. As the wines of emerging regions become cleaner and more consistent, a shift is occurring toward the postmodern mind-set, which honors diversity above standardization. But in the process, competitions have been shown to be increasingly inconsistent in their results. Indeed, the modern and postmodern views can (and probably should) compete within the mind of a single individual judge, so that the score for a specific wine may vary from minute to minute!

We have entered a golden age in which regional character is getting attention and styles are taking shape. Today's most important winemakers, saluted in chapter 12, are regional leaders cementing the styles that their appellations are uniquely capable of, from the Dunns of

Howell Mountain to Johnny McPherson of Temecula to Bruce Zoecklein in Virginia to Murli Dharmadhikari in Iowa.[2] But we have yet to
revamp the consumer's experience to enable a transition from varietal
to appellation thinking and buying. Competitions are supposed to provide a bridge, but they don't.

A TARGET-POOR ENVIRONMENT

Let's face facts: wine assessment in California competitions is a joke.
Recent papers by statistician and Humboldt winemaker Robert
Hodgson on the unreliability of judges and the inconsistency of
awards in thirteen U.S. wine competitions have created a well-
deserved scandal.[3]

Having judged hundreds of competitions over the past thirty years, I
was elated when Dr. Hodgson blew the whistle. Why so? Because in
truth, we saintly judges just make our assessments up. For the consumer, there's no way to tell if a Gold Medal Chardonnay is something
one would wish to actually drink. It's embarrassing.

In Europe, there are clear, well-known definitions of what the wine
of a region is supposed to taste like. The French have known for centuries that varietals vary from region to region and must be marketed as
such. We would never consider jumbling together a Graves, a Chinon,
and a St. Emilion into a grab-bag Cabernet Franc category for judging,
because consumers regard them differently. Why, then, should we judge
Merlots from Spring Mountain, Long Island, and the Snake River
blindly side by side?

Why do we judge today the way we do? When I first began judging
in the early '80s, there were far fewer wineries in California, and nearly
half the wines on the shelf had technical flaws such as VA, aldehyde,
sulfides, or excessive SO_2. Thus it was easy to take fifty California Cabernets, discard the flawed wines, and organize your favorites for Bronze,
Silver, and Gold. In other words, in this tiny world of long ago, varietals
seemed to work as a judging category.

But in truth, this was never a good idea. Today, there are thousands
of Cabernets being grown in hundreds of AVAs scattered across dozens
of states and provinces, and the percentage of seriously flawed wines
has dropped considerably. Almost everything is pretty good. Absent
defining criteria, judges are left to choose among a wide variety of well-
made wines with vastly different personalities, and of course they waf-
fle, as any open-minded expert should.

GOING TO THE DOGS

It seems obvious to me that the primary problem is that judging cannot be effective without targeted profiles. Any of you who have seen *Best in Show* can attest that if we tried to judge dogs the way we judge wines, the breeders would murder us in our beds.

In dog competitions, thousands of entrants are judged according to exacting standards and ribbons awarded based on exacting criteria put forth by the breed clubs and documented by the American Kennel Club. There's a book.[4] Very specific profiles are laid out for each of the 169 approved breeds, and all are unique. An Irish setter and a cocker spaniel, though both are considered Sporting Dogs, are judged by completely different rules. It would be silly to hold them to the same criteria, and sillier still to have no standards at all.

The Experiment

As an outgrowth of my work in defining regional varietal identities for AppellationAmerica.com, in the spring of 2011 I received the cooperation of the Riverside International Wine Competition to experiment, for the first time in any U.S. competition, with the revolutionary concept of judging wines according to regional standards.

For the Petite Sirah category only, judges were provided with the AVA as stated on the label and, if available, regionally based style profile(s) for that AVA. AppellationAmerica.com authorized use of the twenty-one regional profiles that our panel, in conjunction with AVA winegrower associations, had developed for the Best-of-Appellation evaluations.[5]

Petite Sirah was chosen for a number of reasons: wide regional planting, proven response to regional influences, and, most of all, a strong advocacy group ("PS I Love You")[6] that had supported the development of regional style profiles. We already had most of the definitions in the can.[7] Figures 29 and 30 give you a couple of examples.

What Happened

Riverside received fifty-four Petite Sirahs for judging from twenty-six AVAs, fourteen of which we had profiles for, representing thirty-six wines. Thus, 67% of the wines were judged against standards, while the rest were thrown into a grab-bag category as usual, except that they were identified as to region.

TASTE BENCHMARKS	
	Profile #1 **Hard, angular, agreeable style**
Appearance	Dark color with bricky edges
Aroma	High desert vegetation such as sage, juniper, and wildflowers; very closed red licorice fruit aromatics
Flavor	Brutal, uncompromising tannins; guava signature in the finish
Balance	Good mineral energy
PRODUCTION CORRELATIONS	
Terroir	1,400 to 2,600 feet, mostly west facing, thus subject to baking late-day heat; well-drained soils and droughty conditions

FIGURE 29. Appellation America Blue Book entry, Howell Mountain Petite Sirah.

TASTE BENCHMARKS	
	Profile #1 **Refined style**
Appearance	Medium red; quite light for this varietal
Aroma	The very aromas that define Russian River Pinot Noir: cherry, orange blossom, and lilac
Flavor	Round, feminine tannins, bursting with lemon and blackberry on the palate
Balance	The pinnacle of refinement is to be found in the Russian River wines, whose age-worthiness sets them apart.
PRODUCTION CORRELATIONS	
Viticultural	Prone to rot
Terroir	Cool climate and fog influence

FIGURE 30. Appellation America Blue Book entry, Russian River Petite Sirah.

Dan Berger seated me on a panel with winemakers Kerry Damskey and Linda Trotta as well as journalist Mike Dunne. After some initial confusion, the process flowed smoothly and naturally. As I have seen on so many AppAm panels, these first-time participants in judging by AVA groupings were surprised both by the regional character consistency and by how little difference the winemaking choices made compared to the regional variations.

"This is a valuable route to take in evaluating wines," Trotta said. "The key to success is the work that's been initiated with vintners in the appellations to describe the representative regional characteristics. Adjusting the way that I judged the wines to take these criteria into account was a surprisingly quick process."

"The Petite Sirahs from Livermore Valley did have fairly consistent streaks of blackberry, blueberry, black pepper, and sweet tannins," said Dunne. "The Petite Sirahs from Paso Robles tended to be characterized by candied fruit flavors offset against the smell of smoldering briars. Flowers, bing cherries, lemon verbena, and soft tannins ran through the Petite Sirahs of the Russian River Valley. Black-fruit flavors, green herbs, and white pepper seemed to distinguish the Petite Sirahs of Dry Creek Valley."

I find it fascinating the degree to which this holds true despite the absence of regulations in the New World. A combination of natural and human influences is at play. If your tasting room is on Highway 49 in California's Gold Country, you're going to try for softer, oakier wines for the local tourists, while in Napa, you may be more inclined to make classic, austere styles to blow away wealthy visitors from Japan. But clearly, natural influences tend to dominate—though we don't yet understand just how the maraschino cherries find their way into Mendocino reds of all varietals or the darker fruit tones get into Napa Valley wines.

At Appellation America we collect copious technical data on climate, weather, altitude, soils, vineyard practices, and winemaking choices in an attempt to connect these dots. While this is endlessly fascinating work for us eno-nerds, all a consumer needs to know is simply that *these local flavor expressions exist*. The judges need not explain how the character comes to be but, like pornography, simply to know it when they see it.[8]

In general, judging against a standard was perhaps worth a one-rank boost to a wine conforming to its region. More important, it made it easier to allow for outlier styles such as southern Oregon's austerity and the hard tannins of the high-altitude AVAs.

"It makes logical sense to taste a variety defined by appellation, because terroir is going to define that wine, so tasting related wines against each other will better define their virtues," said Damskey. "Tasting Petite Sirahs by appellation generally allows wines to show better amongst their peers. Understanding how an appellation expresses itself makes it easier for judges to discern quality. Tasting by appellation is also less fatiguing than tasting blind with mixed appellations.

There is a sense of expectation when you understand what a terroir should taste like."

I knew the experiment was a success when the panel remarked what a drag it was to have to go back to the old system as we slugged our way through boatloads of randomized Chardonnays.

Whence Come These Standards?

"An important element for judges to work out is the case in which a wine is very well made but may not adhere to the regional descriptors," Trotta observed. "I think that as a panel we worked through that well." In fact, the Christopher Creek '08 Russian River, which was named Best of Class and went on to win the Sweepstakes Prize for Best Red in Show, was just such a wine. Although it was very rich in black cherry, orange, and lilac, the aromatic traits in the standard, and had the expected round, fine tannins, it was extremely dark in color, having been grown in the fog-free end of this long and varied appellation. Its compelling quality made it instantly plain that a second profile for the upper Russian River needs to be added to the standards.

To get the ball rolling, any interested party will do. There is no reason why standards cannot be developed by any journalistic team or by the competition sponsors themselves. Publications regularly churn out articles on emerging wine regions full of descriptive prose that could be used for this purpose, and competitions could collect the best of it over time. But following Europe's lead, the regional winegrower associations should be the final arbiter, and it behooves them to get active in this area. In the AKC, the breed clubs themselves are the source of standards, and among these vested interests is where the political head bashing should properly take place.

PERSONAL SOMMELIER

Competitions exist to serve consumers by connecting them to wines they will enjoy, in the process rewarding wineries that give the people what they want. Absent descriptive categorization, a Gold Medal Chardonnay means nothing, just as it is not helpful to hear the recommendation of a "really good" movie, book, or song absent genre info.

An important manifestation of regional profiling is the development of an open universal language for wine traits. Although this language may never reach consumers, with existing technology, it won't have to.

Five years hence, I predict that your phone will run an app that will sort your preferences into a personal wine list the way Pandora.com allows you to tailor your own radio stations, pairing like with like. Shops and restaurants will upload their offerings; your app will sort them into Joe's Bold Reds, Joe's Crisp Whites under $15, and so forth, providing links to winery blurbs, critical reviews, and user feedback; and you can then refine your personal algorithm with a thumbs up/ thumbs down on your purchase.

This technology will enable consumers to identify their preferences among a huge and growing world of offerings. It will also obviate the need for a European-style system of regulated production.

SOUNDS LIKE A LOT OF WORK

Without question, it's going to take a long time to complete our transition beyond grab-bag varietal categories. But every time we take a baby step toward respecting and advertising diversity, a few good wines on the fringes become more marketable. Giving consumers and the trade a road map to styles can counter the perception of sameness that typecasts the entire state of California. When our wines become once again a navigable adventure, everybody wins.

"To become expert at this, you need to have judges who understand the different terroirs well," cautions Kerry Damskey. That's going to take time. As Mike Dunne puts it, "Whether focusing on origins eventually leads to a heightened understanding and appreciation of wine, let alone improved wine competitions, will only become clear after many, many more vintages."

Still, the sea change in consumer purchasing patterns from simple varietal loyalty to appellation consciousness is already under way, and there is really no stopping it. These things happen fast. Consider that in 1960 it was unimaginable that California table wine production would replace port and sherry. In 1970, no one could predict that Cabernet and Chardonnay would dominate over Burgundy and cheap Chablis.

We have made a solid beginning. The AppAm Blue Book for significant varietal/AVA combinations currently has over three hundred entries. That means a good 25% of the work necessary to characterize the major regions is already done. One area (Petite Sirah) is ready to lock and load into any competition willing to play. Other varietals like Riesling, Chardonnay, and Zinfandel have enough key entries to make a start. When competitions begin providing this aid, uncharacterized

AVAs will have the incentive to add their own standards and so benefit from the competitive advantage they confer.

At the very least, judges ought to be told where the wines come from. This would provide some hint as to style, though judges without a solid regional background would at first be at a disadvantage. But providing judges with AVA information is good judge training in itself, helping everyone to start learning by tasting.

Destiny beckons. Rome wasn't built in a day, and I reckon we'd better get started. In the meantime, it should be plain to even the most short-sighted among us that the Petites at Riverside got a fairer shake this year than ever before.

TAKE-HOME MESSAGES

- American wine is the only commodity that is judged without standards.
- It is imperative that American competitions begin to embrace regional diversity by providing their judges with label information concerning origins.
- The highest priority for regional winegrower associations is to identify and publicize the characteristics of local wine types.

Liquid Music

Resonance in Wine

Annual revenues for music worldwide exceed those of pharmaceuticals. Brain scans of listeners deeply moved by a musical piece show activity in the same cognitive areas stimulated by sex and addictive drugs.[1]

The special allure of wine is similar. There are no $100 beers. We agonize about spending $10 on a bottle of olive oil that will last for months, then cheerfully lay out twice that for a bottle of Cabernet that will be gone in the hour.

In chapter 11, I concluded the section on postmodern principles with a discussion of harmony and astringency, touching on the importance of context for wine sensory properties. Here I want to dig deeper into wine's mystery and advocate for a postmodern view of winemaking as "the practical art of connecting the human soul to the soul of a place by rendering its grapes into liquid music."

This isn't going to work.

It's one thing to hold a reader's interest with well-worn topics like minerality and Biodynamics, even when I bring an unexpected slant. But here I am tackling in prose a realm that is utterly experiential. Without real-life familiarity, you are likely to think I am simply nuts. Merely reading what follows is very likely a complete waste of your time.

So before you read on, I really must beg you to do a bit of preparation. Run down to the store and buy these wines:

1. Glen Ellen Chardonnay from some recent vintage.
2. Some oaky, toasty butterbomb Chardonnay with over 14% alcohol. The Rombauer is great if you can find it.
3. (Optional) A classic-style true Chablis, such as William Fevre or my WineSmith Faux Chablis. This wine is likely to be released much older than the others.

All set? Now, taste the wines. They represent three popular genres of Chardonnay, analogous to movie genres. No. 1 is like a Disney comedy: sweet and shallow. It's a fun wine to make you smile—the "yummy" style. Note that it contains a little sugar to cover up a pressy astringency that appears in the finish.

No. 2 is an action/adventure wine, designed to blow you away with its size—the "wow!" style. Its mild astringency, masked by its margarine fatness, is from oak—a fine, parching/numbing harshness atop the tongue.

No. 3 is the equivalent of a foreign film, stimulating the intellect primarily, the "hmmmm" style. Its astringency is acid- and mineral-based in the finish.

Now go to postmodernwinemaking.com, click on the Wine and Music tab, and find my interview with NPR's Alex Cohen.[2] Open it up, and taste along. As you do, pay close attention to the changes in astringency. Feel free to freak out.

CREDIT WHERE IT'S DUE

This experiment was originally presented as "Chardonnay and the Theory of Deliciousness" at the 1996 American Society for Enology and Viticulture Unified Symposium by a team headed by Bruce Rector, my former boss and guru at Glen Ellen Winery who I mentioned in chapter 11 and who in the late 1980s instigated the Quality Symposia where I was first exposed to the relationship of wine to music. Since then, I have shown this baffling effect to many thousands of participants on a hundred occasions. The result is always the same: deep skepticism followed by exuberant amazement. At this point there can be little doubt that music really does alter the sensory properties of wine.

In seeking an explanation, I was fortunate that my wife, Susan Mayer-Smith, a concert pianist and flautist with a Ph.D. in clinical psychology from the University of Marseilles, was available to help me work up a presentation in Australia in 2007 based on recent advances in music cognition.[3] Recently deceased, Susie had made inquiries in this area that represent a significant contribution to our industry.

The late Don Blackburn, French-trained founding winemaker for Bernardus and an avowed anti-reductionist, devised wine and music pairing methodology as a way to demonstrate statistically significant sensory effects within a holistic point of view. Since they reside in human perception, wine's attributes are innately *subjective*. But Don's experiments showed with a high degree of statistical precision that they are also strongly shared.

Don found modern enology handicapped by a reluctance to explore this vital realm. In scientific circles, "subjectivity" is tarred with a tainted subtext—arbitrary, unknowable, and unworthy of study. Shedding this disdain for things human is an important postmodern skill. While reductionist Aroma Wheel™–type wine descriptors have been of some use, I anticipate that more holistic, anthropomorphic terminology—generous, austere, enigmatic, masculine/feminine, and so on—will hold considerable power as we seek to address our wines' functionality for consumers. Music education shows us that this is an entirely reasonable expectation.

So what the heck is going on?

Wine, like music, carries emotion. Just as we have happy songs and sad songs, wines have emotional modalities. White Zinfandels are silly, happy-go-lucky wines; Cabernets are brooding, foul-mooded, even angry. We will naturally pair up Dixieland jazz or polka with the former, but Beethoven's Fifth, the Doors, or Metallica work better with the latter. That might seem like simple guesswork until you try it the other way around. As Don showed me, *Carmina Burana* actually makes a White Zinfandel seem to have more tannin than a Howell Mountain Cabernet.

Wine acts like another instrument in the ensemble. If it's playing a minor key while everybody else is playing in a major key, the result will be noise.

In the early 1990s, I was privileged to work with neurophysiologist and concert pianist Manfred Clynes, who five decades ago coined the term *alpha rhythms* in conjunction with his oscilloscopic work on frog brains. Clynes's seminal work, *Sentics: The Touch of the Emotions*, concerned itself with a new science focused on the shapes of emotions. His work established the existence of universal shapes that accord with the whole spectrum of emotions. These appear in art and in his experiments were readily generated both by his subjects in Sonoma and by Aborigines in the Australian Outback. Delving together into the relationship of wine and music, Clynes and I were able to classify wines into emotional categories, but we never quite figured out how his shapes manifest in wines.

THE NEW BRAIN TOYS

Until recently, mapping brain function was slow going. The principal resource for a hundred years has been brain injuries, dependent on happenstance to supply subjects with interesting cognitive anomalies. One man, for example, had the back of his head shot off in a war; although he was otherwise normal, he had a hole (a "scotoma") in the middle of his visual field. That's how we first located the visual cortex.[4]

Magnetic resonance imaging (MRI), electro-encephalography (EEC), and positron emission tomography (PET) today allow us to observe live subjects in midthought. Musicologists have been quick to jump on these new tools, and their fascinating cognitive findings have birthed an army of technical papers as well as a host of readable popular articles and books.[5] Wine harmony and balance can be better understood by piggybacking on this research.

In 1993, I began to experiment with adjusting alcohol content. The same wine that was hot and bitter at elevated alcohol became thin and salty at low alcohol, with a balanced wine somewhere in between.

At first I expected that if I graphed preference versus alcohol content, these effects would describe a nice smooth normal curve. But instead we found "sweet spots"—discrete points of harmonious balance separated from each other by terribly disharmonious wines. Figure 31 shows the results of an experiment we did at CSU Fresno on a 1999 Syrah, in which twenty-two judges voted their preferences for blends of untreated and alcohol-reduced components comprising thirty-one alcohol points between 12.5% and 15.5% in 0.1% increments. No bell curve. Instead we have the equivalent of radio stations, with very poor wines just 0.1% away from highly rated ones. At Vinovation we alcohol-adjusted 2,500 wines per year for fifteen years and never saw a bell curve.

Something in our sensory software reacts to fine nuances of difference, sorting harmony from dissonance in a pattern that our judges all perceived intuitively (see sidebar on p. 300). That sounds completely zany until you recognize that this is exactly what music does. The strong

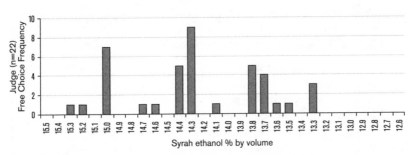

FIGURE 31. 1999 Deiner Vineyard Syrah sweet spot data. Wine at 18.0% original alcohol was blended with a portion de-alcoholized to 10.1% in different ratios to produce 31 samples 0.1% apart. The resulting blends were rated for preference by 22 judges. Multiple preferences were allowed.

nonlinearity we see in figure 31 seems outlandish until you personally experience it.

DISSONANCE VERSUS PREFERENCE

When I pop a cork, I like to test drive with music by sampling free thirty-second clips on iTunes. Matches and mismatches are apparent within seconds.

A frequently asked question is, "Does it matter if I like the music?" My answer is no. There is no song I like less than Iron Maiden's "Run for the Hills," but I have to admit it goes great with my Cabernet Sauvignon, which takes on a round, sweet spiciness. Conversely, my favorite tunes are often just awful accompaniments to the wine I'm drinking.

In 2001, brain imaging showed McGill University researchers Anne Blood and Robert Zatorre that subjects listening to a C–G perfect fifth directed the signal to a "reward system," experiencing a "smooth, sweet" sound. When the same subjects heard a C/C-sharp dissonance, the signal was instead directed to the "fight-or-flight" areas of the brain's limbic system. Dissonant chords were characterized as having a "rough" sound.[6]

My best guess is that this same mechanism routes balanced wines to our pleasure centers, while unbalanced ones trigger our fight-or-flight response. Its function on the palate is an obvious survival mechanism. As hunter-gatherers, primal humans needed to eat. They also needed to avoid toxins and so developed through natural selection a highly refined ability to detect mold compounds, alkaloids, and other nastiness. Put something

Logical Processing Parallels between Music and Wine

Music	Wine
Pitch	Aromas
Timbre	Terroir
Meter	Swirling rhythm
Melody	Anticipation/Sipping
Lyrics	Winemaking story
Tonal context	Style rules
Faults	Technical defects

Many parallels exist between listening to music and wine appreciation. Pitch is the actual frequency of a sound. Its flavor is carried by the timbre, for example a clarinet's smooth, round tone versus the rough, edgy timbre of a saxophone. A wine's aromatic timbre can communicate sense of place. What the pitch *means* is its tonal context (is it the tonic, the dissonant 2nd, the pleasantly harmonic 5th, or the highly anticipatory 7th?) when the pitch is heard in the context of the key signature. In wine, an aroma note can mean different things in different wine styles. For example the addition of muscat to reds is considered cheating. A wine delivers a message of the season, the place, and how it was made that is as clear to an experienced taster as are the lyrics of a song to a devoted band follower. The metered rhythm of music has its analog in the precise swirl/smell/sip of wine tasting, and the way we ignore the glass until desire builds, then resolve the tension with another sip, resembles the repeated building of tension and resolution that characterizes a melody line. Finally, perception for the professional musician or wine taster moves farther and farther away from pure experience into a formatted comparison to some ideal of perfection, with perceived faults looming in the foreground.

in your mouth, and the brain needs to make a snap decision whether to reward the impulse to chew and swallow or to press the panic button and spit it out *now*. Something about wine seems to magnify these sensitivities.

WE HAVE A PROBLEM, HOUSTON

The Chardonnay experiment I described on NPR is an extreme case of "exclusive" pairings; Rector's team went to great trouble to find music that starkly discriminated Chardonnay styles. Even so, most music is exclusive. Open a Riesling, a Sauvignon Blanc, a Pinot Noir, and a

Cabernet Sauvignon, taste them side by side as you sample musical selections, and you'll find that most tunes will work with only one of the wines.

This is a big problem for restaurants, because diners at adjacent tables are drinking different wines. Winery tasting rooms have the same problem. Fortunately, there do exist "inclusive" pieces which resonate with an overall theme. A restaurant's theme may be "romantic get-away," "family joint," or "hip/swank." Every aspect—menu, lighting, decor—should be aligned with this theme. Once properly inclusive background music is selected, the sommelier should always evaluate potential wine list candidates within this environment.

My own wines are Eurocentric and intellectual, so they like Gershwin, flamenco, and Samuel Barber. One of my clients makes very showy, somewhat shallow wines that work very well with big Hollywood anthems such as the *Star Wars* theme and the love theme from *Superman* ("Can You Read My Mind?").

Locating a playlist of inclusive pieces is a lot of work, but the payoff is considerable. Theme music not only boosts tasting room sales, but it is also great for winemakers to blend to. Playing theme music while making blending decisions is the best way I know of for winemakers to stabilize a winery style vintage to vintage—vastly more effective than reducing wine to a grocery list of aroma notes and trying to balance those. I simply haven't found evidence that Aroma Wheel™ elements please my customers as dependably as a well-harmonized style.

Many seasoned wine professionals are disturbed by the possibility that music and other environmental factors could have a profound influence on wine judgment, because a lifetime of quality assessments may go out the window. Too bad. The experience is not entirely in the bottle. Anyone who has purchased a case of wine in hopes of duplicating a peak experience has learned the hard way that the first bottle, consumed in an ideal environment, was much better than the others. Pairing your wine with music greatly improves your chances of connecting with your next bottle.

FINAL CHORDS

Our work as winemakers is to create an elaborate illusion. The euphoria of great wine in perfect circumstances is similar to those peak moments at a rock concert or symphony when our souls feel profoundly connected and our brains don't mind the volume.

Soulfulness is an inherent quality of an artistic product, a message transcending words that the artist vividly shares with an audience. It can be a cello performance, a cheese, a dance, a sauce, or a wine that touches us profoundly. Soulful wines often contain diverse, even conflicting elements such as earth, fruit, and spice, which intertwine to convey a feeling of profound depth. The essence of soulful wine is a deep connectedness, of being shown by another a part of ourselves we did not know existed. The production of soulful wines requires focused artisanal attention that sets aside automatic, formulaic, or cynical blending practices.

When the midbrain's mysterious math determines that this sense of harmony is missing, the limbic system is alerted, and a rough edge attaches to the taste. I believe this explains why 4 ppt of TCA, less than a millionth the quantity necessary to cause physical astringency, nevertheless imparts harshness by masking the wine's fruit.

Our sense of harmony is strongly shared—if the piano is out of tune, everybody leaves the bar; but we also, as individuals, have broadly disparate preferences. Two warring notions, both valid. Lots of people just don't get it about wine. Any kid who has sneaked a taste will tell you that wine is hot, sour, bitter, and harsh. If you are reading this book, though, you somehow got past that. You had a peak experience that turned you into an oenophile.

You may be wondering what hit you. More to the point, you'd probably like to know where can you get more of that feeling, hopefully cheaper and more reliably. I am here to tell you that pairing your wine with music can up your chances big time.

TAKE-HOME MESSAGES

- Wine sensory impressions are highly sensitive to ambience. Music pairing can greatly improve your chances of enjoying a wine.
- Musical pieces are useful in blending to a consistent style.
- The essence of wine is entirely experiential. No amount of Internet chatter can reproduce it in the slightest degree.

Winemaking Basics

Wine is made, in principle and with numerous exceptions, entirely from the fermented juice of grapes. Wine is fundamentally different from beer, which by its very nature is an assembly of ingredients: at minimum, water, barley starches that have been enzymatically modified, and hops. These come from whatever sources and are used in whatever proportions the brewer may desire, whereas wine focuses on the grape's origin. Wine, in its simplicity, is also fundamentally different from distilled spirits, which are by nature highly technological. To make wine, in contrast, grapes may be trodden out by foot, gravity-fed into buried earthen pots, and spontaneously fermented with reasonable results.

THE VINEYARD

Grapes, through millions of years of evolutionary differentiation and millennia of human selection and crossbreeding, now exist in many hundreds of important wine varieties, chiefly from the European *Vitis vinifera,* which contains a staggering array of differently flavored and colored cultivars but is limited in its range by susceptibility to cold and disease. Other grapes of increasing importance include the American species *Vitis labrusca* (e.g., Concord), noted for its grapey "foxy" flavors and its tolerance to cold and disease, and the distinctively aromatic and disease-resistant muscadines *(Muscadinia rotundifolia),* the only grapes that can inhabit most of the southeastern U.S., as well as an extensive and growing menu of hybrids that are proving themselves commercially viable in the American heartland to the great surprise of connoisseurs, myself included.

Grapes are generally grown as single varieties in vineyards, which may contain anywhere from 500 to 10,000 vines in an acre. They may be freestanding or arranged on wire trellises. To prevent attack by the root louse phylloxera, vinifera scions are commonly grafted onto American native rootstocks, which tolerate the pest.

The yearly cycle of a vineyard begins when vines emerge from dormancy in spring, pushing green growing canes from buds formed the previous year, spaced every few inches along last year's woody canes. Within two months from budbreak, tiny flowers bloom on the new canes, generally self-fertilizing, resulting in berries that set and begin to grow through cellular division, forming seeds (Cycle One) as well as vacuoles containing sugars (glucose and fructose) and acids (tartaric and malic) and widely varying levels of tannins in skins and seeds.

Two months later, when these seeds have become viable, berries change color (véraison)—generally becoming black, pink, or golden—to attract birds. Subsequently, cells elongate rapidly, fruity flavors are formed to render berries more attractive to birds, and malic acid is metabolized to provide energy to concentrate high levels of sugar from sap into the berries (Cycle Two).

In summer, vineyard labor is busy weeding, removing unwanted suckers, applying fertilizers, controlling pests, adjusting irrigation, balancing crop and vegetation by manipulating canopy and removing excessive crop load, and training new vines.

Harvest occurs throughout the autumn at a time determined by the cultivar's maturity timetable in the place it is being grown, the type of wine to be made, and the proclivities of Murphy's Law (weather, labor, machinery, and the marketplace). Harvest may be performed by hand, generally in daylight morning hours, resulting in bins of grapes in whole clusters consisting of a stem (rachis) and berries containing juice, skins, and seeds. Mechanical harvesting, which is commonly done at night for its cool temperatures and the convenience of winery day crews, generally removes stems and delivers fruit as whole berries with some degree of juicing.

Following harvest, vines retire into dormancy. Winter work involves pruning back the last year's growth to the desired number and architecture of buds to optimize vine balance in the coming year.

THE WINERY

Red and white wines involve similar processes that are done in a different order.

In white wines, grapes are crushed and pressed in a single operation. The foot-treading of ancient winemaking is now mostly replaced by machinery. Grapes are dumped into a hopper that augers them into a rotating destemmer that knocks berries off the stems. The berries fall through the gap between two rollers set to pop them without crushing their seeds, a source of bitterness. The resulting mass of juice, pulp, skins, and seeds is conveyed into a press, essentially a large screen that separates juice from solids (pomace). Presses have many designs for squeezing pomace to extract remaining juice. Initial free-run juice issuing from the press is the softest in texture, and subsequent juice extracted by pressing is increasingly high in tannins. The creation and use of press wines is a high art.

Juice is fermented under temperature control, generally in large tanks but sometimes in sixty-gallon barrels. Primary fermentation consists of the conversion of sugars, generally 17–25° brix (percent by weight), into alcohol (11–15%) and the production of carbon dioxide. This is accomplished by *Saccharomyces* yeasts occurring in small numbers in vineyards, which can spontaneously ferment, or the must may be inoculated with commercial strains of these organisms. Although other species of yeasts and bacteria can grow in juice, the low pH and high osmotic pressure of grape juice is hostile to human pathogens, and most non-*Saccharomyces* yeasts cannot survive in the resulting levels of alcohol.

Fermentation of whites is normally conducted between 50°F and 60°F in order to preserve freshness and fruitiness. White wine fermentations may proceed to dryness (complete conversion of sugar to alcohol), or, depending on the wine style desired by the winemaker, they may be arrested, usually by chilling, to preserve some sugar sweetness. White fermentations generally take about three weeks.

In the case of red wines, primary fermentation occurs in the presence of skins and seeds. The skins are buoyed by carbon dioxide, and the resulting cap must be regularly remixed into the fermentation by punching down or pumping over. Pressing occurs at the end of primary fermentation. Fermentation of reds is normally conducted between 75°F and 85°F in order to extract and fix color and tannin and create aromatic complexity and nuance. Dryness generally occurs in red fermentations in one or two weeks, but the dry wine is sometimes left in contact with the pomace for a month or more afterward (extended maceration).

The fermentation process results in many types of sediment, aka lees. Gross lees, which include seeds, grape solids, occasional sprinkler heads, and diverse material other than grape (MOG), is discarded. Alcohol also decreases the solubility of the potassium salt of the grape acid, tartaric acid. Crystals of potassium bitartrate, or cream of tartar, fall out of the wine into lees as well. Such crystals, if formed in the refrigerated bottle, are sometimes mistaken for small pieces of broken glass, which can be alarming to consumers. Accordingly, bitartrate precipitation, especially in white wines, is generally forced to completion during the finishing process prior to bottling (cold stabilization); proteins that can cloud white wine are similarly removed by introducing bentonite clay to adsorb them (heat stabilization).

Fine yeast lees may sometimes be preserved and not discarded. These have beneficial antioxidative and sensory properties that may aid in increasing the body and longevity of white wines. In reds, fine lees are destructive to color and may cause dryness if stirred into young wines, but in developed wines over six months of age they may coat tannins and assist longevity. Another high art.

Subsequent to alcoholic fermentations, wines may undergo secondary fermentations by other microbes, chief among them malolactic fermentation, which converts the natural grape acid (malic) into lactic acid, the principal acid in yogurt. Depending on the bacterial strain and conditions of the fermentation, this fermentation will produce a number of flavor elements, most notably the buttery compound diacetyl. Malolactic fermentation also diminishes freshness, fruitiness, and crispness.

Nearly all red wines undergo malolactic, as do many California Chardonnays. Most Sauvignon Blancs, Rieslings, Pinot Grigios, and rosés are prevented from malolactic by addition of sulfur dioxide. These fresh wines are normally not aged but are bottled and released in the spring following vintage for early consumption.

Many sulfur compounds are associated with winemaking. Yellow sulfur dust is applied to vineyards to control powdery mildew and discourage pests. Sulfides are stinky compounds that form in wine and impart a variety of stenches.

Sulfur dioxide is a preservative that is added to nearly all wines, both at the crusher and at the end of primary fermentation, or after malolactic if desired. SO_2 (which creates in wine a family of free and bound sulfites) is an intentionally added preservative, whereas hydrogen sulfide is a stinky aroma defect that is not chemically related and is never added to wine. Excessive sulfur dioxide has a sharp odor similar to a freshly struck match, and is not to be confused with hydrogen sulfide, which has a rotten egg odor. It is unprofessional to speak of adding or smelling "sulfur," as this is imprecise.

It is not possible to be allergic to sulfites, as the human body generates about one gram per day, much more than the quantity present in an entire bottle of wine. Nonetheless, Roman winemaking throughout Europe for several centuries appears not to have used sulfites, and some winemakers believe that the best wines are sulfite-free, just as the world's greatest cheeses are unpasteurized.

Wines whose virtues result from age rather than freshness—Chardonnays and most reds—are aged in sixty-gallon oak barrels for six months to three years. During this time, the wines mysteriously open and develop their flavors much as an aging cheese does, and tannins resolve their harshness and become complex, plush, and supportive of flavors, as in good chocolate. The oaken skin of barrels is slightly porous and contributes to this process, both by allowing minute amounts of oxygen to interact with the wine and by off-gassing microbial aromas such as sulfides, mustiness, and kraut. New barrels also impart vanilla, spice, toast, and caramel aromas, which may be appreciated very positively if not overdone.

Prior to bottling, wines may be filtered by some winemakers to achieve clarity and microbial stability. White wine production was altered forever when sterile filters were introduced in the 1960s that could be integrity-tested by "bubble-pointing," which rectifies the filter's ability to hold gas pressure, guaranteeing that the bottled wine will not referment and explode. This procedure enabled California to convert from port and sherry to off-dry table wine.

Bottles may use natural cork closures made from the bark of cork oak trees, which although traditional and regarded positively by most consumers may harbor musty cork taint (2,4,6-trichloroanisole, or TCA). In recent years, the quest for an alternative closure that prevents cork taint has led to experimentation with synthetic cork look-alikes and screw caps. These closures all have different effects on wine behavior in the bottle during aging.

Winemaking is continually evolving. Most wines today are intended to be drunk within a year of bottling, but many improve if stored at a low and even temperature. The expectation of connoisseurs that wines survive and improve in their cellars is at odds with the typical consumer's expectation that a purchased wine be at its best on the day of purchase. As the American market matures, the balance between these two points of view will need to be balanced as part of each winemaker's art.

RECOMMENDED READING

For a beginner desiring a concise yet comprehensive summary of the wines of the world and the business of wine, you can hardly do better than J. Patrick Henderson and Dellie Rex's *About Wine*, 2nd ed. (Clifton Park, NY: Delmar, Cengage Learning, 2012). Skim it, and then keep it handy as a reference.

In contrast to the vast numbers of wine consumers, there are relatively few wineries in the English-speaking world, so books for this specialized calling tend to be expensive. For beginning winemakers, my preferred general text on modern enology is Ron S. Jackson's *Wine Science: Principles and Applications*, 3rd ed. (Oxford: Elsevier, 2008). New small wineries should also purchase Murli Dharmadhikari's *Micro-vinification: A Practical Guide to Small-Scale Wine Production* (Springfield: Midwest Viticulture and Enology Center, Department of Fruit Science, Southwest Missouri State University, 2001). The definitive guide to chemical analysis of wine is Bruce W. Zoecklein, Ken Fugelsang, Barry Gump, and Michael Nury, *Wine Production Analysis* (New York: Chapman and Hall, 1995).

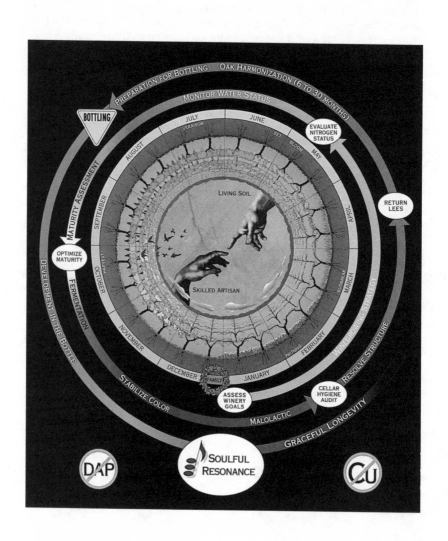

Navigating the Postmodern Calendar

Unlike any other agricultural enterprise or type of cooking, winemaking proceeds at an incredibly slow pace seldom apprehended by those who have not participated in it. Imagine a baker waiting half a decade for his wheat, then placing it in the oven for years and waiting an equal time for it to cool in order to serve it. Winegrowers must anticipate and heavily invest in market trends projected many years into the future.

The Postmodern Mandala, shown opposite, is a circular calendar that depicts the sequence of winemaking activities by overlaying the multiple years encompassing a single winemaking project on the annual cycle of Nature. In general, a winemaker has several vintage chronologies under way simultaneously, nested within this annual rhythm. A contiguous line symbolizing a winegrowing project is drawn outside of the calendar, spiraling outward to symbolize its approach to resolution, passing through its time in the vineyard, then its harvest, fermentation, and the various phases of élevage prior to bottling, finally experiencing the appropriate bottle aging to result in soulful resonance and graceful longevity. Despite the proclivities of circumstance, the intended end of any well-considered project must be contained in its beginning, and vineyard enology strives to unite winemaking goals with vineyard practices.

The black-and-white rendition presented here hardly does justice to graphic artist Bob Lee Hickson's rendering of postmodern winemaking notions, which is best viewed in its interactive version at http://postmodernwinemaking.com/introduction/#calendar.

Within these general phases are markers of particular practices. All terms in the figure are defined in the glossary in this book (also viewable online in an interactive format at http://postmodernwinemaking.com/glossary).

Notes

INTRODUCTION

1. The article can be found at www.wineanorak.com/clark_smith.htm.

2. www.decanter.com/people-and-places/wine-articles/527040/the-decanter-power-list-2011.

3. www.thedrinksbusiness.com/2012/05/alvarez-peters-wine-is-no-different-than-toilet-paper/.

4. Jean-François Lyotard, *The Postmodern Condition: A Report on Knowledge* (Minneapolis: University of Minnesota Press, 1984), vol. 10, 34.

5. Richard Feynmann, *Six Easy Pieces: Essentials of Physics Explained by Its Most Brilliant Teacher* (New York: Basic Books, 1963).

6. Richard Rorty, quoted in *New York Times Magazine*, February 12, 1990.

CHAPTER 1

1. Emile Peynaud, *The Taste of Wine: The Art and Science of Wine Appreciation,* introd. Michael Broadbent, trans. Michael Schuster (London: Macdonald Orbis, 1996). Originally published as Émile Peynaud and J. Blouin, *Le goût du vin* (Paris: Dunod, [1983] 1996).

2. Pascal Ribéreau-Gayon, "The Chemistry of Red Wine Color," in *Chemistry of Winemaking* (Washington, DC: American Chemical Society, 1974), 50–88.

3. Rustum Roy et al., "The Structure of Liquid Water: Novel Insights from Materials Research: Potential Relevance to Homeopathy," *Materials Research Innovations* 9, no. 4 (2005): 98–102.

CHAPTER 2

1. Vernon L. Singleton, "Oxygen with Phenols and Related Reactions in Musts, Wines, and Model Systems: Observations and Practical Implications," *American Journal of Enology and Viticulture* 38, no. 1 (1987): 69–77.

2. A typical 0.45 micron sterile filter strains out particles weighing about 250,000 daltons, with one dalton corresponding to the weight of a single proton or neutron.

3. Pascal Ribéreau-Gayon, "The Chemistry of Red Wine Color," in *Chemistry of Winemaking,* ed. A. Dinsmoor Webb, Advances in Chemistry 137 (Washington, DC: American Chemical Society, 1974), 50–87.

4. *Food Chemistry* 73 (2001): 423–32; www.reeis.usda.gov/web/crisproject-pages/183814.html.

CHAPTER 3

1. Roger Boulton, "The Copigmentation of Anthocyanins and Its Role in the Color of Red Wine: A Critical Review," *American Journal of Enology and Viticulture* 52, no. 2 (2001): 67–87.

CHAPTER 6

1. Vernon L. Singleton, "Oxygen with Phenols and Related Reactions in Musts, Wines, and Model Systems: Observations and Practical Implications," *American Journal of Enology and Viticulture* 38, no. 1 (1987): 69–77.

2. Vernon L. Singleton, "A Survey of Wine Aging Reactions, Especially with Oxygen," in *American Society of Enology and Viticulture, Proceedings of the 50th Anniversary Meeting, Seattle* (Seattle: ASEV, 2000), 323–44.

3. James Harbertson and Sara Spayd, "Measuring Phenolics in the Winery," *American Journal of Enology and Viticulture* 57, no. 3 (2006): 280–88.

4. A. Lonvaud-Funel, "Les aspects microbiologiques de l'élevage des vins rouges en barriques," in *Vème Colloque des sciences et techniques de la Tonnellerie* (Bordeaux: Vigne et Vin Publications Internationales, 2000), 47–51.

CHAPTER 7

1. www.ne-wea.org/LabManual/sour.htm.

2. www.jewishvirtuallibrary.org/jsource/judaica/ejud_0002_0020_0_20616.html.

3. From "Sweetheart Like You," on *Infidels* (Columbia, 1983).

CHAPTER 9

1. C. R. Smith, "Sulfur Dioxide Basics," in *Enology Briefs,* vol. 1, nos. 1 and 2 (Davis: University of California Extension Press, 1980).

CHAPTER 10

1. P. Chatonnet, D. Dubourdie, J.-N. Boidron, and M. Pons, "The Origin of Ethylphenols in Wines," *Journal of the Science of Food Agriculture* 60 (1992): 165–78. doi:10.1002/jsfa.2740600205.

2. Kermit Lynch, "Attack of the Brett Nerds," in *Inspiring Thirst: Vintage Selections from the Kermit Lynch Wine Brochure* (Berkeley: Ten Speed Press, 2004), 293.

3. www.vinovation.com/ArticleWinepH.htm.

4. For more on Integrated Pest Management, see www.ipm.ucdavis.edu and http://attra.ncat.org/attra-pub/ipm.html.

5. K. C. Fugelsang and B. W. Zoecklein, "Population Dynamics and Effects of *Brettanomyces bruxellensis* Strains on Pinot Noir Wines," *American Journal of Enology and Viticulture* 54 (2003): 294–300.

6. www.PLoSOne.org/article/info%3Adoi%2F10.1371%2Fjournal.pone.0036357.

7. N. A. Bokulich, C. M. L. Joseph, G. Allen, A. K. Benson, and D. A. Mills, "Next-Generation Sequencing Reveals Significant Bacterial Diversity of Botrytized Wine," *PLoS ONE* 7, no. 5 (2012): e36357. doi:10.1371/journal.pone.0036357.

CHAPTER 11

1. Richard Gawel, "Red Wine Astringency: A Review," *Australian Journal of Grape and Wine Research* 4 (1998): 74–95.

2. Douglas O. Adams, James F. Harbertson, and Matthew S. Reid, "Quantitative and Qualitative Differences in Red Wine Astringency," (2004), available at www.docstoc.com/docs/4032045/Quantitative-and-Qualitative-Differences-in-Red-Wine-Astringency-Douglas-O.

3. Ann C. Noble, "Bitterness and Astringency in Wine," in *Bitterness in Foods and Beverages,* ed. Russell L. Rouseff (Amsterdam: Elsevier Science, 1990), 145–58.

4. U. Fischer, R. B. Boulton, and A. C. Noble, "Physiological Factors Contributing to the Variability of Sensory Assessments: Relationships between Salivary Flow Rate and Temporal Perceptions of Gustatory Stimuli," *Food Quality and Preference* 5 (1994): 55–64.

5. Tim Hanni, *Why You Like the Wines You Like: Changing the Way the World Thinks about Wine* (Napa, CA: HanniCo LLC, 2013). See for more details www.amazon.com/Why-You-Like-Wines-Changing/dp/0615750885/ref=sr_1_1?s=books&ie=UTF8&qid=1358211249&sr=1-1#reader_0615750885.

6. R. Gawel, A. Oberholster, and L. Francis, "A 'Mouth-Feel Wheel': Terminology for Communicating the Mouth-Feel Characteristics of Red Wine," *Australian Journal of Grape and Wine Research* 6 (2000): 203–7.

7. *Food Chemistry* 73 (2001): 423–32; "The Role of Copigmentation in the Color of Red Wine," www.reeis.usda.gov/web/crisprojectpages/183814.html.

8. Gawel, "Red Wine Astringency," 95.

9. C. R. Smith and K. E. Fugelsang, "Winegrape Maturity Enhancement via Reverse Osmosis," in *Proceedings of the O.I.V. Groupe d'Experts sur la Technologie du Vin, Paris, France* (Paris: Bulletin de l'OIV, 2001).

CHAPTER 12

1. The bottling of table wines containing fermentable sugars requires sterile filters that can be tested for integrity through a procedure called "bubble-pointing." The first bubble-pointable filters were produced in the 1950s by Nuclepore by etching plastic sheets that had been exposed to alpha emissions in nuclear reactors. Prior to World War II, off-dry table wines did not exist, except for those stabilized by funny-tasting chemicals or cooked by hot-bottling, neither of which hit the big time.

2. Clark Smith, "Does UC-Davis Have a Theory of Deliciousness?" www.winecrimes.com/UC_deliciousness.pdf.

3. Mark J. Plotkin, *Tales of a Shaman's Apprentice: An Ethnobotanist Searches for New Medicines in the Amazon Rain Forest* (New York: Viking, 1993).

4. Tom Siegfried, "Odds Are, It's Wrong," *Science News*, March 27, 2010.

CHAPTER 13

1. "The Search for the American Vigneron," www.alicefeiring.com/blog/2010/05/the-search-for-the-american-vigneron-gideon-bienstock.html; Matt Kramer, *Matt Kramer's New California Wine: Making Sense of Napa Valley, Sonoma, Central Coast, and Beyond* (Philadelphia: Running Press, 2004).

CHAPTER 14

1. Randall Grahm, *Been Doon So Long: A Randall Grahm Vinthology* (Berkeley: University of California Press, 2012).

2. Ibid., 222–23.

3. Ibid., 281–86.

4. Aubert de Villaine is co-owner and codirector of Domaine de la Romanée-Conti, a 4.5-acre Burgundy estate that is widely considered to produce among the world's greatest red wines, and director of HdV (Hyde de Villaine) Wines in Napa Valley. With his wife, Pamela, he also owns and runs a domain in Bouzeron called A & P de Villaine.

CHAPTER 15

Dr. Wample requested that I acknowledge the following people involved in these studies: Antonio Odair Santos, visiting scientist from the Brazilian government; Jim Orvis, Oren Kaye, Steve Kupina, John Gonsalves, and Jon Holmquist of Constellation Wines US; and Gregg Berg and Mike Fitzgerald of OXBO International Corporation. In addition, he wishes to thank the American Vineyard Foundation and the Agricultural Research Initiative for their financial contributions.

1. www.soilinfo.com.

2. See Cliff Ohmart, "A New Way to Inspect Your Vineyard's Soils," *Wines and Vines*, September 2009.

3. Sivakumar Sachidhanantham, "Geo-Spatial Modeling of Wine Grape Quality Using Geographic Information Systems," MS thesis, California State University, Fresno, 2007.

4. Thomas Ulrich, "Wireless Sensor Network Saves Water and Improves Grape Quality," *Wines and Vines,* July 2011.

CHAPTER 16

1. Curtis Phillips, "The Renaissance of the Basket Press," *Wine Business Monthly,* April 2005.

CHAPTER 17

1. Napa Valley Vintners, "Climate Change," www.napavintners.com/about /ab_5_climate.aspx.

2. John Williams, "Science of Sustainable Viticulture," www.sarep.ucdavis .edu/resources/sus-viticulture/files-images/Williams.pdf.

3. John Gladstones, *Wine, Terroir, and Climate Change* (Adelaide, South Australia: Wakefield Press, 2012).

4. On the driving force that holds together the phenolic colloids comprising red wine structure, see Peiming Wang and Andrzej Anderko, "Computation of Dielectric Constants of Solvent Mixtures and Electrolyte Solutions," *Fluid Phase Equilibria* 186 (2001): 103–22 (available at http://downloads.olisystems. com/ResourceCD/MixedSolventElectrolytes/Dielectric.pdf).

CHAPTER 20

1. "Not Just Another Bomb . . . but, Much More," http://fermentation .typepad.com/fermentation/2007/09/not-just-anothe.html.

2. www.wineanorak.com/clark_smith.htm.

3. "Alan Goldfarb Wades through the Muddied Waters of Terroir with Randy Dunn," http://wine.appellationamerica.com/wine-review/195/Randy-Dunn-Interview.html.

4. www.winecrimes.com/nytimes.pdf.

5. Matt Kramer, "The Fight for the Soul of Wine," *Wine Spectator,* December 4, 2001; available at www.winespectator.com/webfeature/show/id/The-Fight-for-the-Soul-of-Wine_1088.

6. Don Tapscott and Anthony D. Williams, *Wikinomics: How Mass Collaboration Changes Everything* (New York: Portfolio, 2008), 47.

7. Eric Asimov, "When Technology Is Worthwhile," http://dinersjournal .blogs.nytimes.com/2007/03/06/when-technology-is-worthwhile/, comment #24 by Alice Feiring.

8. Asimov, "When Technology Is Worthwhile."

9. Alan Goldfarb, "Clark Smith Is Vilified for Changing the Way Wine Is Made," http://wine.appellationamerica.com/wine-review/381/Clark-Smith-Interview-2.html.

10. Alice Feiring, "The Feiring Line," www.alicefeiring.com/blog/looking-for-natural-wines/.

11. Grahm, quoted in Jamie Goode, *The Science of Wine: From Vine to Glass* (Berkeley: University of California Press, 2006), 114.

12. Wendy Chapkis, *Beauty Secrets: Women and the Politics of Appearance* (Cambridge, MA: South End Press, 1986).

CHAPTER 21

1. This requires an entirely new science for which Manfred Clynes coined the term *Sentics* in his 1978 book of that name, subtitled *The Touch of the Emotions* (New York: Anchor Press).

2. Murray Gell-Mann, *The Quark and the Jaguar: Adventures in the Simple and the Complex* (New York: Henry Holt, 1994).

3. Sir David Brewster, ed., *Memoirs of the Life, Writings, and Discoveries of Sir Isaac Newton* (Edinburgh: Thomas Constable & Co., 1855), vol. 2, chap. 27.

4. http://biodynamicshoax.wordpress.com.

5. www.planetplutowine.com.

6. "The First Biodynamic Principle: An Interview with Alan York by Deborah Gavito of Counter Restaurant," www.youtube.com/watch?v = CMH_Hq2ZcuQ.

7. Michael Pollan, *The Botany of Desire: A Plant's-Eye View of the World* (New York: Random House, 2001).

8. Sir Isaac Newton, "A Short Schema of the True Religion," available at www.newtonproject.sussex.ac.uk/view/texts/normalized/THEM00007.

9. John Ciardi, "Manner of Speaking" (column), *Saturday Review,* June 2, 1962.

CHAPTER 22

1. Quoted in www.lescaves.co.uk/grapevine/article/two_natural_wine_manifestos_for_the_price_of_one/.

2. A.Y. Smit, W.J. du Toit, and M. du Toit, "Biogenic Amines in Wine: Understanding the Headache," *South African Journal of Enology and Viticulture* 29, no. 2 (2008): 109–27; C.A. Uthurry et al., "Ethyl Carbamate Production by Selected Yeasts and Lactic Acid Bacteria in Red Wine," *Food Chemistry* 94, no. 2 (2006): 262–70; C.S. Ough et al., "Factors Contributing to Urea Formation in Commercially Fermented Wines," *American Journal of Enology and Viticulture* 41, no. 1 (1990): 68–73.

CHAPTER 23

1. On Mega Purple, see www.vinography.com/archives/2006/01/mega_purple_what_crosses_the_l.html. On Velcorin, see Cyril Penn, "Battling Brett with Velcorin," available at www.winebusiness.com/wbm/?go=getArticle&dataId=39048.

2. www.winescience.auckland.ac.nz/uoa/wine-yeast-research.

3. www.ajevonline.org/content/41/1/68.abstract.

CHAPTER 24

1. Iain D. Thomson, *Heidegger, Art, and Postmodernity* (New York: Cambridge University Press, 2011).

2. Arguably the most important enologist in North America, Murli Dharmadhikari has been the force behind the establishment of over seven hundred wineries in the Midwest, more than one hundred in the state of Iowa alone, since 2001.

3. R.T. Hodgson, "An Examination of Judge Reliability at a Major U.S. Wine Competition," *Journal of Wine Economics* 3, no. 2 (2008): 105–13; "An Analysis of the Concordance among 13 Wine Competitions," *Journal of Wine Economics* 4, no. 1 (2009): 101–9.

4. *The Complete Dog Book,* official publication of the American Kennel Club (New York: Ballantine Books, 2006).

5. www.appellationamerica.com/bluebook.aspx.

6. Find this group on-line at www.PSIloveYou.org.

7. You can view the definitions at www.appellationamerica.com. (A month's subscription access will set you back five bucks, but you'll get over it.) While you're there, also check out two pieces I did on Petite Sirah: "PS I Love You— Let Me Count the Ways" and "Sources of Petite Sirah Regional Character," at http://wine.appellationamerica.com/best-of-appellation/Petite-Sirah-Love .html and http://wine.appellationamerica.com/best-of-appellation/Petite-Sirah-Diversity.html, respectively.

8. "I shall not today attempt further to define the kinds of material I understand to be embraced within that shorthand description ['hard-core pornography']; and perhaps I could never succeed in intelligibly doing so. But I know it when I see it, and the motion picture involved in this case is not that." Supreme Court Associate Justice Potter Stewart, concurring opinion in Jacobellis v. Ohio, U.S. 184 (1964), regarding possible obscenity in *The Lovers.*

CHAPTER 25

1. Norman M. Weinberger, "Music and the Brain," *Scientific American,* December 12, 2006.

2. The direct link is www.npr.org/templates/story/story.php?storyId=16372623.

3. Susan Mayer-Smith and Clark R. Smith, "Liquid Music," paper presented at the 13th Australian Wine IndustryTechnical Conference, 2007; available at http://postmodernwinemaking.com/wine-and-music, abridged narrated and unabridged unnarrated versions of the PowerPoint show.

4. H.-L. Teuber, W.S. Battersby, and M.B. Bender, *Visual Field Defects after Penetrating Missile Wounds of the Brain* (Cambridge, MA: Harvard University Press, 1960).

5. Two excellent examples are Daniel J. Levitin, *This Is Your Brain on Music* (New York: Penguin Books, 2006); and David Huron, *Sweet*

Anticipation: Music and the Psychology of Expectation (Cambridge, MA: MIT Press, 2006).

6. A.J. Blood and R.J. Zatorre, "Intensely Pleasurable Responses to Music Correlate with Activity in Brain Regions Implicated with Reward and Emotion," *Proceedings of the National Academy of Sciences* 98 (2001): 11818–23; available at www.zlab.mcgill.ca/docs/Blood_and_Zatorre_2001.pdf.

Glossary of
Postmodern Terminology

Underlining signals terms used in a definition that also figure as entries in this glossary. These terms are hyperlinked in the online version of this glossary at http://postmodernwinemaking.com/glossary.

ANTHOCYANINS These are the <u>phenolic</u> building blocks that when extracted from grape skins give red wine its color. They are also critical to good red wine <u>structure</u>. Anthocyanins act as the "bookends" on the polymerization process, thus the more of these we extract from the grapes at harvest, the softer and finer the <u>tannins</u> will be. Anthocyanins are, unfortunately, not very soluble in wine, so they must be extracted in the form of <u>copigmentation colloids</u>. Since they are positively charged, anthocyanins cannot aggregate by themselves but require monomeric (unpolymerized) <u>tannins</u> to be present to assist the formation of these colloids, which provide a temporary home in new wine for color compounds. From there anthocyanins can become a stable part of red wine through <u>oxidative polymerization</u> and aldehyde bridging, both artifacts of oxygenation. Excessive hang time depletes anthocyanins through <u>field oxidation</u> and is thus deleterious to good structure and longevity.

ANTIOXIDATIVE VIGOR *See* <u>Reductive strength</u>.

AROMATIC INTEGRATION The phenomenon of merging the complex elements of a wine or food into a unified "single voice" through refined <u>structure</u>. The resulting <u>soulfulness</u> is similar to that achieved by a symphony orchestra when all the musicians are in sync. We are moved by structured foods such as lobster bisque, chocolate, and béarnaise sauce when a well-prepared, fine particle size is achieved, resulting in the merging, for example, of the tarragon, fresh onion, mint, and vinegar aspects into a single "béarnaise" flavor. Similarly, properly made wines never need to be over-oaked, obnoxiously vegetal, or unpleasantly alcoholic. Well-structured wines undergoing microbial activity can actually be improved rather than exhibit spoilage characteristics.

BARREL EQUIVALENT The rate of oxygen that a wine receives when stored in a standard 225-liter oak barrel. Approximately equal to 1 ml of oxygen per liter of wine per month. This can also be expressed as 1.5 mg/L/mo. A wine that does not build dissolved oxygen (D.O.) when stored in barrel is required to consume 0.025 mg/L of oxygen per day. Put another way, such a wine would consume 1.0 ppm D.O. in 40 days or less in a sealed container.

BRETT See Integrated Brett Management (IBM).

BRIX Percent sugar by weight present in the juice of grapes. Easily read in the field by refractometer, brix relates closely to resulting alcohol content after fermented to dry wine, which can be closely predicted by multiplying by 0.60. Due to climatic influences of temperature, dew, and rainfall, which vary widely from place to place and season to season, brix is an unreliable indicator of ripeness, which is more closely related to the completion of Cycle Two metabolism.

CLIQUEAGE The introduction of oxygen in tank or in barrel by instantaneous injection as opposed to the slow, continuous infusion that characterizes micro-oxygenation. The term derives from the "click" sound of a radio-actuated solenoid switch that cellar workers use to facilitate a timed burst of oxygen as they climb around the barrel stack and drop a diffuser into barrel after barrel. This "clique" is added to the suffix -age, which in French denotes a process. The results of cliqueage are as opposite to micro-oxygenation as searing is to simmering. Cliqueage pushes a wine along by breaking down its antioxidative power and polishing its tannin, while slow oxygenation builds structure and reductive vigor.

COEXTRACTION A technique for facilitating the extraction from grape skins of otherwise nearly insoluble flavor and color compounds that need assistance to form colloidal beads. The assistance comes from the infusion of monomeric phenols from tannin-rich varieties, often from white grapes. Garnacha in Rioja, for example, is assisted by cofermentation with the skins of palomino, syrah in the Rhône with viognier, and sangiovese with trebbiano and malvasia, mistakenly often supposed only to add aromaticity. Other materials such as untoasted oak, if well cured, can assist extraction, as can teas made from grape stems or seeds. Powdered tannins are polymeric and thus have no coextraction benefits.

COFACTOR CONCENTRATE A filtrate fraction prepared by ultrafiltration that has high coextraction power. Press wine, high in tannic colloids, is circulated against a filter tight enough to exclude colloids until the end of the run, when the concentration of retentate thickens to the point that the colloids merge into a tar; at this stage, the small phenols that cement these colloids come through into the permeate as a concentrate that may be added in very small amounts to a fermentation to facilitate coextraction of flavor and color, thus enhancing varietal and terroir expression.

COLLOIDS Microscopic suspended beads that form in aqueous solutions, generally composed of materials that are not very soluble but that have affinity for each other and can build stable microscopic structures. Phenolic substances form colloids in wine, and almost all the color and <u>tannin</u> of red wine resides in its colloids. Young red wine forms unstable <u>copigmentation colloids</u>, which assist extraction. <u>Oxidative polymerization</u>, if properly orchestrated, can transform these into stable colloids composed of short <u>polymers containing pigment</u>. The finer these colloids are, the more they assist <u>aromatic integration</u> and the wine's resulting <u>soulfulness</u>.

COPIGMENTATION COLLOIDS Young, unstable <u>colloids</u> formed in red wine during fermentation on skins from roughly equal quantities of monomeric uncharged <u>phenolics</u> and monomeric <u>anthocyanins</u>.

COPPER An elemental metal that is used (generally dissolved in the form of copper sulfate) to react with sulfides but that also acts as an oxidation catalyst, thereby short-circuiting <u>reductive strength</u> and diminishing longevity. It is a goal of postmodern winemaking to eliminate the use of copper.

CROSSFLOW FILTRATION Also called tangential filtration. Any of a family of tight (submicron) filtrations in which tangential flow is used to scrub the membrane to reduce fouling. In these strategies the majority of wine is diverted across rather than through the membrane and returned to the feed tank (<u>retentate</u>) while a small percentage of the feed flow passes through the filter (<u>permeate</u>). These include (in descending order of tightness) crossflow clarification, <u>ultrafiltration</u>, <u>nanofiltration</u>, and <u>reverse osmosis</u>. The term is often erroneously employed as a shortened form for crossflow clarification only.

CYCLE TWO The second cycle of grape maturity, during which grapes transform themselves from a bird repellant to a bird attractant, the essence of <u>ripening</u>. Grapes complete Cycle One at about 12 <u>brix</u> (a ripe tomato is only 8 brix by comparison), so they should be pretty good eating. It is therefore essential that they avoid being consumed by birds until the seed matures. Grapes accomplish this through strategies that render them invisible and undesirable: they are small, hard, bitter, low in flavor (except for the bell pepper vegetal flavor camouflage resembling a leaf or stem), tart, harsh, and green. During Cycle Two they transform in six to eight weeks into big, soft, sweet, flavor-filled, highly colored berries with softened <u>tannins</u> and low vegetal aromas, thereby attracting birds who happily consume their seeds and disseminate them elsewhere, along with nutritive dollops of feces.

The balance required to achieve good tannin <u>structure</u> includes adequate levels of <u>flavonoid phenolics</u> coupled with a good supply of unpolymerized <u>anthocyanins</u> from grapes that have experienced a healthy Cycle Two, were harvested ripe but not overripe, and were extracted properly into <u>copigmentation colloids</u>. Good color is the key to good structure.

DAP Diammonium phosphate, an inorganic fertilizer routinely added to fermentations to assure vigorous yeast activity and alleviate <u>sulfide</u> production, a cheap magic trick that novice winemakers employ to please their bosses. Postmodern practice discourages its use. Sulfide production during fermentation is normal and seldom leads to sulfides in the resulting wine. DAP, in contrast, leads to vigorous but incomplete fermentations and sidetracks yeast from creating a <u>nutrient desert</u> beneficial for control of secondary microbial activity in the cellar (see Integrated Brett Management). If we feed the yeasts Twinkies, they won't eat their oatmeal!

ÉLEVAGE A French term for which I have found no perfect English equivalent, denoting the active process after the end of fermentation and before bottling, of elevating, or one might say educating or rearing, the wine to its proper potential. The term is used also for training horses, and good French children are said to be *"bien élevé,"* or properly brought up. The English term *aging* implies a passive process, which certainly does not describe the rearing of either horses or children. The proud discipline of élevage flies in the face of Natural Wine advocates who suggest that passive neglect is the highest form of winemaking and of kowtowing winemakers who (in public) claim to "do the minimum."

The distinction between *"vins d'effort"* and *"vins de terroir"* is an insulting fiction. In reality, to become invisible while showing terroir at its best requires of winemakers a very intense effort.

FIELD OXIDATION The practice of resolving tannins and reductive vigor through extensive hang time. Similar to micro-oxygenation but without the precision that can be accomplished in the cellar. Micro-oxygenation seeks to build a tannin soufflé, an impossibility if the egg is already scrambled when it arrives in the kitchen! Instead of enhancing structural stability, aromatic soulfulness, and longevity, field oxidation usually leads to premature fruit-forward characteristics followed by oxidation, volatile acidity, and dryness. Three weeks' excess in the vineyard robs a decade or more in the cellar.

FLAVONOIDS A subclass of phenolic compounds uniquely extracted from skins and including red wine color (anthocyanins [by definition monomeric] and polymerized pigment) as well as tannin building blocks.

FRAMING One of the seven functions of oak identified in the postmodern system. For wines possessing a rich core of fruit, sweet oak can lead to imbalance. Rather, these wines should be cellared with wood that imparts structure and angularity. Several coopering approaches assist framing. Oak from pedunculated species, or grown in copse habit, will tend to be rich in ellagitannins, which impart framing. Light toasting (spiciness) or very heavy toasting (espresso coffee aromas) are useful for framing, whereas untoasted (coconut) and moderately toasted wood (vanilla) contribute sweetness and should be avoided for this purpose.

HYPEROXYGENATION Introduction of large amounts of oxygen to musts prior to fermentation. While all musts require oxygen to promote yeast health, hyperoxygenation goes beyond this requirement and seeks to promote oxidative browning, polymerization, and precipitation of tannins, usually from white press wines. It has no relation to micro-oxygenation.

IDEAL SOLUTION *See* Solution, ideal.

INTEGRATED BRETT MANAGEMENT (IBM) A strategy analogous to Integrated Pest Management (IPM) but applied to microbiological ecology in the cellar rather than to vineyard ecology. This method seeks to stabilize wine through playing out potential microbial activity during bulk aging so that stable wine can be bottled without sterile filtration. *Brettanomyces* yeast, which in conventional modern wines can impart objectionable earthiness, is controlled through a triple strategy involving complete fermentation to a <u>nutrient des-ert</u>, <u>microbial equilibrium</u>, and <u>aromatic integration</u> resulting from refined <u>structure</u>. Wines cellared in this way display the "good Brett" <u>soulfulness</u> often reported but seldom understood by modern enologists.

INTEGRATED PEST MANAGEMENT (IPM) The promotion of natural ecological balance of flora and fauna in the vineyard. Beneficial insects such as praying mantis, *Anagrus epos* wasps, and ladybugs are utilized to control pest popu-lations as an alternative to absolute control through the use of heavy tillage, pesticides, and herbicides. The resulting <u>living soil</u> appears to impart mineral flavors, <u>antioxidative vigor</u>, and longevity to the resulting wines.

LEES Yeast sediment, usually divided into gross lees and fine lees. Gross lees are the first to settle and often contain harsh and bitter materials. Fine lees, which settle later, can be sweet and creamlike. Suspended lees can be injuri-ous to young red wine by attacking unpolymerized <u>anthocyanins</u> through adsorption as well as enzymatic degradation, resulting in drier <u>tannins</u>. The yeast cells in lees break down over time, and after the wine's polymeric <u>struc-ture</u> is complete, these can coat the structure, rendering tannins softer, fatter, and more available. This process is analogous to the conversion of dark chocolate to milk chocolate by incorporating milk protein. Lees incorpora-tion into wines increases their <u>reductive strength</u>.

LIVING SOIL By eschewing tillage, herbicides, and pesticides as much as possi-ble, the vineyardist can foster a healthy soil ecology. A healthy earthworm population is a good indicator of soil health. Living soil supports the growth of mycorrhizal fungi, which are thought to facilitate uptake of trace miner-als. Wines grown on living soil tend to have enhanced <u>mineral</u> flavors in the finish, <u>reductive strength</u>, and longevity. The pursuit of a living soil doctrine is an effective, practical approach to these ends, one that every grower can adopt because it does not require the extreme restrictions mandated by organic certification.

MALOLACTIC FERMENTATION A secondary fermentation undergone by most red wines and some whites by the action of bacteria similar to those responsible for transforming milk into buttermilk and yogurt. These bacteria consume the grape's natural malic acid and convert it into the less acidic lactic acid, together with by-products such as diacetyl, which is the artificial butter fla-vor used on movie popcorn. Malolactic fermentation diminishes wine's freshness and fruitiness, lowers acid taste, and raises pH. These effects are minimized if malolactic completes during primary fermentation; contact with yeast, moreover, will absorb diacetyl. If, by contrast, malolactic fer-mentation is delayed until wine is barreled down, its action can soften oak <u>tannins</u>.

MATURITY, RED GRAPE From the grapevine's point of view, true ripeness occurs at the completion of <u>Cycle Two</u>, at which point berries contain mature, viable seeds and optimum levels of color and flavor in order to attract birds. This point is characterized by the cessation of sugar transport into berries and of malic acid respiration and by the commencement of <u>field oxidation</u>. Although past practice was to gauge maturity by monitoring sugar content (<u>brix</u>), Postmodernism advocates against this measure of maturity.

Winemakers can assess maturity through berry inspection and sensory evaluation of juice, skins, and seeds, as well as through analytical measures, particularly the quantification of monomeric <u>anthocyanins</u>, <u>polymeric pigments</u>, and <u>oxidative crosslinking</u>. Optimum maturity for winemaking is related to the desired style and the techniques to be employed in the cellar, particularly the desired longevity and the methods contemplated for resolving <u>tannins</u>.

Optimum harvest time often does not correspond with desirable brix. <u>Reverse osmosis</u> is routinely employed to address excessive rain or sugar in berries.

MICROBIAL EQUILIBRIUM The application of <u>Integrated Pest Management</u> techniques to the microbial ecology of the cellar. Controlled microbial competition is encouraged in order to stabilize wine prior to bottling so that sterile filtration can be avoided. Cellar temperatures above 60°F and pHs in the range of 3.70 to 3.85 are beneficial in promoting microbial balance. See also <u>Integrated Brett Management</u>.

MINERALITY A taste sensation characteristic of wines grown on limestone, shale, or schist or in <u>living soil</u> that resembles the aftertaste of a half-shell oyster or of a tiny electrical current in the throat. Minerality can be reproduced by the addition to conventional wine of very dilute tinctures of trace mineral dietary supplements. Wines with strong minerality generally possess more <u>reductive strength</u> than their conventional counterparts.

MICRO-OXYGENATION (MOX) The invention of Patrick Ducournau, a *vigneron* in Madiran who in the early 1990s sought a method to save the local variety, tannat, from extinction. Locals were attempting to globalize by replacing this highly tannic variety with more drinkable grapes such as merlot, so Patrick sought a method to tame the <u>tannins</u>, stumbling in the process upon a complete shift in understanding of wine's true nature and leading to a <u>postmodern</u> school of wine *élevage*.

Patrick discovered that tannat had a huge appetite for oxygen, and if not exposed in youth to many times what a barrel's skin could supply (about 1 ml of oxygen per liter of wine per month) would form dry tannins that would age poorly. The German introduction of stainless steel and inert gas, a boon for Riesling, had thus undermined traditional vinification of reds, tannat being the most extreme example.

Working with Michel Moutounet, director of the Faculty of Oenology at Montpellier, Patrick devised a system for precision oxygenation, metering in minute bubbles of pure oxygen and studying the effects. Treatment became divided into three phases. In Phase 1, red wines, depending on their tannins, could build structure and stabilize color at rates of 10 to 100 barrel equivalents (ml/L/mo.). Rather than become oxidized, they actually increase in <u>reductive strength</u> during this period. After <u>malolactic</u> and sulfite addition, Phase 2 preconditions the wine for barrel at 2 ml to 10 ml by refining <u>structure</u> and texture, balancing <u>reductive vigor</u>, and promoting <u>aromatic integration</u>. Phase 3 occurs post-barrel, when some wines lack reductive strength to remain in barrel but require final harmonization, for example, from the raw tannins newly extracted from deep in wood where toasting cannot reach.

Recent competition from other companies that sell oxygen dosers and diffusers but do not teach the subtleties of the technique to winery clients has led to widespread misunderstanding about the nature of micro-oxygenation. Several vendors of oak alternatives promote the use of oxygen to replace barrels with tanks and to soften the harshness of poorly prepared oak products. Unlike its imitators, Ducournau's company, Oenodev, has consistently stressed high-performance equipment, intensive training, and a sophisticated understanding of _élevage_ principles combined with labor-intensive attention to the wine.

Micro-oxygenation is employed throughout the world today to stabilize, enhance, balance, integrate, and distinguish a wine's true expression. This is essentially the same process the Aztecs taught the Spanish, who passed it on to the Belgians: the refining of cocoa powder into chocolate, through oxygenation (in chocolate making called "conching"). The technique forces the winemaker into close and frequent interaction with the wine, during which issues of balance, timing, and purpose are constantly scrutinized. Its benefits for increasing quality and for acquainting winemakers with wine's true nature far outweigh considerations of cost savings. While micro-oxygenation can be utilized to soften and refine cheaper wines, its highest and best use is to increase the flavor depth, soulfulness, and longevity of the world's top wines.

NANOFILTRATION Crossflow filtration in the range below ultrafiltration and above reverse osmosis, limited to the molecular weight range where monovalent ions can be separated from divalent, that is, between 500 and 1,000 daltons. Since nanofiltration makes a separation in the middle of the wine flavor range, no applications of this type of filtration have been legalized in the United States. This term is erroneously applied in U.S. regulations to loose reverse osmosis (RO) applications below 150 daltons that strip more flavor than tight RO but can remove compounds that do not pass into tight RO permeate.

NUTRIENT DESERT A key strategy of Integrated Brett Management, which works in the vineyard to deliver harvested fruit with healthy nutrient levels so that a complete and thorough primary fermentation is possible without the need for addition of chemical fertilizers. Wines containing in excess of 1.0 gram per liter of fermentable sugar are at risk for nonsterile bottling, but the consumption of micronutrients is equally important to creating a nutrient desert.

OAK _See_ Seven functions of oak.

OXIDATION The progressive deterioration of wine due to exposure to oxygen over time. Late stages of oxidation may be accompanied by loss of aromatic freshness, brown color, aldehydic or nutty aromas, and coagulation of tannins into dry, grainy, dirty astringency and precipitated sediment. Paradoxically, early and skillful introduction of oxygen (micro-oxygenation) does not oxidize wine but rather increases reductive strength, which inhibits oxidation and prolongs longevity.

OXIDATIVE POLYMERIZATION Certain types of phenolics (vicinal diphenols, for you eno-geeks) have the capability to form chains by consuming oxygen. Since the products of the reaction are more reactive than the original reactants, a cascade occurs in which young red wines consume oxygen at a rapid rate and use it to create a rich, light structure. Oxygen thus has the role of a wire whisk in a tannin soufflé. Monomeric anthocyanins are highly reactive with oxygen-activated tannins and are readily incorporated into these chains. Since anthocyanins cannot themselves form polymers (they are not vicinal diphenols), they terminate the polymer, like bookends. The higher the anthocyanin content, the shorter the resulting polymeric pigment and the finer the texture. Oxidative polymerization results in hard tannins that can mature into high-quality structure.

PERMEATE The portion of the feed wine that passes through a crossflow (tangential flow) filter. With tight reverse osmosis, permeate has the appearance of water, and contains only low molecular weight compounds such as water, ethanol, and acetic acid, though looser RO membranes also pass some wine flavor constituents. Permeate from juices contains only water, and is typically discarded. Wine permeates may be subjected to anion exchange to remove acetic acid or to distillation to remove ethanol, after which they may be recombined back into the wine.

PHENOLICS A broad class of organic compounds that contribute many of wine's characteristics, including its color, texture, and many of its flavors. For you chemistry nuts, a phenolic is simply any compound containing a benzene ring (six carbons in a ring connected by double bonds) with an -OH bonded to it. Red wine can be thought of as liquid chocolate, because its phenolics are almost identical. Because phenolics aren't generally very soluble, they exist in wine as tiny suspended beads called colloids.

Aside from many direct contributions to taste (especially bitterness) and aroma (especially from oak), phenolic structure influences aromatic integration of wine aromas and thus is the source of wine's soulfulness. Phenolics are also a source of the reductive strength that protects wine during aging.

Proper artisanal work with red wine requires a good balance of different phenolics such as tannins, anthocyanins, and sometimes oak constituents. Heavily pressed wine fractions are sometimes blended into weak young wines to achieve phenolic balance.

POLYMERIC PIGMENT Tannins and anthocyanins form into chains through nonoxidative or oxidative polymerization. Monomeric anthocyanins are vulnerable to attack by yeast enzymes, sulfite bleaching, precipitation, and even oxygen itself, but polymeric pigment is stable and protected. Polymeric pigment forms colloids incorporating hundreds of chains. The longer the chains, the coarser the texture; the shorter the chains, the softer the wine and the greater its power for aromatic integration.

POSTMODERN WINEMAKING This professional discipline makes use of the benefits of twentieth-century technological innovations but also explores what was lost during the period when scientific enology sought to organize our knowledge of wine and let slip aspects of the ancient wine craftsman's empirical expertise. In the eight millennia preceding the modern era, winemakers labored without the benefit of electricity, petrochemical herbicides and pesticides, or the theories developed by modern chemistry and microbiology. There were no sterile filters, inert gases, electric pumps, or stainless steel tanks, no concept for yeast, oxygen, or chemical preservatives. Wine was expected to be liquid poetry. Ben Franklin called it "proof that God loves us and desires us to be happy." The Romans planted the vine all over Europe and harnessed its seductive power to stabilize an empire for a thousand years. Postmodern winemaking seeks to deliver once again this level of soulfulness. Our job is to steward our vineyards and perfect our cellar techniques in order to bring forth the authentic expression of a distinctive terroir by crafting a refined structure that integrates its aromas into a single voice.

REDOX POTENTIAL That position where a given wine lies on a continuum between highly oxidized and highly reduced. Sometimes referred to as rH, it is analogous to a wine's pH, which designates where the wine lies on a continuum between highly acidic and highly basic. Although pH measures free protons and redox measures available electrons, the latter has proven elusive to measure directly while analysis of the former is straightforward.

REDUCTIVE STRENGTH While imbued with many other meanings, in chemistry reduction is simply the opposite of oxidation, and reductive strength is just a shorter way of saying antioxidative power or vigor. Reductive strength (or reductive vigor) is measured as the rate at which a given wine can consume oxygen without a resulting buildup in dissolved oxygen. Wine in a reduced state is closed in aroma and often produces sulfides, but these traits are not categorically defects, since they indicate the wine's ability to undergo prolonged aging.

An important duty of the postmodern practitioner is to balance reductive strength, a complex task in which wine attributes must be matched with intended style, desired longevity, and closure type. Stelvin closures (screw caps), for example, do not dissipate reductive strength as readily as corks.

Antioxidative vigor derives from at least three sources: phenolic reactivity, lees stirring, and mineral energy. Living soil practices promote mineral energy and flavors.

Phenolic reactivity can be promoted through balanced vines with a healthy Cycle Two, optimum maturity, and adequate coextraction during fermentation. Excessive hang time is particularly injurious to reductive strength, and three weeks beyond maturity can easily rob 90% of vigor and longevity. Paradoxically, micro-oxygenation can be employed in very young red wines to increase reductive strength and longevity. Later in development, reductive strength can be diminished through controlled use of oxygen.

RETENTATE The portion of the feed wine that does not pass through a crossflow (tangential flow) filter and instead is returned to the feed tank.

REVERSE OSMOSIS (RO) An extremely tight filtration originally developed for water purification, with a wide variety of applications for achieving postmodern winemaking goals. Originally utilized in rainy areas to remove rainwater from musts and thus facilitate maturity in wet areas, RO is now widely used in dry areas to remove excessive alcohol, thus facilitating harvest at proper maturity by uncoupling the picking decision from brix. In this application, RO permeate, which contains substantially no flavor or color, is distilled to remove high-proof alcohol and then is returned to the wine. Precise alcohol levels called "sweet spots" are routinely observed, with alcohol content within 0.1% being critical to harmonious balance. Reverse osmosis can also facilitate <u>microbial equilibrium</u> in the cellar through its ability to correct volatile acidity, which occasionally occurs during *élevage*.

SEVEN FUNCTIONS OF OAK Apart from the physical benefits of barrels such as storage, slow oxygenation, settling, and off-gassing, oak extractives are available without the necessity of fashioning a container. Barrel alternatives supplement deficiencies in wines by providing five holistic functionalities and two sorts of flavorings. Proper choice of oak to suit a specific wine should account for its needs for <u>copigmentation</u>, <u>antioxidative vigor</u>, <u>sweetness</u>, <u>framing</u>, and <u>aromatic integration</u> before considering its contributions to flavor in the form of curing aromatics and toasting aromatics. Oak should not be considered as primarily a vehicle for aromatic enhancement without reference to the impact of a chosen wood on the wine as a whole.

SOLUTION, IDEAL In the late nineteenth century, scientists constructed the dilute aqueous solution model to crudely describe the behavior of systems in which water acts as a solvent. The intention of such an idealized model was to enable rough predictions of solution behavior, which may then be adjusted to observed phenomena through the addition of a patchwork of correcting terms. Hence an "ideal" solution was one for which no correction terms need be applied—easy to model but in no other sense desirable. For a solution as complex as wine, this correctional work is usually neglected in practice and the assumptions of the ideal model are taken as a rough guide. Solution-based thinking has shaped the modern view of wine and how we work with it by bringing to bear the powerful tools of analytical chemistry, chemical engineering, and sensory science in an often inappropriate perspective that is hard to see past or even to become aware of.

In 1882, Raoult's Law stated that the volatility of a compound dissolved in an ideal solution is a function of its concentration in the solution and its natural tendency to volatilize (its Henry's Law partition coefficient). This means that if wine is a solution, its sensory properties derive from the concentrations of substances dissolved in that solution. The greater the concentration in the liquid, the more intense its odor and taste. If this relationship is exactly linear, the solution is said to behave "ideally."

One of the key precepts of solution chemistry, ideal behavior assumes that the concentration of a substance in solution (in, say, milligrams of material per liter) is proportional to that found in the headspace, that is, the aroma in the glass. We speak of a "threshold" as the average minimum concentration that a group of subjects can smell. When most winemakers discuss intensities of aromatic elements, they speak in terms of the dissolved concentration in the liquid, not the amount of material in the gaseous headspace they are actually smelling, which is more difficult to measure. The notion of a threshold expressed in this way presupposes, often without realizing it, that Raoult's Law is approximately correct, an assumption that postmoderns emphatically reject as inapplicable to red wine. The presence of <u>colloids</u> is not only the cause of strong deviation from "ideal" solution behavior but also the source of <u>aromatic integration</u> and <u>soulfulness</u>.

SOULFULNESS An inherent quality of an artistic product—be it a cello performance, a cheese, a dance, or a wine—constituting a message, a vivid sharing from an artist that transcends words and touches a receptive audience profoundly. Soulful wines often blend diverse, potentially conflicting elements such as earth, fruit, and spice intertwined in such a way as to convey a feeling of profundity. While the essence of soulful wine is to bring present a deep connectedness, of feeling personally known and understood by another, this connectedness is also achievable through enlightened solitary contemplation of everyday objects. The production of soulful wines requires focused artisanal attention that sets aside automatic, formulaic, or cynical blending practices.

STRUCTURE The physical nature of suspended <u>colloids</u>, which contain substantially all the color and tannin of red wine. Structural finesse is a direct artifact of the ratio between <u>anthocyanins</u> and <u>tannins</u> as well as oxygen exposure. Skillful guidance of young red wine to achieve good structure is called *élevage*.

Red wine is not a chemical solution but derives its flavor properties from its <u>colloidal</u> properties. Indeed, wine's deviation from <u>ideal solution</u> behavior is a good working measure of quality. Good structure alters the aromatic characteristics of wines by sequestering aromatic compounds so that sensory <u>thresholds</u> are not obeyed. Well-structured wines can contain many times the supposed threshold of pyrazines (bell pepper), guaiacols (oak char), and ethyl phenols (*Brettanomyces* yeast) without objectionable aromatic characteristics. This phenomenon is referred to as <u>aromatic integration</u>. Red wines deprived of oxygen in their development or exposed to excessive hang time will make coarse colloids lacking in aromatically integrative properties readily precipitating during aging.

Note: Many English-speaking connoisseurs, critics, and Masters of Wine employ this term in a very different way. Their use does not address any physical arrangement in the wine itself but rather refers to an aesthetic mapping of the elements of balance, such as acidity, sugar, bitterness, astringency, and alcohol. To them, a wine with good structure is one in which these elements together create a focused and harmonious whole, much like the characters in a well-spun narrative or musical composition. The French *oenologues* with whom I have worked use the term *structure* in the physical sense I describe above (indeed, that's where I learned it), and I suspect that, as with the terms *grappe* (bunch) and *raisin* (grape), Anglos long ago simply misapprehended their French acquaintances and gave birth to an English usage that differs in its particulars. I argue for the utility and predominance of my more literal usage, in which the structure exists in the wine itself and not as a human aesthetic theoretical construct.

SULFIDES Stinky compounds reminiscent of rotten eggs, diesel fuel, onions, canned asparagus, or wet wool. Sunlight should never be permitted to shine on a bottle of white wine, as a very short exposure can lead to sulfide production in the bottle.

Sulfide production by yeasts occurs for many reasons and is not always indicative of difficulties. The degree of sulfides present in a wine is important to assess. Small amounts of sulfides will occur in healthy fermentations as consumption during fermentation creates a <u>nutrient desert</u>. Proteins are broken down into constituent amino acids to provide materials for biosynthesis of essential micronutrients. After fermentation, <u>reductive strength</u> from proper red grape <u>maturity</u> or from <u>mineral energy</u> will lead to sulfide production in the barrel and even in the bottle. It is the winemaker's task, through a proper oxygen regimen, to balance this reductive strength against the intention for ageability. Small amounts of sulfides in wines intended for aging are a positive sign that knowledgeable collectors will applaud. Such wines consumed in their youth will benefit from aerative decanting.

SULFITES A class of preservative compounds (unrelated to <u>sulfides</u>) added to wine in the form of sulfur dioxide to control microbial and oxidative spoilage. Wine made without sulfites is the highest achievement of a skilled postmodern practitioner and can result in wine of great terroir expression, similar to the production of unpasteurized cheese. Most wines need sulfites. Certified organic wine is not permitted the use of sulfites, which accounts for its inconsistency.

SWEETNESS One of the seven functions of oak identified in the postmodern system. For wines possessing angularity and <u>framing</u> but lacking a rich core of fruit, sweet oak is a tool for achieving flavor balance. Untoasted wood (coconut) and moderate toasting (vanilla) are useful for this purpose.

TANGENTIAL FLOW FILTRATION *See* <u>Crossflow filtration</u>.

TANNIN The source of structure and texture in red wine. Tannin precursors, notably <u>flavonoid</u> skin extractives, can undergo carefully guided <u>oxidative polymerization</u>; if neglected on the vine or in the cellar, however, they will polymerize spontaneously into less desirable forms. Tannins interact with salivary proteins to form precipitates in the mouth that exhibit a variety of sensory impressions, different forms of astringency, or harshness. Postmodern winemaking uses English names for these impressions that honor the terminology established by French tradition.

Very young red wine always has grainy astringency (thought to be composed of <u>copigmentation colloids</u>), which we refer to as "green" tannin, not to be confused with underripe or vegetal characteristics. If never allowed exposure to oxygen, these tannins migrate during aging into the rest of the mouth, eventually transforming into "dry" tannins, which leave a coarse, grainy impression all over the tongue and cheeks and interfere with other taste impressions. Dry tannin is the only type of tannin perceived under the tongue in the back of the mouth. It is the result of overly polymerized tannin, and its aggressivity should not be taken as a call to age the wine. Dry tannin is unstable and prone to precipitate, hence a marker signifying poor aging potential. Dry tannin can also be present in young wines if produced from grapes left too long on the vine.

In balanced young red wines, early and careful exposure to oxygen quickly transforms green tannin into an aggressive, sheetlike, grippy "hard" tannin that is perceived entirely on the top of the tongue, covering the whole palate back to the throat. This type of tannic aggressivity is a good sign, and such wines will improve with age.

Our picture of the chemistry of this rapid transformation has only recently begun to emerge. When the monomeric <u>flavonoids</u> extracted during fermentation into <u>copigmentation colloids</u> are assisted to <u>oxidatively polymerize</u>, their sensory effects are radically altered within a few days. This process may be assisted prior to <u>malolactic</u> through Phase 1 <u>micro-oxygenation</u>. Surprisingly, this transformation is accompanied by an increase in <u>reductive strength</u>, which results in a temporary closing of the aromas but also increases the prospects for longevity.

As hard tannins evolve in the presence of oxygen, they diminish their grip on the upper palate ("firm tannin") and begin to "melt" from the back palate forward. Tannins in this intermediate stage, melted in back and firm in front, are called "round." Such wines have additional aging potential and are on the right path to tannin resolution to "melted" (sometimes also called "soft," "plush," or "velvet" tannins) as they reach maturity. Melted tannins exhibit great <u>aromatic integration</u> and are generally quite stable. Properly resolved tannins are not a sign of imminent demise or poor longevity. Harmonious wines are capable of palatability in youth without sacrificing age-worthiness.

Oak tannins are perceived as a finely grained "parching/numbing" astringency on the top of the tongue in front but back from the tip. They contain the anesthetic eugenol, which causes a numbing hollowness in this region, surrounded by fine, parching aggressivity. Because of their position on the tongue, oak tannins are easily confused with firmness or roundness.

THRESHOLD A term from modern sensory science denoting the minimum aroma or taste intensity at which 50% of a group of subjects are able to detect or recognize a specific compound. At low levels, subjects are typically able to pick out a spiked sample as different but cannot identify the difference, and thus both detection and recognition thresholds are spoken of. For example, the recognition threshold for the sweetness in water is around 0.5% glucose, but subtle flavor changes are detectable at much lower concentrations. In aroma work, gaseous concentrations are much more difficult to measure than concentrations in solutions. Accordingly, aroma thresholds are generally expressed as solution concentrations. Insidiously hidden in this way of speaking is the assumption that aroma volatility coefficients are similar among our many wines. This has led to much consternation in explaining the differences in sensory assessment related to both recognition and quality judgment in wines containing *Brettanomyces*-related notes. For wines with vegetal pyrazines, alterations in <u>structure</u> using <u>micro-oxygenation</u> lead to large, consistent, and predictable alterations in threshold while having no effect on composition, clear proof of non–<u>ideal solution</u> behavior.

ULTRAFILTRATION (UF) A family of <u>crossflow</u> filtrations one to three orders of magnitude tighter than sterile filtration (1,000–100,000 daltons). UF separates colloids from their solution, and may be used to soften press wines without the volume and flavor losses of conventional fining with proteins such as egg white, gelatin, casein, and isinglass. UF by-products include <u>cofactor concentrate</u> and <u>Xpress</u>.

VÉRAISON The transition of red grapes into <u>Cycle Two</u> during <u>maturation</u> marked by the emergence of red <u>anthocyanin</u> color.

VINEYARD ENOLOGY Distinct from viticulture, a winemaking presence in the vineyard is necessary to ensure that harvested grapes are well imbued with the building blocks of good wine structure, health, and character. We seek to present the distinctive terroir expression of each unique vineyard setting through enhancement of soil ecology, vine balance, and careful maturity assessment. Through skillful artisanship in the cellar with an eye to structural finesse, we can optimize aromatic integration, harmonious balance, antioxidative vigor, and graceful longevity if and only if vineyard enology has met its goals.

XPRESS Named and commercialized by Richard Carey while a professor at CSU Fresno, Xpress is the concentrated retentate of an ultrafiltration of heavy press wine. Xpress may be added when fresh in very small amounts to improve the structure and aromatic integration properties of weak red wines. Micro-oxygenation may be desirable to refine the structure of resulting wines.

Index

About the Author

Clark Smith is one of California's most widely respected winemakers. Besides making wines for Diamond Ridge Vineyards and his own WineSmith brand, he has served the winemaking community for four decades as consultant, inventor, author, musician, and instructor. His popular class on fundamentals of wine chemistry and monthly column "The Postmodern Winemaker" in *Wines and Vines* magazine are industry hallmarks. Founding winemaker for R.H. Phillips in the 1980s, he went on to establish Vinovation, the world's largest wine production consulting firm, to pioneer new winemaking technologies, including patents for volatile acidity removal and alcohol adjustment via reverse osmosis. He holds adjunct professorships at Florida International University and at California State University, Fresno, directing groundbreaking research and teaching online. His tasting panel for AppellationAmerica.com explores winegrowing regions across North America. He resides in Santa Rosa, California.